The VISION of a CHAMPION

Advice and Inspiration from the World's
Most Successful Women's Soccer Coach

by Anson Dorrance and Gloria Averbuch

Foreword by Mia Hamm

Note: This book is intended as a reference volume only. The information given here is designed to provide you with guidance about your involvement in soccer. It is not intended as a substitute for any treatment that may have been prescribed by your doctor. You should seek a doctor's approval before beginning any exercise program.

Huron River Press
3622 W. Liberty
Ann Arbor, MI 48103
www.huronriverpress.com
Huron River Press is an imprint of Clock Tower Press LLC.

Printed and bound in Canada

Reedswain soft cover ISBN 1-59164-024-5

10 9 8 7 6 5 4
Illustrations: Tom Sander
Photos courtesy of: Sports Information Office at the University of North Carolina

- Permission to use "If you let me play..." granted by NIKE.
- UNC players' names include years of college participation in parentheses.
- Statistics as of November 2001.

"The Man Watching" from *Selected Poems of Rainer Maria Rilke*, Edited and Translated by Robert Bly
Copyright© 1981 by Robert Bly
Reprinted by permission of HarperCollins Publishers Inc.

Library of Congress Cataloging-in-Publication Data

Dorrance, Anson.
  The vision of a champion : advice and inspiration from the world's
most successful women's soccer coach / by Anson Dorrance and Gloria
Averbuch.
     p. cm.
Includes bibliographical references (p.   ).
  ISBN 1-58536-055-4
  1. Soccer—Coaching. 2. Soccer for women. I. Averbuch, Gloria, 1951–
II. Title.
  GV943.8 .D68 2002
  796.334'07'7—dc21

                                                                    2002003399

The vision of a champion is someone who is bent over, drenched in sweat, at the point of exhaustion when no one else is watching.

—Anson Dorrance

The title of this book is taken from the above note, originally given to Mia Hamm in 1992, her senior year at UNC, by her coach Anson Dorrance, after he saw her training on her own. Mia included it in the beginning of her 1999 book, *Go for the Goal*.

I would like to dedicate this book to my wife M'Liss
who encouraged me (long before I could see it)
to chase a "life that has exceeded my dreams."

Acknowledgments

Special thanks to:

- The UNC women's soccer staff—Bill Palladino, Chris Ducar, Tom Sander, Delaine Marbry—for their assistance and support.
- The contributors to this book: Bill Palladino, Chris Ducar, Tom Sander, Greg Gatz, Bill Prentice, Ph.D., Tom Brickner, M.D., Don Kirkendall, Ph.D., and Mary Schlegel, M.D.
- UNC soccer alumni and current players—among the best athletes in the world—for sharing their time and their insights: Tracey Bates Leone, Amy Burns, Tracy Ducar, Lorrie Fair, Mia Hamm, April Heinrichs, Rakel Karvelsson, Kristine Lilly, Carla Overbeck, Cindy Parlow, Laurie Schwoy, Tisha Venturini, and Jordan Walker.
- Yael Averbuch, for reading and editing the manuscript with a "player's eye view," and for conceiving of the book's title.
- Readers: Jeff Pill and Angela Kelly.
- For their various contributions: Shira Averbuch, Paul Friedman, Ashu Saxena, Dave Lohse and the staff of UNC Athletic Communications, Pete Dorrance, Tracy Ducar, Ramona Barber of CollegeInfo©, Inc., Dominick Bucci, Ian Brice, Arthur Wells.
- For permission to use their correspondence: Angela Kelly, Maria Glatzer, Ed Leon, Julie Smith.

Contents

Section IV
The Tactical Pillar—COMPETITION

Section V
The Physical Pillar—FITNESS

Section VI
The Psychological Pillar—MENTALITY

Section VII

Appendix I

Appendix II

Foreword

UNC Soccer—Beyond the Game

The University of North Carolina women's soccer is special in so many ways. Its tradition—which is passed down from class to class—is very deep. When I was there, we all shared the feeling that it is an honor and a privilege to play in the program. Every single day you earn the right to be there, and to wear that uniform. Your commitment to yourself, to your teammates, and to that program, is a constant renewal process.

At Carolina, you never have to apologize for wanting to be the best. Anson and Dino (Bill Palladino, Assistant Coach) have created an environment that enables you to reach your potential, both individually and collectively—as a team. As an athlete, you appreciate that environment. The coaches set up a daily competitive challenge. But at the same time it's nurturing, from the standpoint of not feeling that it's wrong to compete, or that you're alone in your pursuit of excellence.

Anson and Dino are the constants. They have been since the beginning of the UNC women's soccer team in 1979. But at the same time, they give a lot of responsibility to the players to shape the program. I think this emphasis on personal responsibility is very unique. There are a lot of examples of how it is cultivated, but one of the best is simply the way a week of practice is structured, and the balance Anson has created in terms of a person's responsibility to herself, and also to the team.

A typical week consists of a game on Sunday, a day off on Monday, and a very difficult, fitness-oriented day on Tuesday. Tuesday is mostly individual work, but at the same time, teammates help each other get through the session by giving their support. Wednesday is one v. one, and small-sided games. That's all about how you personally influence winning. Then, toward the end of the week, and another game, Anson brings the individual back into the team concept, with training that focuses on players bonding.

Every pregame talk he concludes with something that emphasizes group unity. His speeches include comments like, "Isn't it wonderful that you play a team sport, knowing that if you struggle, the person next to you will carry you? Don't ever forget that, because there's going to be a time when others struggle, and you need to carry them." That's the way we always felt about each other. It's why we went out and worked as hard as we did. At UNC you work hard for yourself, to become better, but also to show how much you respect and care about the people around you.

There are a lot of reasons why I feel so strongly about the program, and its successful soccer environment. But for me, even more powerful than the athletics is the strength of the special friendships that are created there. When I think about the best of UNC soccer, people like Tracey Bates (Leone) pop into my head. Tracey is our program in a nutshell. If I could put a face on UNC soccer, it would be hers.

My relationship with Tracey goes back to when I was 14, and she was my roommate as part of a Texas ODP (Olympic Development Program) event—the same tournament where Anson first saw me play. When I got to UNC, Anson wanted me to feel supported, so he asked Tracey if she'd like to live with me. As college roommates, she and I spent a lot of memorable nights talking (and mostly laughing) together, sometimes into the early morning hours.

I still vividly remember Tracey in our fitness tests in my freshman year. We were doing the Cooper test, in which players are required to run at least 7 1/4 laps on the track in 12 minutes in order to pass. Tracey was one of the older players who told the nervous freshmen, "Don't worry, you'll make it. Stay with us, and we'll pace you." She felt it was her mission as a senior to set a welcoming, positive tone for the freshmen.

Tracey was trying to help other people make the standard while she was running herself. Here she was, someone extremely fit, who could have simply gone out and run, made her time, and passed her own test. But it was important to her to push everyone else through it, sacrificing her finishing place to make sure more players qualified. At one point, she was getting close to not making it herself, so Anson yelled out, "Tracey, you have a minute and a half. You better get going." Almost to the end, she had been carrying other people with her encouragement, and then, in the last 30 seconds, something amazing happened. We watched her just start to sprint. She made it.

At the same time Tracey was cheering on the team, it was clear that for some people, it wasn't easy. It was a struggle, and you knew it was going to be that way all year. Maybe that would be the case for four years. But it was also understood that this doesn't mean those who struggled didn't deserve to be there. It doesn't mean they weren't going to help our team, or that they weren't good people.

It was so incredible to see how much Tracey cared. The fitness tests are a freshman's first introduction to the UNC program, and she was carrying on a tradition of encouragement she herself had benefited from. This same system of supporting teammates is one she instills in her own players today, as coach of the United States U19 Youth National Team.

On that day of the Cooper test, the fact that Tracey was willing to do everything she could to help other players pass said everything I wanted to know about the program. The main reason I went to UNC was that no matter what—win, lose, good or bad—those people wanted me to be happy. They wanted me to succeed, and together, we would do whatever we could to ensure that success for each other.

After four years at UNC you think of your teammates as your best friends. They are. The fact that we endured so much together is symbolized by how we saw each other during a typical Tuesday fitness session. During those sessions you can feel as if you're going to pass out. You turn to your teammate and say, "I can't do it anymore," and that person looks you in the eye and says, "I'll get you through it." Regardless of your role—whether it's your day to be pulled through, or it's your day to pull other people through, the fact that your teammates still care about you, that they love you just the same, is what makes the experience so extraordinary.

There was a defining incident, which also happened in my freshman year, when I probably best understood the meaning of the UNC program. It also involved Tracey Bates. A week before preseason of her senior year, Tracey sustained a Jones Fracture (a fracture of the fifth metatarsal of the foot). She had never incurred a serious injury, and her healing, and yearlong comeback to play in her fifth year, were quite remarkable. She and the team were playing against NC (North Carolina) State. I was injured at the time myself, so I was watching the game. At one point, the ball popped out about 25 yards from the goal. Tracey and a very large, physical NC State player went into a tackle for a 50-50 ball. Suddenly, Tracey fell to the ground. She had torn her MCL (medial collateral ligament, in the knee).

There was dead silence, except for the sound of Tracey crying. She was lying on the field, fearing that her season, and probably her career, were over. Bill Prentice, the team's trainer, picked her up and brought her into our van. I walked over to talk to her, and then Anson arrived. He hugged her, and himself began to cry. He was not crying for the player. He was crying for the person, and the pain she was feeling, especially knowing all that she had done to be able to make a comeback.

From the beginning, I knew I had made the right decision to attend UNC. But watching Tracey and Anson at that moment clarified for me the true reason I went there—because it is through this game that we learn the importance of human relationships.

MIA HAMM

Preface

I had just finished scouting the Santa Clara/Florida game in the 2001 NCAA National Championship semifinal in Dallas, Texas, at Southern Methodist University's beautiful new stadium. Florida had come from behind to close the 2-0 gap in the closing seconds to take the game into sudden death overtime. Then, early in the overtime, Santa Clara scored dramatically to meet us in the Championship final. We had beaten an excellent Portland team 2-1 earlier in the day to get to the final, and I was leaving the stadium to rejoin our team at the hotel. Tim Nash was in the hallway as I was walking out. Tim has a rare and penetrating understanding of the women's game, and a real appreciation of the evolution and drama of all these encounters.

> "Anson, I hate to tell you this, but Aly Wagner (the talented Santa Clara attacking center midfielder) has figured it out," Tim said as I approached him. When Tim says something, I listen. He coauthored my first book, *Training Soccer Champions,* and my respect for his opinion is without reservation.
> "What has she figured out?" I asked.
> "In the press conference she said that she understands now what winning is all about. She now knows that it's about grinding it out to the end."

Tim's comment on Aly's understanding was prophetic. Two days later, on a brilliant strike, she stuck a world-class shot into the upper left corner to beat us 1-0 for the 2001 National Championship title. It was not the best of games, but to Santa Clara's credit, its entire team kept "grinding" all game, especially Aly and Danielle Slaton, Santa Clara's superb central defender. Their performance was a statement of this understanding.

In the book I wrote with Tim, I tried to share some of the things I felt worked in developing elite women athletes. It was written for coaches. One of the themes that I tried to drive home was to create environments in practice that would psychologically harden the athletes in training to make them relentless. These sessions were designed to develop the muscle in the middle of your chest: your heart. Your heart doesn't understand systems or shape or tactics, but it bleeds an indefatigable human spirit and, if it's strong enough, it "grinds" away in our game for 90 minutes, or sometimes 150 if necessary. This spirit goes beyond sport. It is the athletic experience at its best, and becomes a statement of your strength of character and who and what you are. When that happens, I feel athletics has value. And I have never been one to think any sport has much meaning without it. Nor do I trumpet the intrinsic value of the athletic arena. I have known people who have been involved in athletics all of their lives who have little moral fiber, and some people without any athletic experiences who are paragons of virtue. The athletic experience only has meaning if we can draw something from it beyond the game. I say this so much our players think it is a cliché: "Athletics doesn't develop character, but it certainly exposes it," and it's true. There is a range of experience in sports that truly tests the human spirit; yes, it can be euphoric, but some of it is not; in fact, at times it is devastating. Your reaction to everything in this range will demonstrate the depth of your character.

Fred Tutweiler shared a powerful Rainer Maria Rilke poem with last year's sophomore class in a personal growth seminar in the spring. I sent it to the entire team at the beginning of the summer with this note:

"Whenever you become afraid of failing to become everything you dreamed of, read the poem Fred Tutweiler shared with us by Rainer Maria Rilke. I have enclosed it for you...because this is how you will grow, 'by being defeated, decisively, by constantly greater beings.' Never be afraid to be the best you can be...hard work will get you there, and remember, no one ever drowned in their own sweat."

The Man Watching

I can tell by the way the trees beat, after
so many dull days, on my worried windowpanes
that a storm is coming,
and I hear the far-off fields say things
I can't bear without a friend,
I can't love without a sister.

The storm, the shifter of shapes, drives on
across the woods and across time,
and the world looks as if it has no age:
the landscape, like a line in the psalm book,
is seriousness and weight and eternity.

What we choose to fight is so tiny!
What fights with us is so great!

If only we would let ourselves be dominated
as things do by some immense storm,
we would become strong too, and not need names.

When we win it's with small things,
and the triumph itself makes us small.
What is extraordinary and eternal
does not want to be bent by us.
I mean the Angel who appeared
to the wrestlers of the Old Testament:
when the wrestlers' sinews
grew long like metal stings,
he felt them under his fingers
like chords of deep music.

Whoever was beaten by this Angel
(who often simply declined the fight)
went away proud and strengthened
and great from that harsh hand,
that kneaded him as if to change his shape.
Winning does not tempt that man.
This is how he grows: by being defeated, decisively,
by constantly greater beings.

So, in this book written with Gloria Averbuch for youth players, I
wanted to share as much as I could about this process taken to another
level. That next level comes through victory *and* defeat. The challenges are
not just physical, technical, and tactical; and as the poem alludes, sometimes your greatest growth periods are going to be when, "what is extraordinary and eternal does not want to be bent by us." And then, what you win
or what you become has much more meaning. This kind of victory you carry
with you wherever you go; it is what you are.

Nothing would have been possible without the remarkable collection
of powerful and talented young women who have inspired me from my first
association with them in 1979. Some of these great people have given generously to this project. Everything positive I have done has been in close
collaboration with the warm center of our program, Bill Palladino. Our cutting edge and energy has been extended by Chris Ducar. The structure and
our protection from the chaos of the universe are provided by Tom Sander
and Delaine Marbry. I am proud and grateful to be guided by two more

friends who are also nationally respected experts that I trust with my life: Bill Prentice and Greg Gatz.

My main satisfaction for what we have done here, however, is seeing the evolution of 15-year-old Yael Averbuch, the prime mover of this collaboration, who asked us the questions she wanted answered in her quest to navigate all the treacherous waters of her sport. I hope in some way we have helped her.

ANSON DORRANCE

A Mother/Daughter Encounter

It began with the dream of my then 10-year-old daughter Yael, and *Dynasty*, the videotape about the University of North Carolina women's soccer. She played that tape so often I swore it would get blisters. At age 12, she and a friend bravely flew on their own to attend UNC girls soccer camp. She wrote an article about what it was like to play on the fabled fields, to be trained by Anson Dorrance, and to listen to the inspirational evening speeches he delivered to the campers.

Spying on her practicing alone in the basement or backyard, I watched her doing the drills she had learned at camp. As time went on, she has added the skills on the UNC competitive matrix, challenging herself to meet the standards of the collegiate stars.

It was Yael, now 15 and just selected to the 2002 U.S. Under-16 Girls National Team pool, who introduced me to the phrases and philosophy that are the core of UNC women's soccer. She had discovered a program, and a coach that fed her independence, discipline, and dedication. She remains unconditionally devoted to the unique and inspiring UNC world, one which, I would later discover, transcends mere sport. It is a world in which women are called warriors; a world in which, even more than their athletic ability, players are valued for traits such as tenacity, resilience, and courage—testimony to the depth and quality of their character.

One day, I was literally chasing Yael down the hallway of our house, trying rather aggressively to impart some parental advice. I quoted from my personal "soccer bible," *Training Soccer Champions*, Anson's first book, which I have read four times. "Anson says good parents can be unbelievable nags...in a positive sense." She turned midflight, and smiling at her own sarcastic wit, responded, "Well, he hasn't met you yet!"

The challenge was irresistible. In the fertile soil of that mother/daughter encounter, the seeds of this book were firmly planted.

From the first trip I took back in 1999, each visit to UNC has been a revelation. After hearing my first Anson pregame team speech, laced with life philosophy, I wept. (Of course, both my daughters rolled their eyes when I told them this.) Subsequently, I discovered that the methodical attention to detail at UNC applies to more than soccer. Education goes beyond the field and into the classroom, where in the off-season players read literature, and learn about leadership and personal development. But there is something else special about the program—a sense of pleasure amidst the hard work. I watched the players in the weight room, where there was as much laughter as lifting. After an exhausting session, athletes somehow found the motivation to shout team chants while doing sit-ups.

Initially, I was surprised by the program's combination of intensity and joy, and how suddenly interchangeable these qualities can be: a fierce tackle followed by an Anson joke. I was impressed by a standard of excellence so expected, and the unquestionable willingness to give one's all, at times to struggle—all for the love of a team and a game. By the time I had done hours of interviews, gathered all the book material, and soaked up the atmosphere through the banter of the players, I understood that the longing of millions of girls to be a part of the UNC program goes far deeper than scoreboard success. Win or lose, UNC soccer reflects an extraordinary sense of camaraderie, and the opportunity to discover a deep sense of one's self.

This book shows you that while skill is essential, what makes a true champion is not just physical ability or soccer talent. Victory only begins on the field. At UNC, it is often outside the white lines that the players' abilities are truly tested, developed, and deepened.

In this book, Anson Dorrance not only defines the technical and tactical tools required to excel, but explores a life view through the value of sport. From him and the UNC program, you will learn that champions are not born, they are constructed. You will learn to empower yourself, and to find both the athletic and personal rewards—and the love of the game—that are the hallmark of his program and of his players. In short, you will acquire "the vision of a champion."

The gift of authorship is the journey one takes toward enlightenment. A writer comes to understand that the process of the work is ultimately what matters, even beyond the result of that work. What Anson gives you in this book is an appreciation of the process—the how's and why's of developing as an athlete as well as a person. He provides meaning and motivation for every level and personality of player. You will come to understand that at UNC, it is the journey that has value. That is why both the individual and the team quest for greatness is every bit as important as the actual achievement of that greatness.

I began writing this book because I wanted to give to others what UNC soccer has continued to give my daughter Yael: The tools to train. The inspiration to excel. The power of a dream. What began as her dream (and a hallway remark) has transcended even my initial expectations, and become what I firmly believe is a unique and valuable contribution to youth sports.

I undertook this project as a gift to my children, but discovered in the end that it is every bit as meaningful for parents, coaches, administrators, and anyone else seeking to truly understand and support youth sports. *The Vision of a Champion* teaches us all how to do our best, and how to get the most of our sports experience.

Above all, this book reflects the spirit of UNC women's soccer. It is that spirit that so powerfully inspires every young player to forever dream the worthy dream.

GLORIA AVERBUCH

Introduction
The 2000 National Collegiate Athletic Association (NCAA) Championship

We just keep going after it and we never quit.
I think that is what is special about our team.

—Meredith Florance,
Offensive Most Valuable Player,
2000 NCAA Championship,
NCAA 2000 College Player of the Year

The ball was dug out of the midfield by Anne Remy, whose heart is as big as a soccer field. She played it down the right flank to Danielle Borgman, who's about the fastest player running with the ball I've ever coached. Danielle ran past her mark and served the ball across. Making the near-post run was Alyssa Ramsey, who fought to get in front of her defender. Because of her size and strength, Alyssa is among the best there is playing with her back to pressure. She also has the tactical decision-making that led her to get in front of the University of California, Los Angeles (UCLA) defense, which was the cornerstone of this scoring opportunity. She cleaned it up, turned, and played it back into the middle of the box to Meredith Florance, one of the best finishers in the University of North Carolina (UNC's) history. She roofed it into the back of the net to get us back into the NCAA final against UCLA. The definitive moment of these championships, this game-tying goal in the final, was built on the best qualities of our game, and of the four players who made it happen. It was Anne's heart, Danielle's athleticism, Alyssa's strength and tactical decision-making, and Meredith's clean technique and focus. That's how championships are won—by a team effort—a collection of the best of all the players together.

The year 2000 provided me with all the ingredients to appreciate the challenges and joys of our sport, and the best possible platform from which to address youth soccer players. That's because everything I could possibly teach you happened in the span of the brief final weeks of the 2000 collegiate competition.

That year, more than any other in our history, our team struggled through a lot of adversity. We came back from being down nine different

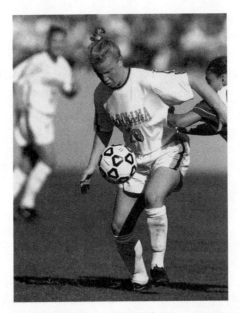

Here's Meredith focusing on her first touch with someone pressuring from behind. It captures her final year for us, when she did everything possible to become the best she could be.

times in the season, the most ever. We were behind three crucial times in the NCAA tournament alone, including both the semifinal and final game. And yet we managed to win, 2-1, in both the semifinal and the final game. One of the most exciting aspects of athletics is the come-from-behind victory. This is even more so in a sport like soccer, in which scoring is so incredibly difficult. The fact that we ultimately prevailed is a tremendous testimony to the skill, commitment, confidence, and relentless effort of our players. It is also a lesson in learning not to panic.

UNC's soccer program has been enormously successful, resulting in our winning 17 of the 20 college championships. That's why the media calls us a dynasty. There were years when we completely dominated women's collegiate soccer. Probably the best example is the "dream team" of 1992. With Mia Hamm on right wing, Kristine Lilly on left wing, Tisha Venturini as attacking center half and a star-studded lineup of quality players in every position, we were destined for greatness. But given the nature of the game, you're never quite sure you're going to win every challenge, so the mission in '92 was basically not to suffer an upset. Back then, it was nerve-wracking for me. But hindsight offers a different perspective; it was needless worry.

Even under the pressure of the Championship final, when Duke scored the first goal, our team went on a rampage, winning 9-1, a Championship margin that showed the awesome strength of that remarkable team.

The 2000 triumph was the exact opposite. Everything was closely fought. Given the evolution of women's soccer, there's an increasing amount of talent, committed programs, and experienced coaches. We certainly had some amazing talent on our 2000 team, but not in an overwhelming sense, like the '92 team. When we won in '92 it was kind of a relief, since I knew we were the best team. We should have won. The year 2000 was different. I was thrilled for everything we overcame, and everything we demonstrated. Our victory surprised a lot of people.

We came into the NCAA tournament seeded fifth, and thus became the lowest seeded team to win. We had suffered three losses within our conference alone. We were behind so often, and had given up so many goals, we became used to pushing through when the tide was against us. Usually a championship team is built on a strong defense. That's something you can bring to every game. A great attack is always going to be inconsistent—at least on the scoreboard—that's the nature of the game. If you have a great attacking personality in soccer you might score five goals in one game but the next game get shut out, even though you may have created the same fine chances you scored on in the previous game. But the nature of defense is that you have the potential to shut everyone out, every game. In 2000, we didn't have the kind of defense that was putting up those numbers. When I refer to the defense, I don't just mean the back three defenders and the goalkeeper. I mean the defensive effort by the entire team.

In addition, the teams we were up against in the semifinal and final games were the number one and number two defensive squads in the country. Neither team had given up more than one goal in a game all season. Until late in both games, we were down one goal to each of these teams. The challenge of playing against their defenses, and trying to come back, was simply enormous, but obviously exciting. This set a wonderful stage.

We struggled with other problems in the season, including injuries to two of our top players, which kept Olympic alternate Susan Bush and senior all-American Laurie Schwoy off the field for much of the season. The inexperience of some of our younger players was also a challenge. But both of these drawbacks only served to demonstrate the strength of a system we switched to five years before.

Our system of play (a semiflat back 3-4-3) is often criticized as being too high-risk. Some say we survive it only because of our "star" players. Throughout the book, however, I praise this system and encourage you to learn it. The 2000 Championship illustrates why, in my opinion, this system takes advantage of the strengths and weaknesses in the women's game and should be looked at as a youth development system that forces every player to play on her edge, and so gain maximal improvement.

Here was our so-called "star" lineup in the final: the left back was a walk-on; the right back was a freshman, starting for the first time in her life; the center back was a transfer who had never started in an NCAA tournament; the defensive midfielder position was shared between a freshman, who had never played our system and wasn't match fit, and her partner, who was still recovering from her fifth ACL (anterior cruciate ligament) tear, and was without her full agility. Yet in both the semifinal and the final, we managed to hold our opponents to a few shots (only four to Notre Dame and three to UCLA), outshooting teams that had not had that happen to them all year. So despite the enormous talent of those players, the success of our system is clearly not built merely on experienced stars in every position.

But victory is never all triumph. In 2000 we had our dark days. The lowest point came after our third loss (we had not had three losses in a season in 20 years), and our second loss in a row. The day following that loss, I was scheduled to travel to Oneonta, New York, to see Carin Jennings Gabarra inducted into the National Soccer Hall of Fame. I had the ticket, rental car, and hotel room already booked. That was an event I did not want to miss, because Carin means the world to me. She was the starting left wing and tournament Most Valuable Player (MVP) when we won the World Championship in 1991. But I had to call to tell her I couldn't go. I explained that I had to help resuscitate this shattered team. She completely understood.

The team was devastated. I spent Saturday with them, trying to reconstruct their confidence. We reviewed all the elements that have made the UNC tradition remarkable, and talked about what we had to do in order to win. A lot of factors influence success, and our team chemistry, of which attitudes and emotions are a part, requires constant attention. Sometimes you have to work off the field just as conscientiously as you do on it.

That's exactly what we did. And the results were evident in the very competitive Atlantic Coast Conference (ACC) tournament. We've won a lot of ACC Championships, and with some amazing teams. But I have not seen us dominate the Conference Championships as thoroughly and overwhelmingly as we did this year in a long time. Quite simply, we rocked. And we did it having come into the event 4-3 in conference play.

That Saturday we had begun to rebuild our winning mentality. We did that with one of the most important steps you will read about extensively in this book: by each and every player stepping up to take responsibility.

Although I stressed to the team not to panic, that should not be confused with being passive. I never want to make the mistake many players and youth coaches do when they use what I think is one of the most destructive phrases in athletics. In a misguided attempt to instill confidence, they say, "Don't worry. It will come. It's going to happen." I use this example when I talk about abdicating responsibility, because, in essence, saying this to a team means: "It will come, but I will have nothing to do with it." That phrase is one I never want to hear from any of the players. It's an attitude that will never get results. The phrase I want to hear on the field is, "Give me the ball. I will make it happen." That's what is critical when you are down—that every player has to feel like she is going to be responsible for the comeback, and that even more, everyone wants that responsibility. One of the most important things I can convey to you is to feel as if you are the margin of victory. Be a part of the reason your team wins. On a day-to-day basis, take responsibility for everything: your fitness, whether you win or lose, whether you get to play or sit, whether you are a positive life force or a whiner, whether you are going to improve that day or "coast." Believe that you are in control of everything.

Another lesson this season emphasized is that the formula for success is no great mystery. No matter what you've been told, or what you assume you have to do to succeed, these pages will stress that successful soccer always gets back to the basics—to technique, to the things you learn as a youth player. A moment in the semifinal game illustrates that.

We were down 1-0 at halftime. The television commentary about unbeaten and number-one ranked Notre Dame had increased in their favor, just as it would when we were behind to UCLA in the final. It was like putting a nail into our coffin, and it made our opponents look like winners already. But it was important for our players not to panic, and to know that we could still win. Due to a commitment requiring each coach to do a halftime television interview during the NCAA Championship games, I entered the locker room late. Everyone was sitting there, silent, concerned about what I would say about their performance. I walked across the room slowly, and hung up my coat. I walked to the drink bin, calmly grabbed a soda, and took a few sips. Putting the drink down, I paused, looked at the players and then simply asked them, "What do you think?" Their answer is unprintable, but truthful. They had played horribly. "To be completely honest," I responded, "I'm very excited, because that is the worst soccer we've played all year, and we're only down one goal." All we needed to know was that we could play better and that we were not dead yet. What is critical when you are down is to know you have hope.

Now, you're playing the number-one team in the country, so people think you are in the locker room coming up with some sort of incredibly elaborate tactical scheme on how to win. But a game is rarely won that way.

I walked over to our junior midfielder Jena Kluegel and pointed to the spot between her feet and said, "That's where I aim if I'm trying to pass the ball to Jena." My advice at the halftime consisted of a review on how to pass the ball to one of my key players, where to pass her the ball, where to aim—which is why you can't take your technical training seriously enough. The game is ultimately won with fundamental technique: receiving, passing, shooting, dribbling, and heading. You can't get good enough at those basic skills.

My main instruction to beat the number-one team in the country is what every quality youth coach is teaching, and every ambitious youth player should be learning. The only difference between what an eight-year-old or a twelve-year-old is doing and one of the women in the NCAA semifinal, or Mia Hamm or Kristine Lilly in the World Cup for that matter, is that you have less and less time as you go from one level to the next to perform your technique, which means you have to be more focused, cleaner, and quicker on the ball. And all of those things you can learn at the most basic level, just by constant practice of the correct technique, done at a quicker and quicker pace. And please understand, you can't ever be skillful enough and you can never spend enough time on this part of your game.

Another one of the basics, and an overlooked aspect of our Championship record, is long-term preparation. Winning is not something built in a day; it is constructed year-round. As always, it comes down to progressive, consistent effort, with a view toward a long-range goal.

After our victory, people wondered what factors helped us to win. "Was it the team's mentality?" Well, yes, but that mentality is built in the off-season, and all year long. As we do every year, we began preparing for that victory on the Tuesday following the 1999 Sunday final game. Every year on that Tuesday we have a team meeting in which we lay out what we have to do to win the next year's title. Obviously, that preparation does not begin with the same sort of intensity to which it ultimately builds by the Championship game, but we make it clear that every player must commit to doing the maximum in every way she can in order for us to be the best we can be. At our level it begins with staying fit. Maintaining fitness is not that difficult. It's getting fit that's hard. The team gets a day off after the Championship game, but I let them know that despite the end of the season, it is obviously a mistake to let their fitness lapse by lying on a couch and eating bonbons, celebrating their last Championship.

What this team fought through in order to win surely took mental toughness. But this mentality was not constructed during the adversity. Actually, those comebacks were constructed in the off-season. My favorite quote about this is attributed to Indiana basketball coach Bobby Knight. "The will to win is overrated in athletics, because everyone wants to win. It's the will to prepare to win that makes the difference."

In the 2000 NCAA final, four players, part of a remarkable team, symbolized the best in the game. The vision of a champion is exemplified by heart, athleticism, strength, tactics, focus, and skill. It all came together in that championship victory. We triumphed that year, and with the same qualities for success defined in these pages, so can you.

HEART

ATHLETICISM

STRENGTH

TACTICS

FOCUS

SKILL

CHAPTER 1

The Dynasty

Beginnings

A winning tradition always starts somewhere. It has roots, and women's soccer is no different. Why is it important for you to know the history of the game you play? For one thing, it's because it has been built from the sweat of previous generations. As female soccer players, you can take pride in the fact you are benefiting from the great players who have gone before you. You are part of a rich and inspiring tradition. Your connection to these great players and their history also makes you a member of the unique women's soccer community. What's more, in understanding the evolution of the game, you will gain valuable insight into your own development as a player.

We are all students of the game, continually learning. Everything I teach my players, and will teach you in this book, can be traced to the University of North Carolina and the U.S. National Team, and how it all began. Much by an accident of fate, I became part of women's soccer history. My involvement in the UNC program dates back to 1979, when a group of campus students petitioned the athletic department for a women's varsity team. I was a UNC student myself, in my third year of law school, and a part-time head coach of the university's men's soccer team.

Spurred by the students' petition, Bill Coby, then head of the Athletic Department, invited me to watch the women's club team. I looked out at the group, moving the ball on the same field where many of the greatest women players in the world would one day practice. "What do you think?" Coby asked me. "They're well organized, with some solid talent," I answered. I had no idea that my response would result in his asking me to coach a new women's team. I had my hands full with my studies, and I enjoyed coaching

Here is yours truly back in his playing days—thick hair and all, 135 pounds, on our UNC soccer venue, Fetzer Field.

the men. But Coby's offer beckoned: I could create a full-time position by coaching both the men and the women. For the next 10 years, I trained both teams—one after the other—for a total of four hours a day. I was eventually forced to give up law school for this job, which now I truly loved.

Just Call Me Anson

This job was a rare and tremendous experience for a young coach. After all, I was only 24 years old. In fact, I was coaching guys I had played alongside just a couple of years before. When I began working with them, there was no way I was going to ask them to call me Coach, or anything else for that matter, other than what they had always called me. That is why, to this day, everyone I work with, no matter what age, calls me Anson. Right from the beginning of my career, I never really wanted a huge distance between myself and the players. I still feel the same way today. So if you ever come to my camp, or have an occasion to play for our great university, just call me Anson. Everyone else does and I hope they always will.

That was exactly how I introduced myself to our first recruit, a player who symbolized the future of our program. It was in 1979, the first year for women's varsity soccer. I invited a goal-scorer from Texas named Janet Rayfield (UNC '79–'82) to visit the campus. A great leader and a wonderful human being (qualities that from the beginning have been essential to my recruiting process and soccer philosophy), she became a four-year captain of the team. Janet remains second all-time in goals scored at UNC (93), surpassed only by Mia Hamm (103). We built our program around her, in the same way that we would one day do with players like April Heinrichs and Mia.

In 1980 we recruited a few more players, and took part in the first women's soccer Invitational Championship at Colorado College. At that time the yearly budget for UNC women's soccer was $5,000. But the cost of going to this Championship alone was $8,500. I explained to the athletic director at the time, John Swofford, that going to the Championship would help us gain a reputation, and recruit other players. When he approved the request—essentially increasing our yearly budget by one and half times for this single event—I knew we were on our way, literally and figuratively.

Our results were unremarkable at the Colorado College Championship, where we won one game, and lost two. One loss was courtesy of Harvard University and a one-year student there named Lauren Gregg. But Gregg was looking for a more high-profile soccer program. We snapped her up. She played on our first two National Championship teams ('81 and '82), and, of course, went on to serve as my assistant coach in the 1991 World Championship and for Tony DiCiccio on the U.S. National Team in its '96 Olympic and '99 World Cup victories.

An accident of fate. That's how I came to coach women that day, watching our club team play. And soon we ended up with a true collegiate women's soccer championship, from which our UNC "dynasty" was born. The first women's national championship happened from a single trip to Detroit. At our own expense, Chris Lidstone, a Colorado coach and organizer of that 1980 Invitational Championship, and I decided to fly to the Association for Intercollegiate Athletics for Women (AIAW) convention. The AIAW, led by a group of great women who worked for equal opportunities, was the first governing body to promote women's collegiate sports. Chris and I went in to campaign for the AIAW leadership to host a women's soccer championship, even before we had any credibility as a collegiate sport.

Although women's soccer did not nearly meet the technical criteria for which collegiate championships are ordinarily granted (such as a certain number of colleges with women's soccer programs), we relied on the beginning of a groundswell of kids playing the game. "There's a youth movement out there, and we have a chance to really do something for a women's sport," we passionately told them. I even remember the analogy we used. We talked about a "big parade" of unbelievable young female soccer players. We said we had an opportunity to lead this parade. Just to show how decisions were made back then, the AIAW leadership left the room, and within 15 minutes behind closed doors, they voted to approve our request. We were stunned but grateful for their decisive support.

Politics being what they are, the NCAA saw something successful and wanted to get on the bandwagon. In 1982 they decided to take over all women's collegiate championships in every sport. Despite the wonderful work of the AIAW, the NCAA had the money and the prestige to offer significant changes, including improvement in the quality of life for the female athlete. But it was the AIAW that had nurtured a product attractive enough for the NCAA to make an offer that no one could refuse. Women's soccer owes the AIAW a great debt.

We hosted the next Championship at UNC in 1981. This time they weren't an invitational; they were official. We wanted to put on a celebration, a chance to promote women's soccer. In order to represent the quality of the game and to enhance its reputation, we invited the best 12 teams from around the country, and made the event a festival. Promoting our game has always been a priority at UNC (something players on the National Team have also been keenly aware of). We even manipulated the media to sell our game. If you look at the pictures from this time, you'll see the players framed by a big crowd, cheering them from the stands. That's because I asked the photographers to take shots that focused the team in front of the largest group of fans, even if the rest of the stands were empty. I guess the tactic worked, because our brochures looked great! Sure enough, the most popular photograph from that weekend is a picture of all of our players in a raised-hands salute, waving to a sole photographer with a huge crowd in the background (over 4,000 people). From looking at this picture, you would not know that with the exception of this one block of excited fans, the 52,000-seat football stadium was empty.

We had phenomenal players at UNC throughout the 1980s and '90s, and women's NCAA soccer participation grew 120% from 1990 to 1996. In fact, I was so busy with the women that in 1989 I dropped the men's coaching position. The women's game had a great future, and we had a chance to continue to prove it. Women's soccer had become the fastest growing sport in the NCAA, the U.S. Women's National Team was making a case for its own international dynasty, and it was becoming the sport of choice for girls under the age of 12. In 1994, for the first time, a predetermined site was

This was our first effort to consciously promote the women's game through the illusion of crowd support. We persuaded our lone photographer to get across the field in our 52,000-seat Kenan football stadium, have the entire crowd sit together on one side of the field, and have them turn to wave at him, so we could capture the entire crowd in the background of that first National Championship weekend in 1981.

established for the NCAA Championship. Rather than in years past, in which the final was held with one week's notice at one of the sites of a participating team, now we set a location early, and had advanced ticket sales. The fact that we managed to sell out our event without ticket buyers even knowing who the teams would be was a true achievement. We may have begun small, but today, more than 600 colleges field women's soccer teams.

As I previously mentioned, there was parallel growth on the youth level. While still a college sophomore I began coaching recreational level soccer—male and female, from young children to adults. We took some of our top recreational players to the International Soccer Camp in Pennsylvania where most of the instruction was from active college players. And in Chapel Hill we saw the youth movement coming from a small number initially that seemed to get bigger every year, with no growth end in sight. Although there was no grand master plan, I could already appreciate that collegiate and youth soccer shared an important connection. All of us seemed drawn into this movement to try to popularize our game.

With the development of collegiate programs, young girls would now have something to point toward—beyond the youth game. From that first Championship, which brought together soccer leaders and players from all over the country, I felt that college soccer was an important key. It combines two wonderful opportunities for females—academic and athletic—a chance for an education and a chance to play soccer, in a sense professionally, since the coaches, uniforms, travel, etc. are paid for by the colleges. College soccer stimulates the development of the youth player. It combines an education with such a wholesome game, an opportunity to continue competing in the sport they love. If done properly, it also provides an opportunity to grow as an individual as well as an athlete.

The Dynasty

- UNC 17-time National Champion (of the 20 years the Championships have been contested), 1981–'00. Carolina has won more NCAA Division I women's national championships than any other Division I women's athletic sport program in the nation.
- 21 successive National Tournament Final Four appearances.
- 14-time Atlantic Coast Conference (ACC) Champions (of the 15 years the Championships have been contested).
- At one time, UNC's winning streak stretched for five years and over 100 games (from 1986–90), three of which were ties. Another streak of 92 wins was established from 1990–94, with no ties.
- Overall record, as of 10/18/01: 500-22-11. As of that date, Anson Dorrance became only the third NCAA Division I soccer coach in history to win 500 games while coaching either exclusively men or women.
- 62 different players have been named to all-American teams or have been all-American honorable mention selections.
- 10 players have been named National Player of the Year.
- 23 times players have been Most Valuable Player at the NCAA Tournament.
- Anson Dorrance named National Coach of the Year on four occasions (once for men) and ACC Coach of the Year six times.
- Coaches and assistant coaches of the U.S. National Team include past UNC players April Heinrichs and Lauren Gregg. Various other past UNC players coach at both the national and collegiate level.
- 24 UNC players played for the Women's United Soccer Association (WUSA) in its first season.

The Dynasty, and the UNC Philosophy

> *No one would have dared to give any less than 100 percent when that Carolina shirt was on her back.*

> —Angela Kelly, member of four UNC National Championship teams ('91–'94)

Women's soccer is part of an incredible athletic tradition at the University of North Carolina. In years past, UNC has been named as having the nation's best NCAA Division I sports program, and in addition to great soccer stars, its alumni include basketball legend Michael Jordan and Olympic gold medal sprinter Marion Jones.

They call UNC women's soccer a dynasty. I'm asked all the time about this dynasty, a term that I recall first appeared in the *New York Times* in the mid-1980s. It is almost impossible to discuss such a title so that it comes out gracefully. I try to address the issue by saying that if we are a dynasty, it is a dynasty of hard work, of year-round play, and of a commitment to striving for excellence. The great names who have been part of our program understood this combination of high achievement and grace. I think one of the most useful lessons I can convey to you as a young soccer player is to grasp what this "dynasty" entails, and how to model your career on this quest for greatness and the critical attitude of graceful humility which must accompany it.

At UNC we do not believe in a sense of entitlement. We never take anything for granted, or stop to reflect on our grandeur. While we celebrate our victories, we acknowledge and learn from our losses. Don't get me wrong, self-confidence is a necessary foundation for soccer, but as soon as you feel you have "arrived," that you are good enough, it is the beginning of your decline. One of the most unfortunate things I see when identifying youth players is the girl who is told over the years how great she is. By the time she's a high school freshman, she starts to believe it. By her senior year, she's fizzled out. Then, there's her counterpart: a girl waiting in the wings, who quietly and with determination decides she's going to make something of herself. Invariably, this humble, hardworking girl is the one who becomes the real player.

One of my favorite illustrations of this is a Calvin & Hobbs cartoon, in which Calvin is flying down the side of the mountain in his wagon, while merrily sharing that he wants his life to be a never-ending ascension. At the same time he is pontificating, he is flying off a cliff into an abyss. This is a wonderful attitude about life. Life is filled with peril, but somehow, with all the danger and prospects of failure, we have to maintain a reckless optimism. So let's dream impossible dreams, a "never-ending ascension," even when there is little evidence supporting it. At UNC, infectious optimism, coupled with dedication and hard work, and a humbling and challenging environment, have helped our sport get noticed.

There is a tremendous significance to the UNC winning tradition—the so-called dynasty—because it has helped showcase women's soccer. From the very beginning at both UNC and on the U.S. National Team, I felt those of us involved had an enormous responsibility to promote the sport. Every top player has worked to sell the game. Before our sport had any real attention, our visibility (stories about our winning streak) gave the national media something to write about, and I think it helped us. If you look at the growth of other major sports, it is the great dynasties that have been at the heart of their popularity—the New York Yankees in baseball, or Michael Jordan and the Chicago Bulls in basketball, and in golf, there is a one-man marketing arm in Tiger Woods. But as soon as Jordan retired and the Bulls went by the wayside, the National Basketball Association became less visible.

Meticulous attention to detail, intense, competitive practices that duplicate the heart of the game, studying every possible tactical scenario—at UNC we pride ourselves on being tremendously thorough. This is a necessity of excellence, and the hallmark of what we try to do. I believe it is also a major contributing factor to our dominance. In our game, everything is choreographed. I use that term because I am married to a dancer, and it best describes how we break down the game. It means everything we do has been rehearsed. No game scenario is left to chance. We dissect the sport: technically, tactically, physically, and psychologically.

One of the benefits of this system to the players is the enormous amount of information we share with them. We give players feedback on everything in practices and games. By the time they graduate, they know so much about the game that each one is prepared to be a fine coach. I know they are equipped to become experts, because so many of our players have gone on to coach at the collegiate and the national level.

Women's soccer has its own momentum now thanks to the overwhelming success of the 1999 World Cup, and the arrival of the nationally visible WUSA. You benefit as a youth from all of this now.

I think people will be shocked at the amount of detail that characterizes our program on a year-round basis, much of it published here for the first time. Appendix II includes the detailed rhythms and programs of what we do. All of this grand choreography and attention to detail is a collaboration of a superb collection of colleagues. In addition to the extraordinary players I have coached, I am fortunate to be surrounded by a number of experts who help create the UNC magic. They have also contributed significantly to this book.

Another aspect of the UNC philosophy is empowering our players. Basically, we teach them to coach themselves. In order to do that, they must take responsibility for all aspects of their soccer and personal development. They are assisted in their development because so much is measured (see the competitive matrix, Chapter 13). They are helped in their personal development because our tradition and senior leadership don't tolerate the selfish or ego-driven personality. They must learn to work independently, maintain year-round fitness and skill, and most important, contribute humanity to the team. This is also your challenge as a developing youth player.

There's a misconception about UNC. Everyone thinks we have a roster of world-beaters. But that isn't the case. Above all, we value people for their humanity. That's what I look for in any player, and it is part of the way we pick our team. Quality human beings are what create the most essential element of any team: great chemistry. We look for positive, hardworking players—the kind you don't hear whine or complain. To make our team, the only requirement is character. You don't have to be a great soccer player; you just have to be a great person. In fact, being great in a sport is totally meaningless unless it has impacted on other aspects of your being.

For example, as I write this book, there is a wonderful young woman on our roster who has never played organized soccer before this, her final year of college. Her name is Julie Smith, and she walked on after a very successful track career at UNC. Although she put in a tremendous effort for us and set a record in one of our aerobic fitness tests, she has very limited soccer skills. You're probably wondering what she is doing on the field with some of the top players in the country, and in the world. It's because we like her and respect her. And having watched the players constantly call out their support to her is a true measure of their character, because they value her as they should—as a person first and a soccer player second. She may not get much time in our games, but she is a valuable member of our team.

Passion and Performance

One of the best descriptions of our program comes from someone who never even played for us. Michelle Akers may be talking about the U.S. National Team in the section below, taken from her first book, but as you will see, what I have sought to contribute to both UNC and the National Team are one and the same. Of course, I didn't ask Michelle to write this, but I am certainly grateful that she did:

I learned a lot from him [Anson] over the years about a great many things. I learned what it means to train for the National Team. What it means to be fit. That detail and precision is an important thing in the game of soccer. How to motivate players. And how to play the politics with the mucky mucks. Anson built the basis of how the current National Team operates and wins by, even now. Prepare and train on our own. Be committed to the one thing you can control—your fitness. Be smart and be aware that your decisions and actions on and

The Tar Heels have plenty of reason to celebrate, having won 17 collegiate National Championships, more than any other Division I women's athletic program in the nation. This earned them the name the "dynasty," coined by the New York Times.

off the field affect the team. Sell the game. Play for each other. Compete with intensity, respect, and guts. Train and play on the edge. We represent the USA—be proud of that and make the USA proud of us.

Standing Fast—Battles of a Champion, by Michelle Akers and Tim Nash, 1997, JTC Sports, Inc.

CHAPTER 2

USA Women—World Cup, Olympics, and the WUSA

Just like the University of North Carolina, the U.S. National Team began with little fanfare. It didn't always play in front of millions of spectators and television viewers, or make the cover of *People* magazine.

The first women's National Team dates back to 1985. It was led by an excellent Seattle, Washington-based coach named Mike Ryan. (I had seen the results of Mike's excellent soccer programs when I flew to his area to recruit players.) The following year I was hired to coach the team. Using the core of the '85 group, I brought in competitive personality players, such as April Heinrichs. I wanted to construct the teams around great performers. To this day, I believe in showcasing exceptional players and their wonderful qualities. The UNC philosophy is to nurture the one v. one artist, the great personalities. That was April—the kind of player who takes over the game and just dominates it. I love that in an athlete.

Although at the time a lot of hardworking coaches were having an impact on the collegiate level, the Americans had no influence in the world arena. Rather, the strength in women's soccer came from the northern European countries, such as Norway, Denmark, and Sweden and a southern European power, Italy. There was a rumor at the time that a world championship would take place in 1990 or '91. In 1987 I decided we had to pick a team in preparation for that event. I had seen a powerful youth group among some U19 National players playing for Hank Leung, our national youth coach, at a tournament in Minnesota, where they actually finished higher than our senior team. So, in a calculated gamble, I picked them all, in the process cutting many of the more senior players. As you can imagine, it caused a huge controversy.

Although as a young, inexperienced team we lost many games between 1987 and 1990 (it also didn't help that the National Team wasn't competing together or practicing much in those years), I still thought we had the potential to be the best team in the world, and of course, over time, we fought our way up to that level. Obviously, what I saw in those youth players is clear in hindsight, which naturally gives all of us vision. Those players, all between ages 15 and 18, included Mia Hamm, Julie Foudy, Kristine Lilly, Joy Fawcett, and Carla Overbeck—who became part of the core of our U.S. National Team that still plays today.

Although we were beset by some injury problems in the first World Championship (notably Michelle Akers, April Heinrichs, Joy Fawcett, and Shannon Higgins), we were still good enough to prevail. Despite the fact that in those days there were barely a scattering of fans to congratulate us, we were proud to return from China in 1991 as the winners of the first Women's World Championship.

Much of what we established in the early years on the U.S. National Team still applies today. It is an important model if you want to reach your maximum potential, and the reason why it is stressed so much throughout the UNC program and in this book. We set standards. One of them was for fitness. Those coming onto the National Team had to perform certain physical tests. It wasn't as if the message was: no pass, no problem. If you didn't pass, you simply weren't brought back to camp. All of a sudden the word went out. If you were going to play for the National Team, you had to take your personal physical preparation very seriously. Even now, we have some tremendously talented girls at UNC who do not start for us because they don't pass the fitness test and someone else—perhaps not as talented a player—does.

In 1994 I resigned as the coach of the U.S. National Team in order to refocus on the UNC. The National Team job was becoming full-time, and college soccer had also become increasingly competitive (this is even more the case today), which required full-time attention. Nevertheless, the National Team leadership stayed in the family. This sense of family is an important feature at both UNC and on the National Team. I think it was perfect that when I resigned, Tony DiCicco, who had been our goalkeeper trainer in 1991, was ready and stepped into place. He is a good man and a fine coach, and all the players liked him. (As of this writing, Tony is commissioner of the WUSA [Women's United Soccer Association]). Now, April Heinrichs, also part of our soccer family, is at the helm of the National Team and is working hard to take our team into an even more competitive future. Creating leaders is part of the tremendous sense of community that is built in this game, and something I also talk about in later chapters.

In the 1995 World Cup held in Sweden the Americans placed third, losing to Norway in the semifinals. In that event I served as a FIFA

(Fédération Internationale de Football Association, the international governing body of soccer) technical director, and thus was not allowed to work at the same venue in which my country's team was competing. I think our result showed how thin the team was. We had lost Michelle Akers when she incurred a head trauma colliding with one of the Chinese players. This compromised our ability to dominate the competition.

One of the dilemmas back then was how little opportunity we had to train and develop our team. There were not high-level leagues or opportunities after college for a large pool of players. This was back when we were just starting to make an investment in United States women's soccer. So '95 was a glaring statement of where we needed to go if we wanted to be consistently competitive at the highest level: we needed to expand our player pool; we needed depth.

The fact the United States then hosted two major events in a row (the 1996 Olympics in Atlanta and the 1999 World Cup), spurred a huge commitment in our development from the U.S. Soccer Federation. Tony and Lauren Gregg expanded the player pool, so the team wouldn't be as vulnerable as it was in '95. It was the memory of that '95 loss, and the continued dedication to hard work, which propelled the team in the first women's Olympic soccer competition the following year in Atlanta. It went from near obscurity in 1991 to 76,481 spectators, a then-record crowd that watched the United States' Olympic gold-medal victory over China.

The '96 and '99 victories were not as overwhelming as some people assumed, but with excellent coaching and organization from the U.S. Soccer Federation, and a tremendous commitment from our core of players, our team was victorious. Also, those players who in 1991 were so young had attained full maturity, which put us in a position in which we were a powerful team.

The U.S. National Team Dream

The U.S. National Team players, coaches and achievements have a strong and enduring connection to UNC.

- Since the founding of the U.S. National Team, a total of 38 different Carolina players have been on the roster at one time or another, including 14 current players. Numerous others have been on Youth U.S. National Teams.
- The victorious U.S. team in the first women's World Championship in China, in November, 1991, was coached by Anson Dorrance. Nine of the 18 on the USA roster played collegiately for UNC.

- Seven UNC players were on the 1995 U.S. World Championship team.
- Seven of the 16 (and three additional alternates) on the 1996 Olympic gold medal team were present or past UNC players.
- Both '96 Olympic assistant coaches, Lauren Gregg and April Heinrichs, are Carolina grads.
- Eight UNC players were on the 1999 World Cup Championship team. Lauren Gregg was an assistant coach.
- Six UNC players, plus two out of the three alternates, were on the 2000 Olympic team in Sydney. April Heinrichs was head coach of that team.
- The 1991 World Championship team, including Head Coach Anson Dorrance and Assistant Coaches Lauren Gregg and Tony DiCicco, was awarded the National Soccer Medal of Honor in August, 2001, by the National Soccer Hall of Fame, only the third time in 20 years this honor has been presented.

Welcome to Women's Soccer, World Cup 1999

The pinnacle of attention to women's soccer came in the 1999 World Cup—16 countries playing 32 games in 10 venues around the United States, and a final in the Rose Bowl in California with a record attendance of 90,185, including the president of the United States. It seems the whole world watched this event, and the thrilling final in which the United States defeated China in penalty kicks. A lot of people may believe that 1999, in and of itself, was the culmination of everything in women's soccer. This may sound shocking, but if that were true, I would consider that World Cup a failure. If you merely bask in the glory, you will suffer from delusions of grandeur. In order to be truly successful, the World Cup had to generate something positive and enduring: continued growth. Fortunately, it directly stimulated the establishment of a new women's professional league, the WUSA.

It is wonderful to be the center of attention, but it won't change the joy and value you find by doing something you love. Obviously having a total of 40 million people watch you play soccer is tremendous. I would love it if that many people always watched. But people didn't come to watch us in the old days and we had a great time. We played for the love of the game and the love of each other. We don't need all the extras for our sport to have value. I think the satisfaction you derive from soccer, and the lessons you learn, go deeper than having 90,000 people in the stands watch you play a final. As Mia Hamm has said, she would still play the game if there were never any spectators. "What I love about soccer is the way it makes me feel about myself," she has said, "It makes me feel that I have something to contribute, and that I can contribute it every day." (The Reluctant Diva, *Sports Illustrated*, Fall, 1997).

That being said, what people, especially young players, got when they watched the 1999 World Cup is enormously important. They understood that women were athletes, that they could truly play this game—with the technical and tactical mastery necessary to perform on such a high level that over 90,000 people would pay to watch. This is what I think was clear when the final became the most-watched soccer game—men or women—in U.S. television history. What I would hope young players got from 1999 is this message: Look at what they can do; you can do it too.

In the previous chapter I spoke of the challenge of continual ascension. Going from the 1999 World Cup to the 2000 Olympics is a case in point. The Olympics posed challenges to the United States, the biggest of which fell to coach April Heinrichs, who had to juggle the wonderful core of veteran players (who some people now call the "91ers") with an outstanding crop of new players in order to continue to prepare for the future. In essence, April's task resembled that in the pre-1991 era—to be competitive now and yet still figure out a way to build for the future. While Sydney was a swan song for some of the veterans (the first major competition without Michelle Akers on the roster or Carla Overbeck on the field), it was also a considerable task for a player like goalkeeper Siri Mullinix, a 21-year-old in her first major international competition.

The United States team had some incredible peak performances in the Olympics and played some outstanding soccer, yet failed to win. But it was not because the team wasn't competitive. I think it was the unpredictable nature of the game, and the fact they were playing basically a one-game series. I feel that if we had played a three-game series to advance in each level, we would still be Olympic champions. The one-game advancement system that is the nature of the championship tournament caught us vulnerable in the final. Scroll back and consider the opening game against Norway (who beat us in the final), which we won soundly, and you can imagine a different outcome in another system.

WUSA (Women's United Soccer Association)

I believe that vulnerability, which the United States experienced in both the 2000 Olympics and 1995 World Championship, is being addressed by the creation of the WUSA. The final developmental piece of the puzzle is now in place with this vibrant and very exciting professional league. The league continues to expand our player base, because rather than have just a small core of players working with the National Team, now there are eight teams of quality players. Rather than a select few coaches of these players, now there are eight new head coaches at the cutting edge of the game in this country. The challenge for April Heinrichs to give her young players experience isn't as daunting, because they are all getting experience on these eight teams. I believe this has put the United States in a truly remarkable and powerful position in the crucial aspect of its future development.

Looking at the creation of the WUSA from a historical point of view, I believe the true value of the 1999 Women's World Cup is reflected in the fact it helped give birth to this league. The WUSA is a dream.

What I like about the WUSA is that I feel it has been created the right way. It includes the community of the U.S. National Team, and maintains the core players of the 1999 World Championship, the concept of the soccer family. Those of us involved have long been fighting for positive leadership in women's soccer, and now we've got it. Everyone in the league leadership has the best interest of the players. The players are a priority, not just items on a business ledger. In addition to their salaries, the players are also sweat equity owners of the league. It's not money they invest up front, it's themselves—their hard work as pioneers—that has been generously rewarded with ownership in a piece of the league. I anticipate that this great leadership of the WUSA's investors and staff will serve as a model for all of us involved in women's soccer at all levels. And it's not just the investors and officers of the league, it is the players as well. Mia Hamm could have commanded the highest salary in the league, but she refused so she could stand on par with all the founding players and make a unique statement in sport by sharing a common salary structure with her teammates of the 1999 World Cup. I hope her spirit will always live on in our game.

It's a brave new world for women's soccer, born of mutual respect and the bond of our community. What I hope for the future of this league is that it can continue to lead just this way. There is, however, a bottom line: television ratings and attendance. We can all make a contribution by helping create a culture of support for the players in this league by watching them play. Every time we buy a ticket or turn on the television to see a game, we are helping our sport and helping ourselves. The foreign players in our league still have a bit more polish in their game because they come from a culture that is used to watching the game at the highest level in their own countries. A part of your climb and improvement as a player will come from how intently you watch and follow the amazing players in this league. So, I am optimistic that this league will be conducted for the love of the game, and that its role models will continue to inspire people in the right way.

See How You Grow

According to the latest statistics of the Soccer Industry Council of America (SICA), (year 2000):

- Total number of soccer players in U.S.: 17,734,000
- Of those, females were: 8,436,000
- Average age of all players: 15.3

You've come a long way, as the cliché goes. The best perspective on how much things have changed would be a look at one of our old UNC brochures I spoke of earlier. It's from 1980, and is on display in the hallway of our UNC offices at the McCaskill Soccer Center. The photo on our first brochure says it all for me. A group of players are on the field, lined up for the picture. The old-fashioned uniforms these star players are wearing don't even match. All of us back then looked like soccer hicks. Of course, we were!

In the first soccer camps we conducted in the mid-1970s there were usually about 60 boys and 40 girls. Of that number, only one or two girls could actually play the game, and maybe four or five would be considered athletes. If we had a girl who could even change direction with the ball, we were ecstatic. It was an added bonus to have one who was somewhat athletic and with a little bit of soccer skill as well.

Everything in women's soccer has changed. As a female player, that, of course, has had a direct effect on you. Now, our annual girls soccer camps fill up early, pushed to their limit with 2,200 players. And while there are no skill requirements to be in the camp, the 40 to 50 elite who make our All-Star sessions are remarkable soccer players and athletes. In the early days, we didn't even take a look at the younger girls. They were very unsophisticated. But then something changed. Our camps have a lot of young talent, even a handful of 12-year-olds, and the standard of these 12-year-olds is getting better every year.

The evolution of quality has been unbelievable. This is reflected in many ways. It's not just the number of players that has grown, it is the quality of play. Across the country, the caliber of the athlete at the youth level has improved tremendously. That's because a larger percentage of elite athletes are choosing to play our game, probably more than any other sport. The 1999 World Cup has had an impact on young girls, who saw this huge, glorious event and thought, "I'd love to play in front of 90,000 fans." They are making soccer their sport of choice. Through the work of the U.S. Soccer Federation coaching schools, the NSCAA (National Soccer Coaches Association of America) and other youth organizations, the average youth coach is becoming so much better. The leadership at the top has improved, as professional coaches are being hired whose sole responsibility it is to develop the talents of extraordinary athletes. The incredible amount of information in books, videotapes, and on the Internet for young coaches and players has added to the improvement.

I mark a significant change in girl's soccer from about 1992, the year after the United States women won the first World Championship. That year, an eighth-grader by the name of Jen Strifer came to our summer soccer camp. Strifer, who went on to play collegiate soccer at Notre Dame, was one of a group of fanatical girls who lived off the inspiration of that 1991 Championship. What I saw was an eighth-grader, from Baton Rouge, Louisiana—not exactly a soccer hotbed—spurred by her dreams of playing on the U.S. National Team. She was a truly extraordinary player. I couldn't believe how good her skills were. After an excellent career at Notre Dame, she went on to sign with the San Diego Spirit of the WUSA.

I noticed the impact of this rise in quality on the elite level a few years ago when coach April Heinrichs invited me to assist with the U16 National Team. What I saw among those players relates to 1991, when I noticed a number of problems in the women's game. One of them was the inability of even our elite players to serve balls over distance. (To improve your own ability at this, and other, skills, see Chapter 14.) The only players at the time who could actually do it well were our strikers, people like Michelle Akers and Mia Hamm. I took our '91 National Team and tested them to see what the average distance was for a ball served in the air. In the clinics I have done, it shocked people when I said the average distance for the left and right foot for these champions was about 27 yards.

But April had two U16 players, Jen Lewis and Catherine Reddick (Catherine now plays for us at UNC), whose average for the right foot was over 45 yards, and whose left wasn't far off. Those two young players—whose technical ability is truly special—could strike the ball significantly further than members of the former National Team. That was when the tremendous evolution of our youth players really dawned on me. In 10 years, we have come light years. In addition, those two girls were from Alabama, a place no one would consider a soccer capital. This told me it was happening all over America.

As a college coach I get the benefits of this growth in girl's soccer. In the old days we recruited college players in single geographical pockets like northern Virginia, Dallas, Seattle, Long Island, and northern and southern California, where soccer was strong. Now they come from all over the country. And there are more of them. In the past, among the 100+ Division I schools, very few of the players could ever have an impact on the best teams.

Now, that's completely changed. Every Division I team has two to three women who could be key players on any top program in the country. And all this talent comes from that great pool of youth feeding into the collegiate level. Now there are phenomenal youth tournaments put on in all four soccer regions of the country.

This has all created an incredible explosion in youth soccer. I'm so excited about it. To be honest, I think those from the United States are going to be overwhelming in the world arena. The rest of the world is going to be playing catch-up with us. They will be forced to react, and to improve dramatically. Perhaps they will surpass us, and we will be pushed to catch up with them again. I am confident, however, that we will lead the way because of the WUSA, our huge numbers, the technology of information sharing, and our commitment to developing the various areas of the game. It is a commitment of leadership, energy, organization, focus, and expertise.

Your Road to the Top

Now that you have a sense of the growth of women's soccer in terms of numbers, opportunities, and coaching, you will be able to appreciate another kind of growth. That's the evolution I referred to earlier that has spurred improvements in the quality of play. This evolution has directly affected the players and coaches I work with, and it forms the basis for the advice I would like to share in this book.

Back when I was coaching both the UNC and the U.S. National Team, I would use the National Team to sort out what needed improvement for the American female player. I would bring those problems back to the UNC practice field and try to solve them. Then, I would take the results and techniques of those UNC practices back to the National Team. In essence, we go to the highest level to see what the biggest problems are, and then we bring it back to the other levels, even to youth players—from which the problems originate.

The National Teams lead the way in this process. For example, one of the biggest problems I saw in the women's game when we first went on the road to Italy in 1986 was how uncomfortable the American soccer player was with her back to pressure (to work on this skill, see Chapter 14). So, when I came back to UNC, we started to design a practice environment in which the women had to play with their backs to pressure. Although we tweak it a bit now and then, the same environment we created back then to work on this skill exists to this day.

But this process goes even further. We continue to try to solve problems, and make improvements in play, in our girls camp even now, and the

19

National Teams are still our role models. I don't work with the National Team any longer, but I watch the team and work with some of the players. A couple of years ago I asked Mia Hamm at our youth camp in London what game in National camp had most helped her. She showed us a six-goal game Tony DiCicco used which teaches defensive principles and changing the point of the attack. We have continued to use and refine this game, even though she introduced it to our campers in the late 1990s.

The purpose of replicating the same practices and games in our youth camps that are played on the collegiate and national level is to show the ambitious camper the highest level. This gives the same sense of inspiration that the '99 World Cup did. One of the fundamental principles of our camp is that we have the girls themselves demonstrate high-level skills. It isn't the male coaches, or even the top female coaches, who do it. It's the campers. We want them to know what they can do, and what they should expect from themselves: to perform at the highest possible level. Of course, they are competing against some of the best players we can find—elite collegiate players—to show how close they are to where their game can be.

CHAPTER 3

Your Game, and Why It's Great

Whether or not you have the leadership presence of Carla Werden Overbeck, the scoring instincts of Mia Hamm, the skill of Lorrie Fair, the consistency of Kristine Lilly, the heading prowess of Cindy Parlow, or the risk-taking courage of Staci Wilson, soccer offers you an enormous range of challenges and opportunities for self-expression. It can be a demonstration of your athleticism, or a showcase of your creativity—an opportunity to test your character, but also an environment to build and nurture powerful relationships.

There is always some way to express yourself in soccer. It's a multifaceted game that offers a never-ending variety of worlds to conquer. You can always improve, and yet, as I elaborate on in Chapter 5, some degree of excellence is actually within reach of us all.

Whatever your level of skill, your temperament, or your talent, there's a place for you in the game. But whether or not you master that role, playing soccer still gives you something—even if you don't always succeed. Whether you win or lose, or progress in a traditional sense (e.g., making a top team as a starter), soccer can be a rich and rewarding experience. That's because, as I point out in Chapter 1, far beyond the external results, it is your effort, and the test of your inner strength, that ultimately can give your game meaning.

I separate soccer from other games. It's a different type of sport, as opposed to just a game, like golf or tennis. The way I qualify a sport is based on its environment. Playing soccer requires taking physical risks. That means there's the potential for injury or pain from someone else (who is also taking the same risks), and that's a tremendous opportunity for you to demonstrate your courage, and the strong mentality, that those risks entail.

Tennis is a noncombative game. You're never going to get hurt in tennis unless you trip and fall coming off the court. The only physical risk is playing at the net and having someone smash the ball down your throat. Soccer isn't like that. Of course, you don't set out to get hurt, or to hurt someone else, but even accepting that possibility takes true bravery. In fact, those who don't play would be humbled, and likely silenced along the sidelines, if they were to step out on the field for even a few minutes and confront a team of opponents trying to cut them down.

The game's physical requirements are extraordinary. Very few sports include demands to the extent soccer does. You can never be fit enough for this game. And it's not just one kind of fitness; it's both aerobic and anaerobic. That is, you need the endurance of a long distance runner—the ability to continue moving for a full game—and the explosive power of a sprinter and a high jumper. Your agility and strength also come into play, along with your skill and finesse. Soccer entails a never-ending circle of improvement. You can always work on various skills and physical aspects of your game, and toughen yourself mentally so you can withstand the pressure. All of this will constantly impact your success.

Soccer Skills

Soccer requires every conceivable physical skill. Here's a breakdown of a typical game for a teenage player:

The distance covered during a game is between 5 and 6.5 miles (2.5 miles for goalkeepers)—constantly walking, jogging, running, sprinting—and in all directions.

Rest pauses are only about 3 seconds every 2 minutes.

Less than 2% of the total distance, or only about 200 yards, is with possession of the ball. So, the majority of the time is comprised of movement off the ball.

There are about 1,000 activity changes in a game, which means a change of speed or direction every 6 seconds.

Games are typically played at 75% of a player's physical limits.

Adapted from material compiled by *Performance Conditioning for Soccer* newsletter in *U.S. Soccer Sports Medicine.*

There's a unique skill component in this sport. Humans are more adept with our hands, and yet soccer requires that you become adept with various parts of the body other than your hands or arms (with the exception of the goalkeeper, of course). So, you are confronted with the enormous challenge of taking away the two body parts that provide the greatest coordination and dexterity, and forced to achieve control with the parts of the body that inherently do not have that advantage.

The magnificence of soccer is in its range of skills. It requires an incredible variety of abilities—from the subtleties of pace and touch, to the violent all-out shot or powerful header, and then back to the textured, bent ball artfully delivered so that it dies softly behind the defense—there are numerous interesting contrasts and variations within the game. These aspects combine to make soccer endlessly fascinating for both those who play and those who watch. And its appeal is universal, because this international game is appreciated the world over.

Consider one of the bizarre dichotomies that make this sport so interesting. It's a team game that also requires individual flair, but a player's singular ability must be executed within the team context. Put simply: the challenge is to become a ball master without becoming a ball hog. That's why the most extraordinary individuals can either elevate, or destroy, their own teams. And yet, while the game-breaker is usually some phenomenal individual effort, the truly great teams are a collection of obviously extremely cooperative individuals.

Even though soccer is a team game, I think we all admire the individual who acts as a hero, fighting the other team on her own. Team games are an attempt to suppress individuality, and yet the classically great soccer player is kind of a rebel against structure and cooperation. Invariably, the type who stands out is not the cooperative team player that athletics purports to admire. It's the April Heinrichs, Michelle Akers, Mia Hamm gimme-the-ball-and-I'll-get-it-done. This shatters the classical concept of the team. Yet in order for an individual to demonstrate this type of rebellion, it must be done within the context of total team cooperation. It's a very wonderful aspect of our sport, yet very bizarre!

Another of the most gratifying aspects of athletics, and of a team sport like soccer, is the social factor. A team is a collection of people who are often totally different from one another, yet they're accepted for some unique or outstanding quality. We all have a range of personality traits, but what's amazing is that on the soccer field, whatever your personal strengths or flaws, you're still embraced as an athlete by your teammates.

Sports can also exemplify equality. There is no greater example of this than the racial divide, which was first crossed in athletics. When blacks and whites started playing together, they saw they had more in common than they had differences. The 1999 Women's World Cup showcased another type of equality. It demonstrated that women soccer players should be respected for the game they play, not the typical female roles they are expected to fulfill.

If your soccer playing is conducted with the proper spirit, you surely have experienced this acceptance for yourself. You may have played with all kinds of girls (perhaps even boys), those who are accomplished or gifted, and those who are more unremarkable players. But even the average player can be fully integrated and accepted in this unique society of sometimes extraordinary athletes. After all, it isn't just soccer that creates bonds. The athletic arena itself forges unique relationships that go well beyond the game itself.

Soccer is a crazy quilt of characters. You surely know this from the social mix on your own teams. That's what makes the game endlessly entertaining. I always share this story with our UNC players. In the mid-1980s we had a player who was a campus social activist. She was really a flake, in a good way—scattered in all directions with her various causes—but I admired and respected her idealism. She was also a tremendous soccer player who I eventually invited to join the U.S. National Team (although she didn't last there).

One day she walked into our office in an angry huff and said to Dino (assistant coach Bill Palladino) and me, "What's this I hear—you're talking about me?" Dino and I readily admitted it to her. "You're right. We talk about you all the time. You're the most entertaining person we know." We meant it. Our players are our lives. They are interesting and engaging for all the right reasons. Sometimes it's because of all the wacko things they do, and sometimes it's because of their unique human qualities that we admire. They're all a part of this great game!

Soccer Personalities

The hang-yourself-over-the-rail confidence of a successful striker; the street-fighting, cocky midfielder; the take-charge attitude of a great goalkeeper; the remarkably responsible and protective, yet savage, defender—all of these personalities have a place on the soccer field. That's another thing I like about this game—whatever kind of personality you have, there's a place for you on the field, a position in which you can find full personal expression. Just as positions favor particular athletic dimensions, they also lend themselves to a specific personality type. (For more on the "personality" of position, see Chapter 17.)

No matter what your dominant quality, you can find a suitable home on the soccer field. In fact, the greatest teams are made up of a perfect chemical blend of differing personalities. That's another fascinating aspect of soccer—watching a player's role grow and change within a team, and seeing what she brings to the table.

But it goes even deeper. Each natural personality can experiment with various other different ones. Soccer allows you to be like an actor, taking on various roles (at various times) which provide both a personal and a team balance. Here are a few of them:

The Warrior

From a 50-50 ball, to a pass that ends up at your feet, to jumping up for a header—every act in soccer, nearly every moment of the game, invites physical confrontation. And in this confrontation, your courage is tested. You have the opportunity to become a warrior.

Michelle Akers is a warrior personality. Throughout her entire career, she constantly battled on the field—never letting a ball go unchallenged, committing her body and her heart to the game. I absolutely love a female warrior like Michelle—a brave athlete challenging an opponent. That's because it's socially unconventional. I admire the warrior even more in women athletes than in men, because women have been socialized not to take physical risks, not to confront or do battle. I love watching their progression— going from the female social dictate of nurturing relationships to this extreme, in which relationships are symbolically shattered. It's great to see the freedom and confidence that female players get when they discover their warrior selves.

In the environment of competitive soccer, the warrior takes risks in all dimensions—physical, social, and psychological. Incurring these risks helps you to understand that you don't have to follow the stereotypical female role of your culture.

The Artist

While the warrior plays like an animal, the artist has perfected the subtleties of the game. Of course, that doesn't mean a player can't take on both roles.

For the artist, the field is her canvas. On it, she delivers bent balls, using the inside and outside of both feet; serves balls with a "user-friendly" backspin that die behind defenses, or that come to rest at a teammate's feet; makes perfectly textured passes—with pace and precise accuracy, so that, for example, if a defender is on a teammate's left shoulder, she delivers the ball to that player's right foot. She employs feints—used to deceive opponents—such as cuts, lunges, or even scissors, stepovers, and Laurie

Schwoy turns. She has perfect touch and plays with such control that the ball stops dead on impact. These are the sophisticated tools with which the artist creates, using subtle soccer techniques that require an extraordinary understanding of the game (as to when to use them effectively) and that are executed from a time-invested foundation of technical training. The artist is also so comfortable with the ball at her feet that she can afford to focus on more strategic areas of the game, since she is the master of the ball. These are the abilities of a Pelé, a renowned artist of the game.

I'd like to see more artistry in female soccer. Currently, there's not enough of this creativity on the girls' side of the game. I think it's missing from the training environment, and in part because sheer dominance over their peers allows good female players to merely use their athleticism—just run right past their opponents—rather than rely on these skills. Therefore, creativity doesn't have to be a part of their repertoire. I think these moves of deception and touch need to be stressed, as does the capacity to serve balls with the correct texture. Of course, skills like these also require an incredible amount of time, devotion, and a disciplined work ethic.

I also don't think enough of us in the women's game watch the game, but we should. Now we have no excuse. The WUSA has all of the remarkable artists in the world assembled in one league for us to admire and study.

The Visionary

As soccer is made up of many requirements, each player is going to have a different balance of abilities, based on her inherent talents, interests, and, on the way she approaches life. Just as there is a place on the field for the warrior and the artist, there is a place for the visionary—the person with the mental as well as the physical gifts.

A fearless warrior, the skillful artist, and general athleticism—these traits in a player are fairly straightforward. Even the inexperienced eye can spot them. Then there's the player who stands out to those who understand and appreciate the intricacies of game—the visionary. The visionary is a soccer genius who has the capacity, poise, and patience to make good decisions under heavy pressure. She has a game sense, which is what you see in players who just seem to know where the ball will go next, and how to respond. You notice it in players especially when you watch high-level soccer in person or on television.

When a visionary gets the ball, she sees the entire field and everyone on it. She has a knowledge of angles, and distances, when and where to move and how to anticipate that movement. When she doesn't have the ball, the visionary plays with her head up, but also on a swivel, looking all over to get a sense of pressure, movement, shape, and opportunity. She is not only thinking about getting into space to receive the ball, but also moving in order to draw defenders with her as well as looking to see who to play the ball to next or what space to attack.

Anticipation is a big part of the visionary's ability—reading the play. This is not a skill a player can exercise in advance, because she doesn't know the circumstances, and the decisions on the field are based on so many different factors (e.g., the shape of the opposing team, whether or not she has possession, the kind of player to whom she is serving the ball, etc.). The visionary is highly skilled at sorting the many different variables that impact her decisions.

I am especially attuned to the visionary because obviously I'm always looking at possible future coaches. Visionary ability entails analyzing the game, what coaches do for their players on chalkboards. In this sense, one element of becoming a visionary can be developed—conscientious study of the game.

It is critical for you as a young player to understand that vision and great tactical minds are built on a complete foundation of skill, so that you can problem-solve individually and hurt the other team tactically. Knowing what to do is easily compromised by being unable to do it. Much of the game is spent with this frustration.

The Construction of Character

In the first two chapters you are introduced to our soccer and life philosophy. I want to expand on what I believe is the most basic value of soccer, and what I will stress throughout the book. It is what makes this a truly great game: the construction of character.

Did you make the cut for your high school varsity or in ODP (Olympic Development Program)? Are you a starting player, or do you wait out most of the game on the bench? The ambition to pursue any goal has value on both sides of the divide, whether or not you are successful in your quest. Both scenarios, success or failure, offer you a tremendous opportunity to demonstrate your value as a person. In a sense, you will always be successful if you keep your heart and head on the right track. Besides, athletic talent is not incredible in and of itself, if it makes a player arrogant or egotistical. In fact, the way you handle failure can be even more important than success, because it gives you an opportunity to demonstrate your nobility.

You have more in common than you might have realized with the great players you idolize, such as Mia Hamm, Carla Overbeck, or Tisha Venturini.

Surely, their success inspires you. But what about their doubts, their failures?

Carla Overbeck, for all of her current greatness, did not start out this way. In fact, her freshman year she did not compete in practice because she did not want to offend anybody. Since we record results in practice, we have a clear record of this. We also have a clear record of her as a senior, dominating and winning everything. She also used to break under the emotional demands of the game. As a freshman starting defender for UNC, in one critical regular season game, she became increasingly down on herself for what she perceived as her vast number of errors. She felt she was letting the team down. At one point, this star player, who later became one of the toughest, most competitive leaders in the game, just "lost it" right on the field. Despite the ultimate victory, this game is known above all—especially by Bill Palladino, who loves to tease her about it—as "The Game in which Carla Cried."

Tisha Venturini is someone that even with extraordinary achievements has come up short. She knows what it means to be cut from a team. A former standout for four UNC championship teams, a member of three World Cup teams and the 1996 Olympic team, Tisha was nevertheless eliminated from the 2000 Olympic team. In my eyes, and of everyone who saw her go through this, she is tremendous for the way she displayed nobility and dignity by moving on and accepting her new role as a professional in the WUSA. She was not bitter, accusatory or petty. Her class and dignity is a wonderful demonstration of her strength of character.

Everyone involved in athletics has an opportunity to demonstrate that her life has a deeper meaning. Long after this game is over for you, you will be able look back proudly on the many times you have handled failure as well as success, and displayed your character. That's something that marks who you are.

The Perfect Game

As a female soccer player, you are benefiting from the many general advantages for girls who play sports. Here are just a few of them:

- Teenage female athletes are less than half as likely to get pregnant as female nonathletes.
- Physical activity appears to decrease the initiation of high-risk health behavior in adolescent girls, such as smoking.
- Research suggests that girls who participate in sports are more likely to experience academic success than those who do not play sports.

- High school girls who play sports are more likely to do well in science.
- Women student-athletes graduate from college at a significantly higher rate than women students in general.
- Half of all girls who participate in some kind of sports experience higher than average levels of self-esteem and less depression.

On the Health Front:

- High school sports participation may help prevent osteoporosis (loss of bone mass).
- One to three hours of exercise a week from the teens to about age 40 may bring a 20–30% reduction in the risk of breast cancer, and four or more hours of exercise a week can reduce the risk almost 60%.

—Facts compiled by the Women's Sports Foundation.

Benefits of Female Sports

This is one of my favorite advertisements. It was a Nike television and print campaign for girls' sports.

If you let me play
I will like myself more
I will have more self-confidence
I will suffer less depression
I will be 60% less likely to get breast cancer
If you let me play
I will be more likely to leave a man who beats me
I will be less likely to get pregnant before I want to
I will learn what it means to be strong
If you let me play sports

CHAPTER 4

Enriching Your Life through Soccer

I had learned what it means to ride the Tour de France. It's not about the bike. It's a metaphor for life, not only the longest race in the world but also the most exalting and heartbreaking and potentially tragic.... The Tour (de France) is not just a bike race, not at all. It is a test. It tests you physically, it tests you mentally, and it even tests you morally.

— *It's Not about the Bike,* Lance Armstrong

I think sometimes we elevate the value of sport for the wrong reasons. In and of itself, it does not have significant value, and the importance we ascribe to it is oftentimes completely overblown or misplaced. But it can have value, if you approach it the right way. I love Lance Armstrong's powerful book, because it is apparent that his physically, mentally, and morally testing sport helped forge a better man. When he faced a potentially fatal cancer, he understood that the sport he loves is not really about the bike. Like all sports, including soccer, it is really about life.

Of course, you don't have to be Lance Armstrong to get meaning from your game. (And sometimes it is just a game.) But as I have found in my own coaching, your soccer experience will be much more rewarding and enriching when you find a deeper value in it.

How are soccer and life connected? As you will soon discover, there is no way in which they are NOT connected. In my first book, *Training Soccer Champions,* I made this point by bluntly saying that long ago I lost interest in soccer as a mere sport. Playing exciting, competitive soccer is what we are proud of at UNC, but there are other, more enduring aspects to our game. They have to do with human relationships, exploring strength of character, and experiencing the emotional risks and rewards that sports offer us all.

Your soccer education may be about the game, but it is also about yourself as a person. Both are part of what I believe you need to understand in order to achieve excellence. Just like many hours of practice on the ball, your personal development is an ongoing process. The road to lasting and meaningful success is a long and often bumpy one. You need to be patient and compassionate with yourself along the way.

The Soccer-Life Connection

Developing the soccer-life connection can be as challenging as developing soccer skills. After all, just because you play the game doesn't automatically make you a better, wiser, and more powerful person. It's not like you wake up one day and you're transformed into a Lance Armstrong.

As you surely realize, while some wonderful things can happen in this game, it can also be filled with adversity. Even though we like to think that if we work hard, positive results will follow, obviously that doesn't necessarily always happen. But if the challenges the game presents weren't difficult, it wouldn't be worth playing. That's why one of the wonderful life lessons of athletics is that success itself shouldn't be the ultimate reward—because there are a lot of people who work incredibly hard and never "make it." What is important, above all, is being in the arena.

I was a philosophy and English major during my collegiate days at UNC. I believe these two areas have banded together to give me a different (some of my players might say bizarre) perspective for coaching. When you talk about the game developing personal character, you deal with a kind of existentialism, the philosophical exploration of our existence.

The credit belongs to the man who is actually in the arena, whose face
is marred with sweat and dust and blood; who strives valiantly,
who errs and comes short again and again; who knows the
great enthusiasms, the great devotions, and spends himself
in a worthy cause, and who, if he fails, at least fails while daring
greatly, so that his place shall never be with those cold and
timid souls who know neither victory nor defeat.

—Theodore Roosevelt

I like this quote from President Theodore Roosevelt because it says that effort is paramount and winning or losing just the scenery behind it. It also inspires us to be resilient, to bounce back. If you don't make the cut in ODP, for example, it doesn't mean you should throw up your hands and say: Why did I waste my time practicing all winter? Why didn't they pick me instead of that other player? Rather, the test is to accept responsibility and take the attitude: What can I do to get better for when I try out next time?

While you can't control the events of your life (like whether you make ODP or not), you can control your reaction to them. "Control the controllables" is the phrase sports psychologists use. You determine your attitude. Will you be able to gain something positive from your disappointments? Will you decide that not making ODP is a great chance to see how committed you are? Will you redouble your efforts, accepting that even with no guarantee of success, just trying out for the team is worthwhile?

Even though sports create an artificial environment, the tests you are given to pass and the emotions you experience are incredibly real. Try to see soccer as a challenging personal adventure, so that when you enter the arena—step on the soccer field—you can willingly face what lies ahead. Ask yourself: What's going to be thrown my way today? How can I demonstrate who I am?

A Laboratory of the Human Spirit

What can you learn about yourself through soccer? One of our major focuses at UNC is how people behave. There's an old sports cliché: athletics builds character. But I don't believe it does. I believe it exposes character. It reveals who you are. The person you are off the field comes onto the field. Then, too, some of the lessons you learn on the field you take off it, and into your life. These tests and how you weather them are determined by your character, and this is ultimately where athletics have value.

Are you a negative life force? Do you criticize your teammates behind their backs or complain that the coach or the system is unfair? Are you the one whining in the back of the line in the fitness session? Or are you like U.S. National Team captain Julie Foudy, who comes to practice every day, and despite having problems like all the rest of us, doesn't reveal a dark side, because she is so powerful and positive all of the time. That's what everyone looks for in the remarkable players—the remarkable personalities behind them.

How do you want to be seen? I confront my players with this question all the time. In everyday life, you may be able to hide character weaknesses, but athletics exposes these weaknesses for everyone to see. Even the greatest phonies among us cannot conceal their true personality by acting a certain role consistently all season. There are too many different situations that draw out all aspects of your character in athletics in general, and in team sports in particular. On the soccer field, you're going to be seen for who you are.

I mentioned Julie Smith in Chapter 1, the walk-on player on our team with limited soccer skills. I chose her because in one particularly grueling fitness test, she ran her heart out—setting an all-time team record. She not only touched each finish line, but repeatedly stepped over it, doing extra in order to prove herself as honorable as well as incredibly fit. I put her on the team because I wanted to show her, and my other players, that if you have that kind of heart—if you are a positive life force—you are an asset for our team, whether or not you can even kick a ball. Her thoughtful post-season message supports my point (see below).

Demonstrating guts or nobility doesn't mean you're a flawless individual. The great thing about the best environments in athletics, and among our greatest teams at UNC, is that while we understand we all have a range of traits, everyone is accepted for the bad as well as the good. Oftentimes it's that understanding of being loved despite our flaws that makes the truly great teams just like family.

Soccer is a great way to work on your personal development, because the game doesn't really matter. It isn't life or death. It's not a paycheck, your survival—at least for young players. But it is a wonderful environment for you to sort out issues that can eventually affect your everyday life— your relationships, your dedication to tasks, and your ability to take hard knocks.

Soccer and life are a lot alike. In both of them, you're going to experience great moments and great people, and, at times, you're also going to see your own efforts, and others', come up short of the line. It's this view of our humanity that makes soccer a fabulous laboratory of the human spirit.

January 15, 2001

Anson,

I finally have the time to send you this long-overdue thank you. I cannot express to you how incredible it was to be a part of the team this year. I think it's the people who make the program so special, and the championships are a compliment to them and to you. I have so many great memories just from this one season. I only made it to the 40s in my first 20s/40s/60s etc. workout attempt before I pulled a hamstring and had to stop. It took me three weeks before I could finish it at an average speed. And then preseason came. My legs have never hurt that way in my life. It's such a different kind of pain than distance running, but I loved the soreness. I remember after our first scrimmage, when it was so evident that I was in over my head, and Susan (Bush) came up to me and said, "Julie, I'd take you on my team any day." I think she could see I was discouraged and knew I needed that. There were countless times when all the girls would get excited when I would finally learn a new skill. Even Branam made me feel at home by bullying me just like the other girls. One day, she picked me up, threw me outside the box, and called me a flea. It was great! Then there was Borgman, Schwoy, Amy, Jules, Anne, Murph, Kimmy, Les, and Hilary, who were constantly encouraging. There was also poor Dino (Bill Palladino). I was always in his groups, but despite my lack of everything, he knew when to bite his lip or when to encourage me.

I just finished the Lance Armstrong book. He says, "There is no reason to attempt such a feat of idiocy other than the fact that some people, which is to say some people like me, have a need to search the depths of their stamina for self-definition. It's a contest in purpose-less suffering." He, of course, was referring to the Tour de France, but it made me think of this past season's soccer endeavors.

If I hadn't made the team, I would have been fine, because I at least tried, but for some reason you kept me on and allowed the program to impact my life. Your program gives people the opportunity to attempt what seem to be "feats of idiocy" to others, but in reality the feat of taking advantage of what the team has to offer is what makes your players strong and amazing people on and off the field. Thanks for bringing me into your soccer family. I hope that in the future, I will somehow be able to give back to the program.

Julie (Smith)

Anson's Reading List

I don't separate soccer and life. That's why it seems everything I read impacts the way I coach, and relate to my players. I share with them everything that strikes me.

You'll notice that especially in this chapter, but throughout the entire book, so much is taken from what I read (some from the classics). Articles and quotes hang throughout the soccer offices, and they are an integral part of my attempts in player development. For example, during the winter holiday break of her junior year at UNC, every player reads *Man's Search for Meaning*, a deeply moving and philosophical book by a Holocaust survivor about enduring the ultimate hardship. Also, during that following spring semester, players read and we discuss a chapter a week from *The Leadership Moment.* I don't make these book discussions separate from the players' soccer experience. I always tie them into the team and the players' lives. We want them to see the correlation. Ultimately, we want them to be great leaders, but above all, thoughtful human beings.

Here's a brief recommended reading list for you:

Training Soccer Champions, by Anson Dorrance with Tim Nash, 1996, JTC Sports, Inc.

Man's Search for Meaning, (most current edition) by Viktor Frankl.

The Leadership Moment, by Michael Useem, 1998, Times Books.

The Road Less Traveled, by M. Scott Peck, 1978, Touchstone, published by Simon & Schuster.

It's Not about the Bike—My Journey Back to Life, by Lance Armstrong with Sally Jenkins, 2000, G.P. Putnam's Sons

Go for the Goal, by Mia Hamm with Aaron Heifetz, 1999, HarperCollins Publishers.

Standing Fast—Battles of a Champion, by Michelle Akers and Tim Nash, 1997, JTC Sports, Inc.

The Game and the Glory, an Autobiography, by Michelle Akers with Gregg Lewis, 2000, Zondervan Publishing House.

The Champion Within—Training for Excellence, by Lauren Gregg with Tim Nash, 1999, JTC Sports.

Sacred Hoops, by Phil Jackson and Hugh Delehanty, 1995, Hyperion.

Greater Expectations: Overcoming the Culture of Indulgence in Our Homes and Schools, by William Damon, 1996, Free Press Paperbacks, published by Simon & Schuster.

Dealing with Adversity

All of us can be wonderful when the sun is shining, but how do you act when it's raining?

If you've had hard times, soccer can be a way to endure them. Having gone through difficulties can also have a positive effect on the way you play the game. If you look at many of the great players—and I have had some in my program—sport is their salvation. Some of them have had rough lives—broken families, difficult financial times, or a painful adolescence. They bring their experiences onto the soccer field. So when they compete, often it is with a sense of fierceness. They play with a sort of "life or death" urgency that separates them from others.

There is another aspect of soccer, and sports, that entails adversity. This is the struggle to succeed. Every single player, no matter what her level, has faced it. And it is a never-ending struggle. Even Mia Hamm, who scored the only goal in the 2000 Olympic semifinal, allowing the United States to advance to the final, is not immune. At the postgame press conference, she was asked whether her talent had begun to erode. According to the *New York Times* (9/25/00), "Her answer was as direct as her play had been. [Said Mia,] "All I have to say is that every single day I wake up, I commit myself to being better. Some days it happens and some days it doesn't. I'm still committed to that. There are games I'm going to dominate and games I'm going to struggle. It doesn't mean I give up." It was surely this inner strength that made her one of those who comforted crying teammates after their defeat in a close Olympic final.

Adversity has a range. On the most obvious level, you face it in dealing with losing. But how you react when the game is over is only part of it. There are many other potentially adverse situations, such as how you play when your team is down, or when the game is tied—or whether you start, how much playing time you get, or how you endure, or come back, from injury. All of these issues test you, and give you a chance to grow as a person.

> *The way in which a man accepts his fate and all the suffering it entails, the way in which he takes up his cross, gives him ample opportunity—even under the most difficult circumstances—to add a deeper meaning to his life. It may remain brave, dignified, and unselfish. Or in the bitter fight for self-preservation he may forget his human dignity and become no more than an animal. Here lies the chance for a man either to make use of or to forgo the opportunities of attaining the moral values that a difficult situation may afford him. And this decides whether he is worthy of his sufferings or not.*
>
> —*Man's Search for Meaning*, Viktor Frankl

I have spent a lot of time telling you how soccer is only a game—that it is relatively insignificant in and of itself, but the way you deal with its challenges is most meaningful because it enables you to strive for something of value beyond the game.

Mia Hamm's quote says it all for me: "I commit myself to being better." Whether or not you make it to your goal, it's your commitment to the quest that's critical. I love the Olympic motto: It's not the triumph, but the struggle. That's what Mia was saying in her quote. What you celebrate in athletics is the struggle. I think too often this gets overlooked, and Mia's comment in the *New York Times* demonstrates that.

Tracey Bates Leone ('85–'89)

A Positive Attitude Can Make You Successful

Your attitude affects everything you do. My husband Ray and I coach together, and we constantly talk about attitude, because it affects everything in life. We believe people are either positive or negative, and that there is no in-between. We categorize the in-between as negative.

When I was growing up, we had to be positive. My dad died unexpectedly when he was very young, leaving my mom on her own to raise three girls, all below the age of five. She was a pillar of strength. She instilled in us all a sense of independence and responsibility at a young age—to carry our load, and to do it to the best of our ability. She did the same, so she was a great role model for us. It's like sports—our family of four was like a little team. We all had to use teamwork to survive as a family, and it has helped us to be successful in life.

When we were young, my mom decided to put my twin sister, Jennifer, and me on two different soccer teams, so we used to play against each other. One of us would go home having lost, and one having won. You can imagine what it was like being in our car. One would be crying and one would be happy. My mom would be very disappointed if we cried. She wanted us to accept the result, deal with it, and be gracious. This is a small glimpse into the many ways she helped nurture a positive attitude and accountability in us.

I think we learned early on to trust people. We weren't threatened by others. Growing up in Dallas, we played team-related games with the kids in the neighborhood. We were constantly put into an environment of working together, and of cooperative learning. We were also on the neighborhood swim team. I remember being so nervous, and feeling so alone when it was time for me to swim my events. We definitely liked team sports better. Every day for hours we played soccer, kickball, basketball, football, and a huge hide-and-seek game that spanned over blocks called "Ditch 'em." We had so much fun growing up.

Being positive in your attitude, and everything you do, can truly make you successful. I'm very short, 4′11″. Being short can be a personal chal-

This is my favorite Tracey Bates Leone photo. During her career our main rival was Central Florida and the indomitable Michelle Akers. For this brief moment in time, 4'11" Tracey Bates is competing with 5'11" Michelle Akers for a head ball. In those days, we used to promote games with posters. Every time we played Central Florida in Michelle's career, we had this photo made into a poster advertising when and where the game would be.

lenge in some things. I wanted to prove that I could be successful in soccer. Everyone has limitations. You can always find areas of strength. What's great about soccer is that you can be any size, and have many strengths. I had to find areas I could control by working hard. For me, those areas were fitness, technical ability, and being positive. I felt that to be great at these things involved commitment, work, and attitude, and I knew I had those qualities. I wasn't going to be the strongest player on the field, but I still had to be as strong as possible. I still had to become the best header I could be, even though I wasn't going to dominate in the air. But I felt I could be the best at commitment, work, and attitude, so I set my sights towards those as being my strengths. What's also nice about these qualities is that you can have them just by a decision you make.

I've had a lot of young players, or parents, approach me. Their coaches have told them they're not going to make it because they're too short, or too small. There are always naysayers out there. Being short has been a good intrinsic challenge for me. I tell those people, "Everyone has strengths. Keep working on your weak areas, but make your strengths flourish. Focus on what you can control—work ethic and attitude. Don't let anyone ever tell you that you can't be great. There is greatness in all of us."

When times really get tough, that's when your true self comes out. Everyone can be positive when she's winning a game, individually playing well, or her season's going great. The real test is facing adversity. Everyone has those adverse moments in childhood, whether they are big traumas—like a death or divorce—or small day-to-day challenges. They are all tests. I think these small challenges helped shape my siblings and me growing up. Mowing the yard, even though you're tired; helping with the shopping and the daily responsibilities—all build a strength and a work ethic. These daily challenges can be as important to conquer as the bigger adversities.

I was very lucky. My coaches were like my fathers. My first coach, Dave Rich, was such a nice, genuine, positive person. He was my "dad." He encouraged me, cared about me, and I wanted to work hard for him. Hard work is such a rewarding quality. It's fairly easy to be positive with hard workers. There's a respect that you gain when you just flat-out work hard. My coaches were important to me, not just as soccer coaches. I hung onto everything they said. I was lucky they were positive. If they had been negative, maybe I wouldn't be where I am today.

I tell the U19 National Team I coach: you need to have staying power to endure the process to make the World Cup team a year-and-a-half from now. You're going to make some rosters, and not make others. How you endure this process, and how you react, will determine where you go. There will be adversity. If it were easy, everyone would do it. There are going to be peaks and valleys for all of you. How are you going to respond? This process can bring out the best in all of you, and wouldn't you rather have the best be brought out of you, whether you make it or not?

There is a deeper measure of success in this process. Human nature is to consider not making the National Team a "failure." Is it really a "failure?" That's how a player who just looks at the surface will see it. But when you wholly commit, and work with all your heart toward a goal in a positive way, that's success. When you do this, even if you don't make it, a feeling of fulfillment still exists. That's success.

It's during the challenge of competition that a player is truly tested. It's when coaches find out the most about their players. That's why Anson makes the environment so competitive, because he's going to find out about you, and you're going to find out about yourself.

The ones who deal with tough, competitive, difficult situations in a positive way usually seem to be the ones who move on, or if they don't, they still feel a sense of reward and fulfillment. If you're positive, knowing that you did everything you could, and in the right way, you might not be immediately rewarded, in terms of making a team or playing time, but you'll be rewarded in your life, because you're going to be a successful person.

You can be pleased with what you're doing, and still not have what you want. It's like the story Anson tells about Kristine Lilly earning the starting position at left midfield over me. I was the reserve player for her. I had to accept that maybe someone else was simply better than I was. I was pleased with how hard I was working, and I was going to continue to work as hard as I could, but Kristine was better. I felt honored to play on that team. It was my job to accept whatever role necessary for the good of the team, but to keep trying to achieve more.

There's something I call the "blame radar." People use the blame radar when things don't go their way. They look to blame everything or everyone else for why they don't get what they want, instead of looking at themselves first. I told the U14's at National camp that if they don't make a team, or a roster, or don't start, human nature is to start to blame. They blame the coach, the field, the weather, an injury—instead of really looking into the mirror at themselves. "What can I do?" is a question they need to ask themselves. When Brandi Chastain scored an own goal in the 1999 World Cup, how did she and Brianna Scurry, the goalkeeper, respond to that moment? The team was down a goal, having scored an own goal in the semifinal of the World Cup in front of millions of people. Talk about adversity! If they had blamed each other, the team probably wouldn't be World Champions right now. But Brandi assumed responsibility, and Bri did the same. They jumped over an astronomical hurdle and won the World Cup. For me, that was a defining moment.

When I'm coaching, I bring up this story a lot. It has to do with the power of a positive attitude in the face of adversity. Shannon MacMillan was cut from the 1995 World Cup team. She had to find a way to deal with that, and come back. In the '96 Olympics she was a starter, and basically played every minute. She was a star. That doesn't happen by accident. In the Olympics, in the biggest moment in her career, she had a tremendously difficult situation to deal with. In the Olympic semifinal the U.S. was playing Norway, a team that included Hege Riise (who now plays for the Carolina Courage), who was voted the best player in the world in World Cup '95. The U.S. coaches had to make a tough decision—how to stop Hege Riise. They brought in Tiffany Roberts, who hadn't played at all in the Olympics. She was called upon to mark Riise. Someone had to be taken out. It was Shannon MacMillan.

There are two great stories here. You've got Tiffany Roberts, who hasn't played a second, about to take on an incredible challenge in the biggest event in her life. Leading up to that, was she whining and complaining and blaming, and, as a result of her attitude, not doing her work? Or, had she worked and prepared for that moment, even though things weren't storybook perfect for her? Had she accepted the responsibility in her training that even though she wasn't playing, she was going to be positive, and commit herself? You're darn right she did. She was unbelievable in that game. She became one of the heroes in the story. She made the decision, which was the margin between being an Olympic gold medalist or not. You never know what is going to be the difference in life.

The other great story is Shannon MacMillan. She got cut in '95, came back to be a star in '96, and then wasn't playing in the semifinal game. She was subbed on, and on her second touch of the ball, she scored the winning goal. She went on to score one of the two goals against China in the final. That made the United States the first Olympic gold medalists in women's soccer.

Who says attitude isn't everything?

Are You Different? Female Versus Male Soccer Players

Many people assume there are athletic differences between male and female soccer players. But aside from the obvious inherent physiological ones, like speed and size, males and females have the potential to play a very similar game. That doesn't mean, however, that there aren't differences. But these differences have to do with social, as well as athletic, factors. Nonetheless, as I have already mentioned, those social factors heavily impact on sports and soccer skills. Some of these are positive, and some are negative. You may read this and think, "That has nothing to do with me." True, you may be an exception, but although these are generalities, most all of us are affected by some deeply-held social beliefs. Understanding and overcoming social obstacles can help make you a better player. It can also enrich your life by making you a more complete person.

How You Play the Game

I wouldn't coach young boys or girls any differently. But that's not the case as they get older, when social influences kick in. Having worked with both male and female players for many years, I have gotten to see some consistent differences. And believe me, those differences exist. I started coaching women with a very aggressive, critical style, the same way I had coached men. After all, I reasoned, they play the same game. This very straightforward approach was successful with men, but it was disastrous with women. The women didn't need the force of my personality (scream at women and you lose them); they needed my humanity. Above all, they wanted me to care about them as people. What they valued was deeper than just soccer. They valued the game in the context of a complex weave of emotions and personal relationships.

While there are many things to be learned from men in athletics (most notably their undying confidence and competitive fury), there are many positive aspects to women's athletics as well. Women seem to play a more honorable game. In women's soccer it's an incredibly entertaining, different type of game—not as fast, but with less stoppage, sometimes a greater flow, not strewn with fouls and more time in play and on the field. The women's game brings to soccer a potentially easier game to follow tactically.

Unfortunately, one of the negative aspects of male sports tends to be the habit of going over the brink. As a result, at their worst, they cheat and fight. I hope we never see in women's athletics the kind of violence that sometimes permeates men's sports. I don't think women's first instinct is to cheat or to injure someone. In general, I think women compete with a spirit of fairness, and have a greater sense of honor and nobility than the men. Of course, time will tell, as women's athletics gets more play and develops higher stakes.

Maintaining this sportsmanship can change the fundamental way the game is played. After FIFA sent referees to work the first Women's World Championship in 1991, they reported that they were exhausted from their efforts. We were all surprised to hear this, and then elated with the reason: the women played within the rules—less fouling, less effort to get away with something, less time-wasting—basically less stoppage, less rebellion, and more cooperation. So the game rarely stopped, and the refs had to run all the time.

There are other aspects of the positive female sociology that impact sports. More often, girls and women play for each other. I think this is part of their capacity to relate to one another. Men have more of a "just get me the ball" attitude; they usually don't care as much if they like their teammates as people. When I was a men's coach recruiting players, they basically wanted to know about scholarship money and playing time. One of my first prominent female recruits was April Heinrichs. I tried to recruit her with the same enticements, but she sort of skipped over that and instead asked: How does your team get along? I couldn't figure out at the time why that made any difference, but each time I called her, she asked the same question. I think I must have vouched for the team as a good group of people that worked well together, as she did agree to play for us. But this was a new experience for me, coming from the men's game. This ability and desire to relate deeply means the potential for powerful team chemistry is greater in the women's game.

In a culture in which women are encouraged to communicate and relate personally, their bonds are generally stronger and deeper. Therefore, the interest in positive team chemistry is greater in the women's game, and the positive impact of that good chemistry is also greater. But this habit of deeper relationships can be a double-edged sword, since it can take team chemistry in the wrong direction. Women can be incredibly demanding; they set very high standards for each other, and they are very sensitive, which is a difficult combination. When people are so sensitive, any negative ripple can be picked up on and magnified. As a result, constructing chemistry is a continuing challenge with a women's team. But once that careful chemistry is achieved, the bond is amazingly powerful and translates onto the field.

While it is my sincerest hope that women's soccer avoids some of the negative qualities of the men's athletic culture, there are some aspects of this culture that women players would be well-served to imitate.

Part of the sociology of girls and women interferes with their development as soccer players. Uninhibited competition is usually harder for females. Because of the importance of their relationships, they struggle with separating competitive anger from personal anger. In general, females don't like direct confrontation. This is true from a very young age. If you look at sociological studies, when girls play they pick nonconfrontational games, like hopscotch or jacks. If two young girls show up at a basketball court, they don't customarily fight for turf in a game like one v. one. Their tendency is to play a cooperative, turn-taking game, like HORSE. But this doesn't train you for the competitive arena. What would really develop the girls in this situation is if they went out and challenged each other in one v. one.

The hardest problem in making females into great soccer players is trying to get them to excel in the one v. one environment—especially against a friend or teammate. One v. one is the most important drill for teaching not only optimum soccer skills but the psychological dimension needed to compete. I cannot stress enough its importance. Some of the most extraordinary female players in the world have evolved going one v. one against boys, who thrive on this type of challenge. A television soccer commentator in the 2000 Olympics told the story of one woman participant who, growing up, disguised herself as a boy in order to play on a team in Brazil—that is, until she got discovered and kicked off.

Use her as an example; imitate the boys. The stress of playing against someone else who is trying to destroy you is wonderful for your athletic development. Jump in and play with your brother or your neighbor. It's not a social struggle, because for these guys, it's not personal; it's not about friendships. One of Scott Lilly's—Kristine Lilly's older brother—favorite stories is about taking his younger sister out in the backyard and pounding her. Obviously he does so jokingly, but he takes full credit for her development as a soccer player. He's probably not far from the truth, because when Kristine got to UNC, the competitive fury we strive to build into our players wasn't new to her. She already had it.

Competitive fury is totally accepted and embraced in the male culture. It needs to be introduced and accepted within the female athletic culture as well. One of the most important points I can stress in this book is to understand competitive anger, and not make it a negative trait or a personal issue. I don't just mean competitive anger toward a rival. I know girls can get fired up to beat their opponents. You need to take it a step further, so that competitiveness is so ingrained and automatic that you use it every time you play, against friend or foe. You want to be on the edge of your intensity without, of course, entering the dark side—which is to maim and mangle the opponent. But I want you to play with physical intensity, to give yourself permission to compete, keep score, not be embarrassed about being a winner.

Michelle Akers, one of the greatest players I have ever coached, has this trait. She is also a consummate Christian. Yet there is no contradiction between those two roles, because when you cross the line and walk onto the field you are in effect embracing a set of rules that demands competitive fire. You can be powerful on the field, yet be a thoughtful and kind person as well. But one of the things you don't need to demonstrate between the lines is the type of kindness you might show outside the lines. Certainly sportsmanship is important, but playing with fearless competitiveness is not unsportsmanlike. Being competitive means being fully engaged in the game, which is actually a sign of respect for your opponent, because to play any easier against an opponent, or against your best friend, in practice is actually demonstrating a lack of respect.

Self-Image

Enriching your life also means expanding it. That's an important symbolic image for female players. Are you big and powerful, or do you prefer to see yourself as thin and fashionable? Is your goal to rule the world, or are you mostly concerned with not taking up too much space? This social factor that impacts female athletes, including the way they play soccer, is their self-image.

I've worked with a lot of the best women soccer players in the world, and I can tell you, they didn't get that way by aspiring to be small and thin. In fact, one of the greatest players, Cindy Parlow, showed all of us she was not embarrassed to fly in the face of genteel female sociology in the things she chose to eat. Growing up female these days is filled with the pressure of trying to look a certain way to gain affection, and the look is hollow-cheeked and paper-thin, which means a diet of watercress and celery. Not Cindy. We give our seniors the opportunity to pick the restaurant on road trips. In Cindy's senior year, she wanted Outback Steak House—much to the delight of the coaching staff. You see, Cindy is a big eater, and proud of it. No body image issues with her!

Eating disorders are common among female athletes, and among women in general. Soccer players are no exception. The best talk I ever heard on this subject was to the U16 National Team when I was an assistant coach to April Heinrichs. Colleen Hacker, the sports psychologist who works with the Women's U.S. National Team, sent a powerful message to this new collection of U16 players that we were training in Chula Vista, California, in 1998. "What is it about us females?" she asked them. "We want to sort of hide away and get as small as we can. And what is it about boys—they seek to rule the Earth? They want to jump into a weight room to become as big as possible and fill up space and be loud and dominant. What is it about us, and our culture, that prevents us from feeling that way? Why don't **we** want to fill up space and dominate the Earth?"

There's a guy who played on the UNC men's soccer team named Chris Carrieri, who was one of the best players and a lot of fun to watch. He left a year early to jump into the MLS as the number-one pick in the draft, with a great collegiate soccer resume behind him, although when he came in as a freshman he was quite small. Throughout his college career he did a lot of weight lifting, and became very powerful. According to the girls on our team, there was a sign in his room that simply said BIG, in huge letters. Even though he was small, he wanted to be big. This is the way men think. In the film *Big*, the actor Tom Hanks is a child who gets his wish to become a grown-up. But if a film titled BIG were about a girl, the first image other girls would have is that she is fat. Our modern culture has made our women, even many of our athletic women, terrified about being "big."

The way Colleen Hacker finished her talk was great. She told the girls, "Let's not be manipulated by our culture and its advertising—the images that we are given of the way we 'should' be. Don't be so weak that you are swayed by the media, by just a magazine photo."

If you work hard, if you do the training we talk about in this book, you're going to be a better soccer player. You are also going to be big and strong and powerful, because you're going to have to get that way to keep from getting knocked off the ball. An important part of what we do at UNC, and recommend to you in the book, is weight, or resistance, training. But there's a persistent negativity among some people about females working with weights. They associate weights with being "big," as if that's something to fear rather than celebrate. Greg Gatz, the Strength and Conditioning coach for our team, who provides you with a program in Appendix I, makes an extremely good point. He says, in essence, "You're involved in a sport that takes power. If you don't have strength, you'll be limited in your performance. Make a decision—do you want to be the best soccer player you can be?" Make that choice. Create your own image of who you are. Don't be manipulated by the culture that wants you to be an ornament.

For Anne Remy ('98–'01), a starting midfielder, and a top scholar athlete, there's never been a choice. That's because for her, femininity and powerful soccer are not at odds. Anne, a pretty blond with long, painted nails, looks like Barbie and plays like Attila the Hun. Everyone on the team has admiration for her. She constantly takes physical risks and doesn't worry about getting her face smashed in. She isn't ruled by her female culture, although she fits perfectly within it. She also fits entirely within the athletic culture.

Anne is one of five children. She says she was always competitive, especially with her sisters, who are four and six years older, both of whom played collegiate soccer at neighboring Duke. She claims her dad (a former track runner) is outwardly sweet, but fierce while playing sports, and her mom, who didn't have the opportunities of her daughters to be a competitive athlete, has always admired and encouraged Anne's efforts. If you ask her how she reconciles her two seemingly opposite sides, she answers with ease, "I feel all of us on this team are that way. We can dress up and 'be girls,' but get out on the playing fields and be animals."

Anne also dates a professional baseball player, a tremendous athlete in his own right, who happens to look like a Ken doll. One spring she went to watch him at training camp. She noticed the other players' girlfriends, mostly pretty but empty, without much ambition of their own. "You're a soccer player?" they asked her, "You don't look like one." Anne was appalled by them. Her mother later told me this incident just added to her daughter's drive to succeed at her sport.

What Anne saw at that baseball training camp drove home the fact that she doesn't want to be a part of a passive female culture. She wants something more out of her life. In my player conferences with her, Anne tells me she basically wants it all, to be the best player she can be. She certainly does not want to be some appendage to a male athlete.

While we're destroying the obstacles that stand in the way of female players, we need to shatter that traditional dream that having a guy is enough. It's not enough. Sure, it can be a very important part of your life, but it shouldn't be your whole life. One of the lectures we give the girls at our soccer camp is to be your own person; don't be some guy's bauble, a decoration on a mantle piece. I tell female players: If you're involved with someone, make sure he is only a part of your life, because be assured, you are only a part of his.

The soccer field is a great place to create a self-image of strength and independence, where you can "dominate the Earth," while a boyfriend watches you from the sidelines!

CHAPTER 5

Toward Personal Excellence

All of Us Can Be Excellent

In 1999, I was invited to lecture on athletic excellence in a freshman honors seminar on campus. The professor had some literature that I found so powerful that I now use it with my team. It has become the foundation of everything we do. I also use it as part of a coaches lecture I give. Below I have adapted it for you.

Excellence is Actually Mundane

Excellence is accomplished through deliberate actions, ordinary in themselves, performed consistently and carefully, made into habits, compounded together, added up over time.

Since it is mundane, it is within reach of everyone, all the time. Please don't confuse this with success. In competitive athletics success is mutually exclusive...there are winners and losers...one team finishes first and another one last.

So this is your challenge:

- through deliberate actions (the things players do in training)
- ordinary in themselves (everyone is doing them, there are no real secrets)
- performed consistently (done on a regular basis)
- and carefully (with high standards and consummate focus)
- made into habits (coached into your technical, tactical, psychological, and physical fabric)

- compounded together (with an understanding of harnessing all the elements)
- added up over time (done when appropriate on a daily, weekly, monthly, and yearly basis).

Daniel F. Chambliss, *Sociological Theory,* 1989

Tactics and Skills

We all know what it takes to develop individual soccer skills: the correct technique, and the enormous time commitment required to do it. I refer not only to team practice, but to your individual work as well. The best example that comes to mind in terms of this skill development is Laurie Schwoy ('96–'00). Laurie was injured off and on for the final two years of her collegiate eligibility, and yet she got better because even while recovering from injury, she continually put in time with the ball, a habit she developed as a young girl. Her skills are so exquisite and remarkable that I call her the female Etchevarry (Marco Etchevarry, known for his ball skills, is a native of Bolivia who plays for DC United of MLS). She can bend balls, lift them and chip them, and even tried a bicycle kick in one of our games. She can go through a "phone booth" (i.e., a small space) of defenders with her skills. She is also brilliant in the air. It all comes from her investment of time in all technical aspects of the game.

When you're developing your skill and physical dimensions, the ongoing factor is perseverance. Sometimes this repetitive work isn't fun; it can be lonely and boring. But it's what will make you exceptional. And skills (together with fitness) is one of the areas of the game in which excellence is completely in your hands. Your work has to be scientific, though. It can't be haphazard. It also has to be structured properly. You have to know the right things to do, and have the right advice. Your advanced training should be properly organized—seasonal and rhythmical (see Appendix II for our Yearly Rhythm). You can do too much, and you can do not enough.

To develop tactically, you have to become a student of the game (see the following chapter). This entails not merely watching soccer, but watching it with a critical eye for your personal development. Let me give you an example of how this has worked at UNC. With a satellite television hookup, I get to see the best soccer in the world. In one game, I saw something that related to my dissatisfaction at the way my team prepared the ball with their first touch. An Argentinean team named River Plate was just exquisite. I noticed how simple their technique was, yet they went through crowded defenses in every direction, and unbelievably quickly. There was one huge glaring difference between these consummate professionals and the way my team prepared the ball. Our players were using the outside of the foot to prepare the ball for penetration or service (as opposed to using the inside of the foot to draw it across and in front of the body). They were complicating their technique, causing them to be off balance. We wanted them to get back to the simplicity of River Plate. In practice I talked to them about the game I'd seen on TV. That became the emphasis of practice for the week. I had discovered and narrowed in on a problem to work on, just by watching TV.

In addition to watching high-level soccer for those who cannot see it live, television helps you to select your role models. Now, all of you can turn on your set and watch the WUSA. Pick out your heroes, and emulate them!

Focus and Discipline

In order to excel at the highest possible level you need to be focused and disciplined. That's because the competitive soccer world is so stressful. For example, athletics demands tremendous fitness. Think of the note I wrote to Mia Hamm, which is in the beginning of the book. Can you drive yourself to get fit, and, after you are bent over in exhaustion from sprinting, can you spend an hour slamming a ball against the wall, or playing one v. one against your friends? Can you drive yourself with self-discipline when others are not there? No one is going to be constantly pushing you, insisting that you get fit or hone your skills. When it truly counts, you're on your own. Your margin of success is based on your inner drive. This focus and self-discipline is also a great element of your character.

Commitment and Courage

You can see examples of commitment and courage in athletics every day. We talk about these traits with our UNC players. When these qualities are lacking, we sometimes tease the players in a light-hearted way, because humor helps lessen the sting when critiquing them. So, we talk about hummingbirds.

One of the crucial aspects when we play with defensive presence is getting "stuck in," a common British expression for an aggressive player who gets in tackles, or sticks her face in where the ball is going, risking taking a knock or getting whacked. This is Michelle Akers's defining quality. We describe those without this all-out physical courage as hummingbirds. They sort of just go humming around the action. They don't get stuck in. Now, to

There are few kinds of players I value more than those who are recklessly courageous. Leslie Gaston, who currently plays for us, is everything I admire as far as the human spirit is concerned.

the untrained eye, the speedy little hummingbird might look like a bundle of energy and hustle. But the hummingbird knows deep down in her tiny little heart that she just doesn't want to get close enough to risk getting hit. So she times everything to get to the play a little late. This is clearly apparent to the trained eye.

In addition to playing good soccer, physical courage means playing with abandon. It is amazingly liberating, and actually a lot of fun, when you allow yourself to just "go for it," to get stuck in. Your capacity to take the risk is also a measure of your commitment to giving your best effort—for yourself and for your team. So, don't be a hummingbird. Be a hawk.

Taking Responsibility

Do you know the kind of player who always finds an excuse when she fails? When something isn't going well, she whines or blames someone else. One of my daughters once came home from high school soccer practice complaining about everything under the sun. I put it all in her lap. If she was expecting any sympathy from me she was going to get absolutely none, because I know how this scenario is played out. From the coach's point of view, this kind of complaining can be unbelievably destructive. So I threw it back at my daughter. "Listen," I told her, "you can solve problems. You make a difference. If you feel cut off, you reconnect with the coach." That's what it means to take responsibility. When faced with challenges, or problems, look within yourself and decide what **you** can do to make things better.

You feel someone did something unfair? Is that your argument against taking personal responsibility? But this is a subjective sport, and besides, the world is filled with injustice. Who promises you justice? Certainly not the referee, whose decisions are irrefutable, regardless of human error. You can't argue away those decisions, no matter how unfair they seem. You only dig yourself into a hole trying.

When I think of injustice, and of the need to take responsibility no matter what, I think of an incident with Cindy Parlow. Cindy is one of the greatest athletes and the finest people I've ever coached. In her freshman year at UNC, we were undefeated, playing Notre Dame in the semifinal on our field, on which we had lost only one game in our entire history up to that point.

A ball was served into the box by Notre Dame, and in an effort to head it out of the goal, young Cindy, a freshman who had left high school a year early, sent it into her own goal. We lost 1-0. We were defeated in the National Championship that year, and we've only lost three National Championships in 20 years.

After the game, I grabbed Cindy as we were heading into the press tent. I knew this was going to be a watershed moment for her. She was going to have an opportunity to demonstrate her character. "Cindy," I warned her, exaggerating a reporter's question just to make my point, "basically what you're going to be asked is, 'What does it feel like to bring down the UNC dynasty on your own?'" Before going into that room, I told her that I wanted her to understand something. "We would not have been in the final if it weren't for you. You're one of the greatest players we've ever had at UNC, and we came into this game 25-0 because of you. There's no way you lost this game for us, but they're going to hang it on you. What you have to do is to take responsibility, and then, in that declaration of responsibility, you are winning an amazing victory." And that's exactly what she did. When someone asked her that question, she started to choke up, and with tears in her eyes, said she took responsibility for the loss. Seeing that exchange, I knew that her whole life she had always taken responsibility up to that moment. And from that day forward, I knew she always would. It was one of the best examples of victory in defeat that I've ever seen in my life.

Learning to Accept Responsibility

Taking responsibility is what Catherine Reddick learned to do in the 2000 season. A high school star, Catherine also played for every age National Team, from U16 to U21. But she came into our program out of shape, and was beaten out for her spot by Julia Marslander, a walk-on. This was a lesson for both of them. Julia showed what hard work can do, and Catherine learned the value of that hard work, and of humility. A lesser human being than Catherine might have whined and complained and deserted the team mission when she was relegated to reserve status, risking havoc with our team chemistry.

Did she quit, or become a negative life force? No, she did the opposite. She took responsibility for the fact she was not starting, and began working her heart out. But just because she got fit, did that mean the whole world had to change for her? She had dug herself a hole, and she was not about to get out of it just because she had rectified her initial mistake. She remained a reserve, and had to live with the fact that although she had a chance to start coming into the season, she had given it away to someone else. Regardless, she kept on working hard and supporting everyone on the team.

Catherine learned that she was paying the price for not being ready when the door was open for her. Now the door had closed, and yet she decided to do whatever she could to help the team. When the door was reopened, this time she was ready, and she understood that she was given a new chance. She was not going to make the same mistake again. In the NCAA semifinal she had a remarkable performance, so we started her in the final—her first start all year. She ended up being a catalyst of the game-winning goal, and winning the defensive MVP in the NCAA tournament, the most important event of the year.

What happened to Catherine is that through adversity she became twice the player she was when she arrived at UNC in August. Part of ascending to greatness is being humbled, and humility is part of your route to the depth of character that I believe is a most essential aspect of your soccer career. Two months later, Catherine had a chance to start for the full U.S. Women's National Team. What an amazing ascension!

Power and Respect

In order to be powerful, you must give yourself permission to be aggressive on the soccer field. Never mind who it is—friend or foe—you play to beat them because that is part of the game. You have to understand the value in doing this (and thus in trying to excel) even if it sometimes separates you from those who don't understand, and you find yourself temporarily unpopular. Popularity and respect are different. Being liked is not as lasting as being respected. You don't want to gain friendship just by being passive, or giving in to try not to offend anyone. That's the way our culture tells girls they have to gain respect. In the long run though, you will gain people's respect, and in a way you'd rather have it, if you go after them on the soccer field.

You're going to gain respect by being a powerful, ambitious player. You're also going to be a tremendously confident and aggressive person who still wants and needs to connect to people, so you should be thoughtful and kind as well. But within the context of the game, I am trying to empower you to tap into that part of yourself that's not afraid of taking physical risks, or even the social risk of jeopardizing friendships. I realize that overcoming negative social pressures can be just as challenging as learning soccer skills. But understanding your priorities will help you to endure the risks, and seek out supportive environments, with people whose goals are similar to yours.

When April Heinrichs first came to UNC she chewed through her teammates in practice. She ruthlessly pounded them. Concerned over her aggressive personality, some of the other players came to me and asked, "What are we going to do about April?" I answered without hesitation. "Clone her," I told them. I wanted everyone to compete like April. I thought it was wonderful.

Being dominant, aggressive, and courageous—that's the powerful part of you. That is the part that is worthy of self-respect, and ultimately, the respect of others.

Leadership

You are also empowered when you assume a position of leadership. One of the biggest issues in female leadership on the soccer field is that players have to find their voice when they compete. Soccer players need to talk on the field, and loudly. Female players are reluctant to do this. Again, I think it's because of the sociological issues. Typically, women are afraid to lead each other verbally, on the field. They feel they will be resented for saying anything. As a result, most feel self-conscious saying anything to others. This is our annual problem in developing our female leadership in the spring, after losing our seniors. A lot of female players know what to do on the field, but they hesitate to say anything to others, like, "Hey, back off," "pull back," or "get wide." So they stand there and watch disaster take place, just because they are reluctant to hear their own voice because they don't want to come across as bossy.

This isn't just an issue for young players. This problem exists on the most elite levels as well. The players on the 2000 UNC team are wonderful, but they don't want to talk on the field. We have a bunch of mute zombies out there; as a result, at times we have absolutely no leadership presence. Even in practice, trying to get them to say something is like pulling teeth. It's such a big problem that we address it in the off-season. We have the players read *The Leadership Moment* (see recommended reading in the previous chapter). We discuss the book, chapter by chapter. One of the chapters is about a smoke jumper who was in a position to save a group of people, but because he is the strong, silent type, he would not say the things he had to in the midst of crisis. That doesn't work in leadership. He knew what to do, but he couldn't communicate it. As a result, he survived but 13 people died.

Carla Overbeck was one of the few players for us who would speak up on the field consistently, and she also used the correct tone. The voice she selected, and the comments she made, encouraged and inspired the other players, but they were not always positive statements. Sometimes she was critical, but she didn't irritate or anger them. The right voice is a combination of tone and the manner with which you command a group. More girls and women need to find this leadership voice, and they have to use it. Otherwise, what happens—although obviously I mean this symbolically—is the smoke jumper disaster.

(For more on developing communication skills, see Chapter 14.)

The Winning Mentality

While evaluating international teams for CONCACAF (FIFA's regional leadership arm) in the Gold Cup, a tournament of National Teams, I was interviewing the national coaches from Mexico, Canada, and China. They told me that what distinguishes the Americans from other countries is their winning mentality. The United States players have an enormous will to succeed, and it is very respected.

This mentality is a description of the strength of your psychological dimension. It involves your capacity to reach down inside and find your

Here's Carla Overbeck celebrating 20 years of her leadership work. She will certainly go down as one of the greatest field leaders in American women's soccer history.

inner hardness. It's what happens when you emerge triumphant from any physical duel or combative situation.

The winning mentality is partly optimism, but mostly it's a combination of focus, pride, competitive anger, relentlessness, hardness, fitness and courage—all of the most descriptive words for competitive athletics. This type of mentality is not about your skills or tactics. What it comes down to is intense desire. To get this winning edge, you need to build an indomitable will. This means you must be relentless; you must never give up.

What I love about this mentality is that it's not a talent; it's not part of a genetic code you're either born with or not. It's a choice, a decision you make to develop it. It is not an easy choice, but it is what is going to elevate you from the ordinary player. The question is: can you make the choice to be indomitable? Of course, having this mentality doesn't guarantee winning, but it's a quality that gives you the incredible strength, power, and hardness that is an element in every consistent winner. You are already aware of our emphasis on one v. one at UNC. We use one v. one as the best training ground for developing the winning mentality. That's because it embodies all of the qualities mentioned above.

The winning mentality is the defining aspect of the National Team and UNC players. But that doesn't mean they have this trait as soon as they get here. Our players are still a work in progress. Most young players are. I can see this in my evening talks on the winning mentality at summer camp. This mentality requires a domination in both practice and games. The girls nod their heads yes when I'm talking about this, but I know what most of them are thinking: that's not me.

We joke with our players all the time (remember the importance of a laugh?). We tell them that we know women have evolved to a higher level—they know their relationships are more important than soccer. That's absolutely true, we say, but forget that for the 90 minutes it takes you to win the game!

Transcending Ordinary Effort

At UNC we talk about transcending ordinary effort. In our girls' camps, for example, if you're doing Coervers (individual ball skills), extraordinary effort means you are on your physical and technical edge. On your physical edge, you're just about to wipe out from these breakneck radical changes of direction you are making at top speed. On your technical edge, you're just about to lose control of the ball. Often you do, because you're going too fast to hold onto it.

Ordinary effort is when you're comfortable. That's mediocrity. A lot of athletes work within their comfort zone, physically and technically. They don't feel like they're going to lose control, or pass out from fatigue. But when you train within your comfort zone, you're not preparing yourself for a match. In a game situation the other team is trying to take you out of your comfort zone. So as soon as they do, you're in unfamiliar territory. You panic. You make a mistake, or lose the ball.

The challenge for you as an individual athlete is to find a way to elevate your environment. This is not easy. You probably have to set your own standards of practice performance. You are part of a team sport in which coaches and your teammates are critical for motivation. It's tough to keep yourself on this edge independently. But this is what sets the truly great players apart. It is their capacity to "flame on" — to hit a button and just ignite. They can do this whenever, and with whomever.

There is no better example of this than our goalkeeper Jenni Branam. (As a sophomore, Jenni was an alternate on the 2000 Olympic team.) What excited me about watching Jenni train in her freshman year was that when she was in goal, every single shot for her was the World Cup. That told me that she was only going to get better every year. And she has.

If you can train like every environment is the World Cup, take it to the most intense level, then your improvement is going to be remarkable. It will separate you from the ordinary.

Mia Hamm ('89–'93)

The Philosophy of Confidence

"The greater the artist the greater the doubt. Perfect confidence is granted to the less talented as a consolation prize." That quote, from the art critic Robert Hughes, was given to me by Colleen Hacker, my sports psychologist.

I think it's most important for people to realize that confidence is a living, breathing thing. It changes every single day. It's not like you wake up one day and say, "I'm confident for the next ten years," and so that's the way you are. It's not like a pill you take. You don't tell yourself, "Alongside my vitamin C, I'll take my confidence pill."

I think from that standpoint, confidence needs to be nurtured. You should practice it just like you do every other skill, whether it's technical or tactical. Confidence takes work. I'm still working hard on it every single day.

Looking back, it's tough to say whether I was confident as a young player. Was I confident in terms of being singled out? No. But to some degree, I had an inner confidence about my abilities. I think I knew I was a good athlete.

As a child, I was probably a more introverted, shy person. Sports were a great outlet for me, and a great opportunity to connect with people. It's what I knew, what I understood, and what I liked to do. I felt a lot more comfortable playing, and competing in sports, than I did in any other aspect of my life.

I don't know if this personality trait is common among my peers. It's not like we've sat down and talked about these issues specifically. I think Kristine Lilly and I probably have a similar personality in this regard, and maybe Joy Fawcett as well.

There's a story that's told about Anson seeing me play for the first time at age 14. He's quoted as saying I ran through the pack and burst up the field. Probably no one would have doubted my confidence if they had seen me on the field as a young girl. But you're different when you're out there. I think when you're in an environment in which you're just playing, you don't

Here's what Mia did best: delighting the large home crowd at Fetzer Field. We consistently draw the largest crowds in the collegiate game.

think about confidence the way people typically do. If you're going to question yourself, you don't necessarily do it during a game, but before or after. If I had been questioning myself and my confidence while competing, I don't think I would be where I am today.

People ask whether crowds, or the aspect of performing, affect my confidence. Sometimes you're aware of the spectators, but a lot of the time, you're not, because you're so focused on what you're doing. That's the case with me, because crowds have never caused me a sense of panic. Confidence isn't at all affected by spectators, or the type of crowds. I think what has more of an impact on confidence is how you're feeling at the moment you're playing in terms of your present or your past successes—or lack of them—and the environment, or the situation of a game.

Can you be overconfident? I don't know if I'd ever use that word. When I think of someone who is "overconfident," I think of a person who doesn't have respect for the game. If you play soccer, you can't be overconfident, because you understand that in this game, anything can happen.

In everything you do—just as it is for me in athletics—there are varying degrees of confidence and doubt. You have different instances in games that either give you confidence, or put a little bit of doubt in your head. As an athlete, you make mistakes. You try to get past them. Sometimes, you have a series of games that take away from your confidence, and then, you have a series of games that help you build it. It's a lot harder to build up confidence than it is to tear it down. That's one of the reasons why a lot of elite athletes use sports psychologists. These athletes are trying to maximize their potential, knowing that the smallest little thing is going to help, or give them that edge. A lot of sports psychology ties into building confidence, such as positive self-talk, mental imagery, having a routine and visualization. All of these are useful techniques to help you maintain a consistent level of confidence.

Confidence is based on certain incidents, the way you play, and things that are said. So much can impact on your confidence, but as an athlete, you try to control it to the degree that you are able. Colleen Hacker, also the National Team's sports psychologist, talks with us about our circle of influence and our circle of control, and understanding that we can't get bogged down in what we have no control over. If you let that happen, then your focus isn't on what is important—making sure that you're there to play.

You learn to understand that just because you have one bad touch, it doesn't mean you have a bad game. You learn to get over things. I've talked a lot about one of my most important lessons, which I learned in college.

When I went to Carolina, I was in a much different environment than I had been in before. I was still one of the better players, but at the same time, I was surrounded by a lot of good players. There were players who had a stronger psychological dimension than I had—players whom I aspired to be like.

What worked for me in terms of building and maintaining confidence was to change my attitude and expectations. I'm a goal-scorer, and rarely are goal-scorers successful. Using goal-scoring to determine my confidence would be like a baseball player banking on the fact that he was going to be confident only when he hit a home run, or, a basketball player feeling that only when he scored 30 or 40 points, or had a triple-double, would he be confident. If it's only at times like these that you're going to gain confidence when you play, you're going to be miserable. So, you have to find things in your game that you can have more control over. For me, that's my defensive effort, and my work rate.

I was not going to put pressure on myself by saying, "I know I'm playing great when I score five goals." Instead, I told myself, "You're going to gain more confidence every time you close down a defender, every time you win a ball, or make a great run, or set someone up," because those were things I had control over. What I found was that it took a lot of pressure off of me, and the goals became a lot easier. I felt that I had a better handle on having more of an impact on my confidence.

Gaining confidence is a result of time and experience, but I have also actively worked to improve it. When I was at UNC, we talked about things, but we didn't sit around saying, "Okay, let's dissect the psychological dimension. Let's analyze how we become more confident mentally." We found ways though. A great example was something that happened during the summer of my sophomore year. I was having a rather bad summer in terms of the way I was playing. I was working at UNC summer camp, and everything about my game felt off. I remember talking to Anson, and saying, "I stink right now. I can't do anything. My touch is off. I can't shoot. I'm this. I'm that."

"You know Mia," he said, "it's simply that you're off balance."

"Really?" I replied.

"Yes, you're just off balance, in your touch, and the way you shoot."

My feeling was one of relief. "Wow, it's not everything; it's just one thing. Now, if I can just focus on that one thing, I'll be okay." And sure enough, that's all I concentrated on in my training. I told myself, "Okay, now just be on balance on your touch; don't lean back; don't lean too far forward; just be right." The next thing I knew, within a week, I was back to being creative and deceptive.

As athletes, sometimes we overanalyze. We think: it's everything. That's not true. It's just the way we view the situation at that time.

I've actually talked a lot about confidence, although it's not like there's a day-in, day-out cathartic episode — "Mia's confidence." With fame, people assume that you are confident. I think it has to do with having success. People may think I go out there every day with an attitude like, "Who am I going to beat up on today?" "Who am I going 'to school' today?" That's not the way I am. Not that I sit around and doubt myself either, but at the same time, I question myself. "How do I feel? What do I need to do? Am I ready for this?" because every game brings about different challenges. If you're playing against a physical defense; if you're playing against a tactical defender; or someone who's extremely fast—it's just making sure to be ready, whatever the circumstances.

In some games, you feel you can do no wrong. Every touch is perfect. Every ball you serve is perfect. Then there are other games when you think, "Have I played before? Is this the first time I've ever kicked a soccer ball, because that's what it feels like right now." It's all so difficult. You're thinking about everything. The fact is, your thought process is too complex for what you're doing.

Confidence improves by gaining more experience, and by succeeding to play at higher and higher levels. The introduction of sports psychologists has also helped, and learning more about how to influence your confidence, and how to control it. This control means that your ebbs and flows aren't as great, that your peaks and valleys aren't as far apart, and that you are in a more consistent state.

My final advice on gaining confidence is to come to grips with the fact that you will have monumental days, and you will have days in which you struggle. Focus on what you can control when that happens, and understand that it is part of your soccer experience.

CHAPTER 6

Soccer Basics

Your understanding of the game is how you see it when you're watching and how you feel it when you're playing.

There's an important quality among great soccer players that I have alluded to in earlier chapters. It is having a soccer sense. While not every good player is gifted with this sense, a great player must be. Some of it seems to be an inborn talent, but as you will see in this chapter, much of it can be developed.

Players with a great soccer sense have a kind of vision—the ability to see and analyze what is happening on the field. This ability is coupled with what seems to be, an internal gyroscope that allows these players to sense pressure, to negotiate their positioning, and monitor the movements of every other player. They can utilize their perceptive and accurate decision-making of where the ball should go, with a kind of timing and execution of play that seems to baffle the laws of physics. Players like this make you wonder how it is possible for a ball and a body to do what they do.

These great players have the capacity to mentally photograph a situation with every look. With one glance, they have a picture of the entire field. Part of that glance absorbs the fact that, for example, their left midfielder is on a full sprint, while the defender is caught napping, and there's a big space over the top, but it's not going to be there in another half-second. So, after a short pause to lull a defender, this kind of player delivers the ball to an onrushing midfielder with perfect timing, pace, and texture that completely shreds the other team's otherwise organized defense.

Exactly what is this ability, and where does it come from? Some people call it an intelligence, and while I'd love to say the people who have a great sense of the game are supremely intelligent (or excel academically), in my experience that's not necessarily the case. Players who make good decisions on the soccer field are not necessarily brilliant people. Certainly, women's soccer seems to draw good students (e.g., at the college level, women athletes graduate at a rate of 10 to 15% higher than their counterparts in the general student population), but I think that's more of a testimony to immersing yourself in the game as a player and a spectator than a correlation between intelligence and soccer ability.

Some of the soccer geniuses I've coached are good students, but some are not. Some of the great students we've had at UNC had absolutely no common sense on the field, whereas others who have played for us don't do very well academically, but in terms of soccer they are sharp as tacks. Not every high-level player has soccer sense. For some, it might always be a mystery. Although those who arrive in our program are highly successful, we are always shocked by how fundamentally underdeveloped some of them are when it comes to soccer sense.

Tactical knowledge is an integral part of good soccer sense. How do you develop that? In our system, the players must be able to verbally describe everything they do, and in detail. When they are asked about strategy, it's not enough to say, "I can do it, I just can't explain it."

Before every game, we discuss tactics. There is always a group of people in the locker room who are very good at verbalizing these tactics. (Unfortunately, they are a minority.) Interestingly, I've discovered that the players constantly involved in the discussions are the ones most willing to attempt the tactical explanations. Sometimes they're right, sometimes not, but those who actively think and attempt to verbalize ultimately develop into great tacticians. Clearly, they are intellectually curious and excited by this aspect of the game, and will explore it verbally because they already dissect it on a tactical level.

There are others who are not at all attentive during these discussions, who look glazed over, or fear they will be called on and exposed for what they don't know. There are all kinds of risk-taking and challenge in soccer. The chance that you will say something incorrect during pregame or practice question-and-answer sessions is part of that risk.

I encourage you not to be timid or apathetic. If you aspire to become tactically sophisticated you should actively pursue this aspect of the game. You have to be interested and attentive in order to explain or form an opinion you are able to defend. You should practice doing this verbally. It takes concentration and study, which this chapter will aid you in doing. Suffice it to say, this is an understanding of soccer at its most complicated level. But when you gain it, you also acquire the deepest appreciation of the game.

*An army of deer led by a lion is more to be feared than an
army of lions led by a deer.*

—Philip II of Macedon
quoted in a leadership team meeting

Integrating Game Sense into Your Play

Soccer geniuses have the capacity to make decisions on the field under enormous pressure. Of course, their gamut of skills is also brought into play, so they are solving problems not just with their minds but with their weapons. That's why developing skills must also be part of developing your game sense.

It is critical for you as a young player to understand that in order to become a tactical genius, you have to be able to problem-solve with every kind of technical tool. After all, you can have a good intellectual understanding of the game without having a high level of technique, and accomplish nothing. Knowing you have to do something, and being able to do it, are two separate things. So, knowing you have to get the ball over to a place right now, and yet not being able to do it, nullifies the understanding that you may have. Obviously, if you want to play at the highest possible level, and to utilize your soccer sense, every aspect has to fall into place.

You can also have soccer sense yourself and not communicate it with anyone. You can excel individually with your positional play, but in order to be ultimately effective, you need to combine your knowledge with communication to your teammates. This is where leadership comes into play.

Leadership is the art of communicating your soccer understanding, both on and off the field. It means driving people to play a certain way with your special understanding of the game. That is done by directing teammates where they should be at a certain time, because their lack of soccer sense hasn't put them in the right position. An ideal team has on each of its four lines (i.e., forward, midfield, defensive, goalkeeping) at least one player with a combination of soccer sense and leadership skills. That leader has the ability to organize her line effectively. Of course, a strong leader on every line is a coach's dream scenario. You have an opportunity to become just such a "dream player," if you understand what it requires.

Many former UNC players possess outstanding aspects of soccer sense. Shannon Higgins-Cirovski ('86–'89), one of the nine former players to date to have her UNC jersey number retired and a U.S. National Team member from 1987–91, is a tactical genius. Her vision was a critical part of her game. Of all the players I've coached, she is the one who came closest to never making a tactical mistake. She saw the field the way I have described above, and coupled that with having the technical ability to carry out her ideas.

Obviously, I'm always looking at potential future coaches. At a certain point, coaches begin to learn from their players. I stopped coaching Shannon when she was a sophomore, and started consulting with her instead. I had so much respect for her that I would ask her questions in order to get a feel for what was going on in the game, and what to do.

Nel Fettig ('94–'97), an all-American defender and WUSA player, is another one of those players with exceptional tactical ability. Most of the time, a coach gets nervous with freshmen and can spend a majority of the game instructing them because they are so tactically naive. I remember early in Nel's freshman year, right in the midst of giving instructions, I realized she understood exactly what to do without Dino (Bill Palladino) or me telling her anything. Suddenly, we sat back and watched Nel perform her magic.

One of the famous clichés in soccer is "the first five yards is in your head." That means that even a slow player—if she is tactically savvy—can outrace a thoroughbred. Nel always had this head start, because she was moving long before the player who was about to serve the ball actually did so. Because she knew what was going to transpire before it happened, Nel had the ability to read a player's body language, and an understanding of where the ball should go. It's a combination of these qualities that gave her such a sophisticated mind-set.

I mentioned at the beginning of the chapter that part of game sense can be developed. One way is through playing other sports. Ability can translate from one sport to another. In Nel's case, I sense that perhaps she had tremendous ability to read the game because it was developed in her elite tennis background (she was a national-caliber youth player). After all, this quality is not just nurtured in our game. If you have it in tennis, basketball, or hockey, you're going to have it in soccer.

There's another aspect to having a good soccer sense. That's the human quality, which I talked about in the earlier chapters. Marcia McDermott ('83–'86), all-American and U.S. National Team player ('86–'88) and the head coach of the Carolina Courage (WUSA), understands the deeper, human aspect of the game almost better than anyone else I've coached. She sees the game within a larger context, and as a result, she understands players as people. To this day, she is also one of my great intellectual colleagues, always recommending wonderful books for me to read, and keeping me on my mental edge.

The capacity to understand and communicate these human issues is a critical element in a great leader. Marcia has that. Most important, her wonderfully deep understanding of the world outside of the game means that nothing intimidates her within the game. When you have this quality, you have the proper perspective on the game, because you have a life outside of it. Then, you have the capacity to be the master of it, because it is not the master of you.

Carla Overbeck ('86–'89)

Being a Leader

I'm not sure whether I've always had the qualities I have today, but I've always been a positive person who has encouraged other people, including my teammates. I guess I got that way from my parents and siblings. My parents have always been very positive, whether about sports or school. Maybe that influence in my life just rubbed off on me. Whatever the reasons, I had leadership experience from early on. In addition to soccer, I was captain of my high school basketball and volleyball teams.

I was never ostracized for being the way I am. I didn't force myself to be this way, either. I wouldn't say that I'm outgoing in a crazy way, but I am outgoing in a reserved, careful way in the sense of how I approach people to say things to them. I try to be friendly with everyone.

I don't think you have to be outgoing to be a leader. I was kind of a shy, timid kid, and a homebody type. I had a hard time my first year away at UNC, because I wanted to stay in Texas and be with my family. I got through that. Fortunately, my parents made me stay. That was probably the best thing that ever happened to me.

Usually, most freshmen make the transition very slowly from high school to college soccer, but because all the defense had graduated my first year at UNC, I had to step into a leadership role right away as a freshman. I would have preferred to sit on the bench that first year, and learn the position as I matured, but I was thrown into it. That turned out to be good for me. As a defender, you have to be a leader and talk, and as a freshman, you're a bit afraid to tell the upperclassmen anything. But it was a role I was comfortable with in my youth, and as I got to know my teammates and learn more about them, and as I got more mature, it became a role I was comfortable with in college as well.

Particularly because I was a freshman, at first I had to try to get the respect of my teammates, whether that was through the way I played, or how I acted on and off the field. I think you have to be secure in your posi-

Over the course of her four-year career at UNC, Carla Overbeck was one of our most improved players. Her improvement came from her desire to become competitive in practice. She developed a passionate desire to see everyone on the field with her compete as hard as possible. This transitioned into part of what Carla understood about everyone who plays the game: they can all make a decision to take their intensity up another notch. This is what she tried to lead, everyone's intrinsic intensity.

tion, because it's kind of frightening to be in a role in which you have to talk to upperclassmen. The first step is to be a voice on the field. Whether it's an instructive voice or not, just be a positive voice.

Why are girls so silent on the soccer field? You want to be liked; you don't want to be perceived as someone who's bossy, and knows everything. While I always wanted to be helpful to my teammates, like anyone else, I also wanted them to have respect for me.

I think if you scream at people all the time, obviously that's not a very effective way to lead and get respect. That's why the tone in which you speak to people is extremely important. If you're constantly yelling and screaming, not many people want to hear that. Even if it's a negative, I think there's a way you can deliver your message in a positive way, just by the tone that you use.

From my past, I know that I have always tried to get to know people as people—what makes them tick, and how to motivate each individual. That's just being a good teammate, being a good leader. I don't think that means you treat everyone the same. You handle every person and every instance differently. One person might be motivated differently than another. Maybe one has a stronger personality, and you can get on her a little bit—not in a mean, attacking way, but in a firm and encouraging way. Maybe there's another type of person who you can't really say anything to in front of others, so perhaps at a throw-in, or half-time, you put your arm around her and say something to her individually. Another type of player might be motivated by having something said to her on the field—not getting in her face, but maybe being a bit harsher than you would to others. I'm a firm believer that you can get on someone, give constructive criticism, even be a bit harsh, but as soon as you see her doing something correctly, you jump all over that. You let her know, "great ball," or "way to get stuck in that tackle"— something to that effect.

If you can understand and be compassionate for every person's position and role, it makes you more aware of what's happening on the field, and aware of the different personalities on your team. It might sound kind of silly, but you should simply treat people the way you would want to be treated. For example, imagine yourself playing for a coach who yells and screams all the time. Would you benefit from that? I certainly wouldn't.

I think it's also important to be a good person off the field. Others have a lot of respect for that. If you see a teammate struggling—maybe to fit in—try to support her. Always be willing to lend a helping hand, whether it's getting someone a ride to a game or collecting the balls after practice— even something small like that.

I was the captain of the National Team, but there have been a lot of veteran leaders. Julie Foudy is an example. She's a vocal leader, and she leads by example—her work ethic is unbelievable. There are a lot of ways to be a leader. You could not say anything during a practice or a game, and work to exhaustion, and I think people would respect that. That's definitely a way of leading. You gain a lot of respect from teammates with a strong work ethic. Kristine Lilly doesn't say a whole lot, but her actions on the field make her a great leader. There's another perfect example on my current team, the Carolina Courage. Hege Riise, from Norway, doesn't say much, but on the field she works in such a manner that everyone is in awe of her. In every game, she shows up to play. She's a winner, and she leads. People want to follow what she does, because she makes such a positive imprint.

You don't even have to play to be a leader. I had knee surgery right before the 2000 Olympics, and didn't play a minute of any of those games.

I knew it was still important to be the voice of the team. But in that situation, it was from the bench. I continued my role by saying encouraging things during the game. Maybe at half-time, Jules or someone else would come to me and ask: what's working, what's not working. Because I wasn't out on the field, I tried to be involved in every other way that I could. Whether it was encouragement, or working to figure out what was wrong, I was going to be there for that team in whatever capacity I was able.

You have to accept your role, and buy into it, and know that every single person—whether it is the trainer, the coach, or the eighteenth player on the roster—is still a part of that team. If you don't buy into that, you're going to be unhappy.

I've been very fortunate throughout my entire career. My time with the National Team is an example. I was with that team for 13 years. Soccer obviously teaches you a lot about skill, but what it really teaches you is about life and being part of a team—learning to work together. What you learn is not only a sport, but something that becomes part of your life once you move away from soccer. I feel very fortunate for the people I've been able to come in contact with during my life. The friends that I have made on the National Team are friends that I will have for a lifetime. They're great players, and great people.

Becoming a Student of the Game

U.S. National Team member Brandi Chastain plays soccer with an amazing level of sophistication. She plays with a lot of subtlety and wonderful deception. She also understands the rhythm of the game. She plays at a pace appropriate to the situation; that is, she knows when to speed up or slow down. She has these abilities because she is one of the best students of the game. Brandi is famous for her passionate interest in watching high-level soccer, and it shows in her playing.

Becoming a student of the game is one sure way to work on your soccer understanding, and will also impact on your soccer sense. This means watching, reading, and learning—in the same way you would with any other subject of interest or importance to you. You can do this by finding yourself teachers—even someone knowledgeable you can talk to along the sidelines. You can learn a lot by attending coaches' clinics or taking a soccer coaches' licensing course. See if you can sit in on these or other classes. Ask your coach for help in your attempts.

To study the game, you have to have a specific aim, such as looking for what makes players sophisticated, or special. You must look with a critical eye, searching for how what you see can impact your own development.

When you watch soccer, you've got two kinds of role models. One is obviously your own gender. But you will always have an even higher level to which to aspire, and that is the men's game. You have to become a student of the game in two "universities." One is that of the elite female player. The other, even higher-level university, is the men's game. We shouldn't be embarrassed to use the men's game as our role model. At times, it is still the game played at its best. Look at it, learn from it, get better from it.

When you have integrated what you see, it can become a part of your game. An example is Cindy Parlow's one v. one skill. It is an imitation of the men's. Most girls and women play one v. one with no attention to what their opponent is doing. They have a preconceived agenda on how they are going to beat a player. They make their moves regardless of what's happening defensively. Cindy beats her opponent with an understanding of what that person is doing (e.g., leaning the wrong way). Taking into account the defender's actions and countering them is the sign of a more sophisticated game.

You consistently hear the same refrain: watch the best soccer. But why? The only way you're going to play high-level soccer is by seeing it first, because you're not going to be able to do it until you understand it. A good coach can talk to you about it, but you need to see it demonstrated in order to imitate it when you play. This exposure is noticeably lacking in the youth game in this country, for both boys and girls. However, with conscious effort, you can incorporate a unique understanding into your game.

Of course, it is fine simply to enjoy watching soccer with no specific aim. But in order to learn from what you see, you have to know exactly what you are looking for. After all, when you watch to learn, you're not just watching—you're seeking to analyze and interpret what you see.

There are all kinds of ways to watch soccer. One is to look at the artistry, that is, the flair and creativity. I think every true fan watches in this fashion. That's how most of us are drawn into the game, which is a great way to view it. Another way is to watch for the power and athleticism; these physical dynamics are also a fairly obvious aspect of what we see.

When you watch the game, see what parts you like. Also, notice the players who are exciting to you. Take it a step further. Find your favorite players and make or buy videotapes of them playing, and learn their moves. (Every great player has signature moves.) Practice them in your backyard or your basement.

A more sophisticated way to watch the game is for its rhythm. Notice how the players calm the game down if it's too frantic, or explode if a defender or defense is lulled or ball-watching. Then, you can fully appreciate that at its best, soccer is basically a game of surges and tranquilities, a rhythm of slow motion and acceleration. It consists of quick, explosive moves combined with slower action in which someone gets the ball, cleans it up, slows it down, recomposes, and then does something dynamic again. It is this change of pace that makes a player or a team unpredictable and hard to defend.

Why is understanding this rhythm important? The less sophisticated a player and a team, the more the game is played with only one rhythm, regardless of the environment. When you think of lower-level soccer, you think about a game of kickball. Kickball is a description of a game in which every time a player gets the ball, she whacks it. That's a game entirely without rhythm, and played predictably, so it is void of the aspect of deception, so much a part of defeating an opponent in high-level play.

A sophisticated player like Brandi Chastain, one who has studied the game, understands its rhythms and how to create them. This kind of soccer is harder to find, as most games you will watch are not played in rhythms. That's why you've got to seek out men's soccer, but not just ordinary men's games, those of the highest caliber.

Another way to look at the game is in terms of shape. Shape is the positioning of the players, or, the attacking and defensive construct. Every team's shape can be different, and yet still be effective. Differing shapes is one of the elements of soccer's variety. Again, at lower levels you can see bad shape (e.g., players bunched into the center of the field). You want to study a game with good shape (e.g., players pushed up and spread wide while on attack), then emulate what you see.

Whether you watch soccer for enjoyment or study, the best way to see is live. Television is useful, but on TV you see only what the camera chooses — the area around the ball. If you want to learn maximally, you have to view the entire field. This means watching the best possible games live. If you're a young boy, try to see the men's U.S. National Team and MLS games; if you're a young girl, watch the women's U.S. National Team and the WUSA. If none of these options are available, find the highest level in your community, such as collegiate, or a very good high school or youth select team.

Think of yourself as a work in progress. Studying various aspects of the game will mold you. Make sure that your palette is filled with elite players in both the men's and women's game, and from that palette you can create your player personality.

Learn by Coaching

Coaching is a great way to learn. When you teach the game, you have to understand it more thoroughly than you do just playing it. Not only will these ideas contribute toward your knowledge of the game, they can also develop your leadership and contribute to team chemistry.

- Lead practice. Volunteer to take all, or part, of a session.
- Coach younger players (including your siblings), and/or a team.
- Assist your coach. You can do this by helping to set up a practice or individual drill, or even writing a lesson plan.
- Clear up any confusion. If a teammate is having trouble understanding something, take the initiative to explain it to her.
- Organize the players. Help them to play effectively in whatever the coach has assigned.
- Demonstrate. You'll perfect your own skills by playing and explaining.
- Coach your partner. When we do pairs heading at UNC, in which players alternate tossing and heading, we ask the tosser to coach the header.
- Rehearse your strategy. Every time we scrimmage (e.g., five v. five), we ask the players to get together to figure out a way to win.
- Make learning a team effort. Speak to your coach about instituting these steps with the entire group.

CHAPTER 7

Technical and Tactical Development

If you had to do one exercise every day...my recommendation is to get a ball and play some kid in the neighborhood one on one. That's going to develop you...if another kid shows up, show a little spunk, play 'em both.

—Anson Dorrance, speaking on the videotape *Dynasty*

Aspiring to Greatness

How do you develop to your ultimate as a soccer player?

A lot of players focus on correcting weaknesses, but as any good coach can tell you, to develop into a great player you have to highlight your strengths.

When forming great teams, a coach tries to expose the collection of remarkable traits of the players, and hide their weaknesses. That doesn't mean that you stop working on your weakness, but you want to focus on getting even better at what you're already good at. Seek to become truly excellent in at least one or two areas of the game. After all, what sets you apart is what makes you great to begin with.

If you are going to rise to the highest possible level, you need at least one quality that permits you to dominate in some aspect of the game. If you want to be truly extraordinary then you need to add more and more qualities. Aspiring to greatness is always an evolution. To achieve it, you have to put time and effort into all areas of your development. You progress on a continuum of ability. Hopefully, in addition to greater skill and a strong fitness base, you can gain more flair, more experience, and more understanding of the game. Also, you can become psychologically harder, and ideally, a great leader as well.

Technical Development

The first stage of your soccer development is to build a solid technical foundation. This means you should get as good as you can at the basic skills: receiving, passing, shooting, dribbling, and heading. Most of these skills are developed simultaneously from a young age, perhaps with the exception of heading, since I believe at first it is physically uncomfortable. (For an explanation, see Chapter 14.)

I've already addressed the importance of working on your skills independently, and you can especially benefit by focusing on traditional weak areas of the women's game (see Chapter 14). Obviously this independent work is usually done in the context of free play, with all of its benefits.

Achieving technical mastery means doing the basic skills in an order of progression. Your evolution entails doing what you first learned, but under increasingly difficult circumstances. First, you have to be able to do the skills at all, so you practice them without pressure. Next, you perform skills with ascending levels of pressure, enabling you to do them with less time and space, and while someone is trying to get the ball from you. Ultimately, you have to develop the ability, and the courage, to perform these skills while an opponent is trying to "cut you in half."

One of the best soccer developmental models is the Brazilian system. Everyone unquestionably agrees that Brazil consistently produces the greatest players in the world, and in the greatest numbers. But the Brazilian development scheme is not a conscious one from an administrative or coaching perspective. It comes naturally from a culture of free play. Even a country like France, which ascended to win the 1998 World Cup in a very stylish (i.e., skillful) way over the Brazilians, achieved its success primarily through one creative player, Zinedine Zidane, who learned to play like the Brazilians do.

The Brazilian model means that after finishing the school day, children head to the Brazilian or French equivalent of a playground. Maybe it's the streets, or a tiny back lot, or an empty field. On their own initiative and without organization, they meet up with friends and just play soccer, imitating the heroes they have grown up watching. This is a youth environment all of us involved in soccer would love to see duplicated in this country.

I think we, as coaches and administrators, have to constantly advocate for the Brazilian-style system of development. Although the American youth soccer movement is tremendous, one of its biggest drawbacks is that it is very structured and organized. As a result, a young person doesn't really get a sense of the freedom to develop her own player personality. I don't think this is good. Instead, I wish there was unstructured, pickup soccer being played in neighborhoods all over the country.

This is a unique opportunity for you to take some initiative and personal responsibility for your own development and, most important, discover the sheer fun of playing pickup soccer. Maybe you can begin to duplicate the Brazilian model by going out into the backyard with your parents or siblings, or whatever neighborhood kids you can find, and just getting touches on the ball. Start a phone chain of friends; convince your school to open the gym in inclement weather; join a racquetball court facility—anything that helps in your efforts to play in an unstructured environment.

Laurie Schwoy ('96–'98)

Playing on Your Own

I work at so many camps where parents come up to me and ask: Who's the best trainer? What's the best camp? It's not about that. It's about spending time with the ball and making this sport your own.

By the time I was 14, soccer was an obsession. I took the ball everywhere. My mom would get mad because I'd grab the living room clock off the wall to make sure I'd stay out two hours exactly, morning and evening. That's how I came up with my soccer creativity: trying to fill the time.

I used to wake up before school at 6 a.m. and go into my backyard to play. My neighbors thought I was crazy. If I didn't play enough that day, and I'd be really tired, maybe I'd go to sleep but wake up at midnight and play at the car wash across the street. People really thought I was eccentric!

I'd do everything with a soccer ball. I always had it in my backpack, no matter where I went. My boyfriend would call, and hearing I was out of breath, he'd ask, "Are you playing in the SISL (Schwoy Indoor Soccer League)?" That was what I called it when it rained and I would play in the basement, a carpeted area that was probably no bigger than five feet by four feet. My backyard was small, too. But you develop consummate ball skills in tight spaces.

I played on the tennis courts. It's the smoothest area. The ball rolls true. It's just you and the ball. I wore out dozens of shoes—dribbling, cutting, stopping the ball. I would play with earphones, holding a Walkman in my hand and dancing with the ball.

Here is Laurie Schwoy obviously in the process of doing something wonderfully creative. She was always fun for everyone to watch because her first touch was exquisite and her skill so extraordinary.

My ball work is a dance; it's choreographed in my head; everything is rhythmic—my touches, my body, my feints, my fakes, my movement. I've done these little moves so many times that it's just a matter of recognizing a situation in a game when to use them. If you were to watch our team play, you could figure out who spent more time with the ball growing up, just because when they get the ball they seem more composed. It's like they've been there before.

When I was a kid, I loved the feeling of beating other kids with the soccer ball—not letting them get it. That's what this individual work gives you—control of the ball.

You've got to love the ball. The ball is the most important thing to me in soccer, and it makes you the best player. The ideal way to become great—a pure soccer player—is to play by yourself, and to discover your own take on the game. It all comes back to time. I can't stress enough that if you spend time with a soccer ball, there's nothing anyone can teach you that you can't teach yourself.

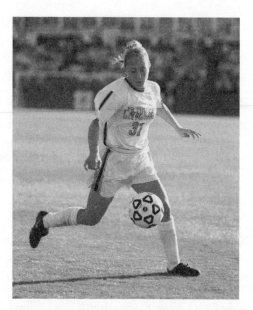

This great photo of Jena Kluegel reminds me of what she did for 90 minutes. Like no other player in the women's game I've ever seen, she is redefining the way women play the flank. I think when people look back on the development of the women's game, and the evolution of elite flank players, Jena will be a part of that history.

Tactical Development

You gain technical proficiency before you gain tactical understanding. Of course, technical skill aids the tactical component of the game. Then, the two of them have to be combined.

The best players have a tremendous tactical knowledge combined with a technical feel for the game. Laurie Schwoy is one of them. She has a tactical understanding of the game, but she feels and plays the game from an artistic perspective as well. You might say she has an understanding of the ball. There are a lot of people who understand the game tactically. Someone in an armchair can do that. But an understanding of the ball is different. You want to aspire to become a player like Laurie, who has both tactical and technical ability.

Before considering tactical development, you should take into account your age. Younger players (under 14) should, above all, focus on mastering the technical aspects of the game. Although advanced tactics may certainly be of interest to younger players in terms of preparation for higher-level play, for the time being they need not place any special focus on the tactical areas described in this chapter. Of course, there is an element of learning proper fundamental tactics at younger ages. Soccer has an infinite variety of situations which automatically teach you some form of tactics. A good coach can guide you by introducing various important basic tactical concepts (e.g., team shape and movement off the ball).

In order to fully appreciate advanced tactical development and how we view it at UNC, I elaborate below on my philosophy of systems of play. This will give you the foundation of understanding that our players must have when we discuss game tactics.

Systems of Play

Obviously, at UNC we're training highly-advanced players. But the concepts described here are not unique to our environment. They are also common in youth development. As you will see, I believe our areas of focus are equally beneficial to your optimum education as a youth player, even though our system is not currently in wide use on the youth level. (Only a handful use it, most all of whom have come to our team summer camp and picked it up there.)

Older players should have a grasp of certain tactical aspects of the game. One of them is shape—that is, where you are on the field in relation to other players. Shape is a result of the system you play. I regularly conduct coaching seminars in which I stress our basic philosophy at UNC—that systems of play can develop players. That is, merely the way you are asked to play can affect how good you become. The most ideal playing systems force you to play at higher and more demanding levels, and thus make you better.

The system we are sold on at UNC is the semiflat back 1-3-4-3. In other words, we play with three backs, four midfielders, and three forwards. I used to skip the number "1" and call what we do a 3-4-3, but recently on a trip to Holland, a very astute Dutch coach asked, "Given the critical role of your goalkeeper in your attacking and defensive shape, shouldn't you call this system the 1-3-4-3?" Of course, he was right.

Basically, the "semiflat back" is a zonal system (see explanation below) adapted from a flat-back three. In the flat-back three, the defenders step up and drop back as a unit. The semiflat back means they angle themselves slightly, based on which side of the field the ball is coming down. In essence, the line slightly tilts. The three backs, of course, are required to defend, but also to begin the attack, which calls upon their playmaking as well.

The system of play (or shape) determines what responsibility a player has. That's why I encourage coaches and players to try to be part of an aggressive attacking system like ours that also insists on every player defending for the system to survive. Because the technical and tactical demands of playing attacking soccer are greater, the player development is greater. In our system, the defenders start the attack and our attackers are our first line of defense. The goalkeeper plays higher (i.e., further forward) than in other systems, and thus becomes more like a "keeper-sweeper," which aids her development, since her area of responsibility grows, and she must also play more with her feet.

It is instructive to look at how our system has evolved. Our original philosophy was simply that we were to attack at all costs. With this as the base of our plan, we started with the conviction that we would always play a three-front. The benefit of doing this on the youth level pays off as much as it has at UNC. That's because the skill and tactical demands on the front runners are the most challenging, and so the more of those forwards there are, the greater the number of players who are getting well-developed.

Another reason we play with a three-front is because I feel that women's soccer has not evolved technically to the extent that women can consistently score with just two front runners (i.e., in a 4-4-2). If you watch the best men's teams, (e.g., the Premiership in England, or Serie A in Italy) the players are so technically and tactically skilled that in their system (4-4-2), two front runners can be productive, even against four defenders. But in the women's game, the 4-4-2 is not as effective.

I believe that this theory is ultimately proved by the fact that in my college coaching experience, the teams that give me the most trouble, and against which I've had the worst record, are those with a three-front. My record against two-front teams (4-4-2) is nearly perfect.

Another issue warrants a three-front for youth development. This may be a generalization, but I have found that for the most part it holds true. The further back a youth player plays in a team's formation, the greater the risk she will suffer limited development (and it's worst of all in a 4-4-2).

In the youth game, the best developed players are the forwards, then the midfielders, and lastly, the defenders. What often happens from one level to the next is that those in the back suffer from lack of progress, because the skill demands and expectations are often so low. As players move on in age or level, a number of midfielders or attackers are positioned back a line (i.e., the forwards become the midfielders, the midfielders become defenders), with the most common collegiate recruiting scenario to convert a gritty forward at a youth level into a skillful defender at a collegiate level. The defenders may end up getting cut, or quit.

Most teams play a 4-4-2, but consider the potential developmental drawbacks of the 4-4-2. Four defenders will not be challenged for a myriad of reasons. One is because they are given the unbelievably stilted task of shutting down only two forwards. In a 4-4-2, with a goalkeeper and four defenders, essentially five players go against two. What kind of defender is sufficiently challenged when she outnumbers the opposition so overwhelmingly? With this miracle of superiority, of course she's able to defend. I think a team could manage this if all four defenders were blind and the goalkeeper had no hands!

In that system, you don't truly need high-level skill to get out of a mess. Every time you turn around, someone's likely to be open, so it's easy to pass the ball around, particularly when you have so many players in the back against so few. Your defending or attacking ability isn't really challenged, because you aren't forced to learn how to play with pressure.

But if teams play three front and three back, I believe they get somewhere. Everyone benefits. In addition to more players playing forward, the backs are forced to learn to defend both individually and collectively, and also how to play with pressure. In this system, a goalkeeper has to be able to play effectively with her feet, so she becomes a more complete player as well, and more a part of the game.

No matter where you play, you want to be "complete." For this reason it's important to be part of a system in which players are not "hidden," in which every player is responsible for both high-level attacking and defending. This is why if you want maximal development, try to play at least some of the time as a forward, ideally in a three-front system.

I want to explain why I attach such great importance for you to focus on defensive skills. One of the biggest problems we face at UNC is that when we recruit a national-caliber front-runner, she invariably has wonderful attacking skills, but no defensive commitment. For our system to succeed, everyone has to defend, because if the front-runners and midfielders don't defend, the three players in the back can get picked apart.

To be a great attacking personality, you have to have talent. But to be a great defender, basically all you need is the intention, or desire. Anyone can become a great defensive presence. My advice to all youth players is: don't be one-sided. Don't be a player who only starts to rev up and try hard when her team has the ball. Be the kind of player who is relentless on defense as well as incredibly mobile and active on the attack. This will prepare you not only to be more effective on your current level, but also to play on even higher levels.

Another quality we try to instill within our system is communication and leadership. We are often playing against flat backs, who, in moving forward as a unit, create a greater risk of being offside. Particularly since at least one of our forwards is going to be in the best position to watch the ball, we instruct the front-runners to yell to each other if one of them is making an offside run, or not making the correct run (e.g., into traffic).

Leadership and communication opportunities exist on the rest of the field as well, as other players in the midfield and defense (and, of course, the goalkeeper) are organizing the shape of their lines.

You need to be more organized in a 1-3-4-3 because you have more people forward, and therefore, you don't have that extra cushion on defense. You have to make the most of the defense you have.

Now that I have made my case, you can appreciate why those of us at UNC have been advocating this system for years. However, support for a 4-4-2 is still overwhelming. The 4-4-2 is what people know, and have copied from what the men play. I feel that the failure to try a different system is usually because of comfort within that system, or because coaches feel they need a greater number of defenders, or perhaps they don't know how to coach another system. There also may be a reluctance to try something that entails such a risk.

I direct these comments to coaches as well as players. Initially at the youth level you might not be as successful in the win/loss column when you try a new system, but when you talk about development for youth players, that does not mean just maintaining the "security" of winning games. It means seeing the larger picture, and your future in the game.

Please don't feel, however, that your game can't develop in other systems. If development is your goal, just make sure you try to select the position that requires the most technical or tactical challenge within that system. Usually these positions are further forward. Obviously I am generalizing. There have been some brilliant players playing in the back of a 4–4–2. Still, I think they are the exceptions.

Zonal Defending

If you buy into our system at UNC, you are committed to play zonally. This is a common system at most levels of play, including ODP and the women's U.S. National Team. You will find it extensively on the college level.

In contrast to zonal is the marking system. Marking means that man for man, each player is responsible for an opponent, no matter where that player goes. On the other hand, in the zonal system, a player is responsible for an area, or zone, of the field (remember, every player on the field has defensive responsibilities). The zonal system allows a team to control its own shape better because in a man-to-man, you are chasing the other team's shape, yet zone requires greater responsibility and decision-making on the part of the players, because frankly, the zone is more challenging to play.

At UNC we began with a combination of man-to-man marking—in which we had two marking backs and a sweeper (against a team playing with a two-front)—combined with zonal defending, which dictated our shape in the midfield and front.

Then finally, in 1996, I made a change. I didn't think we could win the NCAA Championship using our combination system, so on a lark, in the middle of a game in a Houston, Texas tournament, we switched from the combination man-to-man and zone to a straight zonal system, i.e., the flat-back three. It was eye-opening for me. The flat-back three made it nearly impossible for our opponent to penetrate our defense because they didn't have the technical or tactical sophistication. The rest is history. We've gone with this system ever since.

Let me again elaborate on why we chose our system. One of the reasons we play with a three-front is that the other teams are pressed to handle the pressure of three forwards, if those forwards are all working hard. This very lack of success that most teams have against a hardworking collection of three front-runners is why a well-organized flat three zone works. Even though our youth players are getting better each year, they still struggle technically and tactically with pressure.

The trouble with strictly disciplined man-to-man marking is that every serve into your defense, even poor ones, becomes a battle because of your close physical proximity to your opponent. The stunning realization we made after we switched to that zonal defense after years of man-to-man was that the same reason our high pressuring three-front was working—lack of our opponent's technical ability in our zone with maximum pressure—was why our flat-three zone was working. Our opponents struggled to beat our zone because the high pressure defensive effort all over the field caused so many passes to go right to our flat-three defenders and high goalkeeper, who were not necessarily near where the opponent was trying to serve.

Frankly, our technical challenges and tactical inexperience is why beating Norway's flat-back four zone was always so difficult when I was the U.S. National coach. Tony DiCicco, Lauren Gregg, and April Heinrichs, our 1996 Olympic coaches, astutely took our women's National Team to a zone as one of their tactical platforms post-1995 World Cup, and started a National Team winning streak that swept a gold medal in 1996 and a World Cup Championship in '99 as part of our glorious history.

There are other reasons the zonal system is effective. These have to do with traditional weaknesses in the women's game. The high pressure that can be utilized in the zonal system is a great way to play because women have not evolved technically to a level at which they can consistently diffuse pressure. Also, because the women's game is not very developed in long ball service, defensively flooding a zone with players is effective, since you don't have to worry about an attacker switching the field with a long strike, thus leaving your weak side unprotected.

Now that you have an understanding of some of the reasons for our system of play, also understand that a player must have a strong foundation of skills to do well in it, as it quickly exposes players who aren't highly-skilled, or tactically knowledgeable.

Dear Coach Dorrance,

I simply wanted to share with you how our season went this year. We kicked off the season by attending your team camp, which was an exceptional experience for the team, including myself.

Much to the dismay of many of my conservative peers, we played the year with the UNC 3-4-3 system. My girls love this system and any time I even consider switching to anything else, they remark that they "do not want to play down to anyone's level." I have not switched my beliefs. It's 3-4-3 all the way. My observation on this system is that you need to have a deep and talented team for it to work well. This year we had the best team the club has produced, due to the level of talent and the system we train and play with, namely the UNC system. We have scored "buckets of goals."

We won our first tournament, played well at the Region II National League, and won the IWSL U19 A Division (as U16's we played up this year). At WAGS we advanced to the semifinals where we lost 1-0 to the eventual winner. That was a close match. We pounded on them but could not get a goal. As a result of advancing to the semifinals in WAGS, the NSA Lazers earned a National Ranking in the 18th spot. We were unranked going into this season.

Playing in the 3-4-3 system is analogous to walking a tightrope without a net. It simply adds to the excitement of the show. The margin of error is very narrow and it makes your team completely focus during a match.

Respectfully submitted,

Ed Leon
NSA Lazers

Ed Leon has coached the U16 Lazers of the Naperville (Illinois) Soccer Association since they were U9. Above is a portion of an e-mail he sent in November 2001.

CHAPTER 8

Levels of Play

One of the great things about soccer is its versatility. There are so many levels on which to play, and each is worthwhile for various reasons.

No matter what your level of play, you need a reason for what you are doing. It always comes down to deciding what soccer means to you. The critical thing is to make sure that no matter what level you play, you figure out a way to make it fun. You need to get something from your soccer experience, and as long as you can keep returning to the core reason of why you are doing it, then everything is bearable, because there are days when it's hard or painful, and you feel burned out. There are times it isn't fun. But if you can remember how fun it is when you do reach your goal—when you get fit, or healthy, or master a skill, or find the right team—that's what's important.

Recreational

Soccer should be fun. That's a priority in every environment, and best defined by recreational (rec) play. Although you may have left this level long ago, it is worth revisiting. You may find you want a break from serious soccer, whether temporarily or permanently. Or, you may want a relaxed atmosphere that gives you some of the benefits discussed regarding casual play—where you can comfortably practice your skills or take advantage of being a dominant personality. In that case, there's recreational play. Its priority—simply to enjoy yourself—is very appealing to many players, including my own college-age daughter, who currently participates in a coed league as a student at UNC.

Although a score is kept on the rec level, winning or losing is just a context in which the game is framed. In other words, rec soccer is not about competing, it's about playing. The aim should be to leave the field feeling better than when you got there, so everything about the rec environment should be structured to make you feel that way.

Club

When you reach the club level, the game changes. While play is more serious, the creation of a social community is still important. It is critical that on this level, you gain not only playing experience, but that you grow close to a good collection of people—that there is a creation of community. Of course, at this level, there is always a range of playing ability, from remarkable to completely average, which is fine. All players have value within this context, because like in the rec environment, you are there to enjoy the game, each other's company, being outdoors and being physically active. In short, you are there to enjoy life.

Select

The purpose of play changes yet again in the select environment, which is comprised of elite club teams. Certainly, a goal at this level is to be successful competitively. Select should create both an elite player pool and soccer leaders. And while this level is the foundation for developing elite players, this should not be done at the sacrifice of the social connections I mentioned above. The creation of community should still be a priority. Even in select, the mission should be to join a group of friends who love playing soccer together at a high level. Ideally, the select, or elite, club prepares players to compete on ODP, and also prepares them to lead their high school teams, and thus eventually successfully transition to college.

Olympic Development Program (ODP)

The Olympic Development Program (ODP) is the U.S. Youth Soccer national program for identifying and developing high-level players. Beginning anywhere between U12 and U14 (depending on the state), teams of players are selected to represent the state, the region (the country is divided into four regions), and beginning at age 16, youth National Teams. Players are continually evaluated, and being selected once does not guarantee continued participation. ODP is in addition to, not instead of, a club team. Almost all of our players at UNC participated at some level in ODP and/or high-level club teams.

ODP is a collection of competitors (who may, or may not, be friends) who play soccer at a high level. You cross a serious line when you enter

ODP. If you decide to cross this line, you need the mentality to be prepared for it. In trying out, that mentality means that you anticipate making it. You also accept responsibility for the goal of winning.

When I was the women's U.S. National coach, one of the things I consistently did in youth clinics or ODP coaching clinics was to make sure all the players and coaches understood that my job was based on the capacity to do one thing—win. If I couldn't win, I'd be fired. It was that simple. This arena is about winning. In the ODP and National Team structure, this responsibility has to be shared by everyone. If you're not prepared to go into a new situation, and to play to win—in every practice and in every game—you should not get involved in ODP. In ODP (in fact, on any serious team) an important part of your participation is the belief that you are the margin of victory, and the actions you take should make that possible.

Of course, ODP is also about individual player development, but it is development by competing and winning. Obviously, the trouble with this principle is that when two ODP teams play, one will win and one will lose. That doesn't mean the losers are out of the system, but they do have to step up and assume responsibility for this result, and find a way to work through it. That's because in ODP, in one way or another, you are always being evaluated for your ability to compete and to win.

How does this win/loss evaluation work? Teams are judged differently. The way teams from less powerful soccer areas are evaluated is not by whether they can defeat teams from "soccer hotbeds," because that doesn't happen. Instead, they compete against other similar teams, or younger ODP teams.

ODP is an opportunity for you to be showcased individually, but obviously your team success is going to dictate to some extent your level of exposure, because the majority of players who move on in the system are picked from successful teams/states. That doesn't mean successful players from a weak state can't make it. They have, and will continue to do so.

There are myths for selection to ODP, usually among those players not picked. On an 18-player roster, there's usually an eight-player swing between the bottom four who are picked and the bottom four who are not. To some extent, who makes it among them may be luck. People try to make it a science, but for these players it often comes down to who among them happens to play well the day the final decision is made.

None of this undermines the credibility of the ODP system, because it is basically designed not to focus on the bottom players on the State or Regional teams, but to make sure that the top three or four players are picked. Of course, this does not negate the value of ODP for every player who tries out, whether she makes it or not. Each player has the potential to learn something, and to be inspired to work even harder on her game. In addition, ODP is a chance for you to broaden your horizons and gain valuable experience. You play with a collection of different teammates and coaches, under varying conditions, and often away from home. Encountering all of these circumstances prepares you for a variety of environments, and challenges, down the road.

Although it may happen, it is very rare for your climb in ODP to be a continual ascension. You do not necessarily go from one of these playing levels to the next, beginning at a young age and culminating in college or National Team play. Just because you reach one level, you are not guaranteed of making it to the next. Not everyone is a star at a young age. And, in many unfortunate cases, those who are early flames may eventually "burn out."

Trying Out for a Team

Trying out for a team is like any audition—you have to be able to make the most of your abilities, to showcase yourself. There are some practical tips that can help you to do that, as well as a mind-set that will contribute to the value of your tryout experience. It is also insightful to understand the process from a selector's point of view.

The crucial aspect in a tryout is to demonstrate that you will make a difference on the team, and that you are the margin of victory. You do this by highlighting your strengths, and figuring out ways to disguise your weaknesses. For example, if you're an extraordinary header, be absolutely dominant in that area. Get near any air ball to head it. Make sure you're involved in every corner kick and every set piece in which the ball might be served to your head. On the other hand, if your weakness is your touch, for example, don't handle the ball more than you have to. Play it off quickly, before pressure comes. In other words, in any situation, figure out a way to play within your game.

You should go into any tryout very fit, because you never know when you have the opportunity to be selected. Usually there's a single moment when the evaluator has decided to choose you. You do something spectacular, or memorable. But in order to do that, over the course of the tryout you have to get involved in as many situations as possible to showcase yourself. You need the stamina to do that.

Finally, you have to demonstrate to the evaluator that you are psychologically tough and have a powerful mentality. You have to show you have the capacity to take physical risks. If your collisions and injuries are bearable, and are weathered as a matter of course, with no drama or pathetic pained facial expressions, it opens a window to an important part of the competitive personality. This shows your capacity to play contact sports.

If you can demonstrate you are a leader by verbally organizing the team offensively or defensively, that's huge in the selector's eyes. But obviously, don't try too hard, because the false performance of leadership is also easy to see. Be assertive. Show you want the responsibility for the game by demanding the ball, by volunteering immediately to take the penalty kicks, by insisting on taking the free kicks, or by screaming out to the player taking the corner, "Serve my head!" In any way possible, you want to show confidence. In many cases, showing confidence is the first step in actually becoming confident.

If, however, you are timid, or concerned about alienating the other players by being verbal or assertive, you do yourself a disservice. When I'm a selector, I love the player who shows leadership, and who steps right up to take the PKs. I am most impressed by the player who wants to take over, who wants responsibility for victory, and who will lay herself on the line and take the risk of missing that PK.

Sometimes players are instructed, or feel, they must do something different to stand out in a tryout in order to be selected. But just because you jump from your club team to, say, ODP, your game shouldn't change. A quality coach is going to pick out a quality player. Whoever tells you to do something different to showcase yourself obviously has no respect for the selector. Anyone with a clue doesn't need to see a player change her game from what she usually does, assuming she can play. Trust me, if you have good speed of play, decision-making, positional abilities, and skill, you are going to be highlighted. If you can dominate duels in the air, and serve balls over distance, you will be noticed. Players who can carve up defenses on their own will build a case for themselves. Players who can get the ball and go down the field on one of those Mia Hamm/Tiffeny Milbrett/Cindy Parlow runs, that's great. But the player who feels she has to try to do that to showcase herself, and then gets stripped of the ball in the process, is not really going to build her case. You still have to play within your game, and your abilities.

Not Making It—The True Challenge

One of the biggest gripes some people have when they don't make a team is that it has to do with some political process. They blame lack of success on favoritism or prejudice. So, rather than discussing or evaluating failures through lack of ability or performance, the issue is politics. The problem with that specious argument is that it is made by those players on the bottom of a roster. So if you don't want to leave it to chance, don't let it be close. Make a clear statement in the trial about who you are and what you can do.

If you're a good player, you're going to make it. If you're marginal, it may be left up to politics. If you want to be assured of making a team, be one of the top three or four players. Try not to be the 12th through 30th best for an 18-player roster, because in the selector's eyes, players below the top 11 hold diminished significance. You may feel you will improve, benefit from the training, and contribute to the team, but that is not likely what the selectors are concerned with. The selectors are most interested in the truly elite. That is their main responsibility.

The politics of a tryout is well within your control by taking charge of your performance. If you play exceptionally well, if you demonstrate you can help the team win, you will be picked. If politics is a factor in the decision about you, you're avoiding the fact that you need to improve. And as soon as you blame the politics, you're not going to improve. If you're not picked, don't blame the politics, blame yourself, so to speak. As soon as you accept responsibility, the world is your oyster, because now you are not at someone else's mercy, you are in control of your own destiny.

No one is immune to the risks or failures of the tryout process. Even those who have succeeded at the highest levels should never suffer from hubris—a sense of inflated pride and subsequent complacency. A young player might cruise through making higher and higher level teams, but as the competition gets tighter, one day she may be in for a big shock. Even on our level, we deal with recruited players who assume that after making it through youth National Teams, they will just keep ascending, all the way to the full National Team. What they don't understand is that the current members of the National Team hold down spots for years. Mia Hamm or Kristine Lilly aren't going anywhere. Michelle Akers played from 1985–99, so, if you do the math, an aspiring young player has to be the best player in the country for 15 generations of National Teams, and beat out 15 years of challenges, to have a career like Michelle Akers. And this competition—if you use Mia Hamm as an example—begins when you are 15 years old, because that is when Mia was first selected to represent the full National Team. We don't know yet at what age this will end, until the retirement of the rest of the "91ers" (i.e., Chastain, Fawcett, Foudy, Lilly, Hamm, etc.—those who played in the 1991 World Championship).

If you make a team, that's great. But if you don't, you get to demonstrate how determined, strong, and noble you are. Rather than blame politics, or become devastated when your continual success hits a hurdle, take personal responsibility and use a setback to recover and refocus. You weren't selected, so you can begin to figure out ways to improve. You can resolve to come back the next time, and be better. Ask yourself what your weak areas are, and because of this bump in the road, you will give yourself the chance to improve them.

Whether you're chosen or not, you're going to win, because there are wonderful victories in both cases. In fact, I think the higher-level individual can triumph greater in not being selected, because the strength to take responsibility and recommit, or the strength to accept that your best was eclipsed by someone else's best, is a more powerful statement of character than just making the team. Through this adversity, you can grow more as a person, and a part of that growth can be a decision on who you have decided to become as a player.

Playing Up

Another frequent question related to climbing the soccer ladder is whether or not you should play up (i.e., older) in age. And if you do, should it be by one year, or maybe even more. In terms of your soccer development, if you have outgrown a team, it is probably time to move on. Your decision may be made based on many factors: physical size, socialization, or leaving friends or your community—all balanced with your goals.

Whether or not you should attempt to play up may be difficult to evaluate on your own. Your decision should probably be aided by an expert with experience, and who can most objectively judge your ability and the situation. However, this could be complicated if the best person to assess your move is your own coach, who may not want to lose you from your current team. In this case, you might want to seek the advice of others, such as coaches who have seen you play, and/or others who have played up. Also, get as much experience as possible in order to make your decision. You can do this by asking to participate in training and guest play in games for your prospective team, or other teams in that age group. Speak to the coach of the prospective team; ask for his or her opinion, and specifically, about the kind of playing time you can expect if you make the team.

Make sure you move up for the right reasons. After all, you may be taking risks or sacrificing a lot by leaving your current team. It is important for your development not to be swayed in your decision for the wrong reasons, such as simply the status of being with an older and more advanced group of players. Status is not as important as maximal development, as well as being with a group of friends and sharing in an enjoyable experience.

That being said, if you are a serious player, as a general rule you should always play up if you can be a starter with the older team. In fact, you should play at the highest possible level at which you can still be a starter. I've seen an eighth-grader play for a U19 team. Was she a dominant player? No, but by the time she is 18, she is going to be. She has already survived physically, technically, and tactically, so when her athleticism and her body size catch up to that age group, she is going to "own it."

The experience of playing up is worthwhile, although it is likely to be challenging. It can make you play so much faster, and better. You might start out as a role player, but with time, you could grow into a personality and dominate the team. It's a similar experience to playing as a freshman or sophomore in high school or college, where technically you play up by being with older, more experienced players. In these systems, you fit in a little easier each time you move up a year and gain more experience.

If, however, in choosing to play up you're not going to start, I would usually advise against it. Your priority should be playing time and experience, and developing your player personality. If you can only do that on the team you're on, stay there. If you can create a compromise by supplemental training or guesting with an older team, that's fine. But don't quit one team just to sit on the bench for another. (The only exception is if the training environment is so good that you develop from playing against wonderful players in a challenging practice setting. Then the best compromise is to train as much as possible with the extraordinary team, and play on another team you can start for.)

Should Girls Play with Boys?

My guess is that those girls who played with or against boys when they were younger surged in their development—and that development was huge.

While it may seem to be similar to playing up, playing with boys (or men) is a different developmental experience. For largely physiological reasons—but sociological ones as well—boys are simply more physical and generally more skilled than girls. And unlike playing with girls, no matter what their age, you will obviously be visibly different with boys.

Before youth soccer boomed in participation, a lot more girls played on boy's teams. Often, they had no choice. As soccer expanded, however, girls got more teams of their own. While this is great progress, I still recommend you take a cue from what I said earlier about being a student of the game in "two universities," both female and male.

To maximize your development, always play with boys if possible. If you can play on a boy's team, stay with them as long as you can, until they kick you off! Of course, that may not literally happen, but you may eventually be driven away by the physical demands or perceived dangers of playing, or because you are unable to develop your player personality. And, too, there are social reasons or pressures which may eventually affect your decision to stay, particularly if a lack of self-confidence or camaraderie makes being part of a boy's team an unrewarding experience. Usually, the older the players, the more complicated these issues become.

In order to play on a boy's team, or even with boys at all, you will have to be an individual who can stand outside of the norm. You may be stared at, or talked about, and you're likely to be seen as a threat by some people. However, if you are the type who perceives these potential drawbacks as merely more of an opportunity to toughen yourself, and realize that the skills and athleticism of boy's soccer are a great opportunity to elevate your game, you will gain a very valuable experience.

That being said, you're going to have to continually prove yourself. No one owes you a spot, fair playing time, or special treatment. Don't use the fact that you're a girl to rationalize what you feel is unfair. If the boys don't pass you the ball, you'll have to go out and get it. Make it happen. Then, after you've been winning the ball, the boys will sort out that you can play. Just like you, boys want to win. Trust me, if you can play, they'll pass it to you.

Just as with playing up, if you do join a boy's team, make sure you will actually play. It's better to be a starter on a girl's team than never to play on a boy's team. If you can compromise by joining a girl's team and participating in boys' practices or being a guest player, that's certainly good. But don't sacrifice playing on a girl's team just for boys' practices.

If you do choose to play with boys, it is critical you also play with girls as well (such as ODP, guesting, or playing for two teams). One of the problems with playing with boys alone is that ultimately, a girl can't completely develop. Eventually, as the boys get older—about 13 and 14—you'll no longer be a dominant player. You'll basically be a role player (i.e., functional, as opposed to a personality player) in their environment, and believe it or not, that's still going to have some value for you, because the speed of play is quicker. To keep up, you will have to make quicker decisions, and you'll get hit a lot harder. The level of athleticism is also greater. But you won't be the person the ball is pinged into, so you can slice and dice a couple of defenders and drive it into the upper corner of the net—which is what you need to do to express your player personality. That's why you need a girl's team where you can be dominant and express yourself this way.

It's not always practical to join a boy's team. You don't necessarily have to do that to get the experience. While formally playing on a boy's team may not be a viable option, you can absolutely benefit by playing with boys on a more informal level. Find pickup games or some other group. Jump in with an older brother, like Cindy Parlow and Kristine Lilly did. Again, I go back to a line I preach throughout the book: play one v. one, and in this case, with a guy. I don't mean once in a while, or even once a month. You need to do it often, and consistently. As I've mentioned earlier, one of the aspects of playing with boys that makes it easier to do is that the issues that are stressful for girls and women are nonissues against boys. The common female fear of confrontation, or of "offending" a friend by beating her, doesn't exist in an environment with males. You're free to be a warrior, to keep score, to compete, to win. The male culture embraces that attitude.

Almost every great female player I've ever coached has had one of her greatest development stretches while she was playing with boys, and playing them one v. one. Michelle Akers and Kristine Lilly played with boys. In addition to her brother, Kristine grew up five minutes from her cousins, including five boys with whom she constantly played sports. Carin Jennings Gabarra played all the time with her husband, Jim Gabarra, and she became one of the greatest one v. one artists in the world. Mia Hamm played with a college boyfriend for a time, and it markedly helped her game. Cindy Parlow grew up the only girl with three brothers, and played one v. one constantly with her high school boyfriend. I am sure it was a major factor in helping her become the take-on artist she is today.

CHAPTER 9

High School Soccer

Soccer takes on a new meaning when you enter the arena of high school play. While exciting for some, or posing doubts for others, it is a welcome part of the vast expansion over the years in girls' high school sports. Nevertheless, for the serious player entering or already playing in high school, there are many issues to consider.

For the majority of players, which high school to attend is not a choice—you go to the school in your neighborhood or existing system. But some players actually consider, and end up, selecting a high school based on its soccer program. If you are in a position to make a choice, I do not recommend you overemphasize soccer. First of all, I feel a soccer program alone is not worth the added stress of a lengthy daily commute to school. Also, as far as I'm concerned, you go to high school for academics, not for soccer. High school is for developing your intellect—particularly if you are pursuing a college education. Also, the competition at the college level for athletic recruitment or scholarships is very steep. You will not only benefit yourself as a person, but be more attractive to college coaches if you have a good academic record, and have pursued other activities and talents.

It's best to take the attitude that if the soccer team at your local high school is good, that's a bonus. If not, you can still work around it with some of the suggestions offered in this chapter.

To Play or Not to Play

High school soccer may be high-level for some, but it presents questions for the serious player who, above all, wants to maximize her development.

Players who have been part of a serious club team, or have played ODP or other high-level soccer, sometimes express frustration with the quality or system of high school soccer. For this reason, you may be faced with a choice: to play or not to play? After all, you don't have to participate.

Before making this choice, you should understand something fundamentally important about playing in high school. It is not necessarily important to your soccer progression or success. If you're a great soccer player participating in your high school program, you're likely doing it primarily for social reasons, or out of loyalty to your school or community, because you'll actually develop more continuing to play club or other challenging soccer. This is, of course, unless you have an exceptional high school coach or team, or your club team is so inactive during this time that high school play is your only means of organized participation. If you decide to forego high school play, however, you can usually find alternatives. Many serious club teams play year-round, except in places where high school soccer takes most of the players. Then, you are left with finding creative alternatives, or simply deciding that for lack of them, it is best to make the most of high school play.

There is a huge range among high schools. Some school programs are outstanding, and players really benefit. There is often a varying range among team members as well, depending on who graduates or enters. In those programs that are not as good, you can still create your own training environment. In fact, you can set the standard by training hard. A lot of players tend to feel that if the high school team or coach aren't very good, they will be brought down. That doesn't have to be the case. You can still play on the edge of your game, drive your teammates in practice, and help create an atmosphere of competition while maintaining the fun. Use this opportunity to challenge yourself (and others) to achieve by setting goals—such as mastering certain skills—and focus on developing your team's chemistry and your leadership qualities.

If managed correctly, an atmosphere in which you dominate with your ability can benefit you as a player, if you go in with the right attitude and work hard. When I was an undergraduate at UNC, I actually learned how to dribble better by training with the U12 coed teams I was coaching. I'd jump into practice with them and take some risks with the ball while under pressure—balls that I would play off early or quickly if I were playing at a more competitive level. Even though the training environment was, of course, very weak for an adult player, I had an absolute blast, and the kids had a blast trying to take the ball away from me. In the process, I became a better dribbler, and thus, a better player.

While there can be many challenging and worthwhile aspects of high school soccer, it also requires some adjustment. Club and high school play may be quite different, but they can be equally intense (high school is daily, but only one season, whereas club is several times a week, and often all year long), but the added mix of increased academic or social pressures may make maintaining a balance much more precarious while playing high school soccer.

Some express concern over high school soccer adding too much pressure, particularly when adapting to a new experience. I think it's a myth that you can't "have it all." You just have to properly organize your time. Obviously, your first priority should be your academics, and, if you want to succeed in soccer, your second priority has to be your athletic life. What might have to suffer is your social life, but there's time for that later, when things slow down, like postseason, or when you acclimate to your routine.

Remember, too, that soccer is not the only high school sport from which to choose. Taking advantage of other sports can be positive, no matter what your level or aspirations in any of them. Although most high school soccer coaches are teachers as well, and understand the benefits of being well-rounded, beware of those coaches who overemphasize soccer to the exclusion of other sports or activities, particularly if you clearly want to try other things. For example, running track, especially sprints, is good for your speed development and different aspects of your soccer fitness development. Volleyball is good for your jump, basketball for your agility. Field hockey, lacrosse, and cross-country are all viable sports. In fact, most of my great players played other sports in high school, and I think the cross training had some very positive effects.

Whether you choose to play soccer in high school, or instead with an outside team—either way, I believe you can benefit. But unless it totally interferes with your club play or other important aspects of your personal soccer development, I am inclined to favor playing in high school. Although a lot of people think a poor high school team will harm your development, the only thing that's potentially harmful is if you go into the experience with a negative mind-set.

If your high school is the kind that supports athletics, and it is well-run and in the proper spirit, your soccer can be a valuable experience, and a good prelude to various aspects of playing in college.

High School Success

The best way to ensure a successful high school experience is to come into the season prepared. Here's how:

- Check out your high school team. Watch games, and even practices, at least in your eighth-grade year.

- Introduce yourself to the coach. In addition, in the spring of your eighth-grade year, ask the coach for the preseason training and evaluation methods. Ask for specifics on how you will be judged (e.g., fitness, small-sided games, etc.).
- Find a friend. Get to know a player(s) on the high school team, and ask for insight and advice.
- Utilize your club team. Consult your coach for advice on training and preparation for high school, and focus on those important areas in your club team training and games.
- Get fit. Go into the season in good shape, and you'll perform at your best, maximize your chances of making the team or being a starter, and avoid injury or illness (common to incoming students who suddenly increase their training).
- Start early. You can't get fit in one or two weeks of preseason training. (Consult the Summer Training Program in Appendix II.)
- Be self-motivated. Take the initiative to do the necessary training on your own, get whatever help you need, or find a partner to work out with.
- Consider an extensive preparticipation physical. In addition to the required general exam, you might want to see an orthopedist, sports trainer, or other qualified professional to assess your health and/or injury risk.
- Think ahead. Just as you prepare for soccer, see how you might prepare for your academic year. There may be a reading list or other preparatory work you can do during the summer to help you manage your time more efficiently during soccer season.

Transitioning to High School

The most important thing to understand when going from serious club soccer to high school play is that the high school level is likely to be a lower standard, and probably a lot less serious. First, you need to keep in mind that the goals, facilities, and purpose of high school play are obviously not the same as in serious club play. If your high school program is on a lesser level than you are used to, don't condescend when you play. Continue to bring your higher work ethic, your standards, and a positive mind-set to the environment. Everyone will respect you for it, especially your coach and the girls you are playing with. See it as a chance to bring recognition to yourself, your school, and your community. Also, you can look forward to gaining the status and the excellent social and leadership aspects of being on the team. Obviously, your teammates will look to you to lead them.

Serious club playing experience does not guarantee success for every player in high school. Some high schools have challenging teams (better than a player's club), and no matter what their ability, players usually have to prove themselves, at least as freshmen or sophomores. Also, even the best players need to be ready for a new schedule and new demands.

How can you prepare for the experience? High school often includes a two-week (or longer) preseason and tryout process at the end of summer, right before the school year begins. It can be very rigorous, including two-a-day sessions, and just as with the transition to college, many players are in for a shock. You can both survive and show yourself well—thus increasing your chances of making the team—by following the advice given for successfully trying out (see previous chapter). You can also follow the Sports Conditioning workout in Appendix I, and utilize the UNC Summer Training Program in Appendix II.

Your Role and Your Attitude

Success in high school often results in a lot of attention in your community. This should be a wonderful opportunity to shine. Some good players, though, may get caught up in seeing their name in the newspaper, playing under the lights, and in front of the crowds. This can have a negative effect on team chemistry that extends to both high school and club play.

You have to keep high school success in perspective. Some teams dominate because they are loaded with talent, or are in weak leagues. Conversely, if you have a weak team, or you are matched against tough competition, appreciate that you can still have a good experience. Remember that internal motivation—to become a better player and contribute to your team—versus external rewards, such as a winning record or your name in lights, is the most important criteria.

The flip side of being showcased as a star is being a reserve. There is a four-year age span in high school, and while an incoming high-level player may be welcomed onto the team, most have to put in time before they play, or at least become starters.

This is true for any team. If you are sitting the bench, be a positive force. Remember that everyone wants to play. The way you show how badly you want to be on the field is not by complaining about the coach or the other players, or otherwise displaying a negative or noninvolved attitude. Criticizing may be commonplace in some youth programs, but all it demonstrates is lack of character. It's not productive to be a negative force; it helps no one, and you demean yourself.

There's no shame in sitting the bench. In fact, I think it's an incredibly noble mission. It tests the kind of person you are. Even though you are not playing, the question is: will you support the team's mission, the coach, and your teammates? Just as the elite athletes make other players better, the most supportive team players do the same. Whether you are on the field or on the bench, figure out your role, and your challenge, and work at it with 100% effort.

Jordan Walker ('00–)

Thoughts from a Former High School Player

High school soccer is popular where I'm from, and almost all the girls who played on my club team played in high school. I played all four years at Ursuline Academy in Dallas, Texas. As of now, I think we've won 11 or 12 State Championships in a row.

I loved high school soccer. We had a phenomenal coach and a great training environment. My coach was Susan Ellis (UNC, '80–'84), currently assistant coach for the Carolina Courage of the WUSA and a director at UNC girls' soccer camp. Our program was similar to the one at UNC, using the same drills, concepts, and system. I loved the experience of seeing my teammates every day at school, having my friends coming to the games, and the excitement of representing my school. In fact, a lot of high school soccer is like college, just on a lesser level.

I feel that in a lot of ways I got more out of high school soccer than I did from my club team. One of the great aspects of high school is that you really develop a sense of community. Unlike club soccer, in high school you normally train with your team every day, just like you would in college. There are girls from four different years, so you learn how to relate to both older and younger players. You also get to grow into a role gradually, because every year there are relatively minor changes to the team. You learn how to have a sense of respect for the older players and develop a sense of leadership with the younger ones. Practicing that leadership in a high school environment is important, because it is very hard to do that on a club team with equally talented girls who are all the same age. However, in high school you have this natural order of leadership in terms of class rank.

Jordan will always be one of my favorite people because she's such an extraordinary overachiever. Here she is demonstrating back-to-pressure—one of the fundamental warm-ups in our fall rhythm.

Not everyone has the same situation I did. For a lot of people, the coaching and training in high school isn't really adequate. Sometimes it's even detrimental, because you can get used to playing at a lower level. Over time, things such as speed of play and general awareness of the game begin to dull. You're not being challenged. So when you get back to a higher level, such as club, it can take you a while to get out of bad habits. The bottom line is that if high school soccer is your only opportunity to play 11 v. 11 during that portion of the year, I think it's best to participate.

When you're deciding whether to play high school soccer, you have to consider your future. Do you want to play at a top Division I college? Or, do you even want to play college soccer? You've got to try to figure out the best path to your goal, and how—or even if—high school soccer fits into it.

Your decision to play also depends on your time. The 14 or so weekly hours of training in high school, plus all the game time, could mean time away from club or individual soccer that would develop you better. If you decide to play and the level is poor, there are ways to enjoy it, and get around the problems. For example, you have to learn to be careful, since you may be competing against a lot of kids who aren't very experienced, or refs who don't have control of the game. Sometimes I'd play with kids who'd miss a tackle and wind up nailing me because they wouldn't know what else to do. When you're in these situations, you're forced to develop a quicker speed of play, and not be timid (you've got to go in hard) to avoid getting hurt. These forced adaptations can be positive.

High school soccer sometimes means a more relaxed attitude to training and playing than you might be used to. Some players will be in it for pure fun, and that's okay. But if you're a serious player, you may have to push yourself to work hard in practice. You have to be conscious of what the high school program is not doing for you—whether it's fitness or certain ball skills—and make sure you get what you need. In general, you'll have to take care of yourself a little more. If there's a lack of knowledge or facilities, you may have to do things like your own warm-up, stretch on your own after playing, play pickup soccer outside of school to work more on your skills, or consult your club team trainers about medical care.

You can always find unexpected benefits to high school soccer. For those who play serious club soccer, you're likely to be one of the better members of your high school team. You will have the opportunity to present yourself as a personality player, someone who can carry the team on her back. I think that's especially positive for those who have worked really hard and might not get the recognition, say in ODP.

Most of us have to pay our dues. I wasn't a starter in my freshman year in high school. Through the years, there were other players who worked hard and rarely played in games, and this was something everyone noticed. The reserves were able to garner respect based on their work ethic. I always had tremendous admiration for those who maybe didn't play much, but totally busted in practice. You could see them improve over the four years.

Whether you're a captain, or sit on the bench, your role changes over the four years. High school soccer can be the first time you learn to take on roles that are important for the "real world." You may one day be managing a company or be one of many hardworking employees. High school soccer can prepare you for both.

CHAPTER 10

Stepping Up to College Soccer

Living the Dream

If playing college soccer is your goal, it is a worthy one. Of course, there are endless reasons to pursue this level of the sport. Athletically, you are going to be taken to your limit, because obviously the people you are playing with will be equally, or even more, skilled and experienced than you. It is a wonderful challenge. The blend of athletics with college academics is also a unique opportunity to excel at two extraordinary pursuits.

Assuming a college soccer program is properly lead, the best thing about the experience—one that sets it apart from all others—is it will provide you with a tremendous sense of community. This is a community filled with people with whom you will likely be connected long after your playing days are over. They will remain part of your social fabric, and together with them you will follow your college soccer program, riding the roller coaster of its success and failure.

The university doesn't dissolve after you leave. It is a standing monument to the community. You may leave the world of college—go through two or three postgraduate years of searching or doubt about career or other aspects of life. But your school can always draw you back for the stability and sense of belonging it gives you. Even in a program like UNC women's soccer, in which success on the field would seem to be the overwhelming feature, what binds the players are not the wins and losses, or the championships, but the connection to the university and to each other.

Our players are bound together by what they share: the commiseration of surviving fitness sessions, the airplane trips and meals, walking down Franklin Street on Halloween (the main street in Chapel Hill), even agonizing with some of their teammates through a catastrophic injury or personal tragedy—the trauma or joy of four years of great personal change and growth. Every team is a close collection of all of these players' experiences. It is this variety of commonly shared real-life situations that makes our community of soccer players special to each other.

There are so few opportunities presented to us in our lives to gain this sense of community that college offers. This is the rich legacy of the collegiate soccer experience. It is rich while you're living it, and it will remain rich after you graduate.

Choosing a College

If you aspire to play college soccer, you can, because somewhere there's a program appropriate for you. Whether or not it is a Division I team, there are excellent soccer teams for all levels of ability and commitment. Too often a player thinks that if she is not accepted to the school of her choice, she can't play. But there are any number of colleges that can make a "perfect fit." You just have to do your homework to find them.

Colleges range from the highly competitive top-tier of Division I play, which is for elite athletes, to Division II and III schools, whose teams may be organized around their own school populations. Obviously, the challenge is to find a school with the size and location you desire, and suited to both your academic interests and soccer level.

Choosing a college is highly individual. Each person may have different priorities. When we recruit, we try to sell the whole package, because we think we have a unique balance at UNC—academics, athletics, social life, and a climate mild enough to be tolerable during winter and not unbearably hot in the summer.

When looking for a school, begin your task by reading, researching, and speaking to others, including your club coach and current college players, if possible. If you find yourself with a wide-open slate, begin to narrow in on your top selections in your junior year of high school. Then, hone in on about five of them. These should include your "dream school," and several backups.

Once you have narrowed down your choices, the next task is to pay a visit to the schools to which you are considering applying, soccer programs that have recruited you, or otherwise personally contacted you. Prospective student-athletes may be sent recruiting materials beginning September 1 of their junior year in high school, and may be contacted in person beginning July 1 of their junior year in high school. (There are three things a college coach can send to a prospective student-athlete prior to September 1 of their junior year: Camp brochures; NCAA educational informa-

This is one of my favorite pictures of the alumni always being a part of the program. This is April Heinrichs (center) when she was the head coach of the University of Maryland, but also still captain of the U.S. National Team, communing with two of the players she was competing against as a coach, but playing with as a player. Mia Hamm is on the left; Kristine Lilly is on the right.

tion (e.g., NCAA Guide for the College-Bound Student-Athlete); and questionnaires.) The coach will often inform you of available times to meet. The rules permit any coach to speak to any prospective player of any age on campus, and even though a coach can only initiate phone calls once a week beginning July first of a prospective rising high school senior's summer, there are no restrictions on your calling the coach whenever you please.

Assuming you have found your academic match (you may want to research this further on your visit), make an appointment to meet with the soccer coach, and also with several players, if possible. Watch soccer practice during this visit. If soccer is your priority, make sure you are qualified to play on the team. The only way to do that is to actually see the team play. In the fall of your senior year, return to the campus to see a game, not only to further determine if you fit in, but to assess whether you will enjoy playing with this group of girls, and the particular style with which the team plays. Using all of these measures, you will have an overall sense of whether you like the coach, the players, and the team.

When searching for a college, you can certainly utilize the adults in your life. If your youth coach is knowledgeable, he or she can help in recommending or assessing the best colleges for you. Your parents are critical in helping to evaluate your choices, since obviously, they are going to be paying for your education. Listen to all advice carefully, but remember that the most important factor is what YOU think of a school, because you're the one who must live with the decision.

Something else you may not have considered is worth addressing. You don't have to join a team to play soccer in college. If college changes your priorities, and the sport becomes a recreational interest of yours, invest in it on that level. Most large universities have club teams as well as collegiate varsity teams. Clubs require tryouts and include some travel. Obviously, there is a huge difference between varsity and club play in terms of the organization, finances, and the talent, but it is certainly an option. Another option is intramural soccer, which exists in most colleges, and is even less formal than club in that it requires no tryouts or travel.

Maximizing Your Chances

In addition to visiting the school(s), there are other ways to maximize your chances of being accepted in the college soccer program of your choice. Write to the coach(es) early in your junior year, and telephone them often enough so that they become acquainted with you. Then, visit coaches late in that year. Meanwhile, participate in programs that give you high visibility among college coaches. Climb to the highest possible level in ODP; go to major youth soccer tournaments with your club team, and attend the summer soccer camps of the colleges in which you are most interested. Again, consult with youth coaches who may have contacts with colleges.

Most schools with good soccer teams have such camps (with the exception perhaps of some Division II or III schools). Try to attend camp at the school of your choice at least once, preferably both summers before your junior and senior year. In addition to being seen, this will give you another feel for the program, and the coaching staff. There is often a direct connection between the camp and the college program. On one of our recent NCAA championship teams, seven of the eleven starters had attended our summer camp.

One of them is Jordan Walker, who currently plays for UNC. She came to our camp for years. One year, she and her partner from Dallas won almost every camp competition, beating out 400 to 500 other players. She is not a player without weaknesses, but she showed early signs of being the unbelievably hard worker and great leader she has become on our team.

As for the future of young girls, one girl wrote me a letter when she was just 10 years old, begging to get into our camp. (Our camp begins at age 13, with a few 12-year-olds.) She is now a high school sophomore, and has been coming to camp for the past three years. We may end up recruiting her, and it all started with that letter.

Every college has the same bottom line: we're more interested in the players who are interested in us, and taking the steps I have outlined here will highlight your desire to attend the college of your choice.

Be Dynamic

When I was younger, I thought I was going to break Mia Hamm's record and join the full U.S. National Team by age 14. I was a bit of a dreamer. But, I have to say, I was the best player around during elementary school. Unfortunately, I did not develop my talent until everyone had caught up to me.

I want you to know how much the camp helped me. I was in a bit of, well actually, more like a huge, slump. I hadn't played good soccer in quite a while. This was during my sophomore year in high school. During my freshman year of high school, I realized this and began to painfully and slowly climb my way up to the top. I joined better club teams and worked out a lot on my own. Truth be told, I didn't even want to attend your camp because I knew top-level players and coaches would be there to see how mediocre I was at that point. Luckily for me, Coach Dorrance said something to me specifically during camp that rattled within me and has stuck with me till this day, "Be dynamic." The very next play, after those words, I did it. I lost the ball, but a player on my team got it and scored. Coach Dorrance said that I had started it. This made me feel like I could get back to being the player I had once been. I credit that camp, and more specifically, that particular comment, that began the turning point in my soccer career. This year I graduated high school, played on the seventh-ranked club team in Southern California, won the Surf Cup, and got recruited by the University of California at San Diego. I still have to go through the tryout process, but my chances are quite good. So I wanted to thank you for running the camp and for producing so many great soccer players for young girls like me to have as role models. Thanks.

Sincerely,
Marisa Glatzer
Placentia, CA

A portion of a June 20, 2000, e-mail sent to Chris Ducar regarding a camp conducted in Southern California two years prior.

What Colleges Are Looking For

In addition to the obvious—playing ability and experience—at UNC we consider the player as an entire person. We look to see in what other sports she may have competed. (For example, we love sprinters. If a girl is a state 100-meter dash champion, even if she's only an average soccer player, we'll recruit her, because we think we can teach her to play soccer.) We love great leaders, and remarkable students, because whether or not they make a difference on the field, we know their character will have a positive impact on team chemistry.

At UNC at least, the priorities in a college program are not just soccer. That's why it is important not to underestimate the value of having a well-rounded high school experience, including excellence in academics and leadership. Most people are shocked when I tell them we have a no-cut policy. In Division I, this may be unique to our program. A player is not dropped for her lack of soccer ability. (Obviously, what we do is so rigorous that most people who don't feel qualified are intimidated, and don't try out for UNC in the first place.) When we create a team, we look for players who can succeed in at least two out of three general areas: number one, they are positive for chemistry; number two, they are good students; and number three, they are good soccer players. If a person fulfills any two of these criteria, we keep her.

Relative to the success of our program, we have some very average soccer players on our roster, but we want them for their positive qualities as students and people. Helen Lawler, ('96–'99), a valedictorian of her high school class, was outstanding in academics and team chemistry. I loved having her on the team. Her work ethic was off the charts. In fact, it was so good she won quality time in some very important games, including the National Championship final in December of 1997, in Greensboro, North Carolina, against the University of Connecticut. I remember her very classy and thoughtful, "Thank you for letting me play," remark when we subbed her out for a then more rested Robin Confer. I made sure to let Helen know she earned that time with her raw effort. It was not a gift.

An all-around player is a real plus. Nel Fettig ('94–'97) was a high school valedictorian, an all-American for us, currently in UNC law school, and served as my volunteer assistant coach before playing for the WUSA. She's a great example of a player with everything, serving as a wonderful example on and off the field.

People often ask exactly how we form our team, and who ends up playing for us. Recruiting players is a major aspect of college sports, and a full-time effort in our program. In fact, we have greatly benefited in the last few years by having Chris Ducar, also our goalkeeper coach, make recruiting the major part of his job description. In addition to our staff's travel to scout and recruit players, I write between 30 and 40 letters per year to high school juniors around the country, soliciting their interest, and follow up in their senior year with telephone calls and further correspondence throughout the recruitment process.

UNC permits us to recruit four out-of-state residents per year, and one in-state resident. (Admissions standards vary. Some soccer programs allow coaches to bring in from eight to 12 such players.) This means that we can recommend those out-of-state students to the university admissions committee, because it is almost impossible to be accepted to UNC from out-of-state. In addition to recommending one in-state player, another two from in-state might be able to get in on their own. From the five or six players per year that we bring in, three are on some type of scholarship. Very rarely is any one of them on a full scholarship.

The presumption by most players and parents is that everyone who is recruited to UNC (or to most Division I programs) gets a full scholarship. They also assume these players step right in and start as freshmen. This is simply not the case. Nearly one-third of our 26-player roster are walk-ons. A walk-on is a person who comes to a school on her own, without being asked. These players should not be underestimated. They can be integral to the team. In 2000, for example, our starting left back was a walk-on.

A Word on Scholarships

People seem to believe college scholarships are handed out like soccer balls. They talk about college admission and scholarships in one voice. But according to an article in the *New York Times,* not even one percent of those who play high school sports get college scholarships.

Scholarships are often misunderstood, especially in this day and age, when they are equated with athletic worth. I feel strongly that a big mistake of many parents and players is to make scholarships their priority. Unfortunately, for many people, scholarships have become synonymous with a hollow kind of status. The most important criteria is for a player to find the right fit for her, and to be happy, wherever she ends up going to college. That should be the priority, not how much money she will be extended.

Most soccer parents can afford to send their daughters to college. Players who make the amount of scholarship money an emphasis are not the type we actively recruit at UNC. We generally make scholarship offers to players well below what they may be extended by other schools. This certainly sorts out the value system of the young women and parents of those who still choose UNC. It is very unpleasant to me when scholarships become the most critical bargaining chip. Consequently, when this happens, we lose interest, and try to tastefully withdraw our recruitment.

Transitioning from High School to College Soccer

The transition from high school to college soccer can be a severe jump, based on the school you attend. The adjustment to college is compounded by the many social and emotional changes to which you must adapt. Being away from home and making independent choices offers both freedom and responsibility. That's why it is especially important that you come prepared for college soccer. One way to do that is by being conscientious in your fitness preparation (as is also recommended for high school).

Usually the coach of your perspective college will send you material in the summer to help you prepare for the fall season. (See Appendix II for the summer program our UNC players are sent. The same program, which is posted on the bulletin board in our meeting room, is expected to be done by returning players every summer.) Some players use that summer training program to line the bottom of their parrot's cage. Obviously, those players are not going to be ready coming in, and that negative impact can be felt for the entire season. Those who take the material seriously are well-prepared for the college preseason, and beyond.

A common phenomenon among some high school seniors is that once they are accepted to college, they kick back and relax. As soon as they've made a commitment to a school, they think their time is over for proving themselves as soccer players. They go into a kind of maintenance period. This is a huge mistake. Players should understand the competition they face. If someone is coasting, trust me, someone else isn't. There aren't just 11 players on a college team. There are between 20 and 30, and the ones working hard will get the playing time.

Some players who come to UNC are shocked by the expectations made of them. They underestimate the seriousness with which we expect them to do the summer preparation program. Most people are aware of what is expected at our level, but sometimes our recruits can suffer from a kind of hubris, or overinflated pride. Just because they make U.S. National youth teams, they presume no one else on our team can beat them out. But we have players in our program who haven't made any National youth teams who do beat them, because they are working hard, and the "hotshots" aren't.

This does not mean you can't recover from lack of a work ethic, but never presume that if you don't show up, the team will play with only 10 players. Every quality college team in the country has depth. As a recent *USA Today* article shared, there are now more women playing soccer in college than any other women's sport.

CHAPTER 11

Soccer Supporters—Players and Their Parents

*What is true of all the soccer superstars
I know is that these were their dreams,
not their parents' dreams.*

Look out at any youth soccer game, any weekend, anywhere in the country, and you'll see a landscape filled with a vast number of parents. For the most part, they are enthusiastic, supportive adults who have made your soccer career possible. Youth sports is a great opportunity for parents to love, support and teach you, and for you to share a special bond with them. While their involvement can be vital, you should understand the meaning of positive and healthy relationships with your family, and take an active role to help create them. Your soccer relationship with your family is yet another aspect of taking responsibility for your personal development.

Just as you are trying to become a better soccer player, soccer moms and dads are also trying to become better parents. No one is provided with a strict set of guidelines, so the challenge is to understand the relative experience both players and parents are going through. It is useful to be aware of your commonalties: just like players, some soccer parents will be very good, and some will struggle. But like soccer challenges players to find the best in themselves, to learn and grow from difficulties or failures, and to emerge stronger and more capable, it can also provide that experience for parents. This book encourages players to understand and accept their challenges, and to be patient with themselves in their development. So, too, should this be the philosophy for soccer parents.

In my experience, the best soccer parents more or less let their children do their own thing. These parents are not directly involved in their children's soccer, especially not as part of a "management team." They do not coach their players from the sideline, or attempt to solve political problems or serve as enablers of complaining or negativity. They are completely supportive of their players—win, lose, or draw. The bottom line— they fulfill the role of a parent's job, which is basically to love their children.

You can go down the list of American soccer superstars, and almost all of them have what I consider similarly positive parent models. Julie Foudy's parents are great. Michelle Akers has wonderful parents, who have always simply loved her. The same is true of Mia Hamm, whose parents early on removed themselves from anything soccer-related. I believe her dad, Bill, coached her when she was younger, but when she moved beyond him, he simply became a supporter of his daughter. These parents were not managing Foudy, Akers, Hamm, or Kristine Lilly "Enterprises." Of course, they came and watched their daughters play, and hugged them after they won or lost. They were there for them, but they did not serve as a sounding board for the events of the game, or for whether the girls were playing well or not. I also knew that among these players, the passion and success was coming directly from the girls themselves. They were intrinsically driven, not parent-driven. They were intrinsically lead and managed, not parent-lead or managed. What is true of all the soccer superstars I know is that these were their dreams, not their parents' dreams.

I realize times have changed since the formative years of these soccer superstars. The growth of girls' soccer, the media exposure, the college opportunities and the professional league present a much greater risk of an overly-involved parent. I have a real fear for the kids who play with huge amounts of stress put on them, and that the reason a girl is good to begin with may be overshadowed by the expectations of others. The risk is that this type of player will lose sight of her love of the game. I fear she may play for the wrong reason—the vicarious glory of parents, coaches, or any other people.

One poor link does not mean a destructive relationship. A dynamic can work with a psychologically soft player with a strong parent with character, or a powerful daughter who is self-managing with a fragile parent. What doesn't work is a daughter without strong character and the same type of parent. These two, who are not willing to take personal responsibility for anything, bond together and develop a self-righteous, judgmental view of their world, which is especially damaging to the daughter, whose character is being formed. What you have in this dynamic is a player who whines to her parent, and a parent who supports and justifies the whining and then whines to everyone else.

A Healthy Relationship

Almost every stressed-out, self-destructive soccer player is characterized by overmanaging parents. The successful players I've seen at UNC have not had these managerial-style relationships with their parents. One of the best examples is Tisha Venturini.

Tisha was already on the U.S. National Team when I recruited her to play at UNC. She had a difficult time making up her mind which university to attend. (For one thing, she was from California, quite a ways from North Carolina.) In the meantime, I was losing a couple of other players while holding onto Tisha's spot. Eventually, I called her father. Chick Venturini is a very nice guy, so I could level with him. "Tisha is our first choice, but we're losing the rest of our recruiting class waiting for her to make up her mind," I told him. He told me to go ahead and chase the other girls, and that if Tisha decided to come to North Carolina, it wouldn't be dependent on her getting a scholarship. From that conversation, I understood that Tisha was not just a "scholarship commodity" to her parents. These were parents who loved their daughter, and not because she was a talented soccer player, or because through her glory they could participate in her life. Her father's message of unconditional parental support told me that Tisha was going to play for the love of the game. Despite a long commute from California, the Venturinis came to watch the majority of Tisha's games. Sure enough, as I got to know them, my initial instincts proved correct. I consider them two of the finest parents we've ever had connected with our program at UNC.

Cindy Parlow's parents are also exceptional. They helped her to face many hurdles in her career, including her injuries and other challenges, such as skipping her senior year of high school to enroll early at UNC, and the pressures of playing with the U.S. National Team. What I appreciated about the Parlows is that they never let Cindy whine or complain, even though such an incredibly talented girl faced a common and painful dilemma from the envy of other players and parents. Tragically, there always seem to be people who try to tear the great ones, like Cindy, down. But what I admired about the Parlows is that they never permitted Cindy to become bitter or self-pitying. She didn't bow down to people, either. Her parents helped to make Cindy a powerful warrior who could deal with all the issues of being a superstar, without succumbing to a bizarre kind of pressure that seems to follow our young women, that punishes them for being exceptional.

These families were some of the many who have impressed me. How do you know if you have a good player/parent relationship? Sometimes this isn't so easy to determine. It's complicated by the fact that of course, children feel love and loyalty to their parents, and they realize their parents' actions arise from the same love they feel for their children. Parents are people, and they have their own unique personality traits. Some parents seem overly involved, some dads are more involved than moms, some seem to find just the right balance. Some players want an actively involved parent, which makes them feel secure and supported, while others would prefer their parents not even watch their games.

It is important to understand that the same deeper principles I discuss regarding the game should also apply to the relationship between you and your parents. Your value as a person is not determined by how you perform on the soccer field, or whether your investment of time and effort is rewarded with a college scholarship or the ascension onto select, ODP, or National Teams. The value of the game is not the external rewards it provides, but whether you enjoy and can benefit from all the challenges of playing.

What comments or questions parents pose after a game can be revealing. If the first question out of mom or dad's mouth is: Did you win? Did you score? I think there's the potential for an unhealthy view of you and the game. If, on the other hand, the first question is: Did you have a good time? this is an affirmation of a supportive, positive parent who is keeping track of the right emphasis.

[I advise you to get your parents the book *Will You Still Love Me If I Don't Win? A Guide for Parents of Young Athletes,* by Christopher Andersonn and Barbara Andersonn, Taylor Publishing, March 2000].

The way parents can help their children become confident people is *not* by asking first and foremost about the results of a game, or if those parents were there, comparing their children's performance with a rival teammate, getting into the politics of higher-level player selection ("I can't believe you weren't picked for the team."), or by jumping in with both feet and fighting any of their children's battles. I know it can be hard, but a player has to fight her own battles. If sports can have any value off the field, it is in the athletes dealing with these difficult, but ultimately empowering, challenges on their own.

The players who come to UNC struggle to become starters, be dominant, and have an impact. However, if parents don't understand that struggle, they may react inappropriately (i.e., assigning blame, etc.). In our environment, even the greatest players face adjustment difficulties. I know that because when she was a freshman, I told April Heinrichs—one of the greatest players I ever coached—how wonderful it was to watch her dominate in practice and in games. She told me she was shocked to hear that. At the time, she said, she felt she had never worked so hard in her life to dominate so little.

I address this problem of varying perceptions by inviting UNC players' parents to watch our team in the preseason. Those parents who do invariably have a better understanding of what their children are going through; those who don't usually fail to realize that decisions about their player, such as playing time, are based solely on her performance, which, in turn, is dictated by how she meets the challenge of having an impact in a new environment.

Parents who learn to have faith in their children learn to let go of their desire to control and protect. I had one player whose mother gave her a coaching critique after every game. I got the player's permission to talk to her mother. I told the woman, "Listen, I'm the coach. You're the mom. I critique your daughter after the game for soccer. All you have to do is wrap your arms around her and tell her she's a wonderful kid."

I recently had a watershed meeting with one of my freshmen players, whose mother had written me a very critical letter complaining about her daughter's playing time. "You've got a choice," I told the player, "You can select me as your coach, or you can select your mom. But if you select me, you are going to have to support the decisions I make and not become a part of a negative dynamic with your mother. I have a lot of experience in developing players, and I think I can take you to a higher level, but only if you trust me as your coach." She accepted this, and me as her coach. In so doing, things immediately became better with her mother and the girl developed into a superb player.

A potentially very problematic issue between parents and players is college scholarships. It comes up regularly in a sport like ours, in which every roster has more players than scholarship money to support them. Several years ago a 16-year-old ODP Regional pool player failed to make the pool again as a 17-year-old. Her father actually threatened to sue the Regional coach because of what this father claimed was the damage caused to his daughter. Chief among his expressed concerns was the impact not making the team may have on her getting a college scholarship.

The pressure might not always be so extreme. It might be incredibly subtle, so the parents don't even know they're applying it. But there's an expectation that they have invested a lot of time and money in a player's soccer career, and the scholarship is a reward for that, or a return on their investment. If you're playing for a college scholarship, you're playing for the wrong reason, and you're also playing with a lot of stress.

For the most part, parents will respond to what they feel you need and want. It is up to you to communicate that to them. Do you want less pressure, more support? Do you like it when your parents come to watch you play? Would you prefer they not be there? If so, chances are their effect on you is not a good one. Be honest. Tell them, "Mom, Dad, I would love to have you at my games, but when you're there you stress me out." It may initially be difficult for you, but opening some kind of dialogue can only be helpful to everyone.

This is not a decree of divorce. Don't feel you have to banish your parents from your life, or force yourself to become independent of them. Everyone matures at different rates. I don't think someone should accelerate that. Maybe your family bond is extremely tight. There are some parent/ player relationships that are close, and unbelievably great and powerful. I think one of the best is Michelle Akers and her dad. In some ways, Michelle was her own worst enemy as a player, and her dad was always playing devil's advocate against Michelle's own self-punishment. She would come back kicking buckets about having lost, and her dad would get back to basics. "Did you have a good time?" he would ask her. She always knew that win or lose, whether or not she was a great soccer player, she would be loved by her dad. In turn, she has an incredible bond with her father, which is apparent by the love and reverence with which she speaks about him in her books.

Cheering—Do's and Don'ts

Parents often feel an obligation to actively motivate their children, or to serve as cheerleaders for the team. This can spill over to create negative pressure on the child, so that when a parent screams for a player to hustle, or pass or shoot—and in a tone of voice that is the least bit aggressive or negative—what the player really hears is not merely that she is playing badly, but that, "My mom or dad is disappointed in me," or, "I'm not a worthy person." Obviously, parents can participate in helping their children set higher goals or ambitions. But the sideline of a game is not the place to do that.

On the other hand, players should understand that whether or not parents communicate it, they are rooting for them. All of us in the coaching profession realize this. Sometimes parents do the worst things (like blame other people, to protect their children) for the right reasons: love of their children, and wanting them to be successful. While parents have the right intentions, many of them may not understand the correct way of expressing them.

In this case, a player can find the strength of character to act as a guiding light for her parents. She might say: "Mom or dad, I'm playing soccer for myself. Please let me succeed or fail on my own. I hope you are there to support me either way, but let's not blame anything or anyone. I want to take personal responsibility for whatever happens to me."

Make Yourself the Manager

Handling your family dynamics is critical in terms of your development. The first step you can take is not to invite or include your parents to be part of your soccer management team. The more you can do about your game on your own, the more you are playing for yourself. And the more you play for yourself, the less you require from your parents, and the more freedom you will have to pursue something you enjoy for its own sake. Then, the less stress you will have, and long range, the closer you will become to your parents.

There's another reason players have to manage themselves, rather than be directed by parents. That's because the parents aren't the ones having the soccer experience; they can't objectively know what's going on. They aren't on the team, or in the practices. A player comes back and feeds information to a parent, which is taken at face value. "I'm not getting playing time," a girl might complain. Yet the coach might respond to a parent who complains, "I didn't play your daughter because while she is incredibly talented, she got to practice late and thinks she's God's gift, and I am trying to get her back to Earth." She may invent a scenario that protects her. The parents assume everything the player is saying is correct, and armed with what may be skewed information, end up developing a hostile stance toward the coach or the environment. But that coach is surely trying to nurture and develop the player. I have seen very few coaches who don't have the players' development as a priority.

I see a lot of these dynamics not only from coaching and with my own children, but by watching my players relate to their parents. Complaining to the parents is a way to garner support for the reason they aren't playing. It's a self-preservation instinct, but also a way of not taking responsibility. A player complains to a parent, who then jumps in and reacts with this one-sided information. When I explain the problem, the parent might say to me, "Do you tell her? All you have to do is tell her." Of course, I've told the player what to do a thousand times in a thousand different ways. But the message to the player when the parent reacts like this is, "Great, I tell my parents anything and they'll believe me, support me, and protect me from this chaos in my universe...none of this is my fault."

The best answer parents can give when a player approaches them with a problem is, "These are issues you have, so you need to talk to your coach about them. I am sure your coach just wants to help you. I am sure his greatest satisfaction is watching you players get better."

Everyone involved also needs to acknowledge that some of the upheaval may have nothing to do with soccer. It could be other baggage players bring to practice or a game. Emotional extremes are often part of the teenage landscape. Everything seems like a crisis. When you're 15, sometimes even the mere suggestion by your mother that you take out the garbage is like a declaration of war.

The first step in a healthy soccer career is to become your own manager. As you get older, you will develop the strength and courage to direct your relationships with your parents. The earlier and the younger you can begin to do this, the better for everyone. (This independence will also greatly assist you in adjusting to new environments, such as soccer trips, camps or playing in college.) The first step is communication, and learning what you should, and want to, share about your environment. Don't recruit the support of your parents for a situation you can handle on your own. Don't have them dig you out of a hole that you've dug for yourself. A mistake a lot of players make is they require coddling for their failures. Whenever you go home and complain about something, you are soliciting the support of your parents, and asking them to manage your soccer world. Trust me, you don't want your parents in that world. You want them to enjoy watching you be challenged and enjoy that world, but it is your world to manage.

Some parents are not so greatly involved in their children's soccer, including some parents of UNC players. Although it is positive to have parents who come to watch you play, the less involved parents can often be the best ones. Parents like this make it clear that a girl is truly playing, and competing, for herself. While I think a player's career can obviously be enhanced by an involved parent, an overly-involved parent is a more negative scenario than a seemingly apathetic one. So don't feel deprived if your parents are too busy or think it is best not to get deeply involved in your soccer. In fact, in my experience, players whose parents keep their distance actually end up developing faster and better, and with less stress and pressure, than those whose parents want to be involved in everything.

The Beautiful Bond

There are many examples of parents who support their children in every possible way, and players who praise them for it. Over the years, I have seen how much my players love and appreciate their parents. Obviously, I don't see many of the private moments they share, but there are memorable displays. When Meredith Florance was a sophomore she scored the game-winning goal to beat Portland in the NCAA semifinal with just seconds left before penalty kicks to determine a winner. She sprinted to the corner where her parents and entire family had gathered. I could see them all celebrating her success. Obviously, this is an easy time for a parent to jump in and hug a child, but Meredith's parents had always been there for her. In her senior year, I believe they attended every one of her games. You could really sense the parental support she was given every step of the way. The fact that Meredith found her parents after she scored that goal was a great expression of her gratitude to them for that love and support.

CHAPTER 12

The Competitive Cauldron

For a charm of powerful trouble,
Like a hell-broth boil and bubble.
Double, double toil and trouble;
Fire burn and cauldron bubble.

— *Macbeth,* Act IV, Scene I

Soccer is basically a struggle between the ones who want it and
the ones who don't. Every single duel is a statement of
who wants it more.

A keen competitive instinct is what makes you a winner on the soccer field, and it's what you carry with you when you walk off.

If there is a defining aspect of UNC women's soccer, and its success, it is what we call the competitive cauldron. Together with team chemistry and our players' strong personal connection to one another, it is the pinnacle of our program. The great part about the competitive cauldron is that it fosters a quality we can all possess. It isn't a talent we are born with. Competitive drive is not governed by innate ability, but by self-discipline and desire.

An example of this transition into willpower is Meredith Florance ('97–'00), who had three relatively average years at UNC in which she finished 13, 15, and 14 in our competitive team rankings (competitive matrix, Chapter 13 and Appendix II). Meredith knew I wasn't fully satisfied with her performance, and I don't think she was either. I never felt she was reaching her potential these first three years. But in her fourth year, Meredith finished third in the competitive matrix—a huge change in her mentality—

and on the field she exploded, becoming a fantastic player—helping to win our 17th National Championship and winning the Honda Award, one of the four "national player of the year" awards. Her competitive "fire" didn't slowly evolve over those three years, and then peak, like a skill. It was due to her decision to have a new mentality and discipline. When she decided to light that fire, Meredith just flicked a switch and she changed into a powerful competitor. This is within reach of all of us.

Becoming a Shark in the Water

Like the witches' cauldron in Shakespeare's *Macbeth*, the competitive cauldron is similarly furious, a kind of fire into which all the players are thrown in order to develop a mentality for the most critical aspect of sports performance. Competition measures people, but also develops them. Players are always being evaluated in our system and this pressure hardens them in a very powerful way. Teammates are pitted against each other. Those who work harder (because there are always some who do more than others) set a higher standard for the others.

On an individual level, the competitive cauldron creates a relentless, year-round commitment to personal improvement in all aspects of development. If a player embraces this system, she will improve faster than those who don't compete, and elevate every environment she touches. She will become like a shark in the water, relentlessly marauding in every challenge or duel in practice. In addition to giving players a framework for self-evaluation, the competitive cauldron helps them set higher team standards and a team work ethic, because the standard is set by the best player in each category. It not only creates a wonderful environment in which everyone is working; it is also proves there is no mystery to our team's success.

I was inspired to create the competitive cauldron, with its accompanying competitive matrix, early in my career by observing the legendary UNC basketball coach Dean Smith. (Smith is the winningest basketball coach in NCAA history and was the college coach of, among others, Michael Jordan.) He evaluated the practice performance of his players, constantly assessing them. Based on his model, our competitive matrix evolved. It gives a soccer structure to the competitive cauldron. The matrix, explained in the following chapter and in Appendix II, is a ranking of all practice performances. These are posted year-round for the players to see. It also measures improvement (like it did for Meredith Florance), because you can't maximally improve without competing in practice and keeping score.

Competing in practice is the key. We train competitive instinct so constantly that by the time we play a game it comes naturally. You can't expect to fully develop competitive drive just by calling on it during games. As the well-known saying goes, you play like you practice. So you have to compete fiercely in practice to be able to do it fully in a game. The *mentality* of the way you compete—like a battle against your most bitter rival—should be a part of your practice.

The competitive cauldron has changed over time. Every year our matrix is slightly different. Like all of us, I am continually developing as a coach by learning from the game, our players, and the insights of our colleagues—and that's poured into our matrix. If you want to see just how far our program has evolved, compare the matrix in my last book to the one in this book.

One example of this evolution is fitness. Over the years, fitness has become more sophisticated in the matrix. In addition to your mentality and confidence, fitness is connected to your capacity to compete, but also to your year-round discipline and your intensity in this kind of training. Like competition, fitness is not a skill. It requires the discipline to work to get in shape, but also an understanding of what to do and when. To ascend in the competitive cauldron, you have to deepen your fitness base. The competitive cauldron is about outlasting your opponent, physically and psychologically. That's what fitness enables you to do.

One thing I have realized is that to fully develop competitive drive, players need coaches to be demanding of them. In turn, players must be demanding of themselves. They must consistently play on their edge. Most youth players, however, train at a comfortable level. There is nothing wrong with making practice enjoyable, and sometimes comfortable. No one would keep playing soccer if it weren't fun. But in order to improve, and to foster competitive drive, you must consistently push yourself to places that aren't so comfortable. That's how you learn to steel and toughen yourself, and to "break" your opponent.

When we talk to our team about breaking an opponent, we're not talking about physically. We mean psychologically. The ability to break players, which comes from a superior will, creates an undeniable advantage. When you break a player with competitive will, it is not easily visible. For example, parents watching from the sidelines usually can't see it. Breaking a player is clear to a trained eye, however, or an experience understood by a successful player. It means that maybe the broken player is a step late for a 50-50 ball, or hides when she has an opportunity to be involved. The stronger team, or player, may look fresher, as if they are less fatigued. The broken player seems discouraged, and not as interested in playing anymore.

What happens in competitive practices is that you are continually tossed into an arena like a gladiator. You become hardened, and it creates an extraordinary will and confidence and the capacity to excel mentally.

Training in this kind of environment pays off in huge ways. In the 2000 season we were behind nine times in various games, including three times in the NCAA tournament, twice in the two-game Championship weekend alone. In the competitive cauldron, our players had been to "deep down" challenging places many times. Ultimately, they learned to thrive there. In 2000, it was the individual and collective team spirit that had been fostered in a highly competitive system that enabled them to come back, and to triumph. I was very proud of them.

Cultivating Competitive Behavior

You can develop a keen competitive instinct, if you are ready and willing. In fact, you may be doing it without realizing. Just the fact that you play the game is proof. Every time you take physical risks, or beat a player with 100% effort, you get a taste of the quality that we strive to develop in our players at UNC. Here is more you can do to foster it.

- Create a competitive cauldron. We train between 20 and 50 youth teams a year at our UNC summer camp. They take pieces of the competitive cauldron back with them. Check the next chapter and some of the adaptations successfully used by one of these teams. Inspire your own team to give it a try.
- Develop an individual mentality. Take it upon yourself to be competitive in practice, even if others around you are not. Explain your goals to your coach, and ask for his/her support in your efforts.
- Play one v. one. Soccer always comes down to the struggle of one player versus another. Develop your ultimate competitive drive by playing this way.
- Find a role model. Whether it's a WUSA player or an older player in the neighborhood—just as you study the game for its skill, look for players with competitive fire. Study their game, and use them to get psyched.
- Keep it fun. Strengthening your competitive ability doesn't mean it should be all labor and no laughter. Maintain a balance, and, as always, keep the game in perspective.

The Sociology of Competition

People are often surprised that many of the highest level players in the country need to develop competitive skills, but even the best female players aren't socialized to have the competitive drive that males have. I've seen this over the years, even among the players who come to UNC.

I was the U.S. National Team coach for eight years. One of those years I went to Michigan to work with the U14 through U19 ODP teams. At the time, I was trying to show coaches that girls and women could be trained to be competitive. I saw the differences among the players during our one v. ones. I told them to keep score, and to play to win. During the entire drill, I encouraged them, "Keep score! Play to win!"

At the end of the games, the U19 players reported their scores straight down the line, with no hesitation. I went over to the U14s, who were in their first experience in ODP, and pointed to the first pair in line. The girls exchanged tentative looks back and forth, and one finally said, "I think you won." The other reported, "Yeah, 10-0, or something like that." It was as if even reporting a score of one-zero would be a hurtful insult to the winner's partner. In this case, their inability to communicate—assertively and with confidence—was a by-product of socialization, not wanting to hurt peoples' feelings, but also a culture that won't separate competitiveness from personal attack. What this also communicates is that you can teach girls to compete. In this case, by the time they were U19, this competitiveness was part of their new culture—all of the players embraced it.

Players have no problem competing in games, against opponents. Mentally, they create "enemies" out of the opposition, and that makes it easy to battle them. But they have enormous trouble making opponents out of their teammates—especially people they like. The challenge is to change the way we have socialized our girls and young women and make it okay to go after your friends in practice, because currently many feel competition and friendship are mutually exclusive. The intensely competitive practice environment which is expected in our program conditions our players to understand that fierce competition is desirable, even among each other. Ultimately, their relationships, and the team bond, are also strengthened by sharing the intensity of these competitive situations.

The competitive cauldron serves a wonderful function for young women. Throughout the book I discuss all sorts of gender differences between males and females that come into play in athletics. There is even some sociological data supporting these differences. Whenever confrontation is introduced into girls' games, they would rather resolve it than continue the game. Boys are the opposite. They may get into furious, heated arguments about whether the ball or someone's foot crossed the line, but the game is preserved at all costs. If it were girls, any hint of an argument and the game is immediately dissolved. As I discussed in Chapter 4, this can be interpreted positively: girls and women have evolved to a higher level because they understand that relationships are more important than the game. But on the field, competition is the name of the game, and we have to understand it is not personal. That is the way it should be.

Breaking Sociological Barriers

Sometimes, you have to break social barriers to get to your athletic goals.

Like most of you, I'm sure, the girls who come to UNC want two things: to be the best soccer players they can be, and to be accepted and liked by their teammates. Initially, these two aims are at war with one another. We teach the players how to blend them. You can love your teammates, but you have to pound them. It's just that one is done on the field, and one is done off.

I dealt with this somewhat in Chapter 4, but I elaborate again here to emphasize the point. Girls get shortchanged when it comes to learning to compete. They aren't socialized to be blatantly competitive. Even among good female youth soccer teams, raw competitiveness is rare, because society, and the "voices of authority"—coaches, parents, and officials—can have many subtle, and not so subtle, ways of hindering it. But by embracing competitiveness, recognizing its value and developing it properly, we give girls the strength to get the best of themselves. That's because this external competition translates into a personal, inner drive to excel and not make so many things personal issues.

Over the years, I've seen this competitive drive result in enormous rewards for players and teams. However, I recognize that it's easier to say than to do. Initially, it's likely not going to be easy for you to compete this way because you'll feel uncomfortable. Of course, the more you practice it, the more comfortable you'll be. Slowly but surely it will help you to thrive. You will be more successful if you can work with the type of coaches who encourage competitive behavior by praising players for seeking out duels, taking physical risks, being relentless, and positively impacting on winning. Find coaches who continually reinforce competitive behavior, until it becomes a habit in you.

Be ready for the possibility of a rough ride. You have to accept it may be difficult to be socially embraced by your teammates when you are practicing cutting them in half, trying to destroy them.

One of the biggest problems in women's athletics is what I call witch-hunting. I refer to it in Chapter 17 discussing Alyssa Ramsey, one of our players. A person, or a group of people, singles out someone and tries to make her life miserable. Usually, they are jealous of her ability, and, in particular, of her intensity and competitive spirit. They decide not to pass her the ball, to bad-mouth her, or exclude her by not speaking to her or social-izing with her. This can make it a real challenge for the competitive player trying to develop to her ultimate.

All of your life you've been bombarded by society's messages about fit-ting in—and that in order to become popular you have to smile and be co-operative, be cute and sweet and defer to others. That's the way our culture tells girls they have to gain respect. But you're going to gain true respect by being powerful, and yet remaining thoughtful and kind as well. You're not going to be one-dimensional. You're going to be a tremendously confident and aggressive personality who still wants and needs to connect with people. Within the context of soccer, however, you can be empowered to tap into that part of your personality that's not afraid of being dominant, aggres-sive, courageous, and powerful.

If you're doing what's right for you as an athlete and as a person, even if others judge you, I can only encourage you: don't change; don't bow down to anyone; be yourself—because you're going to be the one winning the critical games, and the thing that is most important: everyone's respect. As I've said before, it is better to have that respect, because being popular is so much more shallow. It's temporary; it doesn't endure. It turns and twists with the smallest ripple. Respect is powerful; it's long-lasting. Out of respect can also come affection, but affection is not what you should pursue. You should pursue respect, and the way to gain it in athletics is by competing.

There is a great line in the film *A League of Their Own*, "It's the hard part that makes it special." If developing your competitive drive weren't hard, everyone would do it. It wouldn't set you apart. Ask yourself: Are you special? Are you unique? Are you strong?

Time, Patience, and Perspective

The competitive cauldron is a growth process, no matter who you are. Carla Overbeck comes to mind. When she came to UNC as a freshman from Texas, her adjustment was difficult. Going head-to-head with her team-mates in practice was a shock to her. She didn't want to hurt her friends physically, or to beat them either. She also didn't want to lose, to see her name at the bottom of our competitive matrix posted on the bulletin board. In her freshman year in the one v. one category, that's exactly where her name was. She never won. Over her four years Carla was transformed by an atmosphere that embraced competition. By her senior year, she never lost. She went on to become the captain of the U.S. National Team and the cap-tain of the Carolina Courage of the WUSA. Carla is a leader who drives herself and her teammates to higher and higher levels of performance, and to victory, and she does it by deciding competition is a positive trait.

The decision to have this competitive mentality is not so different from the discipline necessary for developing skills. Both require a significant investment of time, over time. In other words, your technical development isn't an overnight phenomenon. They also have something else in common. Both qualities can also suffer from lapses. Your skill base isn't something you establish and then ignore, assuming you can instantaneously get it back. Competitive drive is the same. Like skill, it has to be maintained and honed. It has to be practiced, and polished, and deepened.

Of course, you don't have to use your intense competitive drive all the time. You'd blow up! We understand this at UNC. It may seem ironic, but the closer we get to championships and big events, the shorter and sometimes more recreational our practices. We don't want the players to implode from pressure, or lose their love of the game.

An important element of the competitive cauldron is keeping things in perspective. There is a time to stoke the physical and emotional competitive fires, and a time to taper them. We also make sure to blend this fierce competitiveness with a continual sense of playfulness, of laughing and joking. The day before a game, there are times when the session dissolves into slapstick comedy. I was recently reminded of this by Will Lunn of the Soccer Hall of Fame, who videotaped parts of the final practice before the Women's World Championship final in 1991, when I was coaching the U.S. National Team. We had just finished some recreational competition in which Tony DiCicco was "butts up" in the goal for the winners to shoot at, and Tony, knowing full well how important it was for all of us to remain loose, toppled over in slow motion following the last shot. The next day, in the fiercest of games, we won the first World Championship. The National Soccer Hall of Fame has this tape. When I see it, it still makes me laugh.

There are other more routine acts that cultivate this spirit. Off the field, we socialize and share meals together. Even in the most crucial aspects of our program, we encourage our team members to remember that enjoyment is the reason they play.

Making the Choice

I recall a soccer camp I conducted some years ago in Columbia, Maryland. We were in a session, and a ball bounced between an absolutely savage girl, and one who was the kind who clearly blow-dried her hair every morning before camp. To get the ball, the savage girl plowed into the blow-dried-hair girl, knocking her down. The blow-dried girl stood up and made the

Here we are resolving another recreational competition—the only way we know how at UNC, which is to get a good laugh. In "Butts Up," the losers pay the "ultimate price" for their failure. From 18 yards out, the winning team fires at their favorite target in the goal.

most candid comment I have ever heard on a soccer field: "If you want it that badly, just tell me. It doesn't mean that much to me." This is a wonderful statement about what happens the entire time in soccer games and practices. Soccer is basically a struggle between the ones who want it and the ones who don't. Every single duel is a statement of who wants it more.

Of course, this competitiveness isn't as relevant when you are younger, when the main focus should be on having fun. But in a sport in which a score is kept, some degree of competitiveness is natural, and should be appropriately nurtured. Even so, not every female player will be anxious to adopt these competitive behaviors. Not every female player will become a savage.

Sometimes there is a player others don't like. They claim she "tries too hard," that she's "too serious," or "arrogant." Many times, it is because this player is fiercely competitive, and others have a hard time with that. If you are someone who decides not to aspire to a higher competitive level, you aren't a lesser human being. You're just a different one. You can still be a wonderful contributing member of society. But you shouldn't criticize someone who you recognize has this empowering, positive quality of competitive drive. That trait is worthy of your respect.

Everyone gets some appreciation of this competitive quality merely from playing the game, even the girl with the blow-dried hair. She gets to be in the athletic arena. She gets to witness, and to respect, the power of the player willing to take physical risks and put it all on the line. Then, too, she can decide whether to adopt this competitive behavior herself.

Finally, understand one thing. You can make the choice to have this competitive quality. It is a worthy choice. It is also wonderfully empowering.

Amy Burns ('92–'94)

Accepting the Challenge

I was recruited to UNC out of their summer camp. I had not played in a very competitive environment in Atlanta, so in the beginning, the training at Carolina was over my head. I was not in great shape coming in, and I really struggled my first year. Almost every athlete who comes to UNC is used to being a star. Like so many players, I was accustomed to starting. Now, I had to come in off the bench.

I didn't even want to play my first game, because I was afraid I would screw up. When Anson told me to warm up, I was almost in shock. I was so nervous. When I got into the game, I actually fell while jogging backwards, even though the ball was nowhere near me!

I called my family so many times, wanting to go home. My parents are big on meeting commitments, and insisted I stay at least one year. I ended up staying for three years, although I redshirted (didn't play) my junior year, and just did the training.

Every year, I considered leaving, but Anson would talk me out of it. The relationships I had with him, Bill Palladino and the girls, and the environment there, were what I enjoyed.

Ultimately, I ended up transferring for my remaining two years of eligibility. I went to the College of Charleston in South Carolina. I knew the men's coach there, since I grew up working at his camp. I was All-Conference my junior year, but the training environment wasn't the same as UNC, and I didn't have the same relationships. I missed all that. I called my mom, and she said, "You're not happy anywhere." After college, I went on to play semi-pro soccer in Charlotte, North Carolina, and now I'm the head women's soccer coach at Wofford College in South Carolina.

Looking back, I realize I missed the opportunity to accept the challenge. When I went to UNC, I was mentally pretty weak. I thought things

I love going to the weddings of my former players, and Amy's was special. I knew she would make her mark and I hear nothing but great things about her as the head coach of Wofford College.

should come easily. I didn't want difficulty. I had never had that. I didn't know what it was like to work. Probably the first three months I was there, I cried to my mom every day. "I want to come home. This is too hard. I can't do it." Only later did I understand that even though I was not starting, I was accomplishing something every day in practice, like making all ten of those 120s.

You start to push yourself, and you get in shape. I was the fittest I've ever been in my life in my sophomore year. I did great on the fitness tests. Times like this make you realize that challenge is what makes the experience enjoyable. Pulling from somewhere deep down may not seem satisfying at the moment, but I understand now that it wasn't the end result (i.e., starting), it was the daily battle that counted. I didn't realize that until after I left UNC.

One of the reasons I was weak is that I was very insecure growing up. Even years after I left, I wanted Anson's approval. I've been working at UNC camp for the past eight summers. This summer (2001) is the first time I didn't need his approval. I'm 27 now. I'm a coach. I know deep down I was a good player. Soccer was my whole life. Everything I did was a reflection of that.

I do regret leaving, but I learned something that maybe I wouldn't have otherwise. It has helped me feel even more tied to UNC. They talk about me as an alumna. I just got married this summer. Anson came to my wedding. That meant more to me than anything.

CHAPTER 13

The Competitive Matrix

The competitive cauldron is concretely expressed by the competitive matrix, which helps players objectively assess their skills in every aspect of the game. The matrix, modeled after watching the organization and accountability of famed UNC basketball coach Dean Smith's basketball practices, was first constructed in the mid-1980s. I also used various aspects of the competitive cauldron when I coached the women's U.S. National Team.

In the early years, the matrix included very few categories, and it never reflected to my satisfaction overall performance. But the longer we've been using it, the more effective it has become. One measure of proof of that is how accurately it reflects the players' abilities. If you look at the 2001 final matrix, the most recent figures as of this writing, with the exception of the injured, the top 14 players on the list are essentially those who, by virtue of ability, get the most playing time, i.e., the 11 starters and three reserves.

The purpose of the matrix, which many people miss when they look at it for the first time, is not to determine the starting lineup. It is to create a climate of competing, and also of self-evaluation and accountability. At UNC, we believe that the only way players truly develop is by competing, so as part of the overall competitive atmosphere (i.e., the competitive cauldron) we create in practice, we give each player an assessment of where she stands in 20 to 25 categories (which is nearly everything in the game, excluding such aspects as physical risks and team chemistry). There are some things the matrix does not address, and I have never sorted out how to measure them objectively. It does not successfully measure an athlete's capacity to take physical risks. Also, it does not measure an athlete's tactical depth. I bounce back and forth on adding these elements as a subjective opinion into the objective matrix to "complete" the review for each player, but I think this muddies the purity of the objective review, and I want the player to always have full control of the rankings. Players tend to take subjective criticism personally, and that can interfere with coaching them effectively.

What You Get from the Matrix

Contrary to what you might assume, the matrix is not for coaches. (I don't need it. I can look at players and evaluate them.) The matrix is for the players. It is a display of their commitment. If a player has been sitting on her butt for the off-season, we'll see it in her matrix ranking. If she's been working hard we'll see it immediately as well. She doesn't have to explain anything, including the choices she has made. It all comes out in the matrix testing.

There are other aspects a player gets from the matrix. She learns that if she wants to change the sociology of her environment—which I discussed extensively in the previous chapter—she has to compete. So, in addition to the fact that every physical and technical component of the game is covered in the matrix, obviously it also evaluates mentality, since the capacity to compete is a psychological measure. The other intention of the matrix is to make every player responsible for her own performance. A player looks at the matrix chart, which hangs on the wall year-round, and is forced to admit to herself where she stands. She may be motivated by good results, or, she may be fueled by the fact that she placed herself 22 out of 25 on the list. If she wants to get higher, she's going to have to do something about it. Over time, we have seen that the matrix demonstrates that an important first step to getting better is a player deciding that it is within her control to do so. The traditional escape into excuses is not easily available when everything is so clearly measured.

Adapting the Matrix for the Individual Youth Player

While the purpose of this book is to give you tools similar to those we provide for our players, several points are important to stress. Don't be too literal. The purpose of reading about the UNC matrix is to be able to get a feel for it, not necessarily to exactly duplicate it. Also, take your time. Don't be in a rush to meet the standards of our program. After all, even most of my incoming players can't meet these standards when they first arrive. Although we give you an idea of how the matrix works at UNC, creating a youth adaptation encourages you to build up slowly, properly, and most of all, to experience improvement. For the matrix to be useful, you must maintain your interest in the program, and also, avoid getting discouraged, burned out, or hurt.

Once you reach high school age you can devote a separate day to fitness on the days you are not playing a high school sport. (Obviously, you will devote less time and/or intensity if you participate in multisport high school competition, or intense soccer programs). Make sure you follow the principles of any workout. That means you should always warm up, cool down, and stretch. Whenever possible, do your running on grass or other soft surfaces. Avoid concrete, hard tracks, asphalt, etc.

Although elements of the matrix are involved in our year-round technical training, we test our players physically three times per year; the best and easiest way for you to use these tests is at the beginning and the end of your season. Testing yourself has value as motivation to work hard in regular training, and to see if you are improving. Some of these tests, particularly the fitness, should be carefully modified for age. Experimenting can help you to evaluate the proper level or amount of work, as can consulting with your club, ODP, or high school coach or other expert, such as an athletic trainer or medical doctor who understands or specializes in sports.

How to Read the Matrix

At UNC, the four tests (done in one day) administered by Don Kirkendall, Ph.D., are given once in preseason (in August), once postseason in February, and once toward the end of spring (late April early May) to see if players have maintained, or improved, their fitness. The entire series of tests, which is done in August only, takes four days to complete (Day 1-Kirkendall; Day 2-120s; Day 3-20s, 40s, 60s, i.e., anaerobic fitness; Day 4-Cooper Test). (For a full account of Kirkendall's tests, check the web at www.us-soccer.com. Go to "coaches," then "resources & materials," and then to "assessment of physical fitness.") The Kirkendall testing is done three times a year, and over the course of a player's four-year career we can track her progress in every physical area.

The tests are combined to give players a guideline of their low and high fitness states, and to help them set a goal for what they can do during the summer to prepare for fall season (which, in turn, will optimally improve their spring results).

(Note the importance of fitness cycles, or periodization. College competition is seasonal, as opposed to most serious youth play which is often equally intense year-round. While you never want to get out of shape, varying the type and intensity of fitness and/or competition is important. (See Tapering and Peaking, Chapter 16).

The matrix chart is a series of two types of tests—fitness and soccer skills. Fitness is related to the kind of "machine" a player is, that is, how well-tuned she is. These fitness tests are also specific to the basic needs of the game. While fitness is an ongoing part of training, fitness testing is conducted only three times per year. Soccer skills, however, are monitored throughout the season and throughout the year, with cumulative scores posted daily in-season and weekly in the off-season.

Soccer-Specific Fitness Testing

Don Kirkendall, Ph.D., conducts and analyzes four of the seven fitness tests (listed below), which he says reveal basic game fitness. He also performs this testing for the men's and women's U.S. National Teams. Kirkendall is on the research faculty at the Department of Orthopedics at UNC. He is also on the Sports Medicine Committee for the United States Soccer Federation (USSF). He began testing our team after the first tests he gave, to the U.S. National Team for the 1996 Olympics in Atlanta.

There is no specific order to most of Kirkendall's UNC tests. The team's players are divided, tested, and rotated. However, players do the beep test last, and usually in one group, to create competition.

1. *Agility*—Studies show that there is a change of speed or direction every five seconds in soccer. Clearly, it is a game of agility. To test this, Kirkendall uses something called the Illinois Agility Run—a series of four cones in a 10-yard by 10-yard box—in which players are timed running zig-zag up and back.

There are many ways to do shuttle runs (sprinting down and back) and zigzag runs, using cones, disks, or lines on a football field. If you want to check your improvement, construct an agility course you can duplicate and keep track of your times. Also, check the Summer Fitness Program for other agility drills.

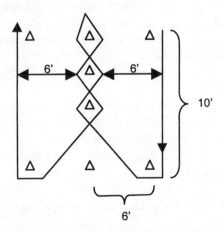

2. *Power*—Vertical Jump. This tests power, another important component of the game. Power increases with strength, and with larger muscle mass. This ability improves over time through about age 15, after which it remains fairly static unless formal weight training is practiced.

Taking a one-step approach, jump up and reach as high as possible. At UNC, a pole with plastic wands is used to measure the jump height. You can jump up and mark the point on a wall with chalk, which can then be measured.

3. *Recovery from high-intensity exercise*—This is tested by running 30 meters seven times. Electronic timers are set up to time players at various intervals, 0–10 meters being explosive speed, 10–30 meters top-end speed (flying 20-meter sprint) and overall speed (30-meter sprint from a standing start). The player sprints as fast as possible, then has 25 seconds to return to the starting line, then sprints again when the recovery period is over. The top speed, average speed, and fatigue (difference of fastest and slowest sprint = fatigue) are recorded for all seven runs.

This test depends on the ability to recover quickly and on maintaining a consistently quick pace. Therefore, your goal is not only to complete the sprints as quickly as possible, but to keep your fatigue index (the difference between the first and the last sprint) ideally to less than 10%.

Without electronic timing, measuring your intermediate times is obviously impractical. In order to adapt these tests, you can do simple 30-meter sprints, and disregard the 10-meter intermediate times. When measuring your running distance in yards, round it off to 33 yards.

Find a place with distinct lines, or make other accurate measures, or use a track in order to retest yourself at the same distance. You can hold the watch yourself (ideally, use a partner to time you). Allow 30 seconds per run (i.e., to sprint, jog back, and recover).

4. *Recovery from moderate exercise*—While soccer includes short bursts of activity such as cruising (moving at a comfortable running pace), sprinting, kicking, and jumping, a majority (65–70%) of the game is played at a walk or jog—a moderate level. To test the ability to recover from moderate exercise, we give an intermittent recovery yo-yo test. This test, also known as the beep test, is done to a tape recording. You can order the tape from Performance Conditioning Soccer by calling 800-487-9984.

In this test, you run at a pace set by the audio tape. Each run is 40 meters total—20 out and 20 back. After each run there is a 10-second rest period. The running speed gradually increases through more frequent beeps until you can't keep up with the pace. The recovery becomes shorter, since you're sprinting faster, but it's still a recovery, nonetheless.

start line (piece of tape)

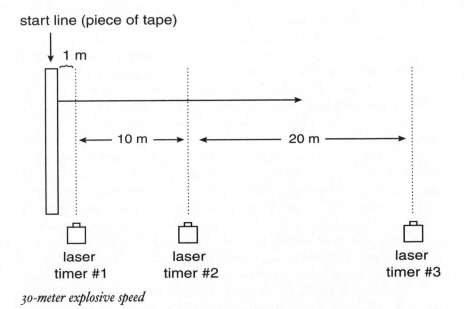

30-meter explosive speed

You can improve this ability by doing approximately a two-mile fartlek run (a Swedish term for "speed play," a run interspersed with random bursts of faster running for varying distances). Choose telephone poles, or distances between parked cars, etc. for your sprint portions. Combine this distance run with some shuttle runs (see explanation in Cones below), to create the components of this test. You can measure your progress by keeping track of shuttle run times.

Don Kirkendall feels that while tests one and two are fairly static in terms of development and are good statements of athleticism, tests three and four are highly affected by training. Tests three and four determine if you have taught, or trained, your body to recover. This is the meaning of endurance. Based on various European studies on all aspects of soccer fitness, one thing sets teams apart: endurance. Endurance has largely been the success of UNC. All things being equal, including the skills and tactical knowledge, the player who runs farther and faster—wins.

That's why Kirkendall stresses that the focus of training should not be on running as hard or as fast as possible, but on the ability to recover—and thus to perform consistently for the entire game. Speed is not particularly sensitive to training, and largely a factor of genetic ability, but endurance (i.e., recovery) is very impacted by training. You can also foster this endurance by practicing the most intense part of the game, i.e., with the ball at your feet (your heart rate and lactic acid production are highest during this time).

Small-sided scrimmages, particularly four v. four, allow for maximum time on the ball and duplicate the components of the full-sided game. The more restricted the space of play, the more you work on the elements of Kirkendall's recovery tests. Also, you can do the fitness with the ball exercises in the summer program in Appendix II.

Another possibility is interval running with short recoveries (e.g., done in Cones or 120s), ideally on soft surfaces and for short distances, such as the length of a soccer field.

Three rigorous workouts per week, spaced appropriately, are ideal to develop and maintain fitness (at UNC these are done with Friday and Sunday games, and a fitness-oriented workout on Tuesday).

Aerobic Fitness

COOPER TEST—This is a 12-minute run conducted on a 400-meter track to measure how much distance is covered. The UNC passing standard is 7 1/4 laps (for all players), which approximately two-thirds of the players (and most of the scholarship players) successfully complete. It ensures that players have worked on aerobic fitness coming into the season. This rigorous test is conducted on day four of testing, which lessens the emphasis on it and helps take the pressure off the participants. This test is not done in practice.

This is a test just for aerobic capacity. You can also run a two-mile time trial, either on a track, or on a two-mile measured road (which can be measured in a car). You do not need to do distance running for soccer, since aerobic capacity is developed while playing, and you should see natural improvement in this area with soccer training. In addition, we have discovered at UNC that anaerobic capacity (sprinting) is more important to do in training, as it more accurately duplicates the requirements of the game.

Unless otherwise indicated, at UNC each of the activities below is done one time per week.

120s—In practice, 120s are done for the first eight weeks of the season, primarily to improve aerobic fitness (the recovery jog). (120s also have an anaerobic component, which is the sprint.) After eight weeks of 120s, we convert to Cones. We also prescribe 120s in the summer fitness program.

120s are done on a soccer field, beginning on an end line. Players make 10 runs, sprinting the length of the soccer field (120 yards) and going past the end line (i.e., not stopping suddenly). They jog back to the start in 30 seconds, and go again after a 30-second rest. The passing standard at UNC for the sprint portion is 18 seconds.

Originally, this drill was done with a 60-second recovery (to jog back to the start) between efforts. The recovery was adapted. Players are now required to get back to the start in 30 seconds (more of a run as opposed to a jog), and then recover for 30 seconds. This more closely duplicates the aerobic requirements of an actual game.

Youth players might want to start out by cutting this workout in half. Do 10 times 60-yard sprints, and jog back in 15 seconds. You then have a 45-second additional recovery. Over time, increase the distance by 20 yards at a time.

CONES—Two-thirds of the way through the season players stop doing 120s in training and begin doing Cones. This is essentially a series of shuttle runs. Players do this because it involves more soccer-specific elements, including anaerobic fitness and agility developed thorough changing directions at speed. Six cones are used in a line, one at the starting line, the rest placed five yards apart, for a total of 25 yards. Players run out to the five-yard cone, then back, out to the 10-yard cone and back, etc. One run (five cones) typically takes the player from 35 to 40 seconds to complete. Recovery is the remainder of 60 seconds (i.e., for 35 seconds work, it is 25 seconds rest; for 40 seconds work, it is 20 seconds rest). One run is repeated 10 times.

Each week in training, players are encouraged to do more repeats in less time (i.e., at least five in 35 seconds, then six in 35 seconds), until in peak season (the week of the NCAA Final Four) they can complete the 10 repetitions in 35 seconds each, which was also the U.S. Women's National Team standard when I was coaching the team. This is a very difficult exercise, and while about three-quarters of our players eventually make the 35-second standard, some complete only five in this time, and a few (mostly walk-ons) get less.

Another note: In Cones, as in the game itself, turning is everything. Turning efficiently will help you shave off time, and also develops agility. Try to reach the cone, or mark, and begin the turn simultaneously, as opposed to reaching the cone and then turning in two separate motions.

Start with five sets of Cones. Over time (e.g., every six months), shorten the rest time as you are able. Any shuttle run, going out and back three to five times (for about 30 to 40 seconds), will give you the equivalent effect. Take the balance of two minutes to recover, and then try to improve it. Be creative; change the running distances periodically.

Anaerobic Fitness

20s,40s,60s,80s,100s—This is a series of sprints in these distances (in yards) to develop anaerobic fitness and explosive speed. It tests players' capacity

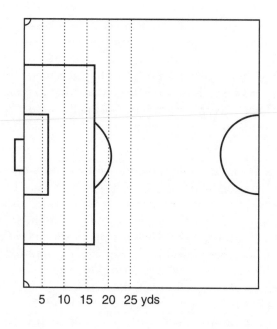

5 10 15 20 25 yds

Cones

to sprint, but also deepens their speed endurance fitness base. The runs are done "all-out," with substantial recovery (e.g., 20-yard sprint, 20- to 30-second recovery). Players are lined up in speed order, fastest to slowest, so they are competing with those next to them. (A player tries not to get beat by the player next to her who is slower on the speed ladder, and tries to beat the player next to her who is faster, and thus, move up the ladder. Players are evaluated by where they finish on the ladder.)

These races are done after training sessions because if they are done at the beginning of a session, and done properly, players will be too wasted to train effectively. While the full distances are used only for fitness testing, in the weekly training players do fewer—12 repeats at 20 yards, and six at 40 yards (postpractice during the season).

Most of you will likely do this on your own, so a ladder is not relevant. Start with 10 times 20 yards, six times 40, three times 60, two times 80, and one time 100. Use the same seconds of rest as the yards you sprint.

Soccer-Specific Skills

ONE V. ONE TO CONES (TOP GUN)—One v. one is used as the major focus of the matrix because it is the core of the UNC philosophy. It involves creativity, skill, and psychological toughness. Also, fitness is a strong component, because some of our one v. one battles are conducted for three minutes at a time.

Although we use cones and a stopwatch, you can do one v. ones with a friend, parent, or sibling. Be creative in constructing your one v. ones, from first player to knock over a cone, to reaching a hedge in your backyard. Make your goal smaller if you're going against a weaker player, and vice versa.

ONE V. ONE TO GOAL—This is another variation, which focuses more on beating a player one v. one on the run. The player has to focus on penetrating a defense in a gamelike environment. At UNC, three players are used, including a goalkeeper. One player standing on the six-yard line (like a goal kick) serves a long, flighted ball to a player standing at the midstripe, who receives it and tries to beat the server who has sprinted out to defend her goal. In this version you also practice long ball service and receiving. The goalkeeper is also scored. If you don't have a goalkeeper you can put cones in the goal to emphasize scoring on the sides of the goal, or insist the finisher hit the back of the net on the fly. Simplify this drill by having a friend knock you a long ball and going against her to goal.

BOGIES IN THE SKY—This one v. one game is played with players checking with their backs to the goal. The server is 35 yards from the goal; the attacker checks off one goalpost while the defender checks off the other. The attacking objective is to face the defender, beat her, and finish. The attacker can serve to the midfielder, but ideally you are training "personality" and want the attacker not to use the midfielder and take it on her own. You also penalize the attacker by allowing an additional defender (and midfielder, for that matter) to join the game for every pass, clogging the box and making it more difficult to score. This, of course, reflects the real game, when you overpass in the attacking box. To complete your attacking training, in the second scenario, the attacking personalities are also playing with a defender on their backs inside the penalty box with service on the ground from the flanks. The emphasis here is to control pressure from behind (get wide and hold the defender off) or check short and brake, keeping the defender on your back while staying in the box, and becoming comfortable playing with this kind of "shielding" in the attacking box. The expectation is still to make something happen and finish or get endline and find a seam through which you can pass the ball for the midfielder to finish. In this scenario from the flanks you can't send a second defender.

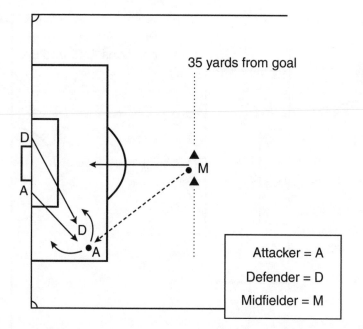

Bogies: Scenario 1

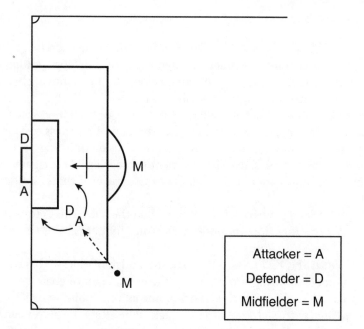

Bogies: Scenario 2

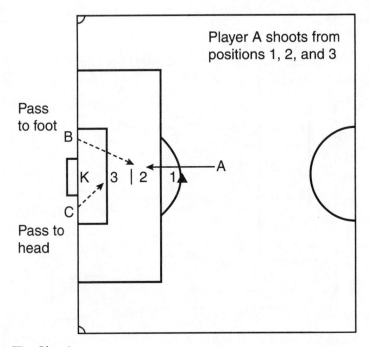

Three-Tier Shooting

THREE-TIER SHOOTING—This is a pure finishing exercise. It gives a player the opportunity to practice three types of finishing—a long-range shot off the dribble (from 22 yards out), a closer shot of a moving ball (from 12 yards out) while she is running, so she has to one-time the ball, and lastly— while still on the run—a ball tossed six yards out to head level. This drill is typically done three times per player, at the end of a fitness session (e.g., immediately after 120s or Cones) in order to focus on finishing a shot while fatigued—often a crucial deciding element for scoring late in a game. Goalkeepers in this drill are also scored. (They take turns if there is more than one.)

    With a friend (or two) who can serve you the balls, this is fun and easy to do. Try variations, like shooting with either foot at various times.

ONE V. ONE SHOOTING—For forwards and midfielders. This is to practice long-range shooting (from outside the box). A pair of goals is set up, 36 yards apart. (Use the midstripe or other line as a midpoint in order to have a marked line, with each goal 18 yards back.) The attacking player can shoot anywhere within her own 18-yard box. Player two serves as a goalkeeper.

After the player shoots, the keeper puts the ball down and shoots, thus reversing roles (i.e., the shooter becomes the goalkeeper, hence must run back to protect her goal). At UNC, the drill is played three minutes per pair. Whoever scores more goals wins. Winners move on to play winners, for a total of four games (also three minutes each). If actual goalkeepers are available, they are used against the better shooters. New pairings are scheduled weekly, so players rotate.

This is a fun game if you have two people. Since the point of the drill is long-range shooting, whatever variation you choose, practice that. You can still approximate this drill on your own. Go to a wall, bring some chalk, walk off approximately 18 yards and draw a line. Also, draw a rectangle on the wall to approximate a goal. Practice shooting from anywhere behind the line.

TRIANGLE PASSING—Triangle passing is done as a fitness day warm-up, before 120s or Cones. It is the best measure of a player's precision in her passing game. It requires a player to play an accurate long ball, and the recipient to take the ball out of the air on the run. It is called "triangle" because three players move in a triangle shape. You can do any drill that requires you to use these skills. Even just two players—one to chip the ball and one to receive the ball on the run—will suffice.

As a warm-up, the ball is passed on the ground. One player starts on the endline, one on the midstripe 60 yards away. The third player is waiting to run outside of three cones set up like a flat back three, 12 yards apart, halfway between the endline and the midstripe. So in the theater of your mind, the server from the endline is trying to get her teammate in "onside" past the flat three. At first players work on bending balls on the ground, splitting the cones using the inside of the feet to bend the ball into teammates running clockwise. This is always easier to understand by seeing it than by describing it, but let me take you through the sequence. Player 1 on the endline bends the ball using the inside of her right foot to player 2, who is running past the "flat three" cones from an onside position (the server's side of the three cones). In a clockwise rotation and with a perfect first touch, player 2 prepares the ball toward player 3, who is on the midstripe. Then player 2 passes to player 3, then player 2 accelerates following the pass. Player 3 now traps the ball dead right where she is standing (and leaves the ball there before she runs), and then bends her run away from the ball toward the flat three cones, continuing in a clockwise pattern. Player 2 gets to the ball before player 3 gets to the cones and bends it with the inside of her right foot, keeping player 3 onside, and the cycle continues. This goes on for one minute 15 seconds, then players go counterclockwise, using the

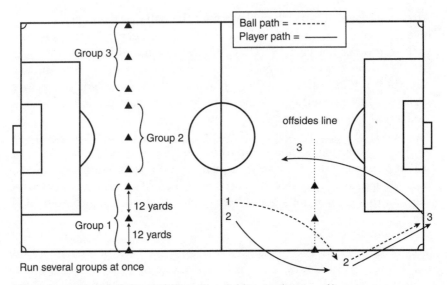

Triangle passing (dash line is ball path; solid line is player path)

inside of the left foot, for one minute 15 seconds. The same pattern goes for outside right counterclockwise and outside left clockwise. In between these one minute 15-second passing exercises, the players stretch different muscle groups. Then the drill progresses to flighted balls, right foot clockwise, left foot counterclockwise, for one minute 30 seconds each, and now it is scored.

If you can serve a ball past the flat three cones with your teammate coming from an onside position that she can take out of the air in stride (without slowing down), you get a point. If your teammate has to slow down, but can still take it out of the air past the flat three cones, you get half a point. If you serve the ball past your teammate in the air and she can catch it before it comes to the endline/midstripe, you also get half a point. After one minute 30 seconds with your right foot counterclockwise, you add up your score. Serving with your left, with you and your teammates running counterclockwise, keep adding onto your score.

Triangle passing is a wonderful technical exercise with a tactical back-drop: serving before your teammate runs offside, playing in the rhythm of the game—accelerating after you pass or bending your run if you are trapping the ball for your supporting teammate.

LONG SERVICE—This drill determines how far a player can strike a ball consistently. Originally it was done in pairs, starting with one player stand-

18, trying to reach her partner, who stands downfield as far as she thinks the ball can be served. She keeps track of where the ball lands. The distances are measured.

With a partner, set up some markers. Strike a long ball to your partner. Have her mark the spot. Move back five paces; see if you can hit it to your partner again. Keep moving back until you can't reach your partner. Do this using both feet.

You can even do this without a partner. Set up cones every five or 10 yards and note where your ball lands. The UNC standard is achieved by reaching one distance five times consistently. When you can do that, move back another five or 10 yards at a time. Track two distances, one for the right foot, one for the left. At UNC, scores are kept for both.

Most of our players are successful from the six-yard line with their dominant foot (54 yards), and from the 18 with their nondominant foot (42 yards). Robin Confer ('94–'97) could do 60 yards with both feet.

The evolution of this is to have players of comparable ability serving in pairs back and forth for a selected distance and for two minutes with the right foot and two minutes with the left foot. Usually, for our team, the players can serve with their right foot a much greater distance, so obviously, when the left foot is being used, they have moved in a bit. Before the two-minute period begins, you and your partner pick a distance to work on. When we do this, we try to line the field with flat cones in five-yard increments and obviously allow a range of distances to select from. For a serve to count, it has to be long enough, but your teammate must be able to take it out of the air as well, so accuracy is certainly going to be a component. With both players serving, get as many repetitions as you can.

LONG SERVICE/LONG RECEPTION (LS/LR)—This is a drill of control, for both server and receiver. It achieves two purposes. One is to serve user-friendly long balls, and the other is to learn to judge and control a flighted ball using a chest trap. Two players are needed, with cones lined at 20, 30, and 44 yards apart. From her starting line, player 1 serves flighted balls past each line of cones. Player 2 must do a chest trap, and bring the ball to her foot, to receive a point. Players then reverse roles. Servers alternate the right and left feet. Players alternate serving and receiving for six minutes straight, but with a running clock every two minutes, one player moves back so the three distances and the number of successful services/receptions are recorded at each distance.

Using the chest can be intimidating for some players. If you're not comfortable with chest control, start by having someone serve you shorter balls until you master the technique. Slowly, you can increase the distance. Then,

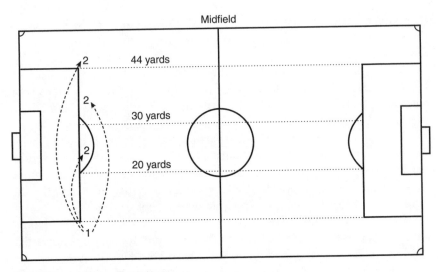

Long Service/Long Reception

try it with someone chipping the ball (or a less skilled partner can punt or throw).

POWER HEADING—This is done in pairs. The server stands on the 18, the header on the midstripe. Rows of cones are set up, at five-yard intervals. The server serves, and the header tries to get the ball to go as far as she can.

A major problem at the youth level (and a challenge at the college level), is the quality of service to head the ball. So what we do is if the ball is not "headable," we work on our clearance and just ask for four head balls before the partners switch places. We record four distances headed and average them each time we do this to get a power heading distance.

Distances increase throughout the season, i.e., 20,25,30,35. At this writing, this is a new drill at UNC, and due to rapid improvement, the distances will likely be extended in the future. You can do this drill just for distance, without a score. Another variation is to have a partner serve you the ball (either chip or toss). See how far you can head the ball back. Measure and keep track of the distances you head.

We are now scoring the clearances as well, on a letter-grading system. If you clear the ball past the server in the air, you get an "A"; if it is short of the server, but has good height and distance, you get a "B"; if your clearance is lacking either height or distance, you get a "C"; if you mis-hit it, and it is either a "grass-cutter," or below head-height, you get a "D"; if you whiff it, or

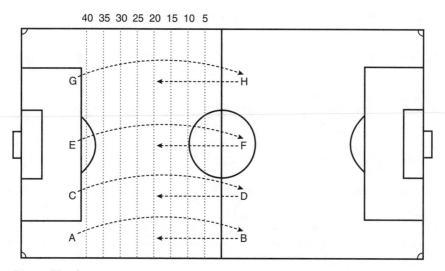

40 35 30 25 20 15 10 5

Power Heading

kick it straight up, you get an "F." You record the "grades" for your clearances that day for your day's clearance grade-point average. Clearing is an incredibly weak area in the women's game. I hope this new grading system will help.

ATTACKING & DEFENSIVE HEADING (A & D)—Like one v. one (to cones), this is a technical duel with a powerful psychological component. The stronger, more courageous player will triumph. It replicates the heading duels that occur in games.

You'll need other people—someone to serve you the ball, and someone with whom to do battle. At UNC it is done with four players, one on each 18-yard line, two on the midstripe. One player on the 18 launches a ball into the partners, one of whom (defending) tries to head the ball to the server, while another (attacking) tries to flick it backward to the other player on the 18. That fourth player serves to the same pair, who reverse roles (attacking, defending) by turning around to face the other server. This is played for three minutes per pair. One point is awarded for each successful header (i.e., getting past your opponent). These duels, conducted throughout the season, create the heading ladder, which is the ranking of all members of the team.

SPEED LADDER—The purpose of this is mostly for evaluation. It groups the players according to speed, who run races against each other. They move

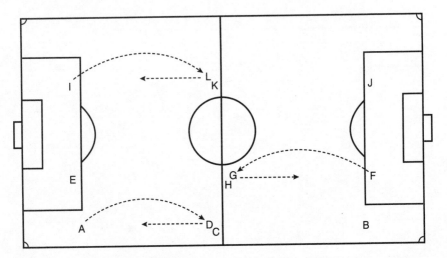

Attacking & Defensive Heading

up the ladder as they beat the runners they are competing against. They do three rounds. Player matchups are determined by previous testing. The pattern here is similar to our test in 20,40,60,80,100.

The speed ladder is ideally conducted once a month, but frankly, we fear straining hamstrings, so we end up doing it only one time per season. Players are lined up in groups of three at the end line. They jog out, and as soon as they hit the 18, they sprint to the midstripe. The winner moves up the line and the losers move down, in a promotion/relegation pattern.

You can do any number of these to get to your true speed, depending on your fatigue level, or what else you have planned that day.

MOST COMPETITIVE—This category is judged on scores kept from half-field games (six v. six), or any small games, which are conducted three to four times per week. The elements of this category, more than any other, develop leadership and the attitude that you are the margin of victory, and will determine the outcome of games. Players get wins, losses, and ties, and they are ranked by winning percentage.

A Note to Teams

Clearly, without a team you don't have a true competitive matrix. A youth adaptation of the matrix is used at UNC summer team camps. That's where we met Ashu Saxena, coach of the Braddock Road Youth Club (BRYC)

Electra in Fairfax, Virginia. Saxena, a national, regional, state, and county youth Coach of the Year award-winner, has regularly attended the camp with his teams. In fact, we liked him so much as a coach we hired him for our camp.

Saxena has successfully used the matrix as a model for his team since 1996, when they were U12, modifying and expanding his developmentally appropriate system over the years, so that it now fits everyone from his BRYC Blue Thunder U10 to his high school and state ODP players. Saxena also uses the matrix for team tryouts and preseason minicamps. He says his Electra team's progress over the years gives credibility to the matrix. They were a Division II team in their league as U12s. By 1999 they were Region I finalists, becoming one of the best teams in the country.

Saxena appreciates the matrix for its objectivity, something difficult to find in youth soccer. "It also creates evidence for the coach. Sometimes, the matrix brings out things I might not see," he says. That objectivity also benefits the player. "Players thrive on factual feedback. It's one thing for me as a coach to tell someone she played well, or needs to work on some aspect of her game. It's another thing to show her where she ranked on a list of skills in order to prove my point."

Based on his experience, Saxena recommends the following for those coaches or players considering using the competitive matrix:

- Understand your goal in using the matrix. Development is always the first priority for a youth player. Obviously, an emphasis on competition and results, or playing college soccer, comes later as you set higher-level playing goals.
- Don't necessarily post the results. You want to protect young players emotionally. Besides, they may not understand that someone near the bottom can still be strongest in another area, such as team chemistry. Explain and interpret results, since it is important to understand that everyone on the team is valued, and that the matrix is only one element of the program.
- Don't just institute the matrix. Talk about it with the team, giving them explanations and a perspective on the results. Put the seriousness in appropriate context, depending on the age and goals of the team. As Saxena points out, "Since self-esteem is often an issue for teens, the matrix can seem rather ruthless. Help players with self-evaluation, to understand their strengths and weaknesses. Have meetings and discuss what areas of the game they want to improve."
- Consider listing different rankings for each category (e.g. fitness, skills under pressure, etc.), so there can be more than one "Number One" player,

seem rather ruthless. Help players with self-evaluation, to understand their strengths and weaknesses. Have meetings and discuss what areas of the game they want to improve."

- Consider listing different rankings for each category (e.g. fitness, skills under pressure, etc.), so there can be more than one "Number One" player, and conversely, so no one appears to be on the bottom for everything. This also helps to better highlight both strong and weak areas.
- Don't rely on the matrix to determine playing time. There are too many intangibles that affect the results of the matrix at the youth level (e.g., some players may have access to personal trainers and so excel in fitness tests; some may be taking time to play other sports, rehabilitate injuries, or pursue other commitments. These all enter the picture.)
- Be ready to adapt the matrix. For example, if players can't hit a 40- or even a 20-yard ball, adjust the long ball service, or replace it with a different skill.
- Use the matrix differently throughout the year. Sometimes, when Saxena notices practice is not as competitive as it could be, he starts keeping more extensive statistics. "It doesn't have to be complicated—maybe points for left or right foot only during passing, shooting, or scrimmaging. Sometimes just knowing we're recording stats is good enough to raise the players' intensity and competitive level," he says.
- Keep a diary or log of your results (you can even do this on a computer). Just the act of writing down what you do helps, as a full calendar can be motivational. Also, it is educational. Over time, you can look back and see what works and what doesn't, and your improvement.
- Be creative. Make up your own matrix drills, such as how many turns a player can make in a set time, or award points for every tackle, shot, pass, or give-and-go in a scrimmage. Have a parent help record scores or give players individual score sheets.
- Reward young players for various strengths. When Saxena does this, he makes sure to give small prizes to everyone present who competes.

Note: Ashu Saxena has detailed records of his UNC competitive matrix adaptations for youth players. Contact him via his club's website at www.brycelectra.com, e-mail AshuS@aol.com or call him at 703-426-8416. To see many of the Competitive Matrix drills, check out the videotapes Training Championship Players and Teams, with Anson Dorrance.

CHAPTER 14

Closing the Gap—Developing Weak Areas of the Women's Game

We Have One Agenda: Excellence

—sign on the wall at the UNC women's
soccer training facility

One humorous perspective on how far women's soccer has come is to look at the early photographs of our teams at UNC. There's one in particular from our brochure in 1980 that says it all for me. The uniforms don't match, and all of us look like soccer hicks. Of course that's because we were!

In the mid-1970s, we conducted coed summer soccer camps with about 100 players, approximately 60 boys and 40 girls. Among those, maybe four or five of the girls were athletes. If we had a girl who could even change directions with a soccer ball, we were ecstatic. It was an amazing bonus to get a girl who was somewhat athletic, and had a little bit of soccer skills.

Today everything has changed. We have 2,200 players per summer in all-girls' camps in six different weeks (we'd have many more, but we quickly close at capacity). The 40 to 50 girls selected for the All-Star sessions at each of the residential camp sessions are remarkable athletes and soccer players.

The evolution of women's soccer has been unbelievable. Everything at the youth level is continually improving. The coaches are getting better, the players are more focused, and more high-level soccer is being played. More books like this one are being written, many seminars and clinics are conducted, and instructional videos are available.

Having said all that, there still exist enormous weak areas with most young female players. This is so universally true that, as I mentioned in discussing the UNC system of play, many of these weaknesses, apparent in ourselves and our opponents, have dictated our tactics of play. If these ar-

Robin Confer, a passionate goal-scorer, striking to goal. She was the beginning of a revolution in youth players who were starting to strike balls powerfully over distance.

eas are weak at the collegiate and even U.S. National Team level, it is clear they need improvement on the youth level.

There are glaring differences between the men's and the women's game, especially in heading and clearing, but hopefully, the overall gap between men's and women's play will close, so that the only remaining differences will be inherent physical ones.

As with everything, awareness of these weaknesses is the first step to improving them. Just as earlier chapters deal with aspects of strengthening your character, I guarantee that if you understand and work on these specific skill areas, it will make you a standout player. You will possess abilities that other female players lack.

In addition to working with your team and coach to develop these weak areas, you can work independently from the tips below, and by utilizing our competitive matrix and Summer Training Program in Appendix II.

Power

Power is a predominant theme of this book. It is what I stress for the psychological side of your game—including leadership. It should also be an emphasis in the physical dimension of your play.

Very few girls strike a ball with power, and we try to recruit every one of them who does. What sets the great attackers apart is the power of their strike. Our all-time ranking of goal scorers is also a ranking of the power with which they hit the ball. Our top five career goal-scorers of all time are: Hamm, Rayfield, Heinrichs, Lilly, and Confer, and they might be the five most powerful at striking a ball. Because we have built our tradition on female players who can hammer balls with power, it continues to pay us back in many ways. A female goalkeeper can't cover a goal as effectively as a man, because she is smaller. If you have someone shoot a ball on the face of the goal with power, it is amazing how many goals can be scored, either directly off a strike or from a keeper being unable to hold onto the ball, or parrying. In fact, our attackers are trained specifically to organize our defense from a keeper parrying the ball or a missed clearance, and we regularly do clinics on this very topic.

The quality that sets our leading scorers apart is obviously their technical training at a young age. Being two-footed is critical, but power comes down to an investment of time—simply going out and practicing. The best example is Michelle Akers. She has an amazing shot because she has worked on it more than anyone else. Ask any U.S. National Team player and she will tell you that at more practices than any other player, Michelle would be out either early or late, working independently on her shooting for 20 to 45 minutes. As a result, she's in a class by herself.

Granted, there is a strength component to the ability to strike balls with power. One of the greatest advantages for young female goal-scorers is that they can develop an effective strike because they physically mature relatively early compared to males, and the strength of their legs and power in their shot can gain a wonderful advantage over the female goalkeepers who are trying to protect a goal designed for men. But it is even more a matter of technique. Striking a ball properly in practice develops both power and technique. Very simply, you need to slam a ball regularly against a wall with both feet. The translation into the power of your strike will be proportionate to your investment of time. You should do this every day of your soccer life, if possible. This type of individual practice will help balance one of the shortcomings of small-group training, because the powerful element of your game is missing in the closed, tight spaces used for developing dribbling and subtle, creative movements and short passing possession.

I think too much youth soccer training is done in small grids and small-sided games, and not enough is devoted to striking for power and over distance (or to power heading as well).

Long Ball Service

My focus on weaknesses in the women's game began after the 1991 World Championship in China. I was the coach of the U.S. team, and although we won, I was surprised by the inability of most of the players to serve long balls over distance.

After we returned from China, I conducted a test to show the players what they needed to work on. I had all of them take two serves with each foot. We measured the distance, and the average of both feet for those World Champions was about 27 yards. Of course, those balls served from the right foot weren't bad, averaging almost 40 yards, and some of the players, like Mia Hamm or Michelle Akers, might have served even further. But generally the left foot—which brought the average down—was a surprise even for them. The disparity between the right and left foot was made very clear.

Developing long ball service became a technical emphasis of our training, and remains so. I took a page from some of the players who did it well in '91, most of whom were the strikers—like Mia and Michelle. Long ball service combines power with technique. Mia and Michelle had those qualities because they practiced them all the time, but practiced them indirectly. The reason they were good at this seemed obvious. Being goal scorers, they spent a great deal of their time striking balls at goal with as much power as they could muster.

Although we still have a long way to go, now there are elite women players who are serving balls a lot further. Several years ago, April Heinrichs invited me to assist with the U.S. U16 National Team. There were two players, Jen Lewis and Catherine Reddick, who in the same test averaged over 45 yards with their right foot, and their left foot was not far behind, maybe a couple of yards. To see these two youth players knock the ball so much further than our '91 World Champions represents a tremendous evolution. Obviously, these two had the ambition to work at it. Now their ability to strike a ball is among the best in the country.

The main impediment to improvement is lack of technical understanding and the lack of practice. (The players who can serve balls over distance practice it.) There is a small element of strength, but usually a lack of strength is caused by a lack of practice. Anyone who goes out and works on long ball service is going to develop a much stronger leg.

Review technique, and then, quite simply, find a partner to serve long balls with, or on your own, strike balls against a gym wall or use the side of your house.

Heading

Heading was also one of the most glaring weaknesses I first noticed in the women's game. That is because I was coaching both men and women, so all my comparisons were made between the two. When I was given my first women's team in 1979, their weakness at heading jumped out at me immediately, and consequently it has been a focus of my coaching from the beginning.

Females are getting better at this skill, but the biggest weakness I still see—even among all-Americans or national youth team players—is that those we recruit out of high school are very average in the air relative to our standards in most other aspects of the game.

Heading is one skill that I do believe is impacted by physiology. I was once told by an expert that the biggest physiological difference between males and females is the musculature in the neck and the surrounding area. Also, there is a substantial difference between males and females in the size and thickness of the skull. Yet, they both head the same ball. Consequently, I think when a woman heads a ball, she is jarred by it—that is, it is physically more uncomfortable—than for a man. Adding credence to this theory, a *U.S. News & World Report* cover story (7/30/01) titled, *Boys, The Weaker Sex? Why girls do better in the real world*, discussed the differences between male and female brains. According to Ruben Gur, director of the Brain Behavior Laboratory in Pennsylvania who was quoted in the article, males have various anatomical brain differences, including a greater volume of spinal fluid, which, says Gur, "means that male brains are built to sustain blows."

Heading has long been debated for concerns regarding long-term injury and cognitive dysfunction. As of this writing, scientists at UNC, led by Don Kirkendall, Ph.D. (see previous chapter), who has previously participated in studies on this subject, were poised to begin a five-year study that will follow elite players. The study seeks to determine definitively whether heading causes long-term injury.

At a 1986 conference on my first tour as U.S. National Team coach, one of the areas of discussion was whether the women should play with a different ball, one which is easier for them to head. I talked to Andy Caruso, who founded the company Kwik Goal, about this. Andy decided to make a special ball for the women—one that was within the guidelines of FIFA, but lighter. He still sells it.

Here is a great example of Alyssa Ramsey laying it all on the line. There are so many wonderful pieces in her game, and the piece we're working on right now is trying to get her to be a more dominant force in the air. This picture captures some of her potential.

When I brought that ball back to the National Team, all the players took a condescending attitude toward it. They nicknamed it the "girlie ball." But whenever we did a heading session, all of them were sprinting and diving after these "girlie balls," because they preferred them over the other balls when they had to head them, and everyone knew these were pretty tough women who we were dealing with. We don't use these balls now since they do not react like regulation equipment (the early prototype sailed), but there are measures that I, and other coaches, take to alleviate the problem of discomfort from heading. Youth coaches could definitely do the same.

The day before the 2000 NCAA Championship final, the main topic of conversation in the pregame conference between UCLA coach Jillian Ellis and me was about the balls. We told the referees that the balls in the tournament were pumped up too high. We asked if the refs could just let a bit of air out, so that they would be easier to play with. The Director of Referees readily agreed, and after doing so, consulted with both Jill and me to make sure the balls were of the proper density for the women. Checking the density of the balls is a measure which we do on a regular basis at UNC, and one

I would also like to see done on the youth level. We don't want our young girls afraid to head, so the balls should not be pumped up to feel like bricks.

If you look at the competitive matrix, you will notice that we do a lot of different kinds of heading practice—attacking, defensive, and power heading. We also try to integrate heading into our other training. For example, whenever we have a shooting practice, as part of finishing, we also include heading crosses into the back of the net.

Again, practice does make a difference. When Cindy Parlow came to UNC, despite her height (5'11"), her most valuable quality was running at people one v. one with the ball. She was a very average header her first year. Now, she is one of the greatest headers on the U.S. National Team and her most intimidating quality is her domination in the air.

Working on this at UNC we determined what has helped us significantly is the following exercise. One player lines up on the edge of the 18-yard box and another on the midstripe (or whatever your desired distance range is). A row of cones (we use five) in gradations of five yards is set up between them. One girl serves the ball, while the other tries to head it past various cones. (Set a specific goal.) When we started doing this, power heading really improved. I believe the reason is that if you set these visible goals for yourself in the form of distances to drive the ball, your body is going to figure out how to reach them.

When we originally began, we had cones only 20 yards away. That was the extent of the players' ability. Now we have them up to 40 yards away. Their capacity to head has been accelerated by setting certain distance standards, and then asking the girls to compete with one another in heading as far as they can.

Communication Skills

"Finding your voice"—that is, talking on the field—is a challenge even on the highest levels. As I write this I am reminded of my last team, the 2000 NCAA champions. Those players were mute. Finding your voice is a sociological issue, and it is a true challenge in coaching young girls. This ability can get better with time, but not without practice.

Very few women or girls are willing to take the responsibility of displaying leadership through communication, because it is stressful. They worry about what others will think of them when they are yelling on the field. They are also afraid of taking on a role that separates them from others.

It's not easy. You can be encouraging, but leading is not cheerleading. It is getting all the players to play their game at a certain standard. To do that, you often have to be critical of them, and they have to accept that. I understand it is painful to stick your neck out and risk being cut off from the group, but that difficulty is part of your evolution as a leader. Remember, what you're interested in is respect, and also effect. Your goal is to be effective on the field, not popular.

To this day, the best communicator I have ever coached is Carla Werden Overbeck. She had a wonderful combination of "bite" and positive tone. I always use Carla as an example of the consummate respected leader. Her voice is the most famous in American women's soccer. It is such a critical aspect of her leadership that she was selected for the 2000 Olympic team even though she had not sufficiently recovered from injury and couldn't play for the team. When I coached her, Carla was always courageous. She was never concerned with what the others thought of her. She was so demanding that she even used to yell at me from the field. "Anson, get so-and-so out of here!" she'd scream at the top of her lungs, because the girl wasn't trying or wasn't effective. Carla wasn't worried about what anyone thought; she was just worried about getting the job done. As a result, everyone she plays with has huge respect for her.

At UNC we are very conscious of trying to get players to be communicative, and constantly work on this in our practices. We always insist that they keep score out loud. (It's amazing how few of them actually do.) If we play a possessional game, everyone has to count out loud. We have players count consecutive passes when they play five v. two or other keep-away games. When players are unmarked, we want them to scream out for the ball. Whenever they don't get the ball, we don't just single out the girl who didn't serve it; we also reprimand the girl who didn't ask for it.

Ask your coach and your peers to help you develop your communication skills. Get into the habit of constant chatter, even if it seems totally meaningless at first. It doesn't just have to be "pass me the ball." It can be supportive or informative chatter (e.g., "I'm behind you." "I'm covering." "I've got this player over here."). Sometimes it will have to be critical. A true leadership voice is, at times, a critical voice. It's not necessarily going to be easy to get the players to perform at a desired standard, and certainly during a game it's going to be tough to always communicate with a measured tone, because to project your voice across the field sometimes destroys the tone that communicates best.

Every female athlete has to find her leadership voice, and she has to express it. But a part of leadership is discovering who benefits most from what kind of direction. Some girls panic when directed on the field, so you must select the appropriate time — say at half-time, or before corner kicks. Other girls are so confident and strong, any kind of communication at any time is fine. Additionally, you have to be strong enough to accept demanding and powerful leadership from others, because we can't call "time out" and bring everyone together and communicate information in paragraphs and in a calm voice. We have to get it out quickly and powerfully.

Again, be the margin of difference. There are so few voices out there that when one finally emerges, it's a wonderful beacon for the entire team.

Back to Pressure

The first time I watched the National Team play was in Italy, after I was appointed their coach. I was stunned at how poorly they played with their backs to pressure (i.e., when you receive a ball with a defender at your back), and overwhelmed with how well the Italians did it. For one thing, our soccer culture had not really prepared us to play without time and space.

During a conversation with Lauren Gregg, former UNC and U.S. National Team player, I picked her brain about how the former University of Virginia (UVA) men's soccer coach Bruce Arena (currently the men's U.S. National Team coach) prepared his team. (At the time, Lauren was the UVA women's coach.) I was always very impressed with the way Bruce's teams played against mine when I coached men, and so whenever I talked to Lauren, I'd ask her what he was up to in practice. Among other things, she talked about his back to pressure drills.

I had never seen Bruce work, so I took what Lauren shared with me and created something I thought was similar. I came up with a back to pressure series that is still one of the most popular coaching clinics that we do (and demonstrated on my videotape series). It is also one of our warm-ups one time per week, once we get to the NCAA tournament. This series begins by working on the techniques of different turns, and progresses by adding pressure in increments, culminating in a full-pressure, one v. one situation. And even though we can only do this warm-up during the NCAA tournament when we have more practice time, all fall we do a training session called "Bogies" (see Chapter 13), in which the back to pressure is done as an individual competition which we record.

You almost can't get enough practice with your back to pressure. Your goal should be to get so good at it that when a teammate serves you the ball, you can play as if you are unmarked. That was my philosophy when I coached the National Team. I wanted my front-runners to be so confident that even if someone was on their backs, they could play as if they were unmarked. They could spin out and face a defender, knowing that the attack wasn't going to break down. That's exactly how the front-runners played by the time we got to the World Championship in China in 1991. The "three-edged sword" of Heinrichs, Akers, and Gabarra was extraordinary with the ball, and very comfortable, even with their backs to pressure. Naturally, all three are exceptional players, but I genuinely believe our emphasis on back to pressure made them better.

Back to pressure is dealt with by a philosophy of confidence. When I coached the National Team, we made a declaration that if one of our players was marked from behind, we would see it as if she were unmarked. That was a statement of our arrogance with someone on our backs. The first step for a player was to decide, "I can play with someone on my back; it's like no one is there." This is the first step in constructing confidence.

The next step was to start practicing in environments that forced the players to mark each other man-to-man anywhere on the field. We conducted a fundamental tactical review: understand there's someone on your back, get a sense of pressure by looking, and then make your first touch away from pressure. When working on back to pressure, focus on the discipline of making that first touch with someone tracking you from behind.

Artistry and Deception

For women's soccer to reach yet another level—and to narrow the gap with the men—there has to be an increase in artistry and deception. This refers to changing pace and direction, and to fakes and feints—all of which are a crucial part of the way the game should be played on a high level. It is also currently a major issue for American women on the national scene, because other countries have this ability better than they do. The Brazilians have it, for example. Their artistry and deception is part of their soccer culture. We Americans have to figure out how to make it part of our culture as well.

One problem is that the women's game does not require the use of this skill. That's because much of the way girls succeed is through superior athleticism, as opposed to creativity. There is often such a disparity in athletic ability among players that girls can just run past an opponent because they are quicker, more explosive, and more agile. They don't have to develop any deception to succeed, so that creativity doesn't become part of their repertoire.

Artistry and deception is another skill we continually work on at UNC. We address it as often as we can—in the off-season, when we do our Coerver warm-ups, or when we play five v. two or six plus one v. three (the three are defenders), I remind the players to buy more time by throwing in a fake, or otherwise freezing the defender. Deception is also used in part of the back to pressure series I described above.

Deception, disguise, and faking are permanent parts of the way men play, and women need them as well. Maybe role models are missing because women's soccer is not universally televised, or high-level women still aren't the best role models for this. Maybe when a female watches a male play with this skill it is hard to relate to him, or to have the leap of faith to believe she can play that way. Maybe a young girl's ambition is too low. It is my hope that with the WUSA, the World Cup, and the Olympics, the play of the world's top women who use these skills will be in tape libraries for millions of young girls to see and study.

Obviously, you need a superior comfort level with the ball to acquire artistry and deception, but part of it is simply experimenting. You'll know you're getting it if you can dip your shoulder in one direction, and the defender falls away and you sprint out of range. Sometimes, before you get proficient at something, you just need to experience that feeling: "Hey, I can do this!"

The critical aspect in developing this skill is doing it on your own. Boys are generally much better on the ball than girls. This has nothing to do with gender differences. It's just that boys handle the ball more on their own. They don't need a social context to play soccer. Girls seem to need someone with them, a girlfriend or a team, in order to play. To evolve as a gender, girls have to get beyond the social aspects of player development. You have to get beyond requiring a friend to be there in order to spend time with the ball.

(Laurie Schwoy was happy on her own. See Chapter 7.)

Outsides of the Feet

The capacity to serve balls with the correct texture—balls that are bent, that have a "user-friendly" backspin so that they die at a player's feet, that are hit with correct pace and precise accuracy so that, for example, they fall at someone's right foot in the event a defender is on her left—every player should have these subtle nuances at her disposal. These are skills that are facilitated by using both the inside and the outside of the feet.

The surfaces most players use to pass a ball are the inside of the feet or the insteps. No matter what their level, very few female players pass or serve balls consistently with the outside of either foot. Some of them do bend balls with the inside of their feet, but almost no one in the women's game uses the outside of the feet, even though this is one of the best surfaces with which to texture a pass or bend a ball.

Actually, bending balls is a form of deception. Although we see it at high levels with the inside of the feet, the minimal use of the outside of the feet is largely from lack of exposure. Female players don't see how often high-level men are doing it, so it doesn't occur to them that it should be part of the way they play.

167

At UNC, we feel that this is a skill that can be acquired with training. We do it as a normal, once-a-week practice to expand and develop our technical arsenal. Although it appears at first glance to be a challenging skill, it is not overwhelmingly difficult.

Balls that are textured, bent, or feathered—these are three great words to describe what you want to develop. But you'll never develop these skills just by trying them occasionally in a game. We practice them with triangle passing (see the competitive matrix, Chapter 13). That is, we focus on bending balls as the players are running in triangle formations. I tell youth players the following: Whenever you have the ball at your feet in practice, just work on bending it. When your teammates are messing around—just arriving or leaving practice—bend balls into the goal using the inside and the outside of your feet. When the coach sets down a pile of balls, pick one out and serve it between two other balls, bending and splitting the two. Find a partner and bend balls to each other. The point is that while you have a minute of free time, you're learning this skill. It is this casual play that can eventually make you a master, because it is difficult to do this in formal training.

Players don't use these skills in games. Most balls are simply driven, or served without any understanding of reception or angle, or splitting the defenders or getting the ball away from the keeper and toward a runner. This is a lack of technical sophistication. Serving bent balls should be a part of your playing personality. If it isn't, you're limited.

Defensive Clearance

The reason we defeated Notre Dame in the semifinal game of the 2000 NCAA Championship was because of a poor clearance by our opponents at the top of the box, which one of our players hammered into the back of the net. In the final game against UCLA, a poor clearance by one of their players resulted in an own goal. Obviously, weak defensive clearance is still plaguing the women's game. (In considering this Championship, thank goodness!)

Part of the problem stems from what Dino (Bill Palladino) and I call "Little League Syndrome." In baseball, when someone hits a fly ball to a decent boy player, he immediately knows where it's going. The same holds true in soccer. Send a flighted ball toward a male and he automatically starts tracking it like it's got radar.

Sighting the flight of the ball is still a challenge in the women's game. If you knock a flighted ball to an average high school girl, she may run toward it, then all of a sudden sense it is going over her head. By the time she realizes, it's too late. Off balance, she vainly tries to correct her mistake. Dino and I think that part of the challenge of clearing balls with either the head or the feet is this sighting issue, caused by the difficulty of girls and women to judge a ball in flight. When a ball is heading toward a female and she needs to clear it, it's an issue of exactly where it's going, so she is rarely well positioned to clear it properly, and she flails at it off-balance, reaching, and it's not decisively cleared high and wide. (Obviously this lack of sighting is also part of issues in such areas as heading, receiving, and goalkeeping).

Of course, there are exceptions. Tisha Venturini can sight a ball superbly. Either she always had this ability or she developed it as a young girl, because when she came to UNC as a freshman she was already the best at it on the team. Michelle Akers also has it. But in the men's game, there aren't exceptions. Men have it as a rule. If they don't have it, it's an exception.

Since I have witnessed this weakness across the board, I seem to feel it might be a physiological difference between men and women. It is interesting that while young girls display superior verbal abilities, from about age 10, boys display greater visual-spatial ability, which is involved in such tasks as manipulating objects in two- or three-dimensional space, reading maps, or aiming at a target.* Perhaps there is a connection, and the ability to sight flighted balls is genetically based.

I do believe this skill can be improved with repetition. You can teach players to sight a ball, but you've got to serve them thousands of balls, like all of us do in training goalkeepers. That's what we do at UNC. We serve flighted balls all the time. It does seem to help, since the seniors are better at it than the younger players. (Try long service/long reception [LS/LR] in the competitive matrix).

When we do our power heading drill, we also get in a lot of clearance skills. That's because one of the most difficult things to do is to serve an accurate flighted ball for a teammate to head. Since I would estimate that at the youth level three-fourths of the balls are going to be poor services, rather than wasting those balls, the receiver, using both feet, should practice clearing by just banging them out, high and far.

Goalkeeping

As in every area of the game, there are some basic characteristics of goalkeeping that are inherently female. However, I would not necessarily

---

* Source: *Child Psychology: A Contemporary Viewpoint*, 5th ed., E. Mavis Hetherington, and Ross D. Parke, 1999, McGraw Hill Companies, Inc.

characterize these as the same weaknesses. You could say that the fact that women, who are built differently than men, are required to play in the same sized goal is an inherent unfairness. With a proper understanding of this position, however, and good training based on that understanding, the female goalkeeper can certainly take command of her game.

First of all, I think that too many goalkeeper coaches coach women the same as they would men. I believe this is a mistake. Men and women are different physiologically, and as a result, their positioning in goal should be adapted.

Most female keepers play too far off their line when they're being shot at. (I am not referring here to the "keeper/sweeper" position we promote at UNC, explained in Chapter 15.) Most females aren't taught to understand their own physiology, and that because of their height (but also the "sighting" issue), the balls often go over their heads. Most female players rarely take a straight shot, but rather, they shoot on a arc, like a rainbow. Thus the ball goes in underneath the bar, but still beats the keeper who is two or three yards off her line.

Because of our system of play, our goalkeepers positioning is radically different than most teams. Although many goalkeepers are trained primarily as shot stoppers, our system requires that we train goalkeepers to be field players first, and keepers second. The modern keeper is one who not only can read the game, but who is very comfortable with her feet as well as her hands. As the following chapter points out, the weakness in female goalkeeping has to do with poor general soccer skills.

In order to prove my point, and enhance their overall field skills, I conducted an experiment in the spring of 2001 with our two great keepers, Jenni Branam ('99–) and Kristin DePlatchett ('98–'01). One played goal while the other played forward; then they switched at the half. Jenni and Kristin did very well; in fact, in our intrasquad 11 v. 11 leagues, Jenni was one of the leading scorers. If you are a goalkeeper, I encourage you, too, to train like a field player.

One of the greatest weaknesses among goalkeepers is their fitness level. A good goalkeeper is required to work on fitness well beyond her teammates, because she does not gain fitness benefits merely by playing games.

High-level youth teams have quality athletes in goal. Top female keepers are also psychologically strong. Many of them, like Jenni, are every bit as courageous as any male keeper. With proper training and experience, there is no more confident or versatile a player on the field than the goalkeeper.

CHAPTER 15

The Art of Goalkeeping

Advice for Every Player

Attention players: This chapter is for everyone. Every position in soccer is interconnected. Just as field players interact—for example, forwards need to understand the actions of midfielders, and midfielders the job of defenders—everyone should be aware of the role of the goalkeeper. From understanding her verbal instructions, to judging the placement of her distribution, no matter what your position, you will have a more complete grasp of the game and how to play it if you know what a good goalkeeper does.

Every player should also read this chapter because of the changing nature of the game, and because the modern goalkeeper is an integral part of the team framework. Also, you may one day end up in goal. A youth player with tremendous athletic ability who can also use her feet is a real asset in goal. There's no better example than our game against Wake Forest in the 2000 NCAA season. Both of their goalkeepers were hurt, forcing them to put a field player in goal. For the first time in our history, Wake Forest beat us, and did so with a shutout. It was a credit to that field player in goal, who made the adjustment to playing this changing and evolving position.

Chris Ducar assisted in writing this chapter. He is one of the best coaches in teaching the goalkeeping of the future. He's done a great job with our UNC keepers and has impacted significantly on the development of the U.S. National Team keepers. His wife Tracy (1999 World Championship team), followed by Siri Mullinix (2000 Olympic silver medalist) and now Jenni Branam (2000 Olympic team alternate)—all UNC keepers—have ascended to the highest level.

Becoming a Complete Goalkeeper

Think back to when you decided to become a goalkeeper. What was it about this position that appealed to you? Was it the excitement and the athleticism of leaping and diving, or was it purely accidental—some coach just put you in goal? After all, what type of child chooses a role that's filled with failure—a position that takes all the blame? Something must have made you successful enough to stay with it.

When Chris Ducar was starting out, he claims, "They always put the 'fat kid' in goal." Now, he says, the game has evolved. "The well-rounded athletes play goal. The goalkeeper is an aggressive, confident person who plays a position that is well-respected, but from which there are also lofty expectations."

No matter what reasons you chose this role, you have selected a specialized, demanding, and satisfying position. Now, we want to show you how to develop and distinguish yourself in it.

A great goalkeeper is a great soccer player, with outstanding agility, tactical awareness, courage, and leadership—all the necessary tools to play the game. In short, unlike keepers in the past, she is a complete player, part of a team that is trained in every skill, and in every competitive circumstance.

Becoming a complete player means understanding your position. Just because you specialize in goal, don't make the mistake of shutting yourself off from the rest of the game. If you train as merely a shot-stopper, you will be very limited. Work on all aspects of your game, especially your foot skills. You'll need this for the high-level skill and confidence required to play this position.

It is difficult to become a complete goalkeeper if the environment is not conducive to your specific developmental needs. Consider a standard soccer practice. Goalkeepers are frequently isolated from the rest of the team. They go off to the side to do their own warm-up, and when they rejoin the group, it is only to play in their position. Of course, keepers in a standard soccer practice work on essential aspects of their game, but the field players learn and practice the entire range of important soccer skills and tactics, all of which the modern keeper needs to master as well.

One of the pinnacles of the UNC philosophy is that to develop into a complete goalkeeper, you've got to become a field player, too. A good practice environment helps you to do this from an athletic and tactical standpoint. Being well-integrated into team practices helps build important social bonds with the rest of the team as well, and makes the players aware of the importance of your position. In many regards, goalkeeping is at times not unlike being a quarterback in football.

Here I am with the brain trust. All the positive things we do at UNC are a collaborative effort. There's not one part of this program, from the beginning, that hasn't been touched by Bill Palladino (wearing cap) and there's nothing in goal that hasn't been positively affected by Chris Ducar (chin in hand).

Even if they are well-integrated into the team, goalkeepers do not traditionally get the fitness benefits of playing in the field. After all, if you share everything with your team you want to get in shape with them as well. But most teams do only limited extra fitness, like sprints or interval training. But you can incorporate goalkeeping skills and get fit within the context of team practice. You can also enhance your understanding of the game, and hence your leadership skills, by playing various positions on the field.

Consider some of the skills of a complete goalkeeper. Higher-level teams utilize the keeper by passing back to her, and although a high percentage of young keepers don't start out by taking their own goal kicks, you should be able to assume that responsibility immediately. We realize that in addition to your specialty training the demands of developing these other skills can be burdensome, but this investment of time and effort is part of transcending ordinary effort, which is addressed earlier in the book.

True, goalkeeping isn't field playing—it is still largely about using your hands to stop the ball. But at a certain point in your development as a player, mere shot-stopping is not enough. That's why at UNC, we stress every dimension of the position.

When we succeeded in recruiting goalkeeper Jenni Branam to UNC, some of the other college coaches called to tell Chris Ducar that they would have taken her as a forward for their programs. That's high praise for Jenni, and a measure of what a well-rounded player she is. That's also the reason she is currently our starting goalkeeper.

As far as Chris is concerned, goalkeeping is the most important position on the field. That's why when he looks for a recruit, he looks for a complete player. "I want a goalkeeper who I see in a small-sided game, and don't even know she's a goalkeeper."

Changing Roles

Sometimes a system of play radically impacts the role of a position. In fact, at UNC, we believe that a system of play can also develop a player. In other words, our system creates a player who can meet the requirements of playing a certain style. This is the case with goalkeeping, which is a demanding position in our semiflat back 3-4-3 system of play. Just as our system of play has evolved over time, so has the role of the goalkeeper.

In defensive systems other than zonal, or flat back, a great deal of responsibility is fulfilled by the sweeper. But in our current defensive system, in a sense the goalkeeper has replaced the sweeper. (We informally call the position "keeper-sweeper".) This requires a goalkeeper with excellent foot skills, decision-making ability, communication, and leadership.

The evolution of the game has expanded all goalkeeping dimensions, including technical, tactical, and psychological. A good keeper is a balance between an outstanding individual and a strong team player. In other words, while individual skills are vital, in the modern game you can't stay inside a bubble, isolated in your little area just to stop shots. The game now requires a larger role. A goalkeeper in our system must organize and guide the defensive unit, and deal with most of the space in and around the 18-yard box.

Among several law changes (including taking unlimited steps and the six-second time limit, instituted in July 2000), another significant change has been the international law that prohibits goalkeepers from picking up a ball deliberately kicked to them by a teammate, instituted in 1993. As of July 1997, goalkeepers are prevented from playing the ball with their hands when it is received directly from a teammate's throw-in. Obviously, these laws have resulted in a greater need for goalkeeper foot skills.

As mentioned above, our goalkeepers have helped to set the standard. But it wasn't always so. We recognize the importance of ongoing development, even in the most elite players. Siri Mullinix, the USA goalkeeper in the 2000 Olympics, came to UNC in 1995. She is an example of someone who had great goalkeeping tools, but who initially wasn't a solid overall soccer player. Her sophomore year was Chris Ducar's first year with our program. The goalkeeping squad at that time also consisted of Gretchen

Overgaard ('96–'97) (an all-American at UCLA before coming to UNC, where she split time with Siri) and Tracy Noonan (a volunteer assistant coach at UNC and 1996 Olympic Team alternate, who later became Chris's wife).

These are all incredible goalkeepers, but when Chris saw them in 1996, he was shocked. He actually said to himself, "We've got some work to do here. They have got to learn to play with their feet." That was when he incorporated an emphasis on strong foot skills as part of our goalkeeping program. In addition to continually refining the goalkeeper fitness standards, he also stresses positioning, communication, and organization of the defense. As we do in other aspects of the game, his focus has also been on addressing some of the traditional weaknesses in women's goalkeeping, such as winning crosses and leadership of the defense.

Become an Attacking Goalkeeper

As the cliché goes, the goalkeeper is not only the last line of defense, but the first line of attack. At UNC, we believe in attacking goalkeeping. This is not to be confused with "kamikaze" goalkeeping, a risky, potentially fatal style in which a player blindly rushes out to any ball served in or around the area. Attacking goalkeeping means that we give our keepers license to take control of the game. We tell them, "If you can win the ball before the shot, do it, because any time there's a shot, it can be a goal." This attacking style of goalkeeping also defines an attitude, just like the warrior personality described in Chapter 3, and also relates to your competitive fury.

One of the things Chris has noticed being done on the youth level is something we also started doing in the early 1990s at UNC. Teams are splitting halves between two goalkeepers. We do this in order to create competition among our goalkeepers and to always have an experienced goalkeeper if one gets hurt. Being required to share time keeps players on their toes, working hard to maintain their place, and depending on the situation, also gives them a chance to play in the field.

Your Development

In addition to the more obvious skill areas, your development should focus on traditional weaknesses in the women's game. These are key areas we work on at UNC, including fitness, communication, and leadership. On the youth level, the focus should be on seeking good coaching, finding role models, and training on your own.

Fitness is an integral aspect of effective goalkeeping. But goalkeeper fitness is a problem even for the women's U.S. National Team, and likely in the WUSA. Although both UNC and the National Team use a competitive matrix which more or less requires the goalkeepers to meet the same fitness standards as field players, it takes a conscious effort to develop this area. Tracy Ducar is known for her dedication to fitness, and when she was at UNC, ultimately finished eleventh out of 24 in our matrix. Some of our top goalkeepers, however, have finished near the bottom of the list.

To excel in this position, you must also develop communication skills. Learn to talk, when to talk, and what to say—and with that skill alone, you will stand out. It's one of the qualities Chris Ducar looks for when he is recruiting goalkeepers. Recently, he picked up a U18 National Team goalkeeper who joined our program in the fall of 2001. When he watched her play, he liked her positioning—no matter where the ball was on the field. He also saw her winning crosses and holding onto them, and diving to make world-class saves. It was her communication skills, however, that ultimately showed him that her knowledge of the game, and of positioning, was superb.

A frequent problem in the area of communication is lack of balance—young keepers either say too much or not enough. You don't want to be a cheerleader, but you don't want to be a silent little mouse either. Also, communicating with your team won't do much good if you don't know what you're talking about. Building a leadership role as a goalkeeper requires a strong knowledge of defensive principles and team shape. When Jenni Branam tells players to "step up," they do it, because they know it's the right command. Another key factor in building your leadership role is learning the strengths and weaknesses of your teammates—to understand who and how to push, or on whom to depend.

Adequate training and good role models are vital. Your development takes patience, hard work, and proper guidance. Perhaps more than any other position, goalkeeping rewards the dedicated player. Tracy Ducar became a member of the U.S. National Team, and currently plays for the Boston Breakers of the WUSA. But she came to UNC as a walk-on. She distinguished herself, eventually gaining a starting position, because of her work ethic. What set her apart was her discipline. She drove herself in the weight room to become as powerful as she could, worked on her kicking game, and always organized her training environment.

When Chris Ducar lived in California in the 1980s, he trained some of the goalkeepers on the youth National Teams, including one perennial number-one youth keeper. That player did not make the full National Team, but Siri Mullinix did. What happened?

When he first met Siri, Chris had never even heard of her. At the youth level, she was a great shot-stopper, but she was not as fit, or as dynamic, as her peers. She had not done anything to truly stand out from the pack. However, she had a huge commitment to working on her foot skills, and her psychological dimension was outstanding. (She is very intense, but also very calm). In her freshman year at UNC, Siri was a reserve. In what has become a feature of our system, she served as an "apprentice" to our starting keeper at the time, Tracy Ducar.

It was Tracy, the first UNC goalkeeper to make the National Team, who started a pattern that has continued with Siri and Jenni Branam. Our next incoming freshman goalkeeper will take advantage of the same system. The new keeper chose UNC over a number of other programs in which she could have been a starter because she saw the long view, and the value of apprenticing herself as a reserve to our current goalkeepers.

Tracy Ducar ('92–'95)

The Importance of Fitness for Goalkeepers

When I got to UNC in 1991, I discovered that the weakest dimension of my game was my physical conditioning. I had never done any preparation on the physical side. We were required to do the Cooper test.* The goalkeeper standard was 6 3/4 laps, which I made within a step. I wouldn't have a problem with that today, but at that point, I had never done any real running. I didn't prepare for the preseason nearly as well as I should have. I didn't heed the advice of my older teammates, who told me to follow the UNC summer fitness program. "There's no way I can do so much stuff," I told myself when I saw the program. So I didn't. The only way I passed the Cooper test was purely on mental strength.

The other test we had to do was 120s. That was the test I failed. I just missed one or two of the sprints. I think it was mental. I didn't push quite as hard for this test, because I didn't realize that if we failed that, we'd be put in the breakfast club. That's the worst thing ever, especially as an unfit freshman. It means you have to get up every morning at about 7 a.m. Daily double sessions become triple, because if you're not fit you have to do a hard morning run. That year, Carla Overbeck was preparing for the World Cup. She was training on her own in the area, so she volunteered to lead the group of us on runs. You take the fittest person, and put her with all of us who failed the fitness tests, and you can just imagine the pain. I wanted to

---

* For an explanation of this and other UNC tests, see Chapter 13.

Few people worked as hard as Tracy Noonan (Ducar) to become the best that they could be. There's no better example than this photograph of her concentrating in a pregame warm-up.

cry every morning when I got up. I hated running, because it hurt, and it hurt because I wasn't fit. I'd never run that much in my life, so I ended up developing stress fractures in my legs. I redshirted (didn't play) my freshman year. This was easily the defining moment for me, when I decided I needed to become fit. I am a firm believer in fitness based on this experience, and on seeing how much better I perform when I am fit.

I think a goalkeeper should be required to be as fit as the field players. I don't like it when my teammates look at me and think, "Oh, you don't have to run as much as we do. It's not as hard for you." They looked at the UNC goalkeepers' standard in the Cooper test, and said, "You only had to run 6 3/4 laps, (as opposed to 7 1/4), I could do that." I don't want my teammates to view my position as an easier one, or that I have an easier way out. I don't want to be that player. I want to be the player who's fitter than the field players, who raises the standard—not the one the standard has to be lowered for.

My goal after my freshman season at UNC was to be able to pass the field player fitness standard, even though the goalkeepers still had a reduced standard. I wanted to raise my level. Now, the UNC goalkeepers have the same fitness standards as the field players.

The average young goalkeeper would argue, "Why do I need to be fit when I'm just standing in goal? I'm not running around on the field. I don't have to sprint." The main reason I feel I play better when I'm fit is mental. It's the confidence factor. The fitness tests we got put through at UNC — the 120s, cones, Cooper test — are physical, but also largely mental. Those who are weak mentally will give in the first moment it becomes uncomfortable, and fail. But when you persevere when it gets tough, and when you pass certain mental hurdles in those fitness tests, you get a real boost in your confidence. Personally, it makes me feel I can do anything. I am mentally and physically ready to take on whatever the opponent can throw at me.

No matter how many games I've played, I still get nervous, so I always reflect on my preparation. Have I done everything in training that I possibly could to prepare myself for this game? Have I done everything in the off-season I could to prepare myself for this season? If I can honestly answer yes to those questions, then there is no doubt in my mind that I'm ready, that I will enter into that game with a confident, positive mind-set. Then, I know I'll play better. But, if in my head I'm doubting—I really didn't work as hard as I could have in the weight room, or, my vertical jump isn't really where it should be, or I didn't do those extra sprints when I should have, or I'm carrying an extra 10 pounds—I'm not going to feel as confident when I step onto the field.

When I talk about fitness, obviously the running component is part of it. But there are other components. I do a lot of agility work, once or twice a week. I use the agility ladder for foot quickness and do a lot of lateral and change-of-direction agility. I do a lot of plyometrics—anything and everything related to jumping. That's unbelievably important for female goalkeepers. Most males can naturally jump much better than women. Obviously, some of it is anatomy. I'm 5'7", and my husband, for example, who's a goalkeeper, is 6'6", yet we still have to cover the same eight-foot-high goal. I think the vertical jump is grossly overlooked in female goalkeepers. I've seen high school seniors who can't even touch the crossbar, yet they expect to go on to play in college.

While I would probably attribute a lot of my development to my years at UNC, what was also important were my years of going to Soccer Plus Goalkeeping School, the camp that Tony DiCiccio runs during the summer. I started going for a week at a time when I was 12, well before Tony became coach of the National Team. That camp was where I developed my technical foundation. I think that's what made me a standout goalkeeper in high school, in North Andover, Massachusetts. It was just being able to catch and hold well, and to dive and catch and hold.

This is very important, because in addition to the fitness issue, I think one of the biggest problems I see in youth goalkeepers is that their technical foundation is weak. They can't catch and hold a ball. They bobble balls that are right at them, and give up costly rebounds. They overlook this simple phase. If you can catch and hold a ball consistently, you'll make a big difference on your team. If you can master the positional and technical aspects of the game early, you will stand out from the masses. That made me a sound goalkeeper at an early age. As a goalkeeper you want to make your life as easy as possible. You don't want to dive if you don't have to. Of course, you will need to know how to dive and will be called upon to make that great extension dive save at some point, but keep that in your bag of tricks only to be pulled out when needed. You want it to appear that every ball is hit right at you because you position yourself well. Most shots that you will face during a game will be hit in the middle third of the goal, so quite simply, you need to be best at handling those types of shots.

I remember taking things from goalkeeper camp and doing them in my front yard. When I do coaching sessions now, I try to show players agility work they can do on their own. They should also do fitness. If they only do fitness for 20 minutes of the weekly session I do with them, that's not enough. Players should devote about one hour per day, six days per week, to developing their physical dimension. (I always take one day off.) I don't expect them to run every day. It can be an hour of lifting, so that's more strength building, or plyometrics, or agility work. It also depends on what they're getting in their club environment. If they're just standing there and taking shots, they're obviously not getting a lot of running. A lot of times at UNC goalkeepers weren't able to get our fitness in during the team's training session, so I would get in my running and lifting before or after practice. I also think it's good for keepers to run to develop an overall fitness base. I work with keepers who can't run for 20 minutes. That's just not good conditioning.

I also try to give the players I work with body-weight exercises, since a lot of young players aren't ready for hardcore weight-lifting. By high school though, with the proper environment and coaching, it can be good to begin a weight-lifting program. It is critical for the players to have supervision from a strength and conditioning coach. Young players lifting too hard or using bad technique at an early age risk getting injured and intimidated by the weight room.

You also need to be realistic with yourself: Are you the right weight? I think young players need to look at that issue seriously. I'm not saying go diet crazy. I don't want to push anyone to an eating disorder. I just think kids today need to be a little more conscious of what they eat. Goalkeepers, in particular, are not participating in team fitness most of the time, so they're not getting the exercise they need. That can make them prone to weight-gain. On the other hand, I see almost as many soccer players who are underweight, and therefore prone to injury and other problems.

I now fully comprehend the link between fitness and weight because of my experiences. I didn't do fitness with my youth club team. We ran occasionally with my high school team, but I wouldn't consider what we did fitness. Thus in college, I put on the "freshman 15" pounds. I've had to deal with dropping some weight and getting myself fitter. It takes time. It isn't meant to be accomplished in a week, or even a month. It is a decision that you make as an individual to lead a healthy lifestyle. That decision became apparent for me in college. I chose to be fit for life. Not only am I a better player because of it, but I am happier, healthier, and a more energetic person.

If you want to be successful at the higher levels, you have to do it all. I never said it was easy. I do it because I enjoy the hard work, love the sense of accomplishment, and because I want to do my best. I am never satisfied with where I am. I am always pushing to achieve that next level within myself.

If you want to excel in this position, if you want to become a champion, if you want to become a professional, you have to take it upon yourself to do extra. A lot of times, you're not going to get proper goalkeeper training. You might not have a good goalkeeper coach. If you do, you're lucky. Most kids don't. You need to take a field player—perhaps a friend—and educate him or her in the training you require. You need to stay after practice, or go early, and instruct your friend, "I need you to hit me some crosses, or some shots." You need to organize your training environment, whether it is doing extra goalkeeper work on the field, fitness, strength or plyometrics. If you're not getting it in your environment, you have to create that environment for yourself. No excuses. If you want to be the best, the responsibility lies solely with you.

The Four Pillars of Goalkeeping

Chris Ducar uses a pyramid model to illustrate the four pillars of goalkeeping. From the base of the pyramid to the top the levels are:

physical, technical, tactical, and psychological. Each component is a necessity which builds toward the next, and all of them continually interact in order to create a whole. Here are some unique tips on developing each of these four pillars.

1. Physical—(power, strength, speed, and agility). Find a local strength and conditioning coach if possible, and focus on your agility, power, quickness, and reaction time. Try this exercise to develop lateral agility. Place two cones, four yards apart. Without crossing your feet, shuffle back and forth between the cones for 20 seconds. Count how many times you succeed in going back and forth. Do this five times, with a 30-second rest in between each effort.

2. Technical—(e.g., how you position your body and hold your hands to make a save). To work on ball handling, play Ten Catches. For each shot you catch, you get a point. Have your partner vary the shots. Make them at different heights and angles, and progressively more difficult. If you succeed in catching all of them, increase the level of difficulty. If you drop two or three, decrease the level of difficulty.

3. Tactical—(the plan of a certain situation, e.g., what you communicate to your defense, or your positioning). Play attacking soccer. Attack the ball before it attacks you. Don't be afraid to take risks. Don't be self-conscious. When a ball is played in the 18-yard box, come out and win it.

4. Psychological—(your mental strength and attitude). Our biggest battle when training female goalkeepers is confidence. Don't fear failure, learn from it. Practice keeping your emotions level. When playing, don't show frustration or excess celebration. Visualize this image: whether you make an unbelievable save or let the ball go through your legs, if a photo were taken of you right after the play, your facial expression would be the same.

Finding a Coach

By the time you reach a certain point, having a goalkeeper coach is a huge advantage. Goalkeeping is a specialized, highly technical position, and it's serious business. If you want to compete at the highest levels, you need every possible edge.

An ideal developmental scenario is to attend a top-level goalkeeping camp in the summers, and continue with specialty coaching and training during your club or school team soccer seasons. Some parts of the country have a lot of goalkeeper camps and clinics, while others have virtually none.

Cities with professional soccer teams, and ethnic pockets of the country, are usually strongest. However, not having these advantages doesn't mean you can't get similar results. In fact, getting ahead independently is an opportunity to once again demonstrate a UNC principle: taking responsibility. You can create your own specialty training environment.

If you can't find, or can't afford, an extra clinic, camp, or private coach, seek out an experienced goalkeeper to mentor or assist you. Also, study your position. Watch goalkeeping instructional videos, and have yourself videotaped. Show the results to a goalkeeper coach to get advice. Watch higher-level games (and goalkeepers) in person, or on television. Pick a player in the WUSA to follow and emulate her. Ask for the help of a parent or someone else to assist you in creating an extra training program. Make sure to practice the exercises described below.

When Tracy Ducar was growing up, she built a program with a combination of expert training and her own initiative. For many years, she attended specialty summer goalkeeping camps. When she came back to high school, she worked with a supportive coach. He wasn't a goalkeeping expert, but he helped Tracy to become one. "You tell me what you want, and I'll set it up," he told her.

Make your assertiveness part of every aspect of your soccer career. Take your program into your own hands. Seek out and find the right atmosphere. When you join a team, choose wisely. Look for a club that promotes "complete goalkeeping." Speak to the coaches and find out their philosophy on developing your position. Let your feelings be known to the coach of your club or your school team about the direction in which you want to develop and improve. Explain to the coach the emphasis you put on gaining the fitness and skills of the field players on the team, and ask to take control of your own training if necessary.

On Your Own

When Jenni Branam was growing up in Southern California, she played a lot of soccer with the Mexican men in her area. They didn't speak a word of English, and she spoke no Spanish, but she didn't let that stop her from getting the kind of experience with these excellent players that she needed, and having fun at the same time.

To get to the highest possible level, you've got to go the extra mile. In this case, that means finding your own, often creative ways of working on your goalkeeping. This singular position, ideal for the independent personality, especially lends itself to this individual homework. Do what Jenni did; take the initiative. Join a second club team to get experience playing in the field. Get some extra goalkeeping practice. It doesn't have to be organized. Go out and play pickup soccer—one v. one, two v. two, three v. three—or just have someone shoot on you.

Here are some easy-to-play games that you can organize on your own.

Keeper One v. One or Keeper Challenge

Set up goals about 20 yards apart. One player starts with her feet, while the other begins in a stalking stance (like ready position, but a stance used for being closer to the ball, so the knees are bent, and the hands are held to your sides with palms facing out). Player 1 tries to score on her partner's goal. The goalkeeper has to do whatever possible to keep the ball out of the net—kick it, shot saves, smother it. If player 2 saves it, she reverses roles and attacks the goal of player 1. You can also do this in small-sided games. It will not only develop your shot-stopping, but you will also get to work on your foot skills and fitness.

Face Off

Find a field-player friend who wants to work on shooting or serving crosses. Instruct her that you need a good warm-up, so have her begin by hitting balls at you (as opposed to into the corners, for example). Shooting at close range is good in order to get a lot of handling, and a lot of repetition. After you are warmed up and the striker begins to vary her shots, do some collapse dives (i.e., dives to the side, landing on your side, without the feet leaving the ground). Remember to work up to a level of difficulty so you are sufficiently challenged, but not overwhelmed.

Wall Ball

Find a wall—at a schoolyard, tennis court, racquetball court, etc. Serve a ball off the wall (at different heights) and work on your handling. Try serving it, spinning around one full turn, and then retrieving the ball. Serve the ball using various distribution techniques to achieve different angles off the wall. If there is grass, underhand the ball off the wall and do a forward roll before collecting it. A corner wall, preferably with grass, is even better. You can practice diving by kicking a ball into the corner and playing the ricochet.

Astro Ball

Go to a pet shop and buy an Astro ball dog toy—a rubber ball with knobs (you can also purchase a reaction ball through fitness and conditioning catalogs). You'll need two players. One player drops the ball, and the other retrieves it after it hits the ground. Catch it as quickly as you can. Award a point for each successful catch. Since the ball bounces irregularly due to the rubber studs, this is a great game to develop balance, agility, and first-step speed.

Crossbar Challenge

This tip comes from professional goalkeeper Tracy Ducar, who feels that vertical jump is one of the most underdeveloped skills in young female goalkeepers. Initially, you may not be able to do these exercises (Tracy couldn't in high school, but mastered them by college), but work your way up to them. From a standing position, try to jump up and touch the crossbar. When you can do that 10 times, try to do it reaching the top of the crossbar. Then, extend your reach and try to touch the bar with your wrist.

Part 2—Have a teammate or coach serve you a cross. After making the save, turn to face the goal, and with a running start, and off of one leg, jump up as high as you can and toss the ball over the bar. Your ultimate goal is to be able to dunk the ball over the bar.

Cross Training

Join a gym or health club in order to play racquetball, or other sports. Racquetball is excellent cross training for developing goalkeeping skills, especially hand/eye coordination. Other good sports or activities for goalkeepers include basketball, volleyball, and roller hockey.

CHAPTER 16

Playing Your Best on Game Day

Excellence is accomplished through deliberate actions,
ordinary in themselves, performed consistently and carefully,
made into habits, compounded together, added up over time.

Game Readiness

Much of game readiness can be summarized by the above quote, which appears in Chapter 5. Your organization—the details of how you approach the game—and the positive habits you develop, are what create your optimum game readiness.

The art of competing depends on being at optimum physical and mental condition at game time. This is called peaking and it does not occur accidentally, but by learning to balance stress (training) and rest (tapering). Understanding how to peak—a concept that is often missing from the intense schedule of youth soccer competition—will greatly benefit your competitive capability.

A tendency among many players and programs is to train in a one-dimensional fashion—continually working long and hard in the erroneous belief that the "more the better." Also, misguided ideas exist, particularly among adults, about the ability of players to withstand seemingly endless loads of training and competing because they are "young and strong." But the same principles of stress balanced with rest apply to all athletes, no matter their age. In order to be in peak form for competition, and keep soccer fresh and enjoyable, you have to learn how to regulate the intensity, and so, how to taper and peak.

I realize many teams do not scientifically taper for competition, and to a degree, I don't necessarily think anything is wrong with that. A high-intensity atmosphere can put positive physical and psychological stress on an athlete. I think it can be useful to train an athlete to play when fatigued. This has been a part of the hardening process that has been the trademark of our player development since we began our UNC program in the late 1970s. However, this "intensity training" has to be done carefully and in context. Also, it should not be confused with optimum readiness for competition, as it is not the way to peak for performance.

Tapering and Peaking at UNC

The ideal preparation for a match is actually a four-day taper, which I will describe later. We never achieve this taper in a collegiate program until the season-end NCAA tournament, because college schedules mostly consist of matches on Fridays and Sundays. (You probably cannot achieve an ideal taper in seasonal club or high school soccer either, due to their game schedules.) Below is an outline of our training program based on our regular season playing schedule. It shows you the rhythm of our week, including tapering for competition. (All drills are described in the competitive matrix, Chapter 13. A reminder: no session at UNC exceeds 90 minutes. I do not feel sessions are productive beyond this amount of time.)

Monday—Possible rest day (e.g., after an away game involving long airline flight) or a short, light, fun practice—mostly shooting.

Tuesday—Tuesday is a physically challenging day in every conceivable way, with a focus on fitness. Following the warm-up (with extensive stretching, sometimes using large rubber bands, also called Therabands), is a technical component, such as triangle passing, with lots of bending ball work and receiving flighted balls, (serving and receiving beyond 20 yards), an aerobic test (120s or cones), followed by skills, purposely practiced when players are fatigued from the aerobic test (such as three-tier shooting and "Bogies").

The session ends with an anaerobic test, so that following the technical work we go right into a 20s, 40s, etc., sprint competition. The players are then thoroughly exhausted, but believe it or not, we're not done yet. They then go to the weight room for a leg-strengthening session.

Wednesday—This is more of a technically and tactically combative day. We play one v. one, attacking and defensive heading, long service/long reception, half-field scrimmages and a short, full-field scrimmage. At the end of practice, we go to the weight room for an upper body session. It is the team's peak day in terms of challenging "psychological warfare."

Thursday—This is basically a technical training day with a few tactics, but almost no physical or psychological stress, as the focus is on emotional bonding. It's a fun session that brings us together and allows a bit of a tapering for Friday. We do most of our attacking-in-the-box tactics, and our shooting and finishing. "Team trains the keeper" (balls served into a crowded box as strikers and defenders go at it) is the only mildly taxing game, but it mostly entails physical risk, since players are maneuvering in a crowded box. The team looks forward to "Team trains the keeper," in which they run around, smashing into each other, scoring goals or saving them. I can tell they've properly tapered by their fun-loving mood when they play this game. We then finish up with all of our set pieces.

Friday—We understand we may enter Friday games a bit fatigued (i.e., not fully tapered). Even though the media makes a huge deal of it if we lose a game, and we are obviously disappointed if that happens, we realize it is not our best effort. An entire season requires long-range training and goals. We save our perfect tapering, and our best effort, for the NCAA tournament.

Saturday—We take off completely. Team training is never conducted on this day. Our players get together themselves for a jog/stretch/massage. Led by our captains, they go for a very slow, 20-minute jog to circulate lactic acid out of their legs, which assists them in recovery for the game the following day. Stretching and massage are also helpful. Players do partner stretching, and partner massage on their teammates' legs. Also, it is a very social gathering. The team enjoys being with each other—a bit of laughing, joking, carrying on, etc.

The Ideal Taper

We get the opportunity to do our ideal four-day taper during the NCAA tournament. I also used this schedule for the U.S. National Team. This taper can be done for a once-a-week game schedule. In this system, the physical day (Tuesday, in the description above) is moved, so it is four to five days prior to the game. For this taper, you might even split that physical day, doing aerobic and anaerobic training on different days. Then, you spread out the other days as well (not necessarily doing that much more work in five days, just distributing it and shortening the practices. So, for example, practices are: day 1–90 mins., day 2–90 mins., day 3–75 mins., day 4–60 mins., day 5–45 mins.).

Although the maximum length of any of our sessions is 90 minutes, leading up to a game, we may shorten the practices so they run anywhere from 75 to 60 minutes. I have found that the best length for a session the day before a game is 45 minutes. For the same reasons described above, "Team trains the keeper" is still the final game in this taper.

Your Warm-Up

There are many other parts of your preparation that get you ready to compete. The pregame warm-up is an essential one of them. My first book didn't discuss this too much since the focus on this aspect of excellence was not as much a part of my coaching at the time, but I have grown to understand its importance.

The warm-up has one function: to prepare you to play. Your preparation in warm-up will dictate your game performance. It should prepare you to be able to play on your cutting edge. The elements of this preparation are physical, technical, psychological, and, to some extent, emotional—which is team bonding and feeling enthusiasm about playing together. Most youth warm-ups, however, only address the physical aspect, but the warm-up has to be as complete, and as perfect, as the game.

Our game warm-up takes about 25 minutes. Based on how cold the temperature is, players should also get out and warm-up again for a few minutes before the second half. The way we view our warm-up is as a minipractice, so it has a lot of different elements that touch on the range of skills players are expected to use. The warm-up is a technical review, so that players basically do everything they are about to do in the game (i.e., receiving, passing, shooting, dribbling, and heading). Like the game, the warm-up has a rhythm. To get into that rhythm, we do knock and move and give and go's. We also review some of the tactical positioning we expect to use in the game.

The warm-up is also designed to build the team's confidence. The physical, technical, and tactical preparation is done with great focus, so players are prepared for the huge pressure of lack of time and space caused by the pressure from their opponents.

If you do the warm-up carefully and with the correct focus, it becomes habit. If you can go into a game optimally prepared, your technique will be exquisite. Of all the players I have coached, Lorrie Fair had one of the best warm-ups. I used her as an example for her teammates. In the four years she was at UNC, she did every aspect of it perfectly. Sure enough, her technique right from the beginning of the game was excellent. It set her apart from most other players.

Lorrie Fair ('96–'99)

Being Game Ready

Why is warming-up important? It's my game preparation. It's mental. It's when I get focused. Actually, I start my preparation the day before the game, with things like drinking water and getting into the right mind-set. A lot of times, I like to feel relaxed before the game, because I think the less I concentrate on what I have to do, the more easily I can let my instincts take over. I listen to music. I get my mind off the game, which is bizarre, because your mind is supposed to be on the game. But if I overthink it, I end up not doing what I've trained my body to do naturally. You can mess up by overthinking.

I find something positive in my life outside of soccer, and I think of that. In the past, maybe this would be a conversation with my boyfriend at the time, or thinking about my family—my sister, brother, uncles—or thinking about something I did. Just not soccer. That's as best as I can explain it.

I don't use these techniques for the game itself, though. As I get closer to game-time, I think it's important to use visualization—to picture myself doing well. I think that's an important asset in an athlete. I'm not necessarily nervous in the warm-up, but I'm nervous when I get out there and it's time to play. If I'm not nervous, I think there's something wrong.

I have game rituals. I put my left stuff on before my right—my left shinguard, left sock, left shoe. Then, I put tape on my left pinkie finger, because that's a Carolina thing. Then, I put tape around my left wrist. Originally, it was to cover a bracelet that my best friend had given me. I didn't want to take it off, so I just put tape over it. As it got worn and broke off, I still wanted to have the tape on, because it's something that I liked. If there's something special happening on the day I play, I write it on my wrist tape. Actually, I've only written on that tape maybe three times.

In addition to helping me prepare mentally, these rituals also help me cope with all the aspects of the game—win, lose, draw, or injury. They also help because they are a habit. They're something that's there for me if I need them. They also let me know I'm in the mind-set that I'm ready to play. The act of doing these rituals is just as important as what they stand for. It reminds me where I came from, and what it took to get here. I think that's important to remember, because if you're an athlete who gets to the top and just kind of blows off all the reasons why, you're not going to be there for very long.

After these rituals comes the actual game warm-up. My physical preparation includes getting my feet used to the surface, and to the conditions.

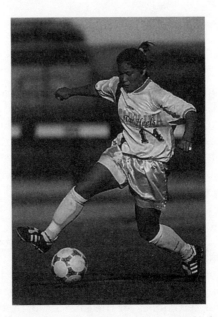

You can see Lorrie Fair's focus, and the pinkie tape on the little finger of her left hand—a good-luck tradition that UNC players continue to this day.

It's also a way to test whether I need studs, molded cleats, or turf shoes. I spend time getting my touch on the ball ready. I get quick touches, and just try to get comfortable. That's important, because you shouldn't get in a situation in which you go into a game and your touch on the ball isn't what it should be because you haven't properly warmed-up. That's something that you can prepare for by warming up properly. Then you don't have to worry about it.

I like to have 35 minutes for a warm-up. Lately, on the (Philadelphia) Charge, we haven't had that much time. But if I do have the time, I do some things on my own. I pop the ball up in the air with one foot, trap it, then tap it up and keep it in the air. I control it so it goes high, low, high, low. Then I switch feet and do it again.

I can't tell you what to do to prepare yourself, because to each her own. Finding what's right is about experimenting. Just like any pregame ritual, just like a way to cope with nerves, it's all trial and error. The best advice I can give is to find ways to cope successfully with nerves, and to develop a warm-up routine. That's totally individual. I've found what's right for me, but I'm still working on it. I'm still trying to perfect my pregame ritual, including what I think about. I'm still trying to perfect everything about my game. Maybe it's just that I'm unsatisfied. I feel I can do better.

My routine changes. Even with the team I'm on now (the Charge), it's a little difficult because it's a new coach, and I'd never done his warm-up before. We talked about it, and adjusted a couple of things, because half the team wasn't getting warm. I'm pretty open-minded to a warm-up, as long as I get ready doing it. It just can't be a little jog and then suddenly sprint and play. That would make me pull a muscle.

I like the warm-up we did at Carolina because it was structured, and we always did the same thing. Sometimes we had less time than usual, sometime more, but it was always the same elements, so there was a ritual. There was a group of three players I was always with. It was the same three people, although, of course, it changed from year to year when people graduated. Sometimes, it was according to position, so I would be with the center midfielders.

Different positions should warm up differently. That's what we did at Carolina. The midfielders and forwards did shooting. The midfielders also had the chance to get the ball from one side of the field to the other by pinging it to an outside midfielder who was running down the line. Our defenders worked on clearing long balls. One defender would hit it to another, who would clear it right back to her with a one-touch.

Then, we had our team warm-ups. We had our two lines at the end, when we were ready to play. It's a sprint, but not all-out. We started off slowly and gradually got faster, so that when we hit the line, we were at top speed. Then we would jog back and stretch.

On the last sprint, we did what's called the Big V, which is still part of the Carolina warm-up. Players are all on the 18-yard line. When Anson says go, the two outside people start sprinting. Once the person next to you takes off, you go. The last people to go are those in the center. So, the sprint up the field looks like a big V, for Victory.

I had the time of my life at Carolina. I dearly miss it. I would go back in a heartbeat. The whole experience was awesome. I thought it was going to be a big soccer factory, with totally one-dimensional college athletes — eat soccer, sleep soccer, dream soccer. My image was ridiculous. I got there and it was everything wonderful I imagined it to be. It was exactly the opposite of a factory.

Anson is a great motivator. He figures out what motivates you as an individual. For example, some people don't like to be yelled at. I like "hard motivation." That is, I don't mind being yelled at if it's truthful, but I don't like it when I'm yelled at as an attack.

Anson doesn't believe in rigid rules because he thinks they display a lack of trust. If a player is given personal responsibility, and she decides she wants to go out and party the night before a game, and she's terrible, she plays like an absolute cone, whose fault is that? Anson would not hesitate to pull that player out. She caused that to happen. With that personal responsibility, we learned that we could be self-disciplined. You don't need rules to tell you what to do. You need to understand that your actions can make or break a team, so all your decisions should be based on what's best for that team.

Anson went to Carolina. He understands what it means to be a student there. He didn't want to prevent us from having the time of our lives in college, because that's what it's about. At the same time, we were out there to win, and that, too, is what it's about. You can be disciplined and have a great time in college. I certainly did. I got to experience college life. Soccer was not the only reason that Carolina was great for me. I went to shows, plays, cultural events, and listened to music. There's always something happening on campus. Any free time we had, we found an activity to do. I think that's what college is about, because how many people are going to continue on to play soccer or athletics? College is all about finding out what you want to do in life. If you're only on a soccer field or in your dorm, you're not going to find it. Anson knows that. He studied for various degrees, but it was only through experimentation that he finally found something that he liked, and felt he was meant to do.

I do a lot of public speaking and appearances. Whenever I speak to groups of kids, I tell them: whatever you do—whether it's soccer or in life—just do it with your heart.

Tisha Venturini ('91–'94)

The Pinkie Tape Story

At UNC, my roommate Angela Kelly and I decided that we would start putting a little strip of tape around our left pinkie fingers for good luck. The team picked up on it and it became a ritual. One year, we went to California to play Santa Clara University. We were having a poor game, and before we knew it we were down by two goals. I was playing near my hometown, and we had never lost before, or even been behind. Here we were, losing by two goals by halftime. We all went into the locker room and I freaked out!!!! I looked around and noticed that not everyone had the pinkie tape on, so I yelled, "Everybody who doesn't have pinkie tape on PUT IT ON NOW!!!!!!"

It was pretty funny because I am usually not very vocal or all that intense, and I just lost it. We ended up coming back and winning 3-2, all because of the pinkie tape!

No matter how much the warm-up is emphasized, very few players focus on it. Most youth girls' warm-ups are performances for the other team, a display of how excited they are about playing. The warm-up becomes a competition between two teams about who cheers the loudest, and who appears happier and more enthusiastic. It's like a show to appear more confident. The warm-up should not be a performance. It's a methodical rehearsal of the game. That's why, when I see the performers, I bring my team together and tell them, "Well, they just won the cheering competition. I guess you're just going to have to win the game."

Most girls also use the warm-up primarily as a social period (which I don't generally see boys do, by the way). They destroy it this way, because there is no meaningful focus on the game itself. Even though the beginning of a warm-up should be slow and deliberate, you should maintain the focus and the perfection with which you perform it. There may be some friendly bonding at UNC, particularly in our warm-up in practice sessions. In training, the players know the level of seriousness of the warm-up by the day's schedule and by my demeanor when we begin, but there are plenty of serious moments. Like all elements of training, practice warm-ups can condition you for competition warm-ups.

Another frequent problem I see with girls' teams is starting the warm-up on time. After everyone is done chitchatting, there's no time to focus, so the warm-up ends up being a total waste, since it does not prepare the team to play. To avoid this problem, try to do a preteam warm-up with a friend. You can start jogging with a ball and pass together before the rest of the team arrives. This allows for some casual fun, without missing out on focus. After all, the warm-up should also be part social, and a chance just to enjoy life.

The Science of Warm-Up

This chapter gives you the benefit of our latest innovations on warming-up. Greg Gatz, our strength and conditioning coach, has introduced us to a routine that makes our physical preparation more scientific, and so, even better. He has been assisted in constructing this warm-up by renowned movement expert Vern Gambetta, president of Gambetta Sports Training Systems, in Sarasota, Florida.

You probably are educated to view a warm-up in the same way most people are—as a way to increase body temperature as well as to naturally lubricate the joints, ligaments, and the muscles used to play. To some extent, this is true. However, the emphasis of a warm-up should also be on activating the central nervous system. This is the body's "command control center," in which all information is processed, such as the movement needed to get you jump-started. This activation is crucial in setting the body's readiness for performing high-level work, and therefore, for playing your best soccer.

The type of warm-up prescribed here is not the usual way teams get ready to play. According to our experience at UNC, and Greg Gatz's observation, athletes who use a warm-up like the one in this chapter, which contains nervous system stimulation, are better able to perform at a higher level, and more quickly, in both practices and games.

To warm-up, most teams do some static stretching followed by soccer skills. However, to perform the most efficient warm-up, traditional static stretching should be interspersed with active movement. In fact, static stretching is best employed as part of the cool-down after playing, both for its calming effects on the body, and to maintain flexibility and help prevent injury.

A warm-up should be thought of as a buildup, in which the activity increases in intensity as it proceeds. The warm-up routine should reach a high point, so that after completing it you feel "revved up" and ready right from the start of play. This alleviates the common physical and mental problem of athletes spending the first part of games in a continuation of an unfinished warm-up.

A warm-up should also be as soccer-specific as possible. In addition to doing skills such as passing and heading, or sprinting and lunging, make sure to duplicate aspects of your play. Since you play in a three-dimensional way, warming-up should duplicate this activity as much as possible. Most traditional warm-ups are multidimensional (e.g., done in many directions), but they are often done in isolated parts, versus movement that is linked together.

Any part of what is provided here can also be used to get ready for coming in off the bench, breaks in play, or at halftime.

Since you do not have as much time during these breaks, you might do an abbreviated version of the warm-up. Whatever you choose to do, the final element should be explosive (something from the last part of the warm-up described below).

Warming Up Well = Playing Well
Traditional Warm-up = Jogging + Static Stretching = five to ten minutes of playing time to reach desired optimal performance level.
Active Warm-up = Dynamic Stretching + Starts/Accelerations + Active Stretching + Ballistic Movements = starting at a higher level of readiness.

How, When, and What to Do

A warm-up is almost always done as part of a team effort (with the exception of rare situations, such as team tryouts). There are several ways you may choose to use the information in this chapter. You might suggest this program to your coach, and/or ask to take on a leadership role by conducting this new workout with your team. You may also choose to create your own individual warm-up, or use any aspect of this program for individual use during breaks in play. Be creative. Take the initiative. The results will be well worthwhile.

Begin with 10 to 15 minutes of general and basic coordinated movement patterns (i.e., jogging, skipping, side shuffling and carioca [also called grapevine step—moving sideways, the feet alternately cross over each other as the hips and torso twist]). Some static stretching may be interspersed in this time frame (e.g., feet together toe touches for the hamstrings, wide splits for the groin, etc.) Ideally, stretching should be done while standing up. This keeps the body in a playing mode, versus sitting or lying down, which, in essence, relays "misinformation" to the brain, since this is not the way you play.

After this initial 15-minute time frame, you may transition into more soccer-specific skills and movement patterns (i.e., heading, cutting, stopping/starting). The key is to increase intensity consistently and gradually, rather than to build up, slow down, then build up again. After doing soccer skills, move into short starts/accelerations—quick bursts of about five to 15 yards in length. If you use hopping, jumping, or any type of ballistic (i.e., explosive) movement, do it as the pinnacle of the warm-up—right before you begin to play.

At the end of your warm-up, try what Vern Gambetta calls the "bodyscan." This is a brief survey of your body. Take two to three minutes to do your own preferred stretching, or use relevant movements to activate areas of the body as you feel necessary. Athletes are individuals, and thus, each one responds differently to the same stimulus.

Below is a suggested sample warm-up, 30 minutes total time.

A. Active Warm-up—Do this portion over 30 to 50 yards, for five to 10 minutes.

1. Jogging with high (overhead) arm swing, also swing arms across the body, like in a running motion.
2. Skipping, both forward and backward.
3. Carioca (explanation above).
4. Backward shuffle/backpedal. This should be done with a quick-step, quick-hand motion.
5. Backward run. A regular backward stride.
6. Snake run (forward run in the shape of an "s").
7. Diagonal run (plant and cut in a diagonal).
8. Jog, skip, run interspersed with 360° turns (after which you continue).
9. Jog and intermittently touch the ground with one hand, alternating hands.
10. Combine movements (e.g., sprint to backpedal, backpedal to sprint, shuffle to sprint, carioca to sprint).

(Add static stretches at any point after step number 3).

B. Dynamic Stretching —Five to 10 minutes

1. Leg swings—front to back, side to side, rotational (high knee, open leg out, keeping knee bent at 90° angle).
2. Moving—high-knee walking, high-knee open leg out, high-hurdle walk (like going over a track hurdle), alternating feet in and out, i.e., pigeon-toed and bird-toed.
3. Lying down—leg crossovers. Lift and cross each leg over the other leg while lying both prone (stomach), and supine (back). Keep your legs straight and your chest or back on the ground.

(A note regarding stretching: Static stretching, better used as a cool-down, can also be done in the warm-up if it is combined with activity. Interspersed static stretching is okay, just don't use it as the end of the warm-up. The key is the heightening of activity at the end of the warm-up—to be able to step onto the field optimally ready to play).

C. Starts/Accelerations (10 to 15 yards), five to 10 minutes, from the following positions:

1. Soccer start (knees bent, feet facing forward).
2. Staggered start (alternate right and left leg, beginning with each foot slightly forward).
3. Balanced start (off of one leg, beginning with one foot slightly raised).
4. Lateral start (facing sideways, step off with your lead leg. Next, step over and lead off with the back foot (i.e., pivot and start). Change the direction you are facing, and repeat.
5. Backward drop step—right and left foot (with your back facing the direction you want to go, this is like a turning start. It's especially good for those who often duplicate this movement in play, like defenders and goalkeepers.)

D. Jumping & Hopping (Hops are lead-ins, of lesser intensity; jumps for the most dynamic movement, done toward the end of the warm-up.)

1. Moving—Do a double-leg jump, then start/sprint for a five-yard burst. Jump 90°, 180°, 270°, 360° turns, sprinting a five-yard burst after each jump. Do a lateral jump with single leg, and then double-leg. Turn and do a five-yard sprint between each jump.
2. In-place jumps—Squat jump, two legs (a regular jump but from a squat position, and landing in a squat position), five repeats.
3. Jump off of one leg, with bent knee and landing with bent knee, five repeats for each leg.
4. Simulated heading jump (do jumping headers without the ball), five repeats.

Cool-Down

After playing, a deactivation of intensity is warranted. You want to put the body back in a relaxed state. But don't do so by simply stopping physical activity just because the final whistle blows. Do some light jogging and thorough static stretching, particularly of the lower body—legs, groin, and hips. Doing this will help revive your legs, and you'll be in a better position to compete again. It is especially important on days you have more than one game. A thorough cool-down is vital in typical youth tournaments, in which you might play up to five games in a weekend. Without proper recovery, the more you play, the slower and more sore you will be, and the greater your risk of injury will be.

At UNC, we cool down as a group. Our cool-down is a total physical and mental decompression. A cool-down can have a social or team-bonding aspect—jogging with friends, talking about the game, laughing and enjoying yourself. It's a good time to support the players who live on an emotional roller coaster, or, comfort your goalkeeper if the ball went through her legs for a goal. I know how important this can be. When I coached the U.S. National Team, Julie Foudy's eternal optimism during cool-downs made her like the beacon in the midst of the team.

Coming in off the Bench

Before players come in off the bench, I usually try to give them a few minutes to prepare, both physically and psychologically. (At UNC, we have preannounced substitute patterns, so the players know when they are going in.) You may not have much notice, but at the very least, try to get your core body temperature up in order to get into the flow of the game immediately, rather than coming in frozen.

Obviously, you should be plugged into the game by having paid attention from the bench. Game analysis and self-analysis is critical. Often, the coach will give you some instructions, but notice for yourself the mistakes being made, and determine how you can try to solve them, and to contribute, by going in.

Some players take a while to get into the game, and some are "fast starters." The best goal-scorer off the bench in the history of our program is Rakel Karvelsson ('95–'98), currently playing for the Philadelphia Charge of the WUSA. When she went in, things happened.

————————

Rakel Karvelsson ('95–'98)

Coming in off the Bench

I grew up playing soccer. I moved to Georgia from California and eventually played for the Lightning Soccer Club. Like every other player who competes at the ODP level, I had set my hopes on playing collegiate soccer. I was looking at several schools, and when Anson called, well, let's just say I was pretty surprised! I had to make a decision. My heart was for UNC, but I was turning down full scholarships elsewhere. Now, I love my grand-

Here's a great shot of Rakel Karvelsson penetrating with the ball in full stride.

father. He is an exceptional man. Apparently he had advised my father that one could always make money, but that a person wouldn't always have this opportunity. I chose UNC.

My parents dropped me off at teammate Sarah Dacey's apartment in Chapel Hill. I can remember the feeling of being on my own for the first time. Our first meeting together as a team was overwhelming. Surrounded by names and well-known players, I was a little intimidated. Then Anson arrived and addressed us casually, welcoming the freshmen and upperclassmen. The way he spoke was so magnetic. I couldn't believe I was actually there.

The girls were very friendly and welcoming, but once we stepped onto the field, it was a battlefield. It took a while, but once I got used to playing at that pace and intensity, I thought to myself, "I can really do this." My confidence gradually started building. I didn't expect to play much my first year, but I had hopes to eventually.

I struggled a lot with how much I played. I wanted more than anything to be out on that field. So, naturally I wondered if I was good enough. I truly felt that I was, but Anson made the decisions on who would start. I never consistently started in my career at Carolina; nonetheless, Anson invested in me. He always gave me what he could. As far as confidence goes,

I had that. I just wanted to be out there on the field as much as possible. Throughout most of my time at Carolina, that was my mind-set. I focused so much on the times I wasn't out on the field, instead of really understanding what my grandfather had said about this opportunity.

I had the experience at Carolina of coming in off the bench to help spark my team. Once I was called by Anson to go in, it was like a rush of energy to get out there. And the talent that surrounded me made it easy to do well. Here I was at the best soccer school in the country, playing alongside the most talented women in the game, and yet I was focusing on the wrong thing. I thought I wanted more than anything to play more. But, I look back now and am thankful for everything.

God has taught me so much through soccer—humility and selflessness. It is such a good training ground for your character, so many emotions and feelings raging all at once. While playing one summer in Iceland, I had been training spiritually as well as physically. Then something happened to me in our most important game of the season. I was completely at peace in my mind. Nothing moved me. I had no thoughts of anxiety or fear or whether or not I would play well. Instead, I was able to move across the field unhindered. I had no recollection of fatigue, or hesitation in my decision-making. I can remember admiring every move and pass that was made by either team. It was incredible. I can't even remember if I played well that day. Somehow, it wasn't important. I wish I had experienced that game sooner, because I know it would have helped my perspective at Carolina.

Looking back, I think the most important thing that matters is your perspective. I wouldn't have known that such peace on the field existed unless it happened to me. I wish I could go back to Carolina knowing that. It would have changed how I felt about not playing as much as I would have liked. I felt free once I was off the bench, but it was a challenge to stay content. I didn't know Anson thought I was the best player coming off the bench. That came as a surprise.

I recall a game when I let the fact that I didn't play almost ruin what turned out to be a blessing. It was the ACC Championship, my junior year. We were playing Clemson in the semifinal. Anson always put me in the first half with about 20 minutes to go. This time, he didn't. I started to feel worse and worse. We were tied 1-1 at the half. At the start of the second half, Anson told me to warm up. It was freezing cold, and I couldn't feel my toes. I got into the game and decided to just run around to keep warm. Well, I managed to score two goals in about 15–20 minutes. It was incredible. I don't think I'll ever forget that, because I was just thinking about how much I wanted to go in, and it was easy to focus on negative thoughts. And then, it all changed in an instant.

Instead of getting down about the fact that you're not in there, you could try to stay positive and ready for when you are called to go in, and make that difference.

There have been a lot of times in my career, and even now in the professional league (WUSA), when I felt I was playing well, but wasn't getting the playing time. And it's then that I remember how easy it is to allow circumstances to disrupt my peace. It is very difficult when you see only what's presented to you at the time.

It's very easy to overanalyze, and do too much thinking on the field. That's when I tend to question myself and hesitate while playing. Then it's not fun for me. But if I can feed into, and maintain that peace within myself, things happen on the field.

Anson has always been strategic in his coaching. He taught us to frame the goal on shots, about box organization, and types of services from the endlines—which were just understood. But within these teachings, he stressed the importance of being creative and always, always having the courage to take players on!

That's one thing I treasure about Carolina. Anson is such a promoter of individualism—taking people on, creative attacking. Instead of being afraid to take on, he made us train and train until we became the best at it. So now I love to do that. That's my favorite part of the game, because I became so comfortable doing it.

I think Anson has been so successful because he invests in each one of his players. He invested in me, and I'm so thankful for it. He believed in me, and I knew that in my heart. I was able to carry that onto the field. When someone believes in you, it's so powerful. I'm so grateful to him for keeping such a high standard for me. He always shared with me what I needed to work on to be better, and now, in the professional league, I know what he's talking about. There's so much more in me that I can give.

Ultimately, I think having to come off the bench is definitely a challenge, and reveals and builds your character, because in the end, everyone just wants to play. That's hard, and always will be. Someone's always going to be better, faster, more technical. Whatever you have that your opponent does not, use it that day to be your best.

Winning and Losing—Keeping Perspective

Is winning everything? I know that's how it often seems, especially in youth soccer. But if you have read my ideas in earlier chapters, you will understand that while winning is wonderful, I believe it is not as important as the kind of athlete—and person—this game helps you to become.

Sometimes it's hard to keep winning and losing in perspective. A look at the sidelines proves that. Even if you feel you can handle the outcome of a game, the adults may have a long way to go. I suggest you give them a great book that I also recommended in Chapter 11, *Will You Still Love Me If I Don't Win?* It describes the overwhelming emotional issues young athletes deal with that parents often don't comprehend.

Winning and losing both have their place. At UNC, you could say we prepare to win by continually losing. Facing the adversity of loss is part of a process that makes you stronger. Danielle Egan ('91–'94), one of our former players, was on a youth National Team that lost a game in Europe. Knowing she was part of our winning program at UNC, her coach said to her in a joking way, "How does it feel to lose?" Danielle answered back, "Coach, at UNC we lose in practice every day."

This is a great statement about all of our players. It's not that they enjoy losing a game, but they can handle it, because they face losing continually. I like this quote from basketball coach Phil Jackson's book, *Sacred Hoops*, "Losing is the lens through which you see yourself more clearly and experience in the blood and bones the transient nature of life." I also like how it can harden you, nowhere better expressed than in Rilke's poem "The Man Watching" in the Preface. The perspective that there is something larger about winning or losing is critical for players, coaches, and parents to understand. While I praise competition, I also think too much of our culture wraps success around winning and losing. Athletics only has value if it has an impact on the people who participate in it. It's what we bring to it that gives athletics that value. If we feel that losing is some sort of anathema, and that we should all punish ourselves following a loss, we have not brought the correct spirit to the game.

At UNC, we've always considered it critical to do our best, but we've never allowed our success to go to anyone's head. We know that it can be gone in a heartbeat. It's the nature of the sport. Even if we play an exceptional game, we can lose with one good shot into the upper corner of the goal by our opponent. We can outshoot a team 40 to one, and still lose one to zero.

Most of us who have competed for a long time understand the enormous value of both winning and losing. If we win, hopefully it doesn't go to our heads. We don't suffer from delusions of grandeur, but rather, we are gracious and kind and yet still focused on continuing our success. If we lose, we maintain that same spirit, but with the determination to recover and play better the next time. How we respond to both winning and losing is our measure as people, and therefore, it is critical to go into competition with the right attitude.

When I think of defining moments in winning or losing, I think of the story I tell in Chapter 5 about how Cindy Parlow displayed such character after our loss to Notre Dame. What also comes to mind is our loss to the University of Florida in the 1999 NCAA final. I do not consider that game a defeat of our team. I believe the team won in the way it lost. All of the qualities about which I speak were evident in our players that day. They were humble, gracious in defeat, and accepted responsibility. Of course, they were disappointed, but they were not crushed. They knew the sun would rise the next morning.

People who understand winning know that there are so many elements that make it fragile, especially in college athletics, in which we play a single-game elimination championship series. There is absolutely no guarantee that even if you work yourself to death, and do everything right, that you will win. Everyone wants to create a formula for success that says if you work incredibly hard, things will always go your way. But they don't. But within the construction of character, you still have to take responsibility for losing. I believe that distributing blame, or making excuses, is a very poor way to approach defeat.

As the expression goes, you want to "control the controllables." Most often, winning isn't one of those. For this reason, I'm always shocked when I hear players say after a game, "I knew we were going to win." What goes through my mind is, "I knew we were going to try hard; I knew we weren't going to quit, but knowing we're going to win..." Every time a player says this, I always cringe. But I never want to disagree, because if that is her mantra for helping her or the team to succeed, I want her to keep it. But I've watched enough soccer games to know there are thousands of ways you can lose, and you can hardly know ahead of time which of them may unfold.

Even though I think our success at UNC is why you're reading this book, it is not our defining quality. Our defining quality is the construction of character, done with a balance created by a laissez faire, light-hearted attitude that is strewn throughout all of our high standards and ambition to be the best.

CHAPTER 17

Being a Team Player

We are talking here about teamwork at a rarefied level,
a swarm of people acting as one.

—From an article on the UNC women's soccer team
in *Fortune* magazine, 1/19/96

On November 20, 1999, Anson Dorrance read this letter from former UNC player Angela Kelly ('91–'94) to his team in the locker room right before an NCAA play-off game, a single game elimination tournament.

Dear Anson:

Hi, how are things going in "Chapel Thrill?" I've been keeping up with the Heels all season, and for the most part, it sounds as if things are going well. A couple of hits, but I always remember you getting excited about possibly losing a couple in the season. Sometimes you tried to schedule difficult situations so that we would lose, so that we would never be complacent. I think it was so you could also be more challenged as a coach.

As you know Anson, the kids seem different these days than we were then. The mentality is different, and there seems to be a tremendous sense of entitlement. Working your butt off just to be a part of the big picture to help your teammates when things aren't going their way— that selflessness is not as prevalent anymore. Maybe we were just so lucky that at North Carolina we would have died for one another because we genuinely cared about each other. Expressing that on the field, working our butts off in practice and in games, day in and day out, was just our way of telling each other that we cared and everyone meant so much. No one would have dared to give any less than one hundred percent when that Carolina shirt was on her back.

At the expense of talking for my friends, there isn't one of us—Vench (Tisha Venturini), Mia (Hamm), Lil (Kristine Lilly), or myself, who wouldn't love to have those days back. Just to feel connected again. All the little things — the high-fives, the band playing, assisting your buddy, clearing the ball off the line, dominating every team that we play. Please tell the team good luck. I hope they can see beyond themselves and their own individual responsibilities. They aren't playing for themselves or the '99 Championship. It goes beyond that. They're playing for their teammates, the tradition, and everyone who's ever been affiliated with the program. We would all die to be back in their shoes.

Angela Kelly ('91–'94)

The Team Bond

What I remember about UNC soccer is not games, or the national championships, but the experience of the family atmosphere.

Cindy Parlow ('95–'98)

Being part of a team has meaning far beyond what takes place on the soccer field. At UNC, the memories our players take with them after they graduate are not so much the championship titles, but the friendship and sense of family that they experience. Interestingly, when you cut a player even from the ultimate level—the U.S. National Team—she'll often say it's not the soccer that she misses, it's the friends. Her social life changes when she is no longer with the team.

The athletic arena forges relationships that are incredibly unique for all different kinds of reasons, some of them quite unexpected. While being on a team reveals everyone's character—good or bad—people form connections regardless of who they are. If your soccer experience is properly constructed, one of the best aspects of being on a team is the sense of belonging, no matter who you are. What makes team sports special is this universal acceptance. The great teams are comprised of all types of people, some of whom may even have limited playing ability, or psychological quirks.

In their everyday lives, these people might not be accepted, but just by virtue of being members of the team, they are embraced and supported.

What you gain from great teams will probably benefit you more as a human being than as an athlete. The team experience teaches you tolerance, loyalty, and gives you a type of long-term security that you will find hard to get in other aspects of your life.

Cindy Parlow's quote emphasizes that teams create a tremendous sense of family. When I resigned from coaching the U.S. National Team, Tony DiCiccio was ready and stepped in. He was family, because he had previously been the goalkeeper trainer, and all the players liked him. April Heinrichs is now at the helm. As a captain of our original U.S. National Team in 1991, she was part of our soccer family. I think this sense of continuity shows how we genuinely believe in ourselves as a community.

Powerful personal connections exist all around you. They are created by the nature of being part of a team, and strengthened by special individuals. When I was coach of the U.S. National Team in the early 1990s, a sports psychologist came to speak. He talked about the tremendous chemistry the team had. "Have you ever thanked the people responsible for it?" he asked. He was referring to Julie Foudy, whom, as I have previously mentioned, personifies the chemistry of the National Team.

Perhaps you know a person like Julie on your team. She obviously has good and bad days, but I know that when I was coaching, we never saw Julie's down times. Regardless of what was going on in her life, Julie just kept giving. She was unbelievably positive and fun to be with, and the comments she made to her teammates were always supportive.

When the psychologist asked that question, I thought to myself, "No, I haven't thanked Julie. I've really taken those kind of people for granted, and that shouldn't be the case." I recall that in a very small ceremony, laced with humor, obviously, we thanked Julie for who she is. Even though it seemed a bit artificial to thank someone in that kind of context, it forced us all to recognize this quality in her, and to remember the people who sustain the chemistry that makes a team great.

What Makes a Good Team

I think a great example of a good team is one that I am currently coaching as I write this book. I've spoken about this 2000 team with both the players and with my staff. This group has all the ingredients of a good team. In my 24 years of college coaching, I probably had the best off-season with them than with any other team. They had all the elements for a good team. It also helped that they were, for the most part, all together in one place. In recent years, we would be missing three to five great players while they were off in residency in the spring, training with the U.S. National Team.

The longer I've coached, the more I've come to realize that having a good team basically boils down to a combination of talent, work ethic and leadership. A good team obviously has a lot to do with the athletic ability of the players, but it also has to do with their motivation and ambition, how well they are led by the upper classmen, and how much they enjoy being with each other.

A team plays well in-season depending on how it constructs itself during the off-season. Every Tuesday in the off-season we conduct a meeting on leadership with the rising seniors. The rest of the team does something similar. This year the rest of the team was part of a seminar called "The Champions' Conversation." It was about personal growth, accountability, and taking personal responsibility for your own success.

A good team is comprised of a community of human beings respected for their humanity, that accepts players of all ranges of ability, and that can figure out a way to handle all their differences, so that despite them, they still connect and bond. A team is defined by its chemistry—how the players click as a unit. Chemistry is established by the individuals. Actually, the measure of good chemistry is the melding of two extremes: the best and most popular player on the roster, and the worst and least popular. If the super stars can figure out a way to make even the most average player feel she is an important part of the team, that's a critical step. If someone is not playing much, and isn't really gaining the benefits or rewards that the starters are, and yet she has a positive attitude—this impacts positively on team chemistry. The possibility of this bond, from top player to bottom, is what makes team athletics special.

Chemistry will always be challenged by differences in players, though, particularly the emergence of a star. In 2000, Alyssa Ramsey, who has played for the National Team, came in as a starting freshman. This threatened the team, particularly the seniors. Their first reaction was to "teach her a lesson" by ostracizing Alyssa socially. The resentment that an older player who doesn't start feels toward the youngest starter on the team made it difficult for a player like Alyssa. In typical female culture, this meant Alyssa was supposed to genuflect and acquiesce to the rest of the team in order to become accepted as a part of it. Of course, that is not desirable in the athletic culture. As a player, it is important that Alyssa maintain a personality that goes out and fights the competition, so it would not be good for her to develop the kind of personality that bows down.

We experienced a stressful few weeks over this wrinkle in our team chemistry. My job as the coach of the team is to support a player like Alyssa, and not let a witch-hunter tear her down in order to elevate or protect themselves. I wanted our leadership to embrace Alyssa's strengths and support them. I spoke to one of the key seniors, who had been a freshman during a similarly rough period for the team. "I want Alyssa to carve you up," I told her. "You don't want her to genuflect to you, because then when we're playing, she won't be a warrior. Let her know she is welcome by saying to her, in essence, "Listen, your whole life your strength has not been embraced by your culture, but you have arrived at a safe haven, because at the University of North Carolina we love powerful, strong, aggressive women like you."

This tension between Alyssa and the witch-hunter threatened the culture and standards of the team. Fortunately, things changed. The team did embrace Alyssa and she went on to a brilliant freshman year. She loves it here. After the team accepted her, I could see her beaming with her teammates. She could feel their acceptance and support, and it was that key senior who protected her, and made it happen.

This type of result is vital to a cohesive team, but a coach can only be a part of it. There are certain people with tremendous character, integrity, and compassion who can hold an entire team together. Elizabeth Marslander ('95–'96) is one of them. She was on the team during one of our most difficult stretches in terms of chemistry, and she had a huge impact. She kept us together, because everyone loved her. She never played, yet she was our team captain. She gave so much without getting anything back.

You may feel that being part of a team with lesser players, even if they are great people, impedes your soccer development. You have to sort out what's important to you. Obviously, some environments—like a team of top performers—are going to make you a better player. Another environment might make you a better person. You may find these two qualities do not exist on one team. Ideally, you can experience both, but be assured, the latter is most important.

What do you do if your team chemistry is bad? Believe it or not, you can have an impact. One of our team books, *The Leadership Moment* (on Chapter 4's recommended reading list), opens with a great quote from John F. Kennedy's *Profiles in Courage*. "To be courageous...is an opportunity that sooner or later is presented to all of us." If you're on a team with bad chemistry, this is your leadership moment. You have an opportunity to turn it around. It's difficult. The soccer is easier. You may see a bad situation, and are shy or reluctant to say or do anything, but a leadership moment is being presented to you. You don't have to do anything, but if you do, you are a leader.

You can see from this photograph the emotional commitment of these teammates. It looks like the soccer equivalent of the "Spirit of '76." You can also see the crowd in the background in a standing ovation—praising the 4-3 overtime game against NC State in the 1990 NCAA quarterfinal, in which the lead changed on three separate occasions. Soccer America has called it the "Greatest Game in Women's Soccer History." Defender Linda Hamilton (left) and midfielder Kristine Lilly (right) assist forward Mia Hamm off the field.

It takes a lot of work, but you can change the team atmosphere by having a persistently positive attitude, by not letting negative or destructive behavior prevail (such as blaming, or talking behind each others' backs). You can try to bring everyone together. This is exactly what Elizabeth Marslander did for us. If you are one of the better players, good chemistry is created by how you bring others within your circle of respect. A younger, or newer, player does this by displaying gestures of support and respect, no matter what her role on the team. In England, young players shine everyone else's boots (cleats). It shows a sense of respect for the veteran players. For example, even though the new girl may be a starter, she may climb to the back of a van, and let the older players sit up front.

In our leadership meetings we try to imprint traditions—what's tolerated and what's not. In the youth game this is mostly left to chance. If you're on a great team with great people, you're lucky. If you are poorly led, by a else), take some responsibility. Change the situation. In other words, be a leader.

Another impediment to good team chemistry is presented by the issue of playing time. The kinds of players we recruit at UNC have always started, so it is hard when they don't. This is always the first challenge to the chemistry. In this case, a logistical step can help. I think one of the mistakes many coaches make is to declare their starting lineup too late. This often causes surprise and disappointment. The sooner the starters are selected, the better, and substitutions based on practice performance should also be clear from the beginning. This gives everyone time to collect themselves and focus on their mission, which is supporting the team in whatever role they are assigned. It also gives the nonstarters a clear message that they have some more work to do to have an impact, and this can be very positive and motivational.

As I said above, maintaining the team bond often falls on the shoulders of individual players. My all-time favorite story on the subject of personal responsibility and team loyalty is one I tell at our girls' summer camps. Tracey Bates Leone ('85–'89) was my starting left midfielder when I coached the U.S. National Team. On a trip to Italy, Kristine Lilly beat her out for that spot. We were staying in a hotel with only one telephone, located underneath a stairwell. Late one night, after I had gone out for a run and was stretching near the stairs, I could hear Tracey on the phone with her mother. "No, I passed all my fitness tests.... No, Anson's not mad at me," Tracy said. Then, bursting into tears she added, "Don't you understand Mom, Kristine is just better than I am."

I could tell that in an effort to comfort Tracey, her mother was giving her every possible reason to pass on blame for not playing, to desert her mission with the team, and Tracey wouldn't accept it. She didn't make excuses for why she wasn't playing; she accepted the reality, which was that Kristine was better than she was.

We won the World Championship later that year, and Tracey was a big part of that. Underneath her photo in the media guide, in answer to the question, "Who do you most admire?" Tracey had said: "Kristine Lilly." That's class. That's honorable. That's depth of character. It's also rare.

The Personality of Position

Despite the fact you're a member of a team, you must still develop your individual player personality. As I mention in Chapter 3, even within the team context, there are varying individual roles. It helps to understand which ones define you.

Over the years I've noticed that fundamental characteristics exist as soon as someone begins playing, and most of these never really change. Obviously, to some degree, players may develop in different areas, but their fundamental style of play will stay with them. Those who are technically creative as youngsters will probably be that way as they get older. Those who rely on their athleticism will retain that as their mark. The 10-year-old who loves the ball may grow up to become an incredibly skillful midfield play-maker or attacking personality, while the player who loves the competition will likely be the defensive midfielder, whose main joy in life is to destroy the creativity of her opposing attacking midfielder.

It isn't that you can't change some players; you can. But I think every person has a secret passion to be a certain type of player. When Mia Hamm was brought onto the U.S. National Team at age 15, she was already a goal-scoring personality. She wanted to score goals in the worst way. After the 1991 World Championship, when we discovered our weakness to serve balls over distance—a skill she had developed well as a striker—we tried to put her in the back to help our poor range of service out of the back. You could see her just wilt under this new assignment. Her personality simply did not take to her playing in a position other than one in which she was scoring goals.

Positions are based on your psychological, as well as your physical, dimensions. There's the assertive, risk-taking personality that is required of strikers—a positive arrogance that's part of the truly extraordinary strikers, as well as of goalkeepers. At the other extreme are the defenders, a remarkably responsible group of people on whom you can build your house. They're a great foundation. They always make decisions for the good of the team. You can rely on them. Then there's the classic midfielder—a confident, pugnacious battler, who's always in people's faces as if looking for fights. This extraordinary midfielder wants the ball the entire time, and duels constantly—not just with her match-up—but against anyone who has the guts to come into her territory. With her extraordinary work rate, she marks out larger and larger territories on the field, restricted only by her fitness capabilities.

You and Your Coach

A major determining factor in the quality of a team experience is your relationship with the coach. Your experience with any coach depends not only on your personal goals and your temperament, but on understanding the dynamics of the coach/athlete relationship.

Many people wonder when more women will get into coaching soccer. I think it's happening. The current international players are going to become our top soccer coaches of the future. Many of them are still playing, but quite a few of our UNC grads with National Team experience have already transitioned into high-level coaching, such as Shannon Higgins-Cirovski ('86–'89), April Heinrichs, and Tracey Bates Leone.

The fact is that currently most girls are coached by men. Male coaches have to adjust to working with females, and female players have to gain some insight into coaching styles. For one thing, you have to be aware that generally speaking, males separate criticism of the game from criticism of you personally. I've found that many girls struggle to tell the difference.

Understanding the motives and styles of your coaches will give you invaluable insight in how to relate to them. The bottom line is that it is a coach's ambition to make you and the team better, and so that coach creates environments to try to make that happen.

If you can keep this perspective in mind, you will be less intimidated or uncomfortable around a coach who may strike you as critical. The point is that different people bring different personalities to coaching. Some are aggressive, some are not. Some screamers are incredibly great coaches, while some quieter ones are horrible. You can't use one quality to determine if your coach is good or bad. Two basic criteria determine the quality of the coach. First, whether you are enjoying the game, and second, whether you are getting better. Sometimes a coach who makes you uncomfortable or upsets you is also making you a better player. And while even though you might love to have a more gentle, nicer person, or a great communicator, some coaches just don't have these qualities.

It will help you to create a positive player/coach dynamic if you continually attempt to see things from the coach's perspective. Most coaches aren't getting paid. If they are, they certainly aren't buying a yacht with their salary. The reason they are coaching is because they are generous human beings, giving of their free time. They would love to believe that what they are doing is helping you and others to become better soccer players and, ideally, good people. Coaches are trying to construct players. No coach wants to destroy a player.

Coaching is not a scientific formula, and it's not a one-way street. I've had the experience of trying to hit some button with a player, and yet to help her get better, or overcome some obstacle, I need to know when something has been particularly helpful, or when it completely undermines that player's confidence. Communicating this is also the player's responsibility. That's why I'm convinced that you can contribute to your environment— set your own standards—and work toward establishing the relationship you want with your coach. Yes, you can make him or her better, but you have to share honestly what you feel.

If you're having a tough time with a coach, try to work through it by using a positive approach. Open up a dialogue. Come up to him or her after something you feel is particularly good and reinforce it. "Hey coach, that was a great session. What I like was…, or, "It's really helping me to build my confidence," or "This was more fun than that," or if you're trying to encourage a change in that person's behavior, "Thanks for not yelling at me. I know it shouldn't bother me, but it does." Maybe with this opening approach, the coach can then share with you why he or she had you do something in particular, even if it wasn't so much fun.

If you feel you simply have a bad coach—one who, despite an ambition to make you better, is either inexperienced or not talented—you can help that person with positive reinforcement. Be assured that if you approach a coach with the proper spirit, and reinforce what is constructive, it will be reinjected into practices and games. If you share with a coach, he or she is going to learn too, and take note of what is positive and helpful.

If you feel the need to be critical of a coach, it should be done with the correct tone and the correct intent. This is just human relations. Criticism should not be done publicly. (Frankly, even praise should be given privately.) The telephone is good, because it is immediate and allows feedback. Those who don't feel they have the courage to be out-front with their comments, or are really struggling, should write a short note or e-mail if they cannot telephone.

It all gets back to your love of the game. You have to find the core reason why you play, and visit that at every opportunity. If, however, despite all your efforts the coach/athlete relationship is destroying you—if it prevents you from enjoying the game or getting better—you have to pull out. There has to be some positive reason that keeps you coming back. If you can no longer find that, you have to take measures to rescue yourself.

All that being said, I believe that the majority of coach/player relationships are positive, or millions of young people wouldn't be playing soccer. Over the years, I have enjoyed the range of player personalities. Obviously, I've had many great experiences, or I wouldn't still be coaching.

Player/coach relationships, constructed by the player based on her needs and personality, can be very different. There are some players who want constant feedback or a strong personal bond, and some who don't want any. Tracey Bates Leone and Mia Hamm are among those with whom I've had very close coaching relationships. Relationships are dictated by the player, based on what she is comfortable with, and her emotional, psychological, and social needs.

There are other relationships that are close, but with players who require little outward connection. They enjoy working themselves hard without our discussing it, yet there is a great mutual respect between us. When Susan Ellis ('80–'84) played at UNC, she never said a word to me. Sometimes, I would say something to her, and she would just nod or grunt, yet Susan is a model of what we do at UNC. I knew when she played she was trying to become the best she could be, and while visibly I had no connection with her, she is now among our most loyal former players. Without my knowledge, during her years at UNC, we were developing a bond so unbelievably strong that if Bill Palladino were to leave us today, perhaps to coach in the WUSA, Susan—a loyal, funny, and tremendous athlete, who has been the Field Director of our summer camps for a number of years and is currently assisting Marcia McDermott with the Carolina Courage of the WUSA—would be the one I'd bring in to replace him.

Another person in this category is Tisha Venturini. She and I may not have exchanged more than four words in the four years she was at UNC, yet we had a great connection. I only knew this because, according to her roommate and teammate Angela Kelly, when I resigned as coach of the U.S. National Team, Tisha was devastated.

You don't have to build an intense bond with your coach. If, like Tisha, you're a self-sustaining, intrinsically motivated person, you just might not need that. But even this kind of athlete has a way of communicating. Just as a few spoken words or an e-mail might help you air a problem, the same gesture can be a meaningful expression of gratitude to a coach. Because the player/coach dynamic can be so intimidating to the player, some of the most powerful messages I've been given by my players have been in a letter or an e-mail. They have made a big difference to me. I have received wonderful letters and e-mails that help make my job worthwhile, some of which you can read in this book. Some players express their gratitude in simple ways, but you never forget it. One day in practice, Raven McDonald ('97–'99) came up to me and said, "Thanks for being my coach." That's all, but I was on cloud nine for a month.

As I've continually said, there is meaning to soccer far beyond the game itself. Your experience being a member of a team is probably the deepest expression of that meaning.

Tisha Venturini ('91–'94)

The Coach/Athlete Relationship

I've been very lucky throughout my career. Since I was a little kid, I did everything on my own. When I was five, I started playing soccer with my brother and his buddies. I loved it, so I never needed anyone to whack me over the head and say, "Come on, don't you want to get out there and play your hardest?" No one had to force me to try; that's something I did naturally.

Every player is different. Some people need a little push from someone, and that's fine. There were several players on our team at UNC who needed that push from Anson, or a little extra attention from him. He was bright enough to know who they were, and when to do that. Speaking for myself, I always did everything because I wanted to. I played from my heart. That made it easier for me in my relationships with my coaches. I've never really relied on my coaches to motivate me to compete. I don't think anyone can do that, because it's something you need to have inside yourself. Support and positive feedback from coaches is always good, but you can't rely on someone else to get you to play. You can't look to coaches to carry you through a game if you're struggling.

I was very shy. That might have partly affected my relationships with coaches. I didn't run right up to them and introduce myself. I didn't hang out with them a lot when I wasn't playing. I'd show up to practice, and listen to what they told me to do. Then I'd do it, and say good-bye at the end of the day. Again, I respected and was friends with these coaches, but they were mostly there to structure the practice and give me advice and feedback.

I wasn't cocky, but I was confident, and secure in my life outside of soccer. I didn't need extra attention. I didn't need praise. I got that from my family. A lot of people I've played with would crumble for a week if the coach yelled at them. I think 80 percent of that probably comes from someone's personality, and her background.

I'm not outwardly really close to people, except for a select few. A lot of kids latch onto a coach because they need someone. I have a wonderful family and group of friends. I'm comfortable with that. A lot of kids don't have anyone, so they completely connect to a coach. Let's say that coach yells at them for some reason, because the coach is going to yell at everybody at some point. I get yelled at all the time. That comes from coaching, not friendship. I think a lot of people get those mixed up. You have to separate them.

The unanimous selection for National Player of the Year in 1994, Tisha was a leader on our NCAA Championship team all four of her years at Carolina. She went on to a career in the Olympics, World Cup and currently plays in the WUSA.

I've had a great history with my coaches. Early on, I think I did more than they expected from me. I come from Modesto, California. There's a lot of soccer there now, but there wasn't when I was growing up. I had my first coach at about age eight. He didn't even know the rules. My early coaches would read the rule book while they were coaching. Everyone was new, so we were all diving in head first together. At that age, you mainly need someone to blow a whistle and say, "Go!" There wasn't much coaching going on at my early level, but I always remember it was very positive. I think that's the way it needs to be when kids are that young. At least up to age 12, soccer is about getting out there and being a team player. It's about fun. It was not much about competition for me at that age, which is what I think it's turned into now. That's terrible. When I was young, we'd go out and have fun, but we didn't necessarily keep score, and there were no negative comments. I was lucky. One nasty coach could have turned me off, and I wouldn't be playing soccer today.

When I was 10, my dad got a call from a boys' travel team. The coach had seen me play, and wanted me to come out for his team. My dad was a little hesitant, but my mom said, "That's great. Let's go." That coach, John Selecky, was wonderful. He treated me like everyone else. He basically opened the door. He told me, "You can play with whoever you want. You're an excellent player with unlimited possibilities. Keep playing and you're going to be great."

Coaches should treat everyone the same, whether you're the star player or never get in the game for a minute. This guy did. He made me feel like part of the team, which I played on for two years. That's when I really started to gain an edge. I was playing with boys every day who were a little faster, a little stronger, a little smarter—and I developed really quickly during that time.

When I got to be about 12 or 13, I was ready to play with girls. Up until age 14, I still had coaches who didn't know too much. One guy was a track coach, so we ran a lot. It was naive coaching, but it was still good, because they were positive people. They might not have been so good at teaching skills, but they were always good at the attitude part and the having fun part. That was okay with me because I did the skills on my own. It might not have been good for other players, but emphasizing fun and not putting pressure on us kept me involved, because then I started playing ODP. That's when I got some serious coaching from some of the best coaches in Northern California.

I had a coach named Rick Caldwell, who is still very big in women's soccer in Northern California. He was a hilariously funny, goofy guy, always telling jokes, but when we'd get onto the field, it was business. We'd play hard. He was perfect for me at age 13. I think he was a great transition coach for playing in college and on the National Team.

Since I was on ODP State and Regional teams, my high school soccer was for fun. I wanted to play hard and to win, and so did my teammates, but it was more about our friendships. I still learned a lot from my coach, Marsha Hoagland, about being a team player and how to become a leader. She made me captain of the team. Later, she would show up all over the country if I had a big game with the National Team. She still comes to my games in the Bay Area.

I felt so much more comfortable in high school. Then, I'd go with the ODP teams and it was a little setback, because I was a bit more shy, and nervous. I wasn't one of the leaders. It was a good balance between the fun of high school, and ODP, where I was taught, and went to play, big-time soccer.

Anson was my first taste of the real deal, though. I was so young and naive when I first got to UNC that I didn't think. I just dealt with it. I don't remember being totally crushed by anything Anson said to me. There were so many kids who would just crumble before my eyes if he'd say something to them. I wasn't going to let that happen to me. Every time he spoke to me, I took it very seriously. He got on me a little and I'd think, "I've got to get my stuff together. I'm not cutting it," because I wanted to play hard for him. I thought he was the most intelligent coach I've had to this point, and I admired everything he said. I took it to heart. I guess he didn't know that.

I waited for every pregame speech of Anson's. They would get me so fired up. Most of the time, I could get myself ready and motivated, but if I couldn't, he did it, in a snap. That was great, but maybe you're next coach doesn't do that, so you have to learn to do it for yourself, and I did. But I took a lot from Anson. He inspired me to play, and gave me the mentality that I was going to be the best.

My current coach, Ian Sawyers (who is Julie Foudy's husband) is very intense on the field, perhaps even more so than Anson. I love it. I've already learned so much from him in just the few months I've been on the team. We're all professionals on the field. We're there to play soccer. That's our job, and we're expected to be good at it. He can have a go at us on the field, but when we come off, he gives us a handshake. That's what's great about a coach like this. He doesn't get so caught up. He can lose it on the field and you think, "My gosh, he's a madman." But he comes off and everything is cool. "Now, did you get that?" he asks. He doesn't yell at us and storm off the field and then go home. He comes over and talks to us and ties it all in. I think that's wonderful. Players here totally respect him.

You have to try to have a good relationship with your coaches. I think you have to listen to them, follow what they're saying, and believe in it. Show respect. Outwardly, you need to demonstrate that you believe in the coach and the team, and that you're a team player. Every coach is different, with a different philosophy, and you're going to have a different relationship with each one.

Some you might not agree with, but it's the way that person is coaching your entire team, and you have to buy into it. If you rebel against your coach or your team, you're not going to last.

It's easy to pick out the player who doesn't show respect, who rolls her eyes when the coach says something. Other players see that and it destroys the team. You need to be as positive as you can, even when you're being criticized. That's the hardest thing to do. But a little bit of criticism makes you a better player, a stronger player—even if you feel the coach doesn't completely know what he or she is talking about.

I've never quit on a coach or a team. I've been lucky that all my experiences have been positive. I know there's some negative situations that I might not relate to, but you always want to outwardly show support for your coach and do everything you can within reason. That's the bottom line. Your teammates will see that respect coming from you.

At the same time, you may have to sugarcoat what the coach says a bit—accept it even with its faults. Ultimately, it's up to you how you're going to play—if you're going to be motivated, or if you're going to make a bad play and let it get to you. You have to be a strong individual player. At a certain level, your coach is there just to guide you, and give a little support and motivation.

On the other hand, don't let a coach totally run your life. It's too easy to get wrapped up in what that person is thinking, or saying. Your coach isn't out on the field with you, and shouldn't be yelling your every move. When game-time comes, you're going to do what you do on your own.

———————

CHAPTER **18**

Becoming the Total Athlete

The fitter you are, the harder it is to surrender

If we want to win next year, basically we need a commitment from everyone in the room that we're going to max out in every way we can, so that we're going to be the best we can be. Does this mean that all of a sudden this becomes a laborious process? No. Maintaining your fitness isn't that hard. What's hard is getting fit. So I think the mistake you can make now that you are relatively fit is to go back and lie on the couch and start eating bonbons. We are meeting right now in order to understand the process, and what we have to go through, to be our best.

—Part of Anson Dorrance's talk at the 2000 edition
of the annual team meeting, held two days after
the NCAA Championship game

Every year, two days after the NCAA Championship, we hold a team meeting. The above quote is part of what I told the team in that meeting in 2000, and in essence, what I say every year. We give the team one day off after the championship, meet the following day, and on day three we begin our defense of that championship, or if we have lost, our assault on the next championship. This is not some vague hope for future success. We are very conscious of the year-round effort it takes to be successful, and how that will get done. There is no reason that the message of that meeting, and the method of preparing our team to win a national collegiate championship, should not include you, the serious youth soccer player.

We believe our program sets a preparation and fitness standard. We are convinced that few other college teams prepare as thoroughly as ours does. We believe that many of the people we play against don't take fitness as seriously as we do, because few people really understand what comprises true fitness. We continually strive to maintain the highest level and standards. True, I think the players we compete with in general have been getting fitter, but as soon as someone meets our standard, we try to raise the bar on ourselves. This is the way we can all help each other get better.

In this annual meeting, we begin a review of all of the elements of athletic success. We believe in constructing athletic bases on a year-round training rhythm, so we don't think there is an off-season for a player's physical development. We believe you should either be maintaining your fitness base, or deepening it. We don't believe in going more than three days in a row without investing in your aerobic base and more than six days in a row without investing in your anaerobic base. If you go longer than this, you lose some of your conditioning. If you don't do something that challenges your agility at least twice a week, you start to lose some of that. In our meeting, we tell the team that our fitness tests, which are conducted when the players return from their three-week winter break, will prove my point.

There are many reasons to get fit. A good fitness program aides your endurance, thus your quality of play. If you are aspiring to join a new team, or starting out on one, there is no greater advantage you can give yourself than coming in as fit as possible. If the tryout process or preseason practice is tough or long, as it is in many cases, being in top condition with these exercises can keep you going strong when others have wilted.

Another aspect of this endurance is the ability to last for the entire season. High school play can include up to three games per week, and no sooner is the season done than players immediately shift to club team play, or begin playing another sport. The college athlete plays up to 24 soccer games a year, and full-time club soccer often includes just as many.

Physical conditioning is definitely a deciding factor in soccer excellence. The message of the 2000 NCAA Championship (and you can see it on any level, time and time again) is that the team that can sustain the highest level of performance (through its fitness and conditioning) has a better chance to win.

My adamant belief in fitness as an essential ingredient of soccer success has deep roots. When I began coaching the women's U.S. National Team in 1991, we set up fitness tests. The players had to achieve a certain standard. If any of them failed, they were cut. All of a sudden, the word went out that if you were going to play on the National Team, you would have to take your personal physical preparation very seriously. The players who learned to meet these standards were only in their teens then. Some of their names are Foudy, Lilly, Hamm, Fawcett, and Overbeck. And their fitness standard—one that also applies at UNC—is maintained to this day.

Making the Decision to Win

From our point of view, and based on our experience at UNC, fitness is one important deciding factor in a player's success. That's why it is an essential aspect of our program. For example, we have some tremendously talented players with the potential to be starters, but they aren't. That's because they didn't pass our fitness tests, and someone else did.

Meredith Florance was the 2000 Player of the Year as a senior at UNC. She had three very good seasons leading up to that, and then an absolutely phenomenal year. The difference in her senior year was that coming in, Meredith conditioned herself like never before. She established a regular personal training rhythm that she had never set up before in her life. In so doing, she completely transformed herself and her game. I told my team in the post-championship meeting that they had to do something similar to what Meredith had done. They had to decide at that minute that they wanted to win the next year. I told them that the 2000 semifinal and final games weren't actually won on a Friday and a Sunday. They were won one year before, when Meredith and the rest of her teammates made the commitment to work year-round, thus making the decision to win.

You have some decisions to make as well. You don't have to be a world-beater to enjoy the game of soccer, but to participate on the highest possible level, and to your fullest capability, you must deepen all of your fitness bases. On top of that, you have to deepen your technical and tactical bases. Sometimes just playing the game will give you what you want, but if you aspire to play at levels like ours, you have to go further. When I'm recruiting a high-level player, I'm always excited to discover that she has participated in some sport or activity that has deepened her fitness bases, and made her a more complete athlete. Doing a strength and conditioning program is one example. Running the 100 or 200 meters in track (which often includes strength and conditioning training) is another. Any activity like this, that promotes explosiveness or strength and requires the discipline and discomfort of pushing physical limits, is a huge plus for a soccer player.

There are good reasons to make your fitness part of a year-round training rhythm. Trust me, everyone who is fit had to suffer at some point. It's work. The process of getting fit can be challenging, but maintaining fitness is not that difficult, as long as you have an understanding of how to do that.

At our annual meeting I discuss how players can maintain their fitness (much of it is in this chapter), and then let them determine what they want to do until we meet up again. My rising juniors and seniors take over their respective leadership duties in directing some off-season team fitness activities. Again, the players must take individual and collective responsibility. For one thing, they have to. That's because NCAA rules do not permit coaches to train their college teams full-time year-round. My parting words in the 2000 meeting were, "You're on your own." And for the next three weeks, they were.

Staying Fit and Sharp on Your Own

On the higher levels of soccer, a great deal of emphasis is placed on individual athleticism. That's one of the things we look for when recruiting players. Athleticism consists of a variety of factors, which can definitely be affected by how much and how hard you work. A part of this athletic ability you're born with, and while you can't change your genetic cards, you can certainly strengthen the hand you've been dealt. Your ability to strengthen that hand depends on your personal ambition. You need look no further for a perfect model of that than to the title of this book, and what inspired it: Mia Hamm, bent over in exhaustion, working out on her own. I loved seeing what she was doing by herself. I knew it was the final piece for her immortality.

What can you do to stay fit in the off-season? To maintain their fitness bases, I invite players on the team to run if they choose. But I advise them not just to go on long, slow distance jogs. This only serves to kill your speed. If you are going to run, do some of it as a sprint. Try a fartlek—after warming up, sprint random distances (e.g., 15 yards to a telephone poll), then jog for recovery. I direct my players to do the fartlek portion of a run for about 20 minutes. But sprinting alone won't do it. You've also got to maintain your agility—if not with soccer, then with something like basketball or hockey. I recall a sprinter on our team who beat all the players running flat-out, but when just one change of direction was added to the test, she went from first place to absolute last.

Fitness should be a part of your foundation, just as it is for us—and built into that foundation are all of the technical aspects of the game, and the study of the game to improve tactically. Following are the soccer skills derived both from what our players do in the off-season on their own, and the more informal spring training we conduct for them as a team. During part of the off-season I also arrange for the team to play some scrimmages with men's teams.

Training Tips

Wall work is what I emphasize the most, which you can also do on your own. Walls are everywhere, but if you fail to find one, try a fence for some of the shooting. Just get closer to it since there is no bounce.

Warm up on the wall with light shooting, just working on pure technique (toe pointed, ankle locked, quick strike). After you've broken out into a light sweat, stretch your leg and groin muscles. Then, hammer balls at the wall. Do this continually, regardless of how the ball comes back at you. Figure out the technically correct way to do a first-time strike. The point is to strike the ball at the wall as hard, low, and as accurately as you can, as if you were finishing.

After the first-touch strikes, we have players clean up the returning balls with one touch, as if they were in a crowded box, and get off a really quick shot. Make sure to do this, and the exercise above, using both feet. Do it for about eight to 15 minutes. The repetitive value of this simple exercise is enormous, because there are so many balls coming back at you.

Next, we have the players move up about two yards from the wall to do some heading. You warm up with some head juggling against the wall. Then, move back five yards, throw the ball up against the wall, and from a standing position, head it into the wall with as much power as you can. Catch it after each header. Then, toss the ball up against the wall so it is now going well above your head, so you have to jump and head it with power. Spend about two to five minutes on this heading.

In our second block of training, we have the players go to the racquetball court once a week. (Depending on where you live, you might want to do this, or something similar, in inclement weather.) We do a combination of turning, passing the ball up against the wall, then turning and passing again to the opposite wall. We do this for one minute, three times, stretching between each segment. A partner counts the number of turns, or balls struck against the wall (of course, we keep score). Then, players team up and play one v. one or two v. two. If you don't have partners, you can still use the wall for the turning and passing, shooting or heading. You can also do volleys off the wall, trying to keep the ball from touching the floor, or quick, one-touch passing, and dribbling. Goalkeepers can use the corners to simulate shot stopping.

For other independent work, we also prescribe the ball gymnastics and figure-eight dribbling detailed in the Summer Training Program (see Appendix II). I also recommend you learn and use Coerver ball skills. We use Coervers as a warm-up all spring. This is good for your skill, agility, and leg strength. If you don't know the work of the Dutch player and coach Wiel Coerver, you can order videotapes from any soccer catalog.

In addition to skills, I highly recommend strength and conditioning, such as the program outlined in Appendix I, as something you should take independent initiative to do. I told the team at our last annual meeting that I'm absolutely sold on weight training, and not just as part of soccer, but as a lifelong activity. This is especially important for females because of the research which confirms that resistance (weight) training is vital for helping maintain healthy bones.

There's an important sociological aspect to weight training. Many young female players are excited about their modern athletic freedom, which allows them to attack in soccer with the same speed and recklessness as young boys. They throw themselves into the fray, and this, coupled with the intense and constant soccer or sports schedule, causes them to get hurt. However, with intense athletics, and the freedom to play physically, comes the responsibility to develop a protective musculature. I notice a dichotomy in girls' soccer. It arises from the clash of the "body image" most young girls and women have to fight, particularly as they go through adolescence. It results in a ridiculous desire to be thin, which is doing enormous harm to our young female athletes, and to all women. Part of the personal conviction about playing powerfully is literally becoming powerful, and developing your musculature is part of that.

Cross Training

In our yearly meeting, I also tell the players that they don't have to focus on soccer in the off-season. There are many cross training substitutes to stay fit and fresh, and to regenerate you, that you can do while you take a break from the game.

In one respect, you can't spend enough time with the ball, or playing soccer in general. By the same token, I'm not necessarily an advocate of 12-months-a-year soccer. There are often some seasons in 12-month soccer that aren't competitive (or maybe there is too much intense competition), and players can either get bored or burned out. Maybe a two- to three-month period focused on another sport would be more stimulating. I think there are many excellent cross training opportunities — sports and activities which allow you to take a break from typical soccer, yet add to the development of your game as well.

As you are aware, cross training (particularly if you combine it with keeping up your soccer skills) can be time-consuming. All of us have a set amount of time each day, so you've got to figure out within each day how to work on everything that's necessary. Since we are part of a highly-scheduled society, you simply have to be extremely efficient with your time in order to do everything it takes to become excellent in this game.

There is also a science to the choices you make. Cross training sports like volleyball and basketball, which include a lot of jumping, starting, stopping, and short accelerations and tactics are good for your soccer. I've also praised running track. I think Tae Bo is great. It provides agility, and touches on strengthening your anaerobic base by doing some of it as quickly as possible.

My current favorite cross training sport for soccer is roller hockey. I don't think there is anything better for soccer agility, conditioning, or the capacity to take physical risks than playing this game. The "old men" (the coaches) on our staff regularly play roller hockey in the off-season, and we invite our players to join in.

Brazil is a good model of soccer cross-training. In the winter, the Brazilians play indoors with a Futsol ball (a weighted, size-three ball, available from soccer catalogs). It's tough to get stripped of this ball, because it's so heavy, so everyone who has the ball thinks he is Pelé. Outdoors, Brazilians play beach soccer. Beach soccer is just plain fun. You can do incredibly creative things with the ball without fear of wiping out and getting hurt. One reason the Brazilians are so good at moves like the bicycle kick is because of the freedom of practicing such moves at the beach.

These two variations, in addition to standard soccer, are their three forms of soccer, so the Brazilians never get bored with the game. Of course, these exciting alternatives have an impact on the 11 v. 11 game. I don't think the Brazilians purposely set out to devise this soccer cross training. They just naturally found ways to play alternative forms of the game. Consequently, they develop tremendous skill.

Supplement this chapter with the Soccer Conditioning Workout in Appendix I.

CHAPTER 19

Maintaining Your Balance

Perspective is critical. I think one of the things that's killing youth sports is that there is no emotional balance.

Soccer can be very demanding. But your desire to be a serious player—and your determination to improve—should not be an endlessly stressful endeavor. Much of this book gives advice on personal management—on everything from your training time to your relationship with your parents. Underlying all of this is your need to create for yourself a balanced environment—on both sides of the white lines.

There are several meanings to finding balance. One is a physical balance that directly involves your soccer playing, and involves complements to intense soccer, such as rest, cross training, etc. This physical balance, in turn, impacts on a social and emotional balance—your perspective on the game, and how it fits into your life. Each aspect of balance should contribute to your continual development as a player and as a person, and should also protect and enhance your love of the game.

Physical Balance

Soccer should be a lot of fun. That's why you play. But as the old saying goes, you can get too much of a good thing. One of the most difficult challenges of coaching is learning to figure out the correct balance for a team and its players. An experienced coach knows when players are wrung out physically, emotionally, or psychologically. He or she knows when to back off and conduct a recreational practice, or even cancel practice and give players a couple of days off. A good coach can shift gears even in the course of a practice, when he or she senses that the stress level is too high and the athletes are struggling.

In coaching schools we talk a lot about the misguided notion of the "more the better." In these clinics we tell coaches, for example, they should want certain practice sessions to end when players still want to play. Even if players are dying to continue, you send them home. Then they're so excited about the next practice that they can't wait to come back. The mistake most coaches make is that players are having such a good time, they keep on going. All of a sudden, players go over the edge and they're burned out. They dread coming back. That sense of dread is what you want to avoid, while that feeling of excitement and readiness is what you want to cultivate. That ensures you also have that feeling on game day.

This is not a contradiction of what I have prescribed thus far. I think the majority of players don't overtrain or overdo it. Burnout isn't usually a result of too much soccer, but rather, a result of an imbalance of soccer. It is more likely caused by an emphasis on organized training and competition, while not enough time or encouragement is devoted to casual play or independent work.

The risk of this imbalance is fatigue or burnout. Be aware however, that these two are not the same. Fatigue is physical; burnout is psychological. If you don't have someone (like a coach) to help you assess burnout, it can be difficult to know if, and when, you are experiencing it. Gauging burnout can be a challenge for a coach as well. A coach has to be able to assess the strength of the players. Is a player tired because she isn't as hardworking or determined as some others, or is she incredibly strong and has pushed herself to exhaustion? Sometimes I assess how to direct my team by asking my most dedicated player how she's feeling. If she admits she's tired, I back off training for the entire team.

The need to strike a balance holds true for competition as well as training. As a player, you obviously have little impact on scheduling games, but understanding scheduling will help you to make crucial decisions. In the 1970s and '80s the soccer community looked toward the wealth of soccer in other countries, and tried to convince coaches to play more games. This country responded, and with a great sense of organization, American soccer created leagues and tournaments that offer endless playing opportunities. Now, young people are often overplaying. The trouble with year-round competition, and tournaments, is that they are potentially a burnout and injury risk. At the end of one of these "marathon" seasons or weekends, many players don't even want to touch a ball. And even the ones who want to are physically spent.

Some seasons or games are not optional, but some are. You need to assess what's best for you. Is a tournament—with up to five games over a weekend—critical for your development? Would a second team, or guesting opportunity, be best replaced by an independent training session alone or with friends? One of the legitimate complaints of the U.S. National Team coaches is that players are playing too many games (even scrimmages), and not sufficiently developing their skills through training. An inexperienced coach assumes that playing 11 v. 11 games is the best way to practice for the real thing. An experienced coach, however, keeps in mind the fact that during an entire game, a player touches the ball for an average of only three minutes. Obviously, training constructed only around 11 v. 11 play is an extreme example, but it illustrates one of the reasons it is important to balance your 11 v. 11 playing with small-sided games—and one v. ones or two v. twos—and personal time on the ball.

A balanced environment also provides variety, which is critical. That's why at UNC we divide training into five or six different blocks, which occur throughout the year (see Appendix II). As I point out throughout the book, a healthy soccer model for variety is the Brazilian system, largely because of the way they integrate various types of play into their soccer environment. Our blocks are derived from careful observation of a physical and emotional balance, and how peaking for competition is best nurtured in our players.

Variety may mean a lighter soccer schedule, but cutting back doesn't necessarily mean you have to lose skills or fitness (During any time of the year, you should still practice your individual soccer skills.). In addition to possible casual soccer play in the off-season, you might want to participate in other sports, such as basketball, volleyball, lacrosse and track, and lifting weights or other conditioning.

At some point, everyone has to rejuvenate. This not only protects you from injury, but also allows your training to take effect and contributes to your improvement. Obviously, one way to rejuvenate is to rest. There's nothing wrong with taking a break. Sometimes, it's even okay to do nothing. When Jena Kluegel ('98–'01), one of our top players, came back from playing with the U.S. National Team in the Algarve Cup in Portugal, she was both physically exhausted and swamped with academics. She asked for a day off from team practice. "Take a couple of days," I told her. An occasional break can be fine, as long as it doesn't become a pattern. If it does become a habit, clearly something else beyond fatigue is going on. If it turns out you want a rest because you're burned-out, you've got to address it.

There are other methods to ensure physical balance and rejuvenation. Besides rest these include massage and proper nutrition and hydration (both before and after practices and games).

Avoiding Burnout

If you have any say in the design of your development, you should seek out variety in your training, using soccer, other sports and cross training. You should also make sure your environment is a positive one.

Soccer will remain fresh, even if you are overloaded with training and tournaments, if you have an experienced and enthusiastic leader who can keep it that way. I think a lot of players burn out, and subsequently quit because they are missing consistently positive, productive leadership. In our ambition to see our children succeed, I think we are overscheduling them. Soccer is part of that. A young person's schedule can be overloaded with activities—soccer, lacrosse, piano, computer class, etc. In addition, parents' overinvolvement in their children's soccer can exert added pressure.

Burnout also happens when people don't have pleasure woven into their environment. Perhaps players don't "stop to smell the roses" because they don't see soccer as a good time, and a refuge from the stress of life. But they have to. In fact, part of a coach's job is to create a fun atmosphere. As a player, it is also your responsibility to enhance your experience with a sense of enjoyment.

Attitude plays a large part in your enjoyment. An example of that is one of our experiences. To raise funds for our program the players run a concession stand at the UNC basketball games. Some years this is a chore. After all, running a concession stand is work. But last year (2000), our leaders were so good at creating team spirit that the players had a blast working the stand. Their attitude was tremendous. They were always smiling and laughing, and committed to their efforts. What was created at this concession stand is a symbol of the best possible team spirit.

As in so many other ways, it comes down to leadership, and it all starts with you and your attitude. How will you look forward to your next soccer experience? What will you do while you are in the midst of that experience? What are you going to bring to it? The right attitude is exactly what we had at that concession stand in 2000. Consequently, it was the best attended, and most outstanding year we've had since we began doing it.

A direct result of burnout is dropping out. But I don't think dropping out always has to do with burning out. The highest dropout rate in youth soccer is among teenage girls. I think there's still social pressure on girls, and a feeling that popular, or feminine girls don't play sports. It's true that even young girls who don't play sports think that Mia Hamm is "cool," but not necessarily because she is a soccer player. It's more because she is attractive, slender, and glamorous. I don't think girls in general yet feel that sport is the "ultimate" group to which to belong. It's still on the periphery.

Girls are still fighting the sociology of their gender. I think it's slowly disappearing, but it still exists.

Another distraction from sports, and part of the negative social pressure that contributes to the dropout rate, is that boys become part of the girls' social landscape. One of the lectures I give to both my freshman players at UNC, and in our girls' summer camp, addresses this issue. A big mistake girls make is completely devoting their lives to entrapping some boy. What helps someone achieve a balanced life is not abandoning herself. What makes a girl attractive is not "slumming around" the mall trying to pick the perfect eye-catching outfit for a guy. What makes her interesting and attractive is to have her own life, and to develop her personal qualities. Those can be strength, athleticism, independence, and ambition.

Emotional Balance

The defining feature of UNC soccer may be our intensity, but what people don't realize is that our environment is also filled with levity. That's what gives us an emotional balance. Even the most serious training is filled with chances to smile, laugh, and have a good time. We celebrate our victories, or tease each other when someone is nutmeged in a one v. one, and just generally have a good time.

This inclination to balance our emotional environment is not a conscious effort on our part, it's just an aspect of our persona and philosophy. I think it also contributes to our success, because we don't agonize or overly soul-search over soccer. We do work hard, and always challenge each other to get to higher levels, but those aren't the aspects of the game we address on a regular basis. What we address on a regular basis is how hilarious, or how "crazy" one of the players is, how funny certain incidents are, and when we're going to get together for pizza.

Part of this balanced view is our realization that soccer is not supposed to be morbid. Intensity is necessary, but it's brief. It's happening while you play, but there are also so many light moments in athletics. If you can't participate in those moments it is bound to make this game very destructive and unhealthy for you. Two players crash into one another; one blows a header—it is turning these experiences into something to laugh about that makes them livable. The day before I wrote this I made one potentially insignificant moment into a humorous and meaningful one using this philosophy. A weak and a strong player were competing in the weight room in a tag-team bench press. I looked at the stronger player, easily matching the tiny weights just lifted by her partner, and I made a gesture to her, like I was lifting that light weight with my little finger, as if to say, "Oh, come on. You can do better than that." She grabbed a heavy weight, lifted it, and turned to me and smiled. In about 20 seconds—without even saying a word—I teased her, challenged her and coached her (by showing her the first weight was too light)—and the whole thing was funny.

As in the rest of your soccer, there is a necessary evolution with attitude. It can take time to learn to balance your view, to recognize the humor, to combine the levity with the intensity—especially if there's no one around to help you do that. Start by looking for the light moments, and participating in them. They are everywhere.

In addition, you need to understand the place of soccer in your life, and make sure that the adults in your life do as well. If you have a passion and an aptitude to aspire to the national level, that's great. But for most players, the chances are soccer will not end up being a career endeavor. They can still go very far, and learn a lot about life, if their soccer is conducted properly. There are many positive reasons for playing, and they should all be supported. In an attempt to be serious, for example, a lot of people shun, or undervalue, the social experience of soccer. But if your team is not social, it has little value. The human relations aspect is what ultimately makes soccer a deep and rewarding experience.

Learning to find your emotional balance is part of your development, just like learning soccer skills or competitive fury. I recognize that the potential of feeling overwhelmed comes not just from soccer, but also from the rest of the stresses in your life. Again, I go back to Victor Frankl (see Chapter 4), who wrote that you can't control the events of your life, but you can certainly control your attitude toward them. Even when you think your whole world is collapsing around you, you can still dictate how you feel about it, how you react. I think that's such an empowering approach—that the power resides in you.

One of the best pieces of advice I ever got was given to me by Murray Strawbridge, my boss when I first entered the workforce as a young man fresh out of college, selling life insurance. This job can be incredibly stressful or depressing, especially when you're not selling anything. Murray used to bring us in to tell us, "Don't take yourself too seriously." That's the critical thing in maintaining balance—while you obviously take what you are doing seriously, you shouldn't take yourself too seriously.

Balance means you also understand the place of the game in your life. As I've said earlier, if you don't have anything outside of soccer, you're going to be governed by it. If it's only just a game for you, you can control the emotional ride, and keep it in perspective. One of the reasons Marcia McDermott, coach of the Carolina Courage in the WUSA, is one of my favorite colleagues is because her tremendous intellectualism impacts on her capacity to coach, and brings balance to the game.

Soccer should be the source of your pleasure, not your stress. The game should be your refuge. Kristine Lilly comes to mind. Whenever she was stressed out in her life, what freed her was just going out and running on the soccer field. It seemed that's where she was free; nothing could touch her in that world.

Kristine Lilly ('89–'92)

Finding Refuge on the Soccer Field

Even when I was very little, the soccer field was a place I enjoyed. I felt good there. I felt free. When you're younger, you don't really think about it so much. You're just out there running around and playing the game.

As I got older—about high-school age—playing gave me a sense of comfort. Soccer came a lot easier to me than perhaps school, or hanging with a big group of friends, or communicating with people. I had my close friends, but I was very shy. The soccer field was a place all that shyness disappeared. I felt comfortable, good about myself, and I was happy. Every time I was on the field, it was like a little retreat. It also gave me an opportunity to release any emotions I was feeling at a time that I didn't express in other ways. I could express anything on the field. I just let it all out, and it was easy. The field was also a place for me to go just to be myself, and not have anything get to me. While it's still one of the greatest places—a place I like to go to get away from everything—I think as I've gotten older, I've gotten a lot better about communicating, expressing my feelings in the way that you should.

Growing up, people knew how well I could play, but they didn't really know that being out on the field gave me comfort. Also, when you're good at something, it's easy to keep going to the place where you do it. That's basically how I felt. I think if you were to ask a lot of athletes, in any sport, they would say they find a sense of comfort in what they do. I think that another part of feeling comfort is the confidence you get when you're good. If I weren't good at soccer, I don't think the field would be a haven for me.

From the beginning, I worked hard. No one ever pushed me in the wrong way. I didn't have any misguided coaches. They basically saw that I had talent, and a love of being on the field, and they tried to help me make the best of it. There were lots of pressures, but my parents were wonderful.

They didn't push me in any way. They just encouraged me and were there for support. Not having that family pressure really helped.

My parents put decisions in my hands, and gave me other ways to look at them. When I was 16, I got invited to the U19 National camp, which was being held in Michigan. They brought in the best players and created what was, at that time, a "paper team." I told my parents that I didn't want to go, because I was afraid. I didn't know anyone; I didn't want to travel; I didn't want to be gone for a week. The only thing they said was, "We'll stand by your decision, but we think this is one step that would help you." I thought about it for a while, and eventually came to the conclusion that maybe it was something I should do. My parents being there for me in this way also made the soccer field a place I always wanted to go.

I think a lot of people have their get-away retreats, whether they sit in a chair, or go to the beach. I think mine has always been the soccer field, even though there are times when I was burned out from playing, and I did need to get away from it. Even then, I think I could still go sit on a field and feel comfort.

Whenever I walk onto a field, whether the ball is in front of me, or I'm just standing there, I feel a sort of peace within myself, even if 90,000 people are watching. At times like this there's that one moment when you first feel the presence of everyone around you. But once you start playing, and get into your zone, that all fades away.

This sense of comfort doesn't mean I'm not nervous. Every athlete has nerves before a game. I think that's natural. Once the game starts, the nerves usually disappear. That's healthy, because if you're not nervous, it's as if you're complacent. If I don't have some nerves, I feel something isn't right, and I have to reevaluate how I'm going into the game. I also think that throughout the game you can go through a loss of confidence, but even if you're having a bad game, it's not like you don't want to be on the field. You still have the opportunity to feel good about yourself there.

I always play with everything that's inside of me. When you see me at the end of the game, I'm really drained. In college, I had a lot going on in my life. I had a lot of emotions that were released on the field, and that really drained me. Going to college is a new situation. You don't know anyone. You're playing a different level of soccer and meeting new people. I really loved my teammates, and I loved playing, so the experience wasn't just about my emotional adjustment. I had a general feeling of, "This is a great place to be right now." I also had similar feelings in high school. I loved the team, but it was a time in my life that a lot was going on for me. While I don't think the soccer field has ever stopped being my refuge, there comes a time when it's not the only answer. In the past, there may have

I have always loved this picture of Kristine. No one could deal with her, and here's an example of how people attempted to—grabbing, pushing, pulling, trying to get her off of her game. But Kristine was just too determined.

been some issues I needed to deal with connected to a particular stage of my life, like starting college.

Soccer wasn't that big when I was growing up, but now, especially for a girl, there are college scholarships and professional soccer—so many different possibilities. It's a very competitive atmosphere right now, especially in club soccer. Parents want the best for their kids, but sometimes they push them for the wrong reasons.

I think there are less pressured ways to learn to be successful. For example, you can develop intensity and competitiveness in a relaxed environment. You may not even know you're doing it. It's amazing. My brother jokes that he made my career by playing one v. one with me, but he did give me a lot. We competed in everything, but we never thought of it that way. He would never take it easy on me, and we wanted to beat each other, but it was never like we felt: we're competing right now. I grew up in Wilton, Connecticut. My cousins—five boys and one girl—lived a five-minute walk away. We played all kinds of sports in their backyard. I think this also definitely played a role in developing my competitiveness.

I never just played soccer. I played basketball and softball in high school. If you're committed to something, and you have some God-given talent, you're going to be good. If you address yourself in ways to get better, like playing another sport, it will help. It also takes your mind off a single focus and lets you relax a bit.

If soccer is getting to be too much, take a break. One of the things I tell high school kids is to get involved in more than one sport. A lot of the time they don't want to do this, but other sports help you in your main one. Also, your life isn't so centered around just one thing: soccer.

I try to get across to the kids in my soccer camp the philosophy that has always been a part of what I do. They should work hard, give 100 percent, but also have fun. Then, it's not so stressful. I also tell them not to be afraid to make mistakes, because that's going to happen.

My perspective on playing the game also has to do with the people on my teams. The 2000 Olympic year was a very long one for the U.S. National Team. We played over 40 games. I was tired from that year, but I knew we were playing in the Olympic final. I stepped it up, and played pretty well, but we lost. You'd think after such a loss you'd feel like, "I hate this," but it was the people surrounding me who I felt the worst about, because I knew how much everyone was hurting.

I think the hardest part was standing on the podium with our silver medals. Not that silver is bad, but when you set your goal to win gold, it is disappointing. I felt the pain of every single one of the players, but when we looked up into the crowd and saw our families, it was the most amazing feeling in the world. They didn't care. They were so proud of us. When I think about all the good things that happen, it's nice to have those same people around me.

You've just got to remember what you're doing. Playing a sport is not life or death. When you lose, it hurts, but it's temporary. When you win, it's great, but that's temporary, too. I have a gold medal from the 1996 Olympics. That's in the past. I'm still proud of it, and I still love the fact I won it, but this is the present. That medal is fairly irrelevant to what's going on in my life right now. I'm trying to win a first-time championship in a professional league. No one really cares about my gold medal. Having that medal is not going to make us win. It's what I do about it, and what I contribute, that matters.

Find what you love. If you love it, work hard at it and enjoy it. Find your own way to do that. If things get difficult, ask for help if you need it.

Love of the Game

I think one of the things that's killing youth sports is that there is not enough emotional balance. Love of the game is what gives you that balance.

I'm a devoted student of Michael Jordan and his success. I think he's one of the greatest examples of someone who has athletics figured out. One of the stories I share all the time is the incredible way he has maintained his love of the game. He understood himself and his love of basketball to such an extent, that unlike anyone before him, when Jordan signed with the Chicago Bulls, he had a "love of the game" clause put into his contract. This meant he could play basketball whenever and wherever he wanted. Most professional teams don't want their athletes taking any unnecessary physical risks (like playing basketball in the off-season) in order to avoid potential injury. But Jordan made it clear that even though he was a professional, he plays basketball because he loves it, and he didn't want anyone to take away this love.

Coaches try to give players some elements of love of the game. After all, we don't want it to be something young players dread, because then we will become a country of soccer players who don't really look forward to playing, and consequently, won't develop the technical mastery to play a game that has any real value. You have to get something back from your investment of time in the sport, and as long as you can keep returning to a core reason why you're working hard, that will make everything bearable. Of course, there are days when training is painful and it's not easy and you do feel burned out. At times it isn't fun to work hard, but if you remember how fun it's going to be when you get fit, or you recover from an injury and you're healthy, or you master a skill and get better, that's what's important. You have to have a reason to want to work.

Why do you love the game? It might be because you like being outdoors, or with your friends, or, like Laurie Schwoy, you love the feel of the ball at your feet. I think for players to be able to endure all it takes to become great, they have to feel that the true value of sport is simply loving their participation in it—for any reason. You have to understand why you play, get at the core reason, and then, revisit that reason regularly. This will keep you excited about playing.

You can foster your love of the game if you figure out what makes it fun for you. Fun can be found in the smaller details of the game. What excites some young players, for example, is juggling. At face value, juggling may seem boring. But if you do it in the context of beating your own record, suddenly it becomes fun. If you've learned to do it with your feet, move to the head, shoulders, outside of the feet, etc. All of a sudden you're doing something a bit more challenging each time. Then you take on some other skill the same way, like bending balls.

Of course, there is a time for physical and psychological challenge. At UNC, this takes the form of competition with each other. But there has to be a time to reconstruct our team spirit. For us, the day before a match is when this happens. When we taper, it's not just physically and psychologically, we also tone down the intensity, and spend time on emotional and team bonding. The off-season is also similarly different than the fall. Most of the off-season is structured around just playing the game—11 v. 11, 4 v. 4, 2 v. 2, 1 v. 1.

Love of the game is not just vital for maintaining your interest in playing, but for playing well. That's why part of the tapering I have discussed earlier includes doing what you love. Before our Friday games, we do a "love of the game" practice. There's no real stress; we do what's fun, what reminds the players of why they started playing soccer in the first place. This practice includes shooting and scoring, hanging out with buddies, joking, teasing, and laughing. It's a "joy of life" practice.

Ultimately, the reason you should be involved in soccer is for the joy of it. If you lose your joy of the game, nothing is possible. There may be times when you feel as if this love of the game is being taken from you. Don't let anyone crush your spirit. Even at the highest level, that's what Michael Jordan made sure to protect himself from. Understand why you love the game and make that the reason you play, regardless of what is happening around you.

CHAPTER 20

Sharpening Your Mental Edge

I want my sons to have the gift of fury. I want them to gobble up life.
I want them to eat life before life eats them.

—*The Great Santini*, by Pat Conroy

The founding principle of UNC mentality is based on this line from *The Great Santini*. I want my players to have the gift of fury. And it is a gift, because not too many players have it. Learn to have it, and you, too, will stand out.

An intense, rock-hard mentality is the cornerstone of our program. Every year, the team votes on the player who exemplifies this quality. "The Gift of Fury" award-winner's name is engraved on a plaque that hangs in our soccer offices.

What stuns a lot of people who watch us play is the intensity with which we compete. This is the mentality that drives our players to work, a relentlessness that prevents them from giving up. This is the philosophy I think is critical to inject into college teams, and one that I have stressed on every level and in every environment—from the U.S. National Team to our UNC girls' camps every summer. Above all other qualities, mentality must be present for achievement. We've had some incredibly talented or fit athletes without this mentality, and in the most important games, they've been useless to us. Of course, you want to cover all the bases—the skills and fitness—but the absolute critical element is your mental hardness and courage, which comes in the form of seeking out responsibility and taking physical risks.

Mentality defines the strength of your psychological dimension, which is your capacity to reach down inside yourself and find your inner hardness.

Staci Wilson ('94–'97), the human embodiment of the gift of fury.

In any physical duel or combative situation, ultimate triumph doesn't come down to skill or tactics. What it boils down to is your will.

This mentality is characterized by a combative, aggressive posture. Your outlook should be that you dominate this zone, this player; you own this game, this is your time, you are the reason your team wins. Mentality is partially optimism, but for the most part, it's a combination of focus, competitive rage, relentlessness, hardness, and courage—all of the words that define combative athletics.

The Evolution of Coaching Soccer Mentality

From the time I can remember I have always kept score. Even as a child, this made what I was doing more exciting. If the environment wasn't competitive, I'd say something to irritate my opponent, just to make sure he tried, because I wanted to compete against others who also wanted to win. This isn't unique to me. I think a lot of people are like this.

This intense, competitive mentality isn't a mystery to those of us who live with it. It isn't as if I woke up one day with a "Eureka!" syndrome, and discovered mentality and how to coach it. I think many coaches, if they have played a sport or been a part of this society, have an innate understanding of this mentality. They recognize the athletes who are competitive—and those who perhaps can't fight through a pain threshold, or take a risk—and they reinforce the competitive attitude. It is the job of a good coach to identify powerful mentality, and to teach, or reinforce it, at every opportunity.

On the other hand, I learned early on that just the presence of my own mentality—my own passion and intensity—did not inspire female players. In fact, it shattered their confidence and created distance between us. The stereotypical youth coach who stands on the sideline and yells at the girls usually just alienates himself from them. Screaming is not an effective motivational tool for developing mentality. I had to find a new way to foster intensity in women. Keeping score became part of the way I train them.

I believe in the benefits of a competitive atmosphere. As a coach, I'm trying to invite everyone else into it. Some players won't come along. If they don't come along in one way, I try to convince them to come along in another way. The classical way for them to come along is to be spurred by the competition itself. Most athletes don't want to see their names on the bottom of our lists. But another way is to convince them of their own potential and let them know that others who became great started exactly where they are now. Being competitive is a decision, not a talent. And we're trying to convince players to make the decision to compete.

Michael Jordan

There is no better example of powerful mentality in athletics than Michael Jordan. What set him apart is not only that he's an extraordinary athlete, but he has indomitable will, and incredible discipline. He carefully takes care of everything before he even steps foot on the court.

Not only does Michael Jordan have the will to prepare, he has a mentality that is second to no one. In his prime, even if a person could stay with him physically, Jordan would eventually break him, because he was tougher psychologically. He wanted it more, competed for it constantly—and even under immense pressure he delivered, because he was so mentally hard.

In his book *Playing for Keeps*, David Halberstam calls what Jordan has a "rage to excel." This, too, sets him apart.

Making the Choice

If you don't have this intense mentality, consider wanting it.

Your goal for developing this intense mentality is to create an indomitable will. It is the quality of being relentless, with a never-give-up attitude. What's wonderful about this mentality is that it's not a talent; it's not part of your genetic code. It's a decision, a choice. You choose to be courageous, and to have a great pain threshold.

It's not an easy choice, but it is one that will separate you from the ordinary. This mentality doesn't guarantee winning, but it is a quality that gives you the incredible strength and power that is an element in every consistent winner.

You don't have to make the choice to develop this mentality. It doesn't lessen you as a human being if you don't choose it. Without it, however, you're not going to be as effective as a soccer player, and helping to develop the best possible soccer player is a part of my job as a coach. It is also my responsibility to make my players into good human beings. So, there is no resentment directed at the player who doesn't have the mentality to head the ball, who avoids a tackle, or won't fight to the next level of fitness. She knows that she's not judged as a person. However, she also knows she cannot be given a powerful role on the team if she is not willing to make these choices.

Make sure you like what you choose. If you don't mind the role you'll play, or the kind of playing time you'll get as a result if you won't make the choices that others will, you are living with your choices. However, if your dream is to play at the U.S. National Team level, you don't have a choice.

The challenge of a coach is to be able to deal with many different types of players, all of whom may have different issues that affect their mentality. In our environment at UNC, I think everyone wants to be intense, and have a powerful mentality. In the conferences I have with each player, I try to get to the core reason why one of them won't be competitive, or doesn't have a strong mentality. My job is to present them with the question: will you choose it? For those who already have this mental capacity, I continually create challenges to stimulate it. For those who have not yet attained that mentality, I try to help them understand why. I try to create a standard for them, a goal to grow and to develop.

When I coached the U.S. National Team, players were selected who had a strong mentality, and we used them as role models. The athlete who was held up as an example while we were building the team was April Heinrichs. After praising her performances, sure enough, others, such as Michelle Akers, jumped into that competitive mode and rewrote their own standards that have made soccer history.

Keep in mind that in every aspect of development there is a continuum for developing this mentality—both in terms of age and level of play. The level of your intensity and mental strength progresses over time, with age and experience. The younger you are, the more relaxed your standards should be. Obviously, the mentality for a U10 player is nowhere near the expectations for a National Team member. A recreational player's mental factor is not the same as it is for an ODP player. At the height of the continuum is a Michelle Akers or an April Heinrichs. If your ambition is to play at the highest level, the closer you can be to players like those two, the better.

April Heinrichs ('83–'86)

The Competitive Personality

The most important thing about being a successful elite-level athlete is your psychological dimension. How do you deal with success? How do you deal with failure? Are you intrinsically motivated? When adversity comes your way, do you embrace it, or shy away from it? Is adversity something you view as positive, or something you fear, because I think we are all riddled with fear, and how we deal with that is very important.

The most achievement-oriented, successful elite-level athletes have an unbelievable knack for embracing adversity and competitiveness. For me personally, it's a question of nurture or nature. Was I born with this competitiveness that just burns? It's a constant flame, and I can't turn it off, and I wouldn't want to turn it off, because I've embraced it. Or was it nurture — that I grew up in an environment in which I was encouraged and allowed to be competitive? In all fairness, I think the answer is a little bit of both. My identity as a child was wrapped up in my success on the athletic field. My social circles were dependent on it. My self-esteem came from that success.

I had a dysfunctional family, and I found activity and acceptance in sports. My brain was captivated, my energies were focused, and I threw myself into it. It was a case of out of sight, out of mind. When I was on the soccer field, all the issues back at home were out of sight; therefore, they were out of mind. On the field, I was committed and winning and feeling great. It wasn't until I was about 21 years old that I realized who I was, and separated who I was from what I did well. Of course, I think some psychologist could have a heyday with that.

I grew up being competitive. I was never shunned because of my competitiveness. I never even realized that I was that competitive. It was who

I was, something I certainly embraced. I was never conflicted about it, and I've never once in my life wavered about my competitiveness. It's probably because I didn't know any better, because no one ever told me otherwise. My parents never communicated, "Could you tame it down a little April, because you're just a little more competitive than everyone else out there?" In the world I was in, never once did I get the feedback that being competitive wasn't feminine. I credit my parents, and maybe the circles that I chose to move in.

I rank this competitiveness as the most important philosophy that Anson and I have ever shared. I wanted that competitive environment. I wouldn't accept anything less than the most competitive environment anyone can throw at me. He recognized that as a good quality, and said: let's duplicate this young lady's experience for every young lady who follows. In other words, I think he recognized this was a quality that he felt would help win games, so let's bottle it up and duplicate it at UNC, so that every young woman who comes here from now on will be in an environment in which she feels socially accepted because of her competitive nature.

I would credit Anson with taking the next step, and that is, he created an environment in which this competitiveness is socially acceptable. In some ways, I think he is 20 years ahead of his time in terms of embracing these concepts. I go back to my childhood, and think that maybe it was 30 years ahead. After all, there are girls today who experience being socially ostracized because their parents and peers don't think it's cool to be sweaty and competitive.

A girl doesn't have to be in the situation I was to embrace that competitive world. If she doesn't have it, or didn't grow up with it, or it wasn't nurtured over time, then she has to nurture it. It doesn't come from parents; it doesn't come from coaches (although Anson would like to think it does). In my opinion, the motivation has to come solely from within. Coaches can motivate in the short term. They can do long-term goal-setting. Parents can want their kids to be on the National Team, or choose soccer over football or dolls, but at the end of the day, the athlete is going to be confronted with what she truly wants, and how badly she wants it. It must be her will to focus her energy, to prepare herself to ultimately achieve her goals.

A girl definitely needs social support for her success. If she's in an environment in which being competitive is socially or culturally frowned upon, or not appreciated for its full value, it's going to be difficult for her to embrace it. On the other hand, if she is in what Anson calls a competitive cauldron, the acceptance and nurturing of competitive juices, a fiery spirit and a hate-to-lose mentality—if there is consistent feedback that this is

This is one of my favorite pictures of April, because it captures so much of what I loved about her—her speed, determination and competitive nature.

healthy and positive, I think a young girl can embrace and nurture competitiveness over time. It can become a part of her fabric.

In the speeches I do around the country, one of the topics I address is the three levels of competitiveness. I don't care if you're talking about the National Team, college, or high school soccer, you can rate every athlete on the team and place her in one of three different categories. The third-tier competitor is the person who thinks she's competitive because she's on a sports team. Her parents, peers, and coaches all think of her in the same way. The second-tier competitor is on a sports team, and is competitive when the coach draws a line on the field, there's an out-of-bounds, score is kept, and at the end of some time, or a number of opportunities, there is a winner and a loser. The first tier, number one competitor, is what I call a natural-born competitor. Whether she's on a soccer field with a coach and a score, on her own in her backyard juggling, in a classroom taking a test, or licking stamps—she always competes.

This analysis encapsulates sports in general. For example, coaches can teach a player how to head. We do a drill, teach heading technique through progression—using the neck, forehead, torso, the timing of a jump, etc. How do you teach competitiveness? You have to train it the same way you would a skill or fitness. You don't do it once a month. You have to put the athlete in a competitive environment every single day. Either you win or lose, and either you get used to losing or you get used to winning. And once you get used to winning, it's addictive, and you don't ever want to go back to losing. You also understand as an athlete that there are some days you can control winning, and some things you can't control about winning or losing.

How do you evaluate a competitor? How long does a loss sit with her? How much does it fester in her brain? How committed is she to preparing herself so that she doesn't lose very frequently? I believe that the difference between a natural born-competitor and everyone else is how long a loss lasts, how personally she takes it, and how committed she is to ensuring she doesn't lose very often. For me, that's what separates the natural-born competitor—or the warrior, in Anson's language—from everyone else.

I would submit that there are possibly three qualities that are interlinked, but also mutually exclusive in some ways. They are competitiveness, work ethic, and performance. Work ethic and competitiveness are things that you can bring to the field every day, and that you can control every aspect of. Performance-born competitor, or a warrior, in her mentality is that her competitiveness, work ethic, and ultimately, her performance, are all tied in.

Every team has a plethora of second-tier competitors. You're really lucky if you have one or two natural-born competitors. The players who are third-tiers just aren't going to make it on the team long-term. They might survive four years at UNC, but they're not going to be starters. They might survive and be named to the women's National Team, but they aren't going to become veterans.

Even on the National Team, we have all three levels of competitors. They aren't all number ones. As a coach, the challenge is to get all the threes to become twos, and all the twos to totally embrace competition 100% of the time and become ones, like natural-born competitors. Anson has done a great job over time of training twos to become ones.

Self-Talk

Most all the great players do some form of self-talk before they play. This self-talk is in the form of a mantra—which refers to a word or phrase that is silently repeated as a part of meditation. Self-talk is a review of who you are, and what makes you special—a positive statement about you and your game. Every player has a quality she takes pride in. Self-talk is a silent affirmation of who you are, why you play, and why on a particular day you are going to play well. Your mantra might be, "I'm the best player here," or, "No one can take the ball from me."

Psychological Readiness

Some people are internally focused and motivated. They know how to ready themselves to compete. I can see them preparing before every practice, and every game, so I don't even discuss their readiness with them. Others, however, are on an emotional roller coaster, which may cause them to play brilliantly one day, and horribly the next. Their first touch may be exquisite, or it may desert them entirely. I try to help those who are inconsistent. Self-talk is one way to do that. They also have to learn to focus, and to feed off of what happens in the game. The winners know what to do. They know when to turn on their focus and intensity, and when to compete.

We know that intensity, characterized by a competitive fire, translates into hard mentality. Sustaining that intensity with focus and concentration is the key. An athlete who has focus can maintain this intensity for the entire practice or game. Players with a weak mentality drift in and out of focus. The analogy I use is that anyone can run the first quarter-mile of a marathon, but can that person also sprint the last lap after running 26 miles? Any player—even one with the weakest mentality—can be intense or courageous for a brief moment. While that's certainly commendable, it's not what you're after. You want to be able to summon this fury for the entire competition.

The true art of intensity is to blend it with composure. The best description of this composure comes from the famed UCLA basketball coach John Wooden, who tried to teach it to his players. "Move quickly but don't hurry," he said. Basically, this means you're going as fast as you can, but you're not hurrying. You're not in a panic. It's a wonderful statement of control, which takes great psychological skill and guts. It means you have the confidence to remain composed when the world around you is like a tornado. It's like great firefighters who remain calm when the rest of us would not. They weren't born calm; this was trained into them. In the same way, you can learn to have it. The way we do it at UNC is to put players into the tornado so often in training that they aren't panicked by it.

Developing Mentality

You develop your mentality in the same methodical, purposeful way as everything else I discuss in the book. At UNC, we do it by keeping score in all of our soccer, and by consistently using one v. one as the best training ground (one v. one is about domination, both physically and mentally). In addition to a sense of hardness, and taking physical risks, mentality entails the capability to fight through various pain thresholds. This requires inner drive and intestinal fortitude, because to reach your ultimate fitness level or put yourself in the midst of physical risk can be painful.

We want our players to make the decision to have a powerful mentality. Keeping score is part of our attempt to recreate players mentally. If something is missing, we want to supply it. In addition to the training environment, we do this in meetings and discussions during the off-season, in which we teach players to develop a strong and positive outlook. Peer evaluation, and individual evaluations done by everyone, also give players the responsibility to assess each other's mentality.

We also use goal-setting. We do this in our group discussions on leadership and personal growth, but we also do it one-on-one, in the player conferences I mentioned earlier. We begin with a review of a player's academic achievements and goals, because after all, UNC is an educational institution. The underlying team goal is that every player maintain over a 3.0 grade point average (GPA). A lot of them are well above that, and set even higher goals for themselves. We have academic standouts on the team, such as goalkeeper Kristin DePlatchett ('98–'01), who has between a 3.9 and 4.0 GPA every semester.

Next, we review career ambitions, so players can prepare for their future. Some want to be doctors, lawyers, teachers, or various other such professions. In our program, many also have higher soccer aspirations. The great benefit of being in a program like ours is that I can point out a long string of immortals who have played at UNC. This creates an expectation of greatness here. In the past, the ambition of the great players was to make the U.S. National Team. Now, it is also to become professionals. Any player with the goal to play professionally, however, also has to declare a backup career in our meeting.

With their goals in place, I help players to construct their days. While the main goal for the player who wants to go to medical school is academics, she still works to be the best soccer player she can be. The person who seeks to become a professional soccer player might be asked to do something extra, like deepen her fitness bases during periods when others might be taking breaks, work at soccer camps in the summer if her long-range goal is to coach, and basically construct a lifestyle that will prepare her for her athletic profession.

We also review concrete, interim goals. There are thousands of ways you can use concrete goal-setting. You can set up disciplinary structures for yourself to help you improve as a player, such as spending 20 minutes a day working on the wall, five minutes a day on long-ball service with a neighbor, going out with Mom and Dad and trying to beat them both in one v. one, etc. You can also set game goals. If you're a striker, your goal might be to get a shot off in the first five minutes, or, if you're a flank midfielder, it might be penetration down the flank at least three times, or get backpost to head the ball at least once a half. You can also create goals to make various teams.

We provide our players with feedback, based on their goals. If you state your goals to a coach or teammate, it could help you to get some support and advice. I think goal-setting measures are positive, as long as you are not crushed by any failures, and you can continue to set new goals once your current goals are reached.

Tactical Agility

Having a strong mentality also means understanding when to exercise it. Most female players don't overdo intensity, but there are situations not worth taking physical risks, or some environments where you should pull back and preserve yourself—such as if you're distributing your energy for a long weekend tournament, or you're already winning a game by a big margin there is no reason to take a life-or-death risk in a 50-50 challenge with a goalkeeper. You don't need to demonstrate your mental toughness then. Other environments or situations don't require intensity—like juggling a soccer ball for fun.

One of the most incredibly powerful players is Michelle Akers. Her intensity and toughness was such a feature of her play that she often couldn't rein it in when she should have. The team would be winning by 6-0, and a 50-50 ball would be rolling out-of-bounds, but Michelle would still try to save it, risking shredding her knees or getting cut in half by a defender. That's just who she was. As much as I wanted to preserve that intensity when I was coaching her, I also wanted to preserve her health, so in our coach/player conferences I would talk to her about what I call tactical agility. This means the understanding of how and when to use the intensity and mentality I've described in this chapter.

I told Michelle she needed to avoid contact that wasn't significant, and that what she risked in stepping in to take an unnecessary hit was not worthwhile. Of course, the irony is that because of her wonderful mentality over the course of her career, her body paid a huge price. Still, my admiration for this remarkable woman was also tied into this wild recklessness I tried to change. Although rarely does an overly-intense player like Michelle need to be managed, you still need to be aware that there are some environments in which intensity, such as in the form of taking physical risks, can be counterproductive.

Getting the Message

Acquiring mentality is a crucial part of your developmental challenge. It helps to understand this mentality by having concrete examples. Like any soccer skill, which you learn by demonstration, it is easier to understand how mentality works if you see how a coach might communicate it, or teach it.

Overall, I believe female players are getting mentally tougher. I notice this on a youth level, particularly in my recent work with the ODP Region III teams. But like all players, including those at UNC, young players are a work in progress. In the ODP training several years ago, we addressed the issue of mentality by using one girl in particular as an example. Although she was a talented player, she avoided heading the ball. A lot of players make subtle choices—timing a tackle just a bit late to avoid possibly getting hit, or making sure to be slightly out of the way when an air ball comes toward their heads. My task as a coach is to know when they're doing this, and call them on it. When we noticed the girl in ODP who avoided heading, we set her a goal: one header per game. We turned it into a kind of joke—the entire bench cheering for her when she finally headed a ball. Underlying the laughter, though, was an important message. There was an expectation that everyone was going to head the ball, even if they didn't like it, or it was painful.

I believe there are right and wrong ways to send a message. When trying to get a player to fight through her pain threshold, and to deepen her risk-taking mentality, a lot of parents and coaches make a big mistake. When an athlete gets knocked down or falls, for example, they go rushing out like the player is in her final death throes. She's not; she's just in a little pain. When someone goes bolting out onto the field any time a player is clipped, banged, or bumped, subconsciously the player thinks: this is how I get attention. But that's a negative dynamic. That's why I purposely don't go out onto the field when my players go down.

Of course, there are times when players are truly hurt. We certainly support them in that case. But most of the time it isn't catastrophic injury,

Here I am standing next to Dick Baddour, my Athletic Director, with the team, celebrating our program's 500th win.

it's just getting whacked in the shin or getting the wind knocked out of them. Yes, that hurts; it's frightening, but it's part of the game.

You can survive the bone-jarring pain of a tackle and not flinch. Pop up and deal with it. What a coach or parent should compliment is the player who, despite getting absolutely hammered, immediately gets up. Then the athlete gets the message that taking physical risks is praiseworthy.

When I was coaching men at UNC, I had a really nice player named Billy Probster. We were in practice, and in a very vicious tackle, he was absolutely hammered to the earth. He was rolling around on the ground, screaming and writhing. I silently stood over him, watching, as he continued to roll around, screaming. Finally, I said, "Billy, I know it hurts, but if you were to die now, is this the way you'd like us to remember you?" Everyone found this hilarious. Even Billy started laughing. The message was clear: don't writhe around when you're smacked. Pain is manageable. You can deal with it. Like Billy, given the chance, you can even laugh at it.

The Vision of a Champion

Mentality is the defining quality that allows you to utilize all of your soccer abilities. It all goes back to what I say in the introduction of the book—the vision of a champion is exemplified by heart, athleticism, strength, tactics, focus, and skill.

Appendix I

Soccer Conditioning Workout

We think it is critical to share the entire foundation of everything we do in our program. We consider Greg Gatz an addition to our coaching staff. It is his sole responsibility to make our players quicker, faster, and more agile, and at the same time, help protect them from injury. The program in this section will also contribute to your mental hardening, which takes place in all aspects of our program. I wanted a forum for Greg to share with you everything that he does.

This section has been written with the assistance of Greg, the Director of Strength and Conditioning for Olympic Sports at UNC. Greg is one of a series of strength coaches the team has had, but he's been our best. In addition to training our current teams, he has worked closely with past UNC and U.S. National Team players such as Carla Overbeck, Mia Hamm, Lorrie Fair, and Cindy Parlow.

The importance of strength and conditioning cannot be overstated. That's because the overall fitness it provides is generally lacking among competitive soccer players. For all of its tremendous development, American youth soccer's focus on specific skill training and competition comes at the expense of general physical development. And it shows. Even at our level, we have players arrive at UNC unable to do even one push-up or pull-up.

There are several reasons to undertake a program like the one included in this chapter. The program addresses the "missing link" in most soccer programs. It creates a more well-rounded athlete, with an ability to better utilize the entire body in the most coordinated matter. This increases the level of soccer performance. Finally, it helps keep players injury-free, and it is also an important tool in injury rehabilitation.

To understand the importance of fitness, you must view it in totality. The primary goal in a good soccer or athletic program should be to integrate (and enhance) all components of fitness. This is contrary to an isolated approach. With the proper resistance work, for example, the focus is not on body building, but rather, on building yourself as a total athlete. The exercises in this section are geared toward this athleticism, as well as to soccer-specific skills. They emphasize not just strength and conditioning, but coordination, speed, agility, power, and balance. They are dynamic (i.e., they entail continual movement), as opposed to a more limited aspect of strength training, which isolates muscles, or entails simply running and lifting weights with machines, for example (which, by the way, if done properly, is still preferable to doing no strength and conditioning training at all).

Playing Injury-Free

Given the physical demands of competitive soccer, if you haven't yet been injured, you're the exception. Strength and conditioning is probably the single most important step you can take to protect yourself against injury.

While you may have heard a lot about strength training and injury prevention, you may not understand the connection. Consider the knee, for example, one of the greatest areas of injury in female soccer players. By doing the exercises in this section, you activate the supporting tissue in the ligaments surrounding the knee joint. In addition, your ankles and hips work in unison to provide further protection. (That is why the goal of a good program is always to train the "whole versus the part".)

Soccer is a year-round activity for many players. The better your "structural integrity"—that is, the stronger the muscles and connective tissues—the more you will be able to withstand the wear and tear of so much intense play, and the better you will be able to perform.

Injury often plagues serious players, and can jeopardize their careers. Cindy Parlow spent two years with a nagging hamstring problem. Cindy, who had a tendency to overstride instead of using short steps to accelerate, worked with Greg Gatz on some acceleration drills, including using an ABC ladder (i.e., agility, balance, coordination. You can make a version by laying out rope on the floor in a stepladder pattern). This helped her to learn movements that promote getting the feet down quickly during acceleration, thus emphasizing the pushing mode, as opposed to the pulling mode she was formerly using, which tends to cause stress on the hamstrings. Greg also helped Cindy strengthen her hamstrings by doing lunges and step-ups.

You've heard the expression "Let nature take its course" to describe the natural healing process. But modern theory dictates doing active rehabilitation. Perhaps the best testament to the value of this active rehabilitation is Carla Overbeck, who had knee surgery in June, shortly before the

2000 Olympic Games in September. Carla was facing difficult odds. The doctors told her it was questionable that she would heal in time for the Olympics. "It's going to take four months," they said. "I don't have four months," she replied. She worked with Greg, and was so motivated and aggressive in her rehab training that she healed in time to make the team.

Back to Basics

How many of today's young players spend the majority of their childhood just running, jumping, and playing on their own? The truth is that with the advent of organized sports there is very little free play, which is the way children naturally build a strength and fitness base.

Once upon a time, children created their own general fitness. Even traditional girls activities contributed. Hopscotch and jump rope are excellent plyometrics. (Plyometrics, also called jump training, are reactive movements and counter movements.) These traditional girls games utilize similar movements to those in some of the exercises prescribed here. It is important to do fitness activities—specifically those including balance and agility—in childhood. That's because in addition to establishing lifelong habits, much like learning a foreign language, there is a window of time during youth in which optimum physical abilities are established. (This is why adults have a harder time than children learning to speak French, and playing soccer!).

Due to this lack of a general fitness background, a variety of activities are prescribed here which address physical development—such as increasing strength, coordination, agility, and balance. In fact, Greg Gatz believes that even children at the very beginning of their development—as young as 10 years old—should add some general physical activity to their soccer skills in the form of fun games which require basic, general movement patterns.

Finally, a strength and conditioning program can be a lot of fun—at least it should be. From lunges, which are reminiscent of taking "giant steps," to tossing medicine balls—these exercises resemble the games children play. The UNC team certainly seems to have a good time doing them. That's why in the Olympic Sports weight room, you'll find the players laughing as much as lifting, raucously counting off their reps as they work out, and developing their team spirit as much as their fitness.

How the UNC Program Works

The program in this section is based on building "movement as opposed to muscle," which is the phrase popularized by renowned sports performance specialist Vern Gambetta, president of Gambetta Sports Training Systems in Sarasota, Florida. The program is also designed to be sports specific. Since soccer is played in all dimensions (i.e., left, right, back, forward, up, down, etc.), you have to be strong in multiple directions. In standard weight training, movements are done primarily in one plane (direction), leaving a player deficient, and also vulnerable to injury, in all the other directions.

The periodization, or cycles, of training given in this chapter include a preparation phase, a strength development phase, and finally, a maintenance phase.

These exercises are adapted from the program we use at UNC. There is no "science" to this adaptation; most programs need to be personalized. You will likely find your own best mix by experimenting with what is prescribed here.

Women at the Top

When the big-name players on the U.S. National Team were at UNC, they didn't have access to the exercises here. In fact, even after ten years on the National Team, it was only when they came back to work with Greg Gatz that they learned to incorporate this type of strength and fitness program into their routine. They still periodically return; they appreciate the resources we have.

About eight weeks after the 1999 Women's World Cup, Mia Hamm came to Chapel Hill to hold her fund-raiser celebrity golf tournament. She brought Brandi Chastain and Julie Foudy into the weight room to train during their stay. What they saw impressed even those accomplished veterans. Former UNC players have said that when they go back to U.S. National training camp, the others have told them, "You're lucky to have those strength training resources."

Teams in the WUSA employ full-time strength and conditioning coaches. In their very first season, players talked about how these coaches had them doing things they had never done before.

Considerations for Creating a Program

While it is optimal to include every possible cutting-edge technique to develop yourself as a player, you have to be realistic. Your time and energy are limited, so you must undertake the most efficient program, and one that you will stick with. Keep in mind that consistency is key, so take on only what you believe you can do over the long run. Start conservatively, particularly if you are new to this type of work. You can always add more later. It's okay to be a little bit sore after your first few workouts, but persistent soreness or difficulty completing the exercises means you should probably cut back the weight and/or the number of repetitions.

Undertaking this, or any such program, should be done with the advice and/or supervision of a professional. In addition, you can consult a coach, player, or other athlete experienced in this area. You should be instructed on how to do the exercises safely. Avoid attempting an exercise with too much weight, or doing something risky you have not tried without supervision. In any outside facility or program, work with a certified trainer. If you are working at home, do so with adult supervision.

To help you structure any strength and conditioning program, take into account the following:

1. What is your age? This has two meanings: your chronological, or actual, age and your physiological age. For example, some 12-year-olds are postpuberty and fully developed, while others at age 14 are still growing. Your physiological age should help you to determine the amount and level of appropriate strength training. It is recommended as safest at prepuberty to use your body weight only and avoid external weights (e.g., push-ups use body weight as resistance; a weighted-bar for bench press is an external weight). Postpuberty and more advanced athletes may graduate to external weights.

2. What is your training age? This refers to how much sports or physical activity you have done. Are you a relative beginner, or have you participated in years of soccer, and/or other such activities? The stronger your general conditioning background, the greater the amount of work—i.e., more weight or repetitions—you'll be able to do.

3. When are your sports seasons, and what do they consist of? This will determine how to proportion the amount you do. Those on soccer teams that compete in fall or spring, for example, might want to focus on strength training in the off-seasons (winter and summer), and do a lighter, more "maintenance program" during their competitive phases.

4. What is your level of commitment? Be honest with yourself. Don't compromise soccer skills training. On the other hand, even if strength training conflicts with skills practice, consider fitting in a minimal amount of conditioning. At the very least, injury prevention, which is an important aspect of these exercises, is a vital investment of your time. (At a minimum, a couple of sets of push-ups, lunges, crunches, and single-leg squats—done in that order—can be performed casually, even while watching television.)

Priority Strength and Conditioning

Whether you are short on time, or limited in energy, keep these priorities in mind:

Work from the inside/out—as Vern Gambetta suggests. Start from the core, then strengthen the extremities. The order of your strength priorities are:

1. The core: abdominals, lower back, hips and groin—your power center. All movement goes through, and is generated by, the body's core.
2. Bottom up (legs to waist).
3. Top down (shoulders to waist).

EQUIPMENT (Do It Yourself—gym membership not necessarily required!)

- Medicine Balls—These come in both kilograms or pounds of weight, and are made in leather or hard rubber. (Get the rubber for bouncing off of walls). Purchase at least one in the four- to five-pound range.
- Dumbbells—Three to 20 pounds, made in increments of five pounds. If you buy a dumbbell set, you can create what you need.
- 12"–18" stepping box or bench (6" for beginners).
- A jump rope.

Program Design

Ideally, you will need a minimum five- to eight-week block in order to adapt to, and gain benefits, from this program. Beginners will notice a marked strength difference within several weeks. More advanced athletes may not recognize more subtle changes, but you will still gain overall athletic benefits (e.g., balance and body control in addition to strength) and help yourself to prevent injury. Also, strength training must be constantly maintained to show results.

Assuming you play high school soccer in the fall, the program would best be done during the summer. If you play regularly in the spring, you could also begin in the winter. Do these workouts by allowing for at least one day's rest prior to competition, and at least one day's rest in between sessions.

(In season at UNC the program is done on Tuesdays and Wednesdays [but different parts of the body—Tuesdays are the lower body, and Wednesdays are the upper body]. For the first month, players go to the weight room four times a week. For the rest of the four-month off-season, they go three times a week. In summer we suggest in our Summer Training Program [see Appendix II] that players do conditioning and weights at least twice a week in preparation for the fall season).

The program is separated into phases. The first phase is two weeks of general preparation. The second phase is five to eight weeks (as time allows) for developing overall strength in order to get you ready for the requirements of playing. There is also a pre- and in-season program to maintain the strength levels. The majority of fitness work can be done by goalkeepers, with small modifications to emphasize mostly high-intensity short sprints and lots of agility work. However, the exercises provided here would be the same for them.

Devoting two sessions per week to some strength and conditioning is an excellent supplement to your soccer program. You can continue aspects of this program all year long as part of soccer, or as part of a cross-training routine. Be creative. You can also incorporate parts of this program into your warm-up or postpractice routine, such as doing one or two quick sets of squats or lunges. Engage your teammates in a group effort.

- Do 12–15 repetitions of each exercise, with 30 seconds rest in between each set, and one minute rest between each of the two to three complete sets of all exercises. As you get more into strength training, you will use heavier weights and take longer rest intervals. When doing body circuits, maintain a controlled, even movement.
- As you gain more experience, follow the UNC routine: one day more strength-oriented, the second day more power-oriented. Do the power workout closer to game day, as it more closely duplicates the rigors of play. In order to activate the nervous system, some elite athletes even do a light power-oriented workout in the morning before an afternoon game.
- Warm up for 15 to 20 minutes by jumping rope or going for a light jog (about five to 10 minutes), and then going through exercises that move the body as a whole. Use some of elements of the soccer warm-up prescribed in Chapter 16. Don't just do static stretching. Your warm-up for this program needs to be movement-oriented.
- Cool down by stretching. Do not omit this phase. Every muscle that is strengthened should also be kept flexible.
- Do these exercises in the order in which they are given here. This order is by design. A good circuit training regimen works and rests different muscle groups in a coordinated manner.
- In doing these exercises or selecting your weights, if you cannot comfortably achieve at least eight repetitions, lower the weight or modify the exercise.

- Medicine ball rotation, overhead chop and squat and press exercises can also be done with a weight(s), such as a two-and-a-half to five-pound dumbbell(s).
- Soccer is played three-dimensionally—with lots of changes of direction and regrouping of the muscles and the body to make plays. A three-plane movement is great fitness preparation. In addition to straight forward, do your exercises, especially the leg work (e.g., lunges) also at angles (i.e., 45° to the side and 90° to the side).
- To a degree, most of these exercises can work many parts of the body. Provided in parentheses are the main body areas strengthened.

Weeks 1–2 — General Preparation. If you've been in an ongoing strength and conditioning program, you may choose to bypass this phase.

Total Body Circuit Exercises

Medicine Ball Rotation (strengthens primarily the core—i.e., lower back, hips, groin and abdominal muscles)
　　Stand with your feet shoulder-width apart, knees slightly bent (we call this soft knees). Hold a medicine ball with your arms extended in front of you, elbows slightly bent. Rotate your trunk to alternate sides (right and left). Twist as far as comfortably possible while still maintaining upright form. Either keep your head facing forward (which works your trunk more), or if your head rotates with your body, you will work the shoulder area as well.

Push-Ups (strengthens primarily chest and shoulders)
　　Place your hands on the ground, slightly wider than shoulder width. Keep your body in a flat plane, making sure not to raise your buttocks in the air. If you cannot accomplish a minimum of eight, modify the push-ups by placing your knees on the ground with your feet lifted up in the air. If you use correct form—i.e., your body doesn't buckle or bend—you are also using the body core, thus activating all of its muscles.

Bodyweight Squat (strengthens primarily the legs)
　　Stand with your feet shoulder-width apart, hands behind your head. Squat down, keeping your heels on the floor and your upper body upright, until your thighs are nearly parallel to the ground, but no lower than parallel. Keep your head upright, looking forward. Stand up and repeat. If you do this properly, it also forces the muscles of the lower back to contract, and work. If done improperly, the back bends and relaxes.

Once you're comfortable, and doing the movement with correct form, add resistance (either hold a medicine ball or dumbbells at the chest, or use a weighted bar held behind the neck).

You should do this exercise with supervision, as you can hurt yourself with incorrect form.

Medicine Ball Overhead Chop (strengthens the body core)
Stand with your feet slightly wider than shoulder-width apart, knees slightly bent. Holding a medicine ball (or a two- to four-pound dumbbell) above your head with arms extended, bend down as if you were chopping wood, bringing the ball down between your legs. Keep the arms straight throughout. Swing the ball in a full arc. Bring the ball back above your head and repeat.

Dumbbell Curl and Press (strengthens primarily the biceps and shoulders)
Stand with your feet shoulder-width apart, knees slightly bent. Holding the dumbbells with your arms hanging at your sides and your palms facing forward, bend your elbows and bring the dumbbells up to your shoulders. Then, turn your wrists so your palms are facing each other, and extend both hands up and overhead. Make sure to extend your arms completely. Keep the body trunk stable while doing the exercise. Reverse the direction (i.e., bring dumbbells to the shoulders, then turn your palms facing forward, then curl back down to your sides). Do this exercise in one continuous motion.

Alternate Front Lunge (strengthens primarily the gluteals [buttocks] and quadriceps)
Stand with your feet shoulder-width apart, hands at your sides. Take a step out from your body, extending one leg in front of you as far as comfortable while still maintaining your balance (do not step so far that your knee extends in front of your toes). The heel of your back foot should come off the ground. Step back and repeat, stepping forward with the opposite leg.

Medicine Ball Squat and Press (strengthens the total body)
This is done in the same way as the body weight squat, only holding a medicine ball (extended out in front of you, or over your head, each of which forces different core muscles to be activated. Alternate arm position with each rep, or do one set of each).

When you rise up from the squat, extend your hands overhead pushing the medicine ball straight up. Bring the ball back down to your chest and begin the squat. Remember: do this exercise in one continuous motion.

If you use dumbbells you have the option of working one hand at a time, which develops more coordination, and may also facilitate strengthening a weak side.

Incline Pull-Ups (strengthens primarily the arms and upper back muscles, also develops posture)

You'll need a bar for this. If you do soccer practice in a park, look for some monkey bars.

An incline pull-up lessens the difficulty of a standard pull-up, which you can do instead if you are able, or try the flex arm hang—hanging for a time with bent elbows.

With your head facing a bar, heels on the ground, toes pointed upward, keeping your body in a supine/parallel position, grab the bar and pull yourself up to your chin.

You can make an incline pull-up easier by bending your knees and keeping your feet flat on the floor. As a general rule, the further away your limbs are from the center of your body, the more difficult the movement.

Standard pull-ups are notoriously difficult. Most players at UNC can do eight to 12 at most. Some players can't do any. On the other hand, at one time Carla Overbeck could do 20.

Alternate Step-Up (strengthens the legs)

Facing a bench or step, step up with one foot, bringing the other up, but without putting the trailing foot down on the step. Bring the trailing foot back down first, then the stepping foot. Alternate feet on step-ups. Keep your arms hanging at your sides, and your posture upright. Also, try step-ups at various angles.

Abdominal Crunches (strengthens the abdominal muscles)

Do regular crunches (i.e., sit up part way, but not all the way), and combine these with rotational crunches, in which the body twists while coming up, so the elbow points toward the opposite knee.

Off-Season Weeks 3–10

Day 1

- Medicine Ball Rotation
- Medicine Ball Overhead Chop
- Abdominal Crunches
- Alternate Step-Up

- Medicine Ball Squat and Press
- Push-Ups
- Dumbbell Curl and Press

Day 2

Day 1 focused on strength, Day 2 develops more power (e.g., throwing an object). These are both components of soccer.

Medicine Ball Chest Pass (strengthens primarily the upper body—shoulder, chest and arms)

This exercise resembles a basketball chest pass. Stand with your feet shoulder-width apart, knees slightly bent. Face a partner or a wall. Hold the ball with your fingers spread and your palms facing forward (like a goalkeeper), and extend the elbows out to your sides. Push the ball with an explosive thrust. Catch the ball and repeat.

Medicine Ball Soccer Throw-In (strengthens primarily the shoulder muscles, and activates core)

Do this just like a soccer throw-in, to a partner or against a wall.

Medicine Ball Rotational Throw (strengthens primarily the core)

Start the same way as you do for the Medicine Ball Rotation. Twist to your right, swing forward and toss the ball in front of you—as though you were throwing a bucket of water. Alternate throwing from the left and right sides.

- Incline Pull-Ups
- Alternate Front Lunge
- Abdominal Crunches
- Single Leg Squat—Do this as you would a regular body weight squat, but while raising one leg off the ground. This focuses on strengthening one leg (and ankle) at a time, and also works on balance.

IN SEASON (Try to do this on days off of soccer practice and/or games.)

Day 1

- Push-Ups
- Incline Pull-Ups
- Squat (with external weight)
- Alternate Lunge

- Alternate Step-Up
- Abdominal Crunches

Day 2

- Push-Ups
- Incline Pull-Ups
- Medicine Ball Chest Pass
- Medicine Ball Soccer Throw-In
- Medicine Ball Rotational Throw
- Abdominal Crunches

Staying Healthy—Sports Medicine for Females

The overall responsibility of our medical care, headed by Bill Prentice, Ph.D., includes the challenge of all aspects of sports medicine. At UNC we are fortunate to have the staff, facilities, and cutting-edge philosophy that has helped to set the standard in sports medicine. Part of sharing with you the depth of our program is including some of the wealth of experience in this field. This section, written with the assistance of some UNC sports medicine staff, contains vital information that can make an enormous impact on your soccer career. After all, nothing is more important than staying—and playing—healthy.

I attribute our success to many factors, most of which have to do with skill, conditioning, mentality, and teamwork. But I always include our medical staff, notably our trainer, Bill Prentice. Soccer is a contact sport, and the extraordinary capacity to care for and rehabilitate our injured athletes so that they can resume competition is what Bill brings to the team. Consequently, there are some seasons we get to the NCAA Championship game because of Bill.

Obviously, the intention here is not to provide you with a complete sports medicine guide in one chapter, but rather, to give you a sense of the overall importance of health and injury care and prevention, and how it affects you. It is particularly useful for you to be aware of some of the medical issues which are especially prevalent among female soccer players.

College is the first time away from home for many of our players. Before coming to UNC, they always had their parents to take care of them. Being on their own is a learning process. We are fortunate to have a state-of-the-art staff and facilities to be able to assist our players in regard to their health. With the resources of one of the country's best college sports medicine staffs, there is daily interaction between the athletes and our physicians, athletic trainers and physical therapists, as well as numerous graduate and undergraduate student trainers. Many of these staff members also attend games and daily practices.

As part of a UNC medical staff of eight physicians and 10 staff athletic trainers, we have a team orthopedist, Bill Garrett, M.D.; team physician, Tom Brickner, M.D.; and team athletic trainer, Bill Prentice, Ph.D. Brickner and Prentice have assisted in writing this section. In addition to serving as our team physician, Tom Brickner treats between 300 and 400 athletes from nine different teams in the course of a year. Bill Prentice has been the athletic trainer for our team since its inception in 1980. Among his numerous awards is the 1999 Most Distinguished Athletic Trainer Award, presented annually by the National Athletic Trainers Association.

Check It Out

Tom Brickner and Bill Prentice together conduct yearly preparticipation examinations of all of our players. The main purpose of these exams is to get a baseline knowledge of the players' health, and to identify any potential problem areas. Dr. Brickner's exam is similar to the one you are given by a family physician or pediatrician, except that he takes a more thorough look at the musculoskeletal (muscles, bones, and joints) system. Both Brickner and Prentice deal with injury prevention and treatment. Prentice, for example, often discovers preexisting conditions such as joint instability caused by previous ankle sprains which have not been properly rehabilitated. In addition to these annual examinations, our team fitness and conditioning tests provide both coaches and our medical staff with important health and injury information. For one thing, the more fit a player is, the less likely she is to get injured.

Tom Brickner recommends a yearly soccer preparticipation physical for all young players, because they are rapidly growing and thus, changes occur. You may already get a yearly physical with your pediatrician or primary care doctor, which can also serve the purpose of a preparticipation exam. Always make sure to discuss your athletic participation with your doctor.

To keep on top of your health it is important to understand your needs as an active soccer player. Take advantage of expert advice when necessary. For example, our medical staff establishes communication with incoming freshman to make them aware of their health care needs, and refers them to other available medical staff—such as a psychologist or a nutritionist— if indicated.

The Triad

It is important to be informed about common trends that exist, particularly among female athletes. One is the "female athlete triad," a syndrome that has been highly researched and publicized. The triad, a phrase coined in the early 1990s at an American College of Sports Medicine meeting, refers to three health areas which impact on one another—disordered eating, irregular menstrual cycles, and bone health. Disordered eating patterns (obsessive dieting or calorie restriction, and exaggerated avoidance of fat, and such diseases as anorexia and bulimia), together with exercise, may result in a loss of nutrients, weight, and fat stores. The result can be a disruption in the production of the hormone estrogen, which regulates the menstrual cycle. Subsequently, amenorrhea, the loss of the menstrual cycle, may occur. In females, estrogen plays a large role in bone growth, development, and maintenance. While exercise does promote health, including bone density, a lack of this hormone may nevertheless result in a weakening of the bones, making them more susceptible to stress fractures, and eventually leading to early osteoporosis (brittle bones). Compounding the problem is that this potential disruption of bone growth comes precisely at an age when a female accrues 60 to 70% of her bone mass.

In an average taken of various sports, 30% of female athletes have an eating problem, as opposed to 10 to 15% of the general population. In some sports, the number may be as high as 70%. The "triad" is often seen among those who are highly trained and who fit a particular profile—compulsive, high achievers, strivers, goal-setters, and perfectionists.

At higher levels, athletes often look for anything to fine-tune themselves. They may go to an extreme with training or diet that often leads to problems. The general population of women includes a lot with eating disorders. In the athlete, this may come from a desire to find an edge—perhaps an attempt to feel quicker or more fit by modifying her nutrition. This well-intentioned desire for an edge can get distorted and intensified, until it becomes unhealthy.

Some female athletes view losing their period as a sign they are in shape. In fact, they may even be told by their doctors that this is the case, and not to worry about it. However, those who have not had a period in three consecutive cycles should see a medical professional. After ruling out other causes or conditions, hormone treatments (such as birth control pills) may be prescribed to promote bone health.

Cindy Parlow ('95–'98)

Eat Well, Drink Well, Play Well

I majored in nutrition at UNC because I loved math and science, and I knew there was some connection among these fields. By the time I was a sophomore, I learned how nutrition is useful in sports. What I learned began to influence the way I ate. It has also influenced my goals. I'd like to use nutrition studies to work with kids one day, perhaps in a hospital setting.

I eat differently now than when I was younger. I make wiser decisions. I basically try to avoid fast food altogether. But I used to eat a lot of junk food, particularly back in high school. I was terrible. I'd eat at MacDonald's with only an hour-and-a-half to two hours in between games. At tournaments, when we didn't have much time, I didn't eat very well. If the team went to Wendy's, and the coach told us to get baked potatoes, I had to have a huge burger, too. At the time, I needed the calories, because if I didn't eat enough, I'd get a headache. I didn't really start to think about this until college. Fortunately, that fast food didn't have a negative effect on me. I wouldn't change what I did in high school, because I enjoyed my time with my friends. I'm not saying you can never go to MacDonald's, but I wouldn't eat this way now before a game.

I grew up playing soccer in the South. When you're really hot, you lose tons of fluids. In high school, I wasn't great about drinking water. It was all sodas, or nothing. I never noticed the effect of dehydration until I started drinking more. I didn't put lack of fluids together with the fatigue I would experience, particularly in the last 15 minutes of a game. Sometimes after playing, I'd get headaches from dehydration and not eating enough calories. I'd even get muscle cramps. Now, I've completely changed. At every meal, every day, I drink a quart of water. On game days, I drink water throughout the day in addition to at meals. The National Team stocks Gatorade and water, but before games I drink just water. I grab five bottles. I'm amazed at how wonderful a "nutrient" water is.

I'm pretty regular in my training and competing eating patterns, which I started in college. I try to eat an hour to an hour-and-a-half before practice and four hours before a game—a high-carbohydrate meal (and a good-sized portion), such as spaghetti or baked potatoes. I avoid things like soda and beans before a game. I still love my sodas, but I only drink them after a game, or during the week. Sometimes, I'm hungry before a game, so I'll eat a half a Power Bar (all of us on the National Team usually eat some kind of

There are few players with Cindy Parlow's psychological dimension. She is one of the fiercest competitors and most physical personalities I've ever coached. She is the consummate creative personality on the ball, and devastating in the air.

sports bar), or drink some Gatorade. There's a famous ritual at UNC, a candy bag for during the game. It's just for fun, though.

The team eats pregame meals together at UNC. I missed the pregame team meal once, and ate on my own. I felt weak and tired when I played, without my usual strength. It obviously wasn't a good meal. The team eats every meal together. It builds chemistry. It brings us all together; we tell stories and have a good time. All of us eat well, although Jules (Julie Foudy) does have to have her doughnuts whenever she gets them. Players on the National Team sometimes come to me for advice on nutrition.

Eating with the team is part of a consistent routine. It's comfortable not having to think about preparation. You have the game meal, attend the pregame meeting, get dressed the way you like to, do the same warm-up—there's no mystery about what's going to happen. You know you're ready to play.

I think a lot of women, especially in sports, tend to avoid certain types of foods—like protein, or those with fat. Physically active females have to learn to understand that they need these foods. I'm a huge carnivore, but if you don't regularly eat meat, there are other ways to get protein. Also, there are huge misconceptions about fat content in food and weight gain. While

I try to avoid fast food pretty much all of the time, I do eat foods with fat, such as beef, chicken, and dairy products (which are also important to get calcium). I eat very sensibly, but try not to eat the same foods all the time. I'm not a late-night eater, either. For breakfast, I'll have a bowl of cereal, a banana and some water before morning training at 10 a.m., and keep drinking water throughout the day, unless it's really hot. Then I'll have some Gatorade as well. My main course at lunch is baked chicken, potatoes, and salad or a turkey and cheese sandwich. Dinner is hot food, some protein like chicken or fish, mashed potatoes, broccoli or cauliflower, soup, water, maybe a soda. If I eat sweets, it's a brownie or cookie after dinner.

In elite athletics, obesity isn't really an issue. It's anorexia and other eating disorders. I know this problem may be on the rise, at least in college athletics, and it's made worse by the pressure society puts on women to be thin. It's amazing to me. I hope those who have an eating disorder can recognize their problem, and get some help. Unfortunately, sometimes they have to hit rock bottom before they do.

I've always been a big eater. I come from a loving family. I'm the third, and the only girl, of four kids, and having meals together as a family has always been a special occasion for me, but I spent my entire college career trying to put on weight and gain muscle. I'm 5'11", and at UNC, I was 125 pounds, my skinniest ever. Now, I weigh between 145 and 150 pounds. I've had quite a few friends who want to lose weight, no matter how skinny they are—even if it makes them poorer athletes. It's usually not about the way they play, or even the way they look, it's the way they feel about themselves. After all, the one thing you can control is what you put in your mouth.

I don't like the word diet, period. If you're changing what you eat for a few weeks in order to lose weight, that's a diet. I'm into common sense. If you need to "diet," you probably need to change your lifestyle. That's real change.

Common Health and Injury Problems in Females

Female athletes are prone to certain conditions. Anemia, which can be thought of as "low blood" or "tired blood," is more frequent in females than in males because of the monthly loss of blood during menstruation. This creates a higher need for iron, an important mineral in the diet and from supplements. Anemia causes such symptoms as fatigue, a feeling of burnout or mild depression, and recurrent illness or injuries.

Tom Brickner also sees a lot of health-related psychological symptoms among women soccer players, such as stress, anxiety, depression and burnout. (The medical signs of burnout include fatigue, decreasing performance, and loss of interest and/or enthusiasm.) Hard training makes players more susceptible to these health and injury problems, and increases the chance of a compromised immune system, perhaps making players more susceptible to viral infections. You should see a medical professional if you experience any of the above symptoms, or health conditions such as fever, coughing, or diffuse muscle aches, any of which persist longer than one week. You can avoid many of these problems with a commonsense approach, using proper hygiene such as stringent hand washing; not sharing water bottles or cups, glasses, utensils or food; covering your mouth when coughing; getting sufficient rest, etc.

One of the most common problems Bill Prentice sees, aside from ACL injuries, is chronic ankle sprains (in both men and women) due to weak ankles. He prescribes the ankle strengthening exercises below, and in fact, will not let a player who suffers from recurrent ankle problems return to training if she is not performing these exercises.

Ankle Strength Prescription

To strengthen and stabilize ankles, purchase a wobble board (from a sports conditioning catalog), or make one, using a half-inch piece of plywood cut into a circle 24 inches in diameter and a wooden croquet ball sawed in half and nailed to the middle of the board. Every day, stand on the board and rock back and forth (on a homemade board) or a roll around (on a wobble board) about 20 to 30 times in each direction, making sure the edges of the wobble board touch the floor. This action strengthens and stabilizes the ankles, while helping to provide them with control. You can also try doing single-leg squats (see page 269) on a cushion, or any surface that wobbles. Try doing the squats barefoot, and with your eyes closed.

According to Bill Prentice, following knees and ankles, the most common injuries are lower extremity muscle strains. In order of frequency, these strains occur to the hamstrings, groin, quadriceps and calves. Without a doubt, the best prevention for these strains is stretching. Stretching is vitally important for general flexibility and injury prevention, and you should do it consistently. Some teams stretch as part of a warm-up, which is fine. Research shows, however, that the best time to stretch for injury prevention is immediately following physical activity.

In addition to flexibility, work hard on soccer-specific strength. You can do this with the program of exercises as described starting on page 266, which also includes flexibility.

General Signs of Injury and Home Remedies

General signs of injury include swelling, warmth or redness of the skin to the injured site, decreased range of motion to the joint, obvious visual deformity, difficulty or inability to bear weight, feeling of instability, and feeling of locking or catching in the joint.

If injuries do occur, your best and safest bet is to apply an elastic compression wrap, and ice and elevation applied as soon as possible following injury for 20 to 30 minutes. Repeat this cycle as often as possible for 24, preferably 48 hours, following injury. Stretching and range of motion exercises can then be used to regain movement.

You may experience muscle soreness after a hard workout, which you can best alleviate the following day with general movement or doing a light jog and stretching, which increases circulation and removal of lactic acid, an excess of which causes the soreness. DOMS, or delayed onset muscle soreness, means that while you may not feel sore at first, symptoms heighten up to 36 hours following activity, and should then subside. Treatment of minor muscle aches includes having parents or friends massage the affected muscles, or you can even try self-massage, by hand or with devices sold to assist you. If you're not feeling significantly better with minimal rest, it is probably best to consult a medical professional.

The Knee

In an athlete the knee is very vulnerable to injury. This is particularly true in the female athlete. Bill Prentice ranks injury to the ACL (anterior cruciate ligament) as the number one knee problem he sees in female soccer players, and in his practice, the numbers are on the rise. He has seen these problems since the beginning of the UNC program, and among the current players he mentions is Leslie Gaston, who has had six ACL reconstructive surgeries!

Female athletes in jumping and cutting sports such as soccer and basketball show a higher incidence of this knee injury than males in the same sports. Serious knee injury is six times higher in female soccer players than in male players, and knee surgeries (such as to repair the ACL) make up 70% of all surgeries for girls.

There are various theories as to why ACL injury occurs so frequently in female athletes. Some believe that it may be related to female hormones causing joints to be more lax, or anatomical (physical) differences, such as pressure exerted on the knees due to wider hips in females. Tests show that women athletes typically have stronger quadricep muscles (front of the thigh) than hamstring muscles (back of the thigh), and this strength imbalance may cause a tear of the ACL. However, other experts attribute the problem not to anatomical or physiological causes, but to differences in training and coaching. These experts contend that despite advances in women's sports, attention by coaches and physicians to female athletes has lagged in comparison to male athletes. Studies show inadequate training may be rectified by specialized programs, including jump training (plyometrics) and stability exercises. Specialty training in female athletes has been shown to decrease by 50% the type of knee action that causes ACL strain. Prevention of this, and other, injuries through overall body strength and stability is why programs such as those in the Soccer Conditioning Workout section (this Appendix) are so important.

Bill Prentice suggests that the best way to prevent ACL injuries is to strengthen the muscles and tendons that surround the knee joint. Even if you can't do the exercises in the Soccer Conditioning Workout section, he recommends simple knee extensions (while sitting, raising your lower leg with weight attached to your foot or ankle, in order to strengthen the quadriceps [muscles in the front of the thigh]; hamstring curls [while lying on your stomach, raising weight from your ankles up in the air toward your back; strengthens the back of the thigh]; and toe raises [while standing on the edge of a rise, such as a stair, raising up on your toes; strengthens the calf]). If you don't have access to a weight room, try squats with a bag loaded with books or other weight to strengthen the quadriceps, and do lunges (described in the Soccer Conditioning Workout section) for the hamstrings. Do ten repetitions of each exercise, for a total of three sets, two to three times per week.

Here's a test for your ACL: Studies show that when they jump, half of women land in a potentially dangerous position. Their legs may be nearly straight, or their knees slightly turned in or out. Try this test to determine if are making this potentially problematic landing, which can throw the knee joint off balance, causing the ACL to snap. Jump down from a 12-inch stair or bench, then freeze. Take a look at your position. Make sure your knees are slightly bent and in line with your hips and feet. If not, practice your landings. It could protect you from knee problems.

Female Matters

Adolescent girls who are serious about sports should be aware of issues concerning their menstrual cycles. Although menstrual irregularities in active females are more researched among those who are at greater potential risk of health problems (i.e., runners, dancers, gymnasts), information on soccer players is harder to come by. That's the conclusion of Mary Schlegel, M.D., Clinical Assistant Professor of Obstetrics and Gynecology and Director of Women's Health for Student Health at UNC Chapel Hill. However, informal discussions among players do reveal that there are those who experience delayed or irregular menses.

Here's what you should know. The risk of delayed or irregular menstrual periods can have a negative effect on bone density, up to 60% of which is laid down at menarche (during the beginning of the menstrual cycle). According to Dr. Schlegel, late puberty is defined as having no period by age 16, or no secondary sexual development by age 14 (e.g., breast growth and pubic hair). The average age of the first menstrual period in the United States is 12 (down from age 16 in the past 100 years). Family history, diet, height, weight, and percentage body fat have a big impact on when stages of sexual development occur.

"Eating disorders are a problem which can overlap with the effect of exercise on the menstrual cycle. I don't want to discourage girls from intense sports, but I think we have to individualize some recommendations. Some girls will be at much greater risk to their bones than others."

If you have a late, or an irregular menstrual cycle, or any questions or concerns, you should consult a medical professional, preferably one who has some experience treating athletic girls.

When to Sit It Out

For Tom Brickner, what stands out about working with the team is the intense competitiveness and strong will of the players. If they are hurt, he says, they don't want to be told what they can't do. "What CAN I do to remain active?" is their question. This toughness helps them to persevere through illness and injury, an attitude that is bred throughout all the players, and often exists in high-level sports. What is also helpful is that at a high level, the players tend to be very attuned to how they are feeling.

It may seem hard to believe, but players like Mia Hamm and Kristine Lilly were forced to sit on the bench to rest injuries. Susan Bush, Tiffany Roberts, Lorrie Fair—all U.S. National players—have also sat out a lot of practices and games. But it's not just the big names; it's done with everyone. In our system we must, by necessity, learn how to rest injured players in order to get them healthy for crucial games. So we are more prone to sit them out when necessary, and not to take any risks in less difficult games.

As Bill Prentice points out, our philosophy is based on our ultimate goals. Our team expects at least to reach the NCAA Championship tournament. So, instead of having players play through an injury during the regular season, they sit it out, and thus are ready to play when it is most crucial for us, and for them. In fact, so prevalent is this routine that for the entire year of 1999, we didn't have everyone available to play until the semifinal Championship game! Susan Bush sat out the 1999 season for weeks with hamstring and ligament strains. She did supervised rehabilitation, came back, and was named an MVP in the NCAA final.

Many times, the coaches or the media praise those who play through injury. Bill Prentice says he's not overly conservative about resting players, but he tells those who are reluctant to do so that there's a good reason for it. "We don't need you for practices, we need you for games," is his point. He says it's hardest to convince freshman to sit out even practice. "They're used to being patted on the back for toughing out an injury. They're concerned with what Anson will think if they sit out practice. Just think how concerned he'll be if you pull up injured and have to sit out three weeks instead of a few practice days," counters Prentice.

The Psychology of Injury

The evolution of women's soccer at UNC reflects the history of the women's collegiate game. The scheduling of play is a lot tougher than it used to be. Consequently, resting players is a lot more relevant now than in the past. Before 1985, just a small collection of teams comprised our true competition. Now, any collegiate team can beat us. In the old days, it was simple to rest players, since there were more easy games, and you could even play people with some minor injuries, because the intensity of the matches varied tremendously.

Bill Prentice's job is to try to determine whether an injury is truly real or not, which isn't always easy. After a while, you get to know the "mindset" of the players you're coaching. While some "tough it out" to the point they cause themselves serious injury, others may feel unable to participate with relatively minor ailments. This may be a way to protect their fragile psychological dimension. For example, there is sometimes a complex dynamic between young soccer players and their parents. Parents may have a greater ambition for their children's success than the players themselves. Believe it or not, this is true even in our environment. We have some players at UNC who hide behind an injury, and it protects them from their fear of the wrath of their parents. Then, they don't have the pressure of trying to live up to their mom's or dad's expectations. The other side of the equation is that minor aches or pains can become a psychological problem that parents create. They make a big deal out of a bump or bruise, or take their player to the doctor or orthopedist every time she gets a minor injury.

Try to be open and honest with yourself, and your parents and coaches. On occasion, Tom Brickner says, an athlete confides in him, "I just need a break." But most are reluctant to openly admit this, because even if they realize it, they don't want to disappoint or upset adults.

On the other hand, aches and pains are your body's messages. Don't ignore them. You shouldn't be cavalier about injury, or just try to play through it when it's serious. Knee or ankle injuries, and muscle pulls, can be crippling. You shouldn't push through injury that can damage you long-range. There's a difference between a relatively minor problem and something that doesn't resolve in a couple of days. Young people heal quickly, but if you experience any of the signs of injury mentioned above, or persistent pain or soreness for two to three days, it should be evaluated by a medical professional.

By the same token, this is a contact sport, and those who don't like contact shouldn't be playing soccer. Besides, "hurt" is a broad category. While ligament damage and severe muscle strains and pulls warrant rest, everyone in soccer plays with cuts and bruises, slight strains or other minor injuries. You've got to listen to your body, use your experience, and seek out the advice of those you know and trust to help you determine when to play and when to rest.

About UNC Women's Soccer

National Champion: 1981, 1982, 1983, 1984, 1986, 1987, 1988, 1989, 1990, 1991, 1992, 1993, 1994, 1996, 1997, 1999, 2000

ACC (Atlantic Coast Conference) Champion: 1987, 1989, 1990, 1991, 1992, 1993, 1994, 1995, 1996, 1997, 1998, 1999, 2000, 2001

Eleven players to date have had their Carolina numbers retired. They are #2 April Heinrichs, #3 Shannon Higgins, #7 Robin Confer, #8 Debbie Keller, #13 Tisha Venturini, #14 Lorrie Fair, #15 Kristine Lilly, #19 Mia Hamm, Cindy Parlow's #22, #27 Staci Wilson, and Meredith Florance's #28.

University of North Carolina Tar Heels
    For more on UNC women's soccer, check on the web at: www.TarHeel Blue.com, www.ncgsc.com, www.dynastysoccergear.com

Resources

Training Soccer Champions, by Anson Dorrance with Tim Nash, 1996, JTC Sports.
Goal! The Ultimate Guide for Soccer Moms and Dads, by Gloria Averbuch and Ashley Michael Hammond, 1999, Rodale Books.
Carolina Women's Soccer, media guide, UNC Athletic Communications.
Nothin' Finer— Carolina: The History of the University of North Carolina Women's Soccer, by David Smale, 1993, The Donning Company, Publishers, Virginia Beach, VA.

Videotapes:

Dynasty, University of North Carolina women's soccer, 1995, JAMB Productions LLC, Chapel Hill, NC.

Training Championship Players and Teams, 1998, JAMB Productions LLC, Chapel Hill, NC

Twenty-First Century Soccer Recruiting—
The Internet

Listed below are websites that will supply you with information that can help you with the college recruitment process. New sites are springing up daily. Be sure to check the links at these websites for other related sites.

collegesoccer.com
Exceptional Information. One of the best places to learn about different college programs. The section on the National Scoreboard provides constant updates of college scores. The College Soccer News section highlights fast-breaking stories. The Next Wave section details where senior recruits have signed. Explore all the areas and don't forget to check out the link section.

ESPN.go.com
Click on the section that says college sports. Once in that section, click on the soccer areas for current articles and scores in men's and women's soccer.

naia.org
This is the official website of the National Association of Intercollegiate Athletics. Information is available on schools with soccer programs that are affiliated with the NAIA.

ncaa.org
This is the official website of the National Collegiate Athletic Association. Information is available on schools with soccer programs that are affiliated with the NCAA. Check out the NCAA Eligibility Rules, NCAA Clearing-house, NCAA Soccer Championships, etc.

njcaa.org
This is the official website of the National Junior College Athletic Association. Information is available on schools with soccer programs that are affiliated with the NJCAA.

nscaa.com
This is the website of the National Soccer Coaches Association of America. It services all different coaching levels. Check out the News module. Although many of the articles will not apply to the student-athlete, the site has very thoughtful articles about different aspects of the college soccer scene. Also, the NSCAA soccer rankings of all the college associations and the conference rankings are updated regularly during the season and are very helpful. It also includes information on soccer programs at junior colleges.

socceramerica.com
Soccer America is often referred to as America's No. 1 soccer news weekly. This is the website of that highly respected publication. One click on the College module will bring up a variety of articles on men's and women's college soccer. The coverage is especially good during the fall college season. Check in often to keep up with the ups and downs of the fall competitions. The organization also puts out weekly rankings during the season.

Soccerbuzz.com
Soccer Buzz is a free magazine on the Internet that is devoted to women's collegiate soccer at the NCAA Division 1 level. It provides detailed information on teams, players, games and coaches. Game results are provided by NCAA member institutions and posted as they are made available. This sit is chock-full with all kinds of detailed information. It is worth your while to check every nook and cranny. Don't forget to look at the links!

Soccerinfo.com
This site offers college scores and schedules as well as conference information. Scores are usually posted within 24 hours of college matches. It is unusual to find NCAA, NAIA, and NJCAA information all on one site.

CollegeInfo©, Inc., Copyright 2000
Kent & Ramona Barber, W. Des Moines, IA

Appendix II

The Essence of the UNC Soccer System

Yearly Rhythm

We're sharing with you our organizational playing and developmental structure. The yearly rhythm is an overview of how each part of the year has its own special training and player development emphasis. It's a breakdown of the different things that we do during various periods.

Competitive Matrix

The competitive matrix is basically a report card for practice performance in the fall. The reason we record everything is to create practice intensity. But the reason we organize the matrix is for players' postseason goal-setting, and to make it clear to each player what areas she needs to work on for her continued development.

Training Blocks

Training blocks are expanded portions of the yearly rhythm—a competitive breakdown of some parts of that rhythm, with names and competitive ranks substituted for names of training environments.

Conditioning Test Charts

These test charts are the physical aspects of the competitive matrix—athletic and strength training performances—broken down into rankings.

These are the results of tests administered by Don Kirkendall, Ph.D., and Greg Gatz.

Long-Range Tracking

This is another way to organize the competitive matrix and the conditioning test charts in a format in which the players can see their own progress athletically—in terms of strength development—and their technical development, over the course of their collegiate careers.

Summer Training Program

This is a packet we send out each summer to the new and returning players to prepare for the fall. It can be used in part or as a whole for soccer conditioning for players in the off-season.

Self/Peer Evaluation

These are our core values, put into a format in which each of the players can evaluate herself against these values, and when appropriate or necessary, evaluate teammates.

North Carolina Women's Soccer Yearly Rhythm

In Season

Aug 12–31: Preseason
  TWO-A-DAYS—until classes start (5 days)
    1. Testing in morning (1.5 hr)
      • day 1 - Beep, Agility, Vert. Jump, Speed Testing w/Don Kirkendall
      • day 2 - 20s, 40s, 60s, 80s, 100s
      • day 3 - 120s
      • day 4 - off
      • day 5 - Cooper
    2. Training in afternoon (1.5 hr)
       regular training
       (2 x 1.5 hr) training sessions per day until classes start
  ONE-A-DAYS—until first game (2 weeks)
    • regular training with emphasis on scrimmages, choreography, starter and reserve units formation
    • establish speed ladder
    • lifting Tues., Wed. (1 hr each)

Sept 1–Nov 9: from first game until NCAA Tournament (2nd week of Nov.)
  Play Fri., Sun.
  20 min. team jog and stretch Sat.
  Mon.—Back to Pressure warm-up, shooting games (1 hr)
  Lifting Tues. (lower), Wed. (upper) (45 mins each)
  Train Tues., Wed., Thurs. (1.5 hr each)
    Tues.—Triangle Passing warm-up, 120s (cones start 2nd week of Oct just before conference tournament), 3-Tier Shooting, Bogies, 20s-40s
    Wed.—6+1 v 3 and combination game warm-up, 1 v 1s (alt to goal and cone by week), power or attack and defensive heading, 5 v 5s, 11 v 11
    Thurs.—5 v 2 warm-up, paired footwork out to 18 and back, 4 corners flank serving and finishing, attacking box finishing, set plays, team trains the keeper

Nov 10–Dec 4: NCAA Tournament (4 weeks)

Play Sat.

Off Sun.

Lifting: Circuit training once a week (1 hr)

Train Mon., Tues., Wed., Thurs., Fri. (length dependent on day)

> Mon.—(1:15) Triangle Passing warm-up, cones, 3 Tier Shooting, Rickys*
>
> Tues.—(1:30) Combination game warm-up, 1v1s (alt to goal and cone by week), attacking and defensive heading, 5 v 5s, 11 v 11
>
> Wed.—(1:30) Back to pressure warm-up, Bogies, power heading, 5 v 5, 11 v 11
>
> Thurs.—(1:15) 6+1 v 3 warm-up, Long Service/Long Reception, Attacking & Defensive Heading, 5 v 3 from midstripe, knock it back where it came from finishing, 11 v 11
>
> Fri.—(:45-1:00) 5 v 2 warm-up, paired footwork out to 18 and back, 4 corners shooting, paired heading, set plays, team trains the keeper

Free Kicks and PKs taken by artists after every practice

Dec 5–Jan 6: Exams and Break

Players on own to run, lift, maintain fitness

Off Season

Jan 7–Feb 6: Interim Training

TESTING with Don Kirkendall (beep, agility, vertical, speed)

TESTING with Greg Gatz (weight room)

> (players may train only 8 hr/week structured, 2 with coaches)

Lifting

> – 4 times a week x :45 = 3 hr (M,T,TH,F)
>
> – 2 x regular, 2 x circuit

Basketball, Hockey, Tae Bo, or "Spinning" - 2 times a week x 1 hr = 2 hr

Group run - 2 times a week x :30 = 1 hr

---

*Rickys—Relays. The team is divided into 4 equal groups in a 50y x 50y square. Four players (one from each group) race to the corners, then tag teammates. Do this for 3 cycles. Shrink the box (25y x 25y), change the running direction, repeat the race. Optional: a middle square, measured somewhere in between the above two (e.g. 35y–40y).

Training 2 times a week x 1 hr = 2 hr
    4 players per group (session)—groups assigned based on class schedule
        Triangle passing warm-up
        1 v 1 in 20x20 field w/ full-sized goals
        2 v 2 in 20x20 field w/ full-sized goals
        Power heading/Clearing
        Long service/long reception
        Long service
        Long Range Shooting

Feb 7–Mar 9: Indoor Off-Season
    Lifting 3 times a week (M,W,F) 1 hr each
    Train 4 times a week in the evening (1 to 1.5 hr each)
    • 5 v 5 on basketball court with minigoals and size 3 ball
    • 11 v 11 vs. college boy's intramural team
    • 5 v 5 and 11 v 11 on AstroTurf
    • 1 v 1, 2 v 2, shooting, heading on racquetball courts with reg ball
    • Teams are drafted by rising seniors

Mar 10–19: Spring Break

Mar 20–April 15: Outdoor Off-season
    Lifting 3 times a week (M,W,F) 1 hr each
    Games on weekends (5 playing dates max. per NCAA rules)
    Train 3 times a week in the afternoon (1.5 hr each)
        Mon. - Speed training
        Tues. - Scrimmage with college men's team, Triangle Passing, Bo-
            gies
        Wed. - 11 v 11 from player draft (players drafted by 2 new captains
            each week), 1 v 1 to goal, long service/long reception, power
            heading/clearing, technical shooting
        Thurs. - Speed training
        Scrimmage:
            11 v 11 starting front 6 + reserve back 5
            vs. starting back 5 + reserve front 6
END OF SPRING TESTING with Don Kirkendall (beep, agility, ver-
    tical, speed)
END OF SPRING TESTING with Greg Gatz (weight room)

April 16–Aug 11: Summer Break
    Individual Training
        UNC Summer Skills Conditioning Program
            Ball Control and Agility
            Technical Speed, Pure Speed, and Endurance
            Strength and Flexibility
            Shooting and Heading
        UNC Summer Speed Program (20s, 40s, 60s, 80s, 100s)
        UNC Summer Lateral Speed and Agility Program
        UNC Summer Anaerobic/ Aerobic Fitness Shuttles
        UNC Summer Strength Program

University of North Carolina Women's Soccer Competitive Matrix
2001 Final Statistical Composite Rankings

Category	Preseason Testing							Aerobic Fitness					Bogies		1v1's	1v1's to Goal	
Sub-Category	Ave Spd	Fastest Spd	Aa Fit	Accel	Agil	Vert J	Beep	Cooper	120's	Cones	Test	Season Comp	Offensive	Defensive		Offensive	Defensive
Sub-Cat Multiplier	1/2X*	1/2X*	1/2X	1X	1/2X	1X	1X	1/2X	1X	1X	1X	1 1/2 X	2X	2X	4X	2X	2X
Category Multiplier	5X							2 1/2 X					2X		4X	4X	
Rank Player — 00,99,98 Ranks																	
1. Kluegel, Jena 3,7,9	3	3	5	16	7	10	1	1	1	1	1	3	3	1	4	11	6
2. Roddick, Catherine 11,-,-	10	17	4	18	9	5	12	16	14	12	8	12	8	10	2	2	3
3. Gaston, Leslie 14,17,-	4	2	11	2	12	4	7	6	4	15	5	8	1	13	11	8	18
4. Remy, Anne 6,2,13	7	8	9	7	6	5	5	4	7	9	7	9	5	5	10	9	5
5. Ramsey, Alyssa 9,-,-	7	12	5	16	4	12	3	6	9	10	5	7	14	3	3	5	2
6. Borgman, Danielle 1,9,14	2	1	15	12	3	5	3	2	12	1	3	5	10	5	1	6	4
7. Randolph, Sara -,-,-	6	7	10	5	2	12	3	5	1	1	3	4	6	3	7	4	12
8. Bush, Susan 8,6,-	1	6	6	3	1	9	5	8	4	1	4	2	7	1	8	13	7
9. Felts, Anne -,-,-	16	20	8	17	18	17	7	6	6	1	4	6	4	12	4	10	8
10. Morrell, Anne -,-,-	11	19	1	22	13	3	15	12	19	20	10	14	2	5	15	1	1
11. Tonucchia, Maggie 7,-,-	11	15	7	14	4	1	17	19	13	10	10	11	19	14	12	12	14
12. McDowell, Mary -,-,-	4	12	2	15	15	12	3	3	1	1	10	15	11	11	6	15	16
13. Walker, Jordan 16,19,-	18	21	3	23	20	12	13	9	10	1	13	19	18	22	9	18	17
14. Ball, Elizabeth 19,22,-	21	13	21	8	19	18	16	18	22	16	12	19	20	18	13	3	10
15. Watley, Carmen 17,-,-	8	2	19	11	4	9	18	9	9	17	1	1	9	5	16	7	9
16. Whittier, Amy -,20,-	8	5	18	10	11	12	9	7	16	14	5	13	16	9	19	16	11
17. Smith, Jane 23,-,-	15	9	14	4	7	5	11	15	17	20	12	16	12	17	14	20	19
18. Costa, Johanna 21,23,22	13	18	12	11	21	11	9	11	15	1	15	17	21	21	17	19	13
19. Winslow, Laura -,-,-	13	13	22	19	10	23	21	14	11	19	11	10	17	18	17	17	15
20. Gervais, Sophie -,-,-	20	16	19	13	14	20	20	17	17	18	17	17	13	15	20	21	21
21. Blomgren, Leigh -,-,-	19	10	20	1	17	21	17	13	23	23	16	21	22	15	22	14	20
22. Ball, Susie 24,-,-	22	24	16	20	22	22	22	20	26	26	18	22	15	20		22	22

Category	Preseason Testing							Aerobic Fitness		Bogies		1v1's	1v1's to Goal
Sub-Category	Ave Spd	Fastest Spd	Aa Fit	Accel	Agil	Vert J	Beep	Cooper	120's				
Sub-Cat Multiplier	1/2X	1/2X	1/2X	1X	1/2X	1X	1X	1/2X	1X	2X		4X	2X
Category Multiplier	5X							1 1/2X					
Rank Keeper — 00,99,98 Ranks													
1. DePlachett, Kristin 2,2,2	8	3	13	9	16	2	14	10	8	1		3	2
2. Braun, Jenni 1,1,-	17	11	17	6	5	12	17	18	24	3		1	3
3. Simmons, Katie 3,-,-	23	22	23	21	23	18	23	21	20	2		2	4
4. Winget, Aly -,-,-	24	22	24	24	24	24	24	26	25	4		4	1

University of North Carolina Women's Soccer Competitive Matrix
2001 Final Statistical Composite Rankings (Continued)

Three Tier Shooting 1X	Shooting 1/2X	Triangle Passing 1X	Long Service 1/2X	LSP,R 2X	Heading Power I 1X	Heading Power II 1X	Heading A&B 2X	Most Competitive 4X	Total Points	Player	Rank
10	22	11	3	9	8	14	11	3	209.0	Kluegel, Jena	3,7,9	1
5	21	5	1	1	1	1	5	10	233.3	Reddick, Catherine	11,~	2
9	9	4	10	3	2	2	3	4	241.0	Gaston, Leslie	14,17,~	3
1	1	12	14	6	4	10	6	7	247.5	Remy, Anne	6,2,13	4
8	3	10	4	2	10	4	4	16	349.5	Ramsey, Alyssa	9,~	5
16	15	6	7	16	15	16	12	8	254.0	Borgman, Danielle	1,9,14	6
3	6	2	6	5	12	11	16	17	266.5	Randolph, Sara	~,~	7
21	4	4	16	10	14	14	16	12	289.0	Bush, Susan	8,6,~	8
14	13	19	10	3	19	9	14	6	298.5	Felts, Anne	~,~	9
6	9	13	7	12	9	7	10	5	319.0	Morrell, Anne	~,~	10
7	2	3	14	18	7	3	1	1	336.0	Tomecka, Maggie	7,~	11
19	15	15	5	11	6	5	8	12	344.5	McDowell, Mary	~,~	12
12	19	1	9	8	7	12	17	2	409.8	Walker, Jordan	16,19,~	13
4	13	8	2	7	3	5	2	14	416.0	Ball, Elizabeth	19,22,~	14
22	4	15	13	15	5	13	12	19	416.5	Watley, Carmen	17,~	15
15	9	17	17	13	18	21	7	11	455.5	Whitley, Amy	~,20,~	16
18	6	21	20	14	13	8	9	15	488.0	Smith, Jane	23,~	17
11	15	9	20	9	16	18	20	9	499.0	Costa, Johanna	21,23,22	18
17	6	18	21	24	21	17	21	20	609.0	Winslow, Laura	~,~	19
13	19	20	22	22	20	15	14	18	616.0	Gervais, Sophie	~,~	20
2	15	13	17	23	17	19	18	22	631.0	Blomgren, Leigh	~,~	21
20	9	22	24	18	22	20	19	21	706.5	Ball, Susie	24,~	22

Three Tier Shooting 4X	Triangle Passing 1X	Long Service 1/2X	LSP,R 2X	Most Competitive 4X	Total Points	Keeper	Rank
2	6	10	16	2	135.0	DeFlaschert, Kristin	2,2,2	1
1	25	16	25	1	300.0	Braxson, Jenni	1,1,~	2
3	24	25	20	4	262.5	Simmons, Katie	3,~	3
4	23	20	21	3	286.0	Winget, Aly	~,~	4

Notes: Final rankings for each category are indicated in boxes (1 to 22); Ranking is multiplied by multiplier (importance of category); All categories' multiplied scores are added for total.
* Central players (Felts, Tomecka, McDowell, Walker, Reddick, Gaston) have multiplier 1/2 of other players' (1/4 X).
** Large italic # ranks derived from comparable drills since players did not participate in tests.

University of North Carolina Women's Soccer
Training Blocks
Spring 2001, Part I

Long Service / Long Reception

		Ave Succ Serve/Session			
Rank	Player	20 yd	30 yd	44 yd	Total
1. EB		8.8	7.6	2	18.4
1. Gaston		10.4	6.4	1.6	18.4
1. Ramsey		10.8	6.4	1.2	18.4
1. Tomecka		8	7.6	2.8	18.4
5. Kluegel		10	6.4	1.6	18.0
6. Reddick		10	6	1.2	17.2
7. Remy		8.8	4.4	1.6	14.8
8. Ball		6.8	6.8	0	13.6
9. Smith		6.8	6	0.4	13.2
10. Branam		6.4	4.4	0.8	11.6
10. Watley		5.6	5.2	0.8	11.6
12. DePlatchett		5.6	·3.6	2.4	11.6
13. Costa		6.8	2	0	8.8
14. Young		5.2	2.4	0.4	8.0
15. Simmons		3.6	2	1.2	6.8
15. Whittier		4.4	2	0.4	6.8

2 v 2

Rank	Player	% Won		Record	
1. Remy		73.3%	9	2	4
2. DePlatchett		70.0%	9	3	3
3. Branam		63.3%	8	4	3
3. Reddick		63.3%	8	4	3
5. EB		60.0%	7	4	4
6. Costa		56.7%	7	5	3
7. Smith		53.3%	6	5	4
8. Kluegel		50.0%	4	4	4
8. Ramsey		50.0%	6	6	3
8. Tomecka		50.0%	5	5	2
11. Gaston		46.7%	5	6	4
12. Whittier		45.8%	4	5	3
13. Watley		41.7%	2	3	1
14. Young		30.0%	3	9	3
15. Ball		26.7%	2	9	4
16. Simmons		10.0%	0	12	3

Long Service

		Distance Served		
Rank	Player	Right	Left	Total
1. Reddick		48	36	84
2. Branam		44	37	81
3. Gaston		45	34	79
4. Ramsey		43	32	75
5. EB		42	33	75
6. Watley		35	35	70
7. Tomecka		44	26	70
8. DePlatchett		43	26	69
9. Whittier		30	30	60
10. Kluegel		36	23	59
11. Remy		35	23	58
12. Smith		28	26	54
13. Costa		26	27	53
14. Ball		30	22	52
15. Simmons		28	21	49
16. Young		26	19	45

Triangle Passing

Rank	Player	Succ Serves per Session
1. Remy		3.1
2. Reddick		2.4
3. EB		2.2
3. Ramsey		2.2
5. Tomecka		2
6. Gaston		1.7
6. Kluegel		1.7
8. DePlatchett		1.1
9. Branam		1.0
9. Young		1.0
11. Costa		0.9
12. Whittier		0.7
13. Watley		0.6
14. Ball		0.5
15. Smith		0.4
16. Simmons		0.1

Power Heading

Rank	Player	Distance (yd)
1. Remy		24.6
2. Tomecka		24.2
3. DePlatchett		22.4
3. Reddick		22.4
5. Gaston		21.6
6. Ramsey		21.0
7. Branam		20.8
7. Kluegel		20.8
9. EB		20.0
10. Smith		19.6
11. Watley		19.2
12. Simmons		19.0
13. Ball		18.8
13. Young		18.8
15. Costa		18.4
16. Whittier		17.7

Group 1
Remy
EB
Watley
Ball

Group 2
Branam
Simmons
DePlatchett
Costa

Composite

Rank	Player	Ave Rank
1. Reddick		3.4
2. Remy		4.2
3. Ramsey		4.4
4. EB		4.6
4. Tomecka		4.6
6. Gaston		5.2
7. Branam		6.2
8. DePlatchett		6.6
9. Kluegel		7.2
10. Smith		10.6
10. Watley		10.6
12. Costa		11.6
13. Ball		12.8
13. Whittier		12.8
15. Young		13.2
16. Simmons		14.6

Group 3
Gaston
Kluegel
Smith
Tomecka

Group 4
Reddick
Ramsey
Whittier
Young

University of North Carolina Women's Soccer
Spring 2001, Part II

4V4

Turf

Team	Record			Pts	GF	GA
1. Royal	4	0	1	9	59	22
2. Yellow	2	2	1	5	36	30
3. Red	1	3	1	3	23	38
3. Orange	1	3	1	3	21	50

Carmichael

Team	Record			Pts	GF	GA
1. Yellow	3	1	0	6	60	44
1. Royal	3	1	0	6	44	23
3. Orange	1	2	1	3	25	45
4. Red	0	3	1	1	36	53

Team

Racquetball

Team	Record			Pts
1. Royal	3	0	1	7
2. Orange	1	2	1	3
2. Yellow	1	2	1	3
4. Red	0	3	1	1

11v11

Regular

Team	Record			Pts	GF	GA
1. Orange	1	0	3	5	3	1
1. Yellow	1	0	3	5	3	1
3. Royal	0	1	3	3	1	3
3. Red	0	1	3	3	1	3

2v2

Racquetball

Team	Record			Pts
1. Orange	6	2	1	13
2. Yellow	4	4	1	9
3. Royal	2	3	0	4
4. Red	1	4	0	2

OVERALL COMPETITION

(4v4 + 11v11)

Team	Record			Pts	GF	GA
1. Royal	7	2	4	18	104	48
2. Yellow	6	3	4	16	99	75
3. Orange	3	5	5	11	49	96
4. Red	1	7	5	7	60	94

Game vs Men's Team

Team	Record			Pts	GF	GA
1. UNC Women	2	1	1	5	10	10
2. Intramural Men	1	2	1	3	10	10

GOALSCORING BY TEAM

Royal

Remy	41
Tomecka	34
Watley	15
Branom	11
Ball	10

Red

Walker	25
Gaston	10
Borgman	10
Young	8

Orange

DePlatchett	17
Smith	14
Ramsey	11
Whittier	10
Costa	6

Yellow

EB	32
Reddick	30
Kluegel	26
Simmons	0

4v4 Leading Scorers

Rank	Player	Goals
1.	Remy	39
2.	Tomecka	34
3.	EB	29
3.	Reddick	29
5.	Kluegel	26
6.	Walker	24
7.	Watley	15
8.	DePlatchett	14
8.	Smith	14
10.	Ball	12
11.	Ramsey	11
12.	Branam	10
12.	Gaston	10
14.	Borgman	9
14.	Whittier	9
16.	Young	7
17.	Costa	6
18.	Simmons	0

11v11 Leading Scorers

(men's game + intrasquad)

Rank	Player	#Goals
1.	DePlatchett	3
1.	EB	3
3.	Remy	2
4.	Ball	1
4.	Borgman	1
4.	Branam	1
4.	Reddick	1
4.	Walker	1
4.	Whittier	1
4.	Young	1
11.	Costa	0
11.	Gaston	0
11.	Kluegel	0
11.	Ramsey	0
11.	Simmons	0
11.	Smith	0
11.	Tomecka	0
11.	Watley	0

Leading Scorers

Rank	Player	Total #Goals
1.	Remy	41
2.	Tomecka	34
3.	EB	32
4.	Reddick	30
5.	Kluegel	26
6.	Walker	25
7.	DePlatchett	17
8.	Watley	15
9.	Smith	14
10.	Ball	13
11.	Branam	11
11.	Ramsey	11
13.	Borgman	10
13.	Gaston	10
13.	Whittier	10
16.	Young	8
17.	Costa	6
18.	Simmons	0

Individual Most Competitive

(individual's record on 4v4, 11v11 teams)

Rank	Player	% Won	Record		
1.	Reddick	77.3%	7	1	3
2.	Watley	75.0%	5	0	5
3.	Remy	73.3%	10	3	2
4.	Ball	71.1%	11	3	5
4.	Tomecka	71.1%	11	3	5
6.	Kluegel	67.9%	8	3	3
7.	EB	57.9%	8	5	6
8.	Smith	50.0%	6	6	7
9.	Costa	41.7%	4	7	7
9.	Borgman	41.7%	1	2	3
11.	Whittier	40.0%	3	6	6
12.	Ramsey	33.3%	0	2	4
13.	Gaston	23.5%	1	10	6
14.	Walker	22.7%	1	7	3
15.	Young	20.0%	0	9	6

Rank	Keeper	% Won	Record	
1.	Branam	70.0%	6	2	2
2.	Simmons	57.9%	8	5	6
3.	DePlatchett	44.7%	5	7	7

R-ball Turning Series

Rank	Player	Shots
1.	Remy	537
2.	Kluegel	526
3.	Reddick	498
4.	EB	493
5.	Whittier	492
6.	Tomecka	490
7.	Costa	476
8.	DePlatchett	469
9.	Smith	461
10.	Ramsey	439
11.	Watley	411
12.	Young	409
13.	Ball	386
14.	Simmons	369
15.	Gaston	348
	Borgman	
	Branam	
	Walker	

Racquetball 1v1s

Rank	Player	% Won	Record		
1.	Remy	94.4%	8	0	1
2.	EB	83.3%	10	2	0
2.	Reddick	83.3%	5	1	0
4.	Kluegel	77.8%	7	2	0
5.	Tomecka	75.0%	9	3	0
6.	Whittier	66.7%	2	1	0
7.	Costa	55.0%	5	4	1
8.	Smith	54.2%	5	4	3
9.	Gaston	38.9%	3	5	1
10.	DePlatchett	37.5%	4	7	1
11.	Ramsey	30.0%	1	3	1
12.	Ball	25.0%	2	8	2
13.	Young	11.1%	0	7	2
14.	Simmons	0.0%	0	12	0
14.	Watley	0.0%	0	3	0
	Borgman				
	Branam				
	Walker				

Royal	Yellow
Remy	Kluegel
Branom	Simmons
Ball	Reddick
Tomecka	EB
Watley	Murphy

Orange	Red
DePlatchett	Borgman
Costa	Marslender
Whittier	Young
Smith	Gaston
Ramsey	Walker
McDonald	Florance

University of North Carolina Women's Soccer
Spring 2001, Part III-1

Weekend Game Stats

Player	Shots	Goals	Assists	Pts
Ramsey	5	3	1	7
Remy	12	3	1	7
Walker	8	2	1	5
Kluegel	10	1	2	4
Tomecka	2	1	0	2
Borgman	8	0	1	1
Branam	8	0	1	1
DePlachett	0	0	1	1
Reddick	6	0	1	1
Ball	0	0	0	0
Costa	2	0	0	0
Gaston	0	0	0	0
Smith	3	0	0	0
Watley	0	0	0	0
Whittier	0	0	0	0
Young	0	0	0	0

Draft 11v11 Most Competitive

Rank	Player	% Won	Record		
1. Costa		87.5%	3	0	1
1. Kluegel		87.5%	3	0	1
1. Tomecka		87.5%	3	0	1
4. Gaston		75.0%	1	0	1
5. Ramsey		62.5%	2	1	1
5. Smith		62.5%	2	1	1
5. Walker		62.5%	2	1	1
5. Young		62.5%	2	1	1
9. Ball		50.0%	1	1	1
9. Watley		50.0%	0	0	1
11. Borgman		37.5%	1	2	1
11. EB		37.5%	1	2	1
13. Reddick		12.5%	0	3	1
13. Remy		12.5%	0	3	1
13. Whittier		12.5%	0	3	1

Rank	Keeper	% Won	Record		
1. Branam		62.5%	2	1	1
1. Simmons		62.5%	2	1	1
3. DePlachett		50.0%	1	1	1

Overall Keeper Stats

Keeper	Goals	Games	GAA
Simmons	0	1.5	0.00
Branam	3	2.4	1.25
DePlachett	9	3	3.00

Men's Game Lead Scorers

Rank	Player	Goals
1. EB		2
2. Borgman		1
2. Branam		1
2. Reddick		1
2. Remy		1
6. Ball		0
6. Costa		0
6. DePlachett		0
6. Gaston		0
6. Kluegel		0
6. Ramsey		0
6. Simmons		0
6. Smith		0
6. Tomecka		0
6. Walker		0
6. Watley		0
6. Whittier		0
6. Young		0

11 v 11 Leading Scorers (Intrasquad)

Rank	Player	Goals
1. Walker		6
2. Branam		3
2. Reddick		3
2. Remy		3
5. Ball		2
5. DePlachett		2
5. Kluegel		2
5. Smith		2
9. EB		1
9. Gaston		1
9. Tomecka		1
9. Young		1
13. Borgman		0
13. Ramsey		0
13. Simmons		0
13. Watley		0
13. Whittier		0

Weekend Scorers

Rank	Player	Total # Goals
1. Ramsey		3
1. Remy		3
3. Walker		2
4. Kluegel		1
4. Tomecka		1
6. Ball		0
6. Borgman		0
6. Branam		0
6. Costa		0
6. DePlachett		0
6. EB		0
6. Gaston		0
6. Reddick		0
6. Simmons		0
6. Smith		0
6. Watley		0
6. Young		0

Overall Scorers

Rank	Player	Total # Goals
1. Walker		8
2. Remy		7
3. Branam		4
3. Reddick		4
5. EB		3
5. Kluegel		3
5. Ramsey		3
8. Ball		2
8. DePlachett		2
8. Tomecka		2
12. Borgman		1
12. Gaston		1
12. Young		1
15. Costa		0
15. Simmons		0
15. Watley		0
15. Whittier		0

Front 6/Back 5 11v11 Most Competitive

Rank	Player	% Won	Record		
1. Kluegel		100.0%	5	0	0
1. Ramsey		100.0%	4	0	0
1. Remy		100.0%	5	0	0
1. Walker		100.0%	5	0	0
5. Ball		60.0%	3	2	0
6. Borgman		50.0%	2	2	0
6. Watley		50.0%	1	1	0
8. Whittier		40.0%	2	3	0
9. EB		33.3%	2	4	0
9. Reddick		33.3%	2	4	0
9. Smith		33.3%	2	4	0
12. Costa		0.0%	0	5	0
12. Gaston		0.0%	0	1	0
12. Tomecka		0.0%	0	5	0
12. Young		0.0%	0	5	0

Rank	Keeper	% Won	Record		
1. Simmons		66.7%	4	2	0
2. Branam		60.0%	3	2	0
3. DePlachett		28.6%	2	5	0

University of North Carolina Women's Soccer
Spring 2001, Part III-2

1v1s to Goal

Offense

Rank	Player	Points	Runs	Ave pts/Run
1.	Reddick	54	19	2.84
2.	Ramsey	37	14	2.64
3.	Watley	11	5	2.20
4.	EB	37	17	2.18
5.	Remy	39	19	2.05
6.	Tomecka	30	15	2.00
7.	Walker	35	18	1.94
8.	Kluegel	23	13	1.77
9.	Borgman	24	14	1.71
10.	Costa	26	17	1.53
11.	Whittier	12	14	0.86
12.	Young	8	13	0.62
13.	Smith	9	16	0.56
14.	Ball	2	13	0.15
	Bush	0	0	
	Gaston	0	0	

Defense

Rank	Player	Points	Runs	Ave pts/Run
1.	Reddick	53	15	3.53
2.	Watley	12	4	3.00
3.	Smith	38	13	2.92
4.	Ramsey	23	8	2.86
5.	Borgman	22	8	2.75
6.	Tomecka	32	12	2.67
7.	Costa	32	13	2.46
8.	Remy	31	13	2.38
9.	Young	18	8	2.25
10.	Kluegel	19	9	2.11
11.	EB	23	11	2.09
12.	Ball	19	11	1.73
13.	Walker	24	14	1.71
14.	Whittier	17	10	1.70
	Bush	0	0	
	Gaston	0	0	

Goalkeeping

Rank	Player	G Allowed	Runs	Ave G/Run
1.	Branam	8	49	0.16
2.	DePlatchett	11	49	0.22
3.	Simmons	13	49	0.27

Long Service / Long Reception

Rank	Player	20yd	30yd	45yd	Total
1.	Reddick	18	12	4	34
2.	EB	19	11	3	33
3.	Kluegel	17	8	3	28
4.	Tomecka	14	11	0	25
4.	Walker	16	8	1	25
6.	Ramsey	15	8	1	24
6.	Smith	14	8	2	24
8.	DePlatchett	12	9	1	22
9.	Remy	9	11	1	21
10.	Costa	12	7	0	19
11.	Ball	8	8	0	16
11.	Borgman	9	7	0	16
11.	Branam	7	8	1	16
14.	Whittier	8	4	1	13
15.	Watley	9	3	0	12
16.	Simmons	6	5	0	11
17.	Young	6	4	0	10
	Bush	0	0	0	0
	Gaston	0	0	0	0

Power Heading

		Semester	Ave Distance				
Rank	Player	Ave	19-Mar	26-Mar	02-Apr	09-Apr	16-Apr
1.	Ramsey	26.67		26.00	25.75	28.25	
2.	EB	24.81	28.00	20.00	23.75	27.50	
3.	Reddick	24.50	30.00	23.25	17.50	27.25	
4.	Remy	23.38	20.25	24.00	25.50	23.75	
5.	Tomecka	22.19	22.75	19.25	21.25	25.50	
6.	Watley	21.75				21.75	
7.	Walker	21.19	22.50	19.25	23.00	20.00	
8.	Smith	20.69	23.75	18.75	19.75	22.50	
9.	Borgman	20.00	20.00		21.50	18.50	
10.	DePlatchett	19.83		18.25	22.50	21.75	
11.	Simmons	18.56	18.75	18.75	13.25	23.50	
12.	Kluegel	18.25		14.50	19.50	20.75	
13.	Costa	17.60	13.75	18.75	16.00	22.25	
14.	Ball	16.50		17.00		16.00	
15.	Young	16.00	12.50		15.50	20.00	
16.	Whittier	15.92		21.25	11.25	15.25	
	Branam						
	Gaston						

Long Service

Rank Player	Total Distance	Player	R Distance	Player	L Distance
1. Reddick	88	Reddick	50	Reddick	38
2. Kluegel	83	Kluegel	45	Kluegel	38
3. EB	81	EB	46	EB	35
3. Ramsey	81	Ramsey	45	Ramsey	36
5. DePlatchett	78	DePlatchett	45	DePlatchett	33
6. Tomecka	75	Tomecka	46	Tomecka	29
7. Remy	74	Remy	40	Remy	34
8. Borgman	73	Borgman	38	Borgman	35
9. Branam	72	Branam	36	Branam	36
10. Walker	71	Walker	38	Walker	33
11. Costa	66	Costa	39	Costa	27
12. Watley	64	Watley	36	Watley	28
12. Whittier	64	Whittier	34	Whittier	30
12. Young	64	Young	40	Young	24
15. Smith	59	Smith	40	Smith	19
16. Simmons	58	Simmons	33	Simmons	25
17. Ball	56	Ball	33	Ball	23
	Bush	0	Bush	0	Bush	0
	Gaston	0	Gaston	0	Gaston	0

University of North Carolina Women's Soccer
Conditioning Test Charts
2001 April (4/28/01) Wt Test

RANKED BY APRIL RESULTS

Reach (in)

Rank	Player	Feb '01	Apr '01	% change
1.	Tomecka	92.5	92.5	0.0%
2.	Simmons	91.0	91.0	0.0%
3.	Ramsey	90.0	90.0	0.0%
4.	Branam	88.0	88.0	0.0%
5.	Bush		85.5	
5.	EB	85.5	85.5	0.0%
7.	Ball	85.0	85.0	0.0%
7.	Reddick	85.0	85.0	0.0%
7.	Smith	85.0	85.0	0.0%
7.	Whittier	85.0	85.0	0.0%
11.	Borgman		84.5	
12.	Young	84.0	84.0	0.0%
13.	DePlatchett	83.5	83.5	0.0%
14.	Walker		83.0	
14.	Watley	83.0	83.0	0.0%
16.	Costa	82.5	82.5	0.0%
16.	Gaston	82.5	82.5	0.0%
18.	Remy	81.5	81.5	0.0%
19.	Kluegel	81.0	81.0	0.0%

Vert Jump (in)

Rank	Player	Feb '01	Apr '01	% change
1.	DePlatchett	25.5	26.00	2.0%
2.	Watley	25.0	25.50	2.0%
3.	Gaston	22.5	22.00	-2.2%
4.	Branam	18.0	21.00	16.7%
4.	Kluegel	21.0	21.00	0.0%
6.	Remy	20.5	20.50	0.0%
7.	Borgman		19.50	
7.	Costa	19.0	19.50	2.6%
7.	Smith	18.5	19.50	5.4%
7.	Tomecka	19.5	19.50	0.0%
11.	Bush		18.50	
12.	Ramsey	15.5	18.00	16.1%
13.	EB	17.0	17.50	2.9%
14.	Simmons	14.0	17.00	21.4%
14.	Whittier	17.0	17.00	0.0%
16.	Young	15.0	16.50	10.0%
17.	Walker		15.00	
18.	Ball	15.0	14.50	-3.3%
	Reddick	20.0		

Broad Jump (in)

Rank	Player	Feb '01	Apr '01	% change
1.	DePlatchett	90.0	95.0	5.6%
2.	Kluegel	87.5	90.0	2.9%
3.	Gaston	87.0	88.0	1.1%
4.	Watley	87.0	86.0	-1.1%
5.	Remy	80.0	85.0	6.3%
6.	Tomecka	85.0	84.0	-1.2%
7.	Borgman		83.0	
8.	EB	83.0	82.0	-1.2%
9.	Branam	77.0	81.0	5.2%
9.	Simmons	75.0	81.0	8.0%
11.	Ramsey	77.0	80.0	3.9%
12.	Reddick	84.0	78.0	-7.1%
12.	Smith	75.0	78.0	4.0%
14.	Bush		75.0	
14.	Costa	75.0	75.0	0.0%
14.	Whittier	67.0	75.0	11.9%
17.	Walker		72.0	
18.	Ball	65.0	70.0	7.7%
19.	Young	67.0	69.0	3.0%

Sit-ups (/min)

Rank	Player	Feb '01	Apr '01	% change
1.	Costa	64	64	0.0%
2.	Branam	58	63	8.6%
3.	DePlatchett	52	54	3.8%
3.	Kluegel	53	54	1.9%
3.	Walker		54	
6.	Ramsey	43	52	20.9%
7.	Borgman		51	
8.	Bush		50	
9.	Ball	48	47	-2.1%
10.	Reddick	35	46	31.4%
10.	Remy	36	46	27.8%
12.	EB	43	45	4.7%
12.	Watley	50	45	-10.0%
14.	Gaston	43	43	0.0%
15.	Tomecka	32	42	31.3%
16.	Simmons	25	34	36.0%
17.	Smith	28	30	7.1%
	Whittier	34		
	Young	37		

Push-ups (/min)

Rank	Player	Feb '01	Apr '01	% change
1.	DePlatchett	48	68	41.7%
2.	Borgman		61	
3.	Costa	46	60	30.4%
4.	EB	60	56	-6.7%
5.	Whittier	16	50	212.5%
6.	Remy	38	49	28.9%
7.	Kluegel	58	48	-17.2%
8.	Ramsey	36	47	30.6%
8.	Reddick	47	47	0.0%
10.	Branam	32	44	37.5%
11.	Walker		43	
12.	Gaston	28	42	50.0%
13.	Bush		40	
14.	Smith	24	34	41.7%
14.	Tomecka	27	34	25.9%
14.	Watley	35	34	-2.9%
17.	Young	16	33	106.3%
18.	Simmons	22	30	36.4%
19.	Ball	12	17	41.7%

Pull-ups (reps)

Rank	Player	Feb '01	Apr '01	% change
1.	Branam	4	7	75.0%
1.	DePlatchett	5	7	40.0%
1.	Ramsey	0	7	up
4.	Borgman		6	
4.	Kluegel	4	6	50.0%
4.	Remy	4	6	50.0%
7.	EB	3	5	66.7%
7.	Whittier	5	5	0.0%
9.	Bush		4	
9.	Watley	6	4	-33.3%
11.	Gaston	4	2	-50.0%
11.	Smith	0	2	up
11.	Tomecka	1	2	100.0%
14.	Reddick	0	1	up
14.	Young	0	1	up
16.	Ball	0	0	0.0%
16.	Costa	0	0	0.0%
16.	Simmons	0	0	0.0%
16.	Walker		0	

Med Ball Push (Bench) (ft/in)

Rank	Player	Feb '01	Apr '01	% change
1.	Borgman		14.0	
1.	Branam	13.5	14.0	3.7%
1.	Tomecka	13.5	14.0	3.7%
4.	DePlatchett	13.0	13.5	3.8%
4.	Gaston	11.5	13.5	17.4%
4.	Kluegel	10.5	13.5	28.6%
7.	Ramsey	11.5	13.0	13.0%
7.	Reddick	13.0	13.0	0.0%
9.	Simmons	11.5	12.5	8.7%
10.	Ball	9.0	12.0	33.3%
10.	EB	11.0	12.0	9.1%
10.	Remy	10.5	12.0	14.3%
13.	Bush		11.5	
13.	Costa	11.0	11.5	4.5%
13.	Smith	10.5	11.5	9.5%
13.	Watley	10.0	11.5	15.0%
17.	Young	11.0	11.0	0.0%
18.	Walker		10.5	
	Whittier	10.5		

3 Cone (30 sec)

Rank	Player	Feb '01	Apr '01	% change
1.	Costa	30	33	10.0%
2.	EB	31	32	3.2%
2.	Kluegel	29	32	10.3%
2.	Reddick	28	32	14.3%
5.	Gaston	29	31	6.9%
6.	Borgman		30	
6.	Branam	28	30	7.1%
6.	DePlatchett	30	30	0.0%
6.	Watley	28	30	7.1%
6.	Whittier	25	30	20.0%
11.	Ramsey	29	29	0.0%
11.	Remy	30	29	-3.3%
11.	Smith	25	29	16.0%
11.	Tomecka	28	29	3.6%
11.	Walker		29	
16.	Ball	23	28	21.7%
16.	Simmons	23	28	21.7%
18.	Bush		27	
18.	Young	27	27	0.0%

Ave Rank

Rank	Player	Ave Rank
1.	DePlatchett	3.75
2.	Branam	4.62
3.	Borgman	5.62
3.	Kluegel	5.62
5.	Ramsey	7.37
6.	EB	7.62
7.	Tomecka	8.25
8.	Gaston	8.50
9.	Reddick	8.57
10.	Remy	8.75
11.	Whittier	8.83
12.	Costa	8.87
13.	Watley	9.25
14.	Young	10.00
15.	Bush	11.37
16.	Smith	11.50
17.	Simmons	12.50
18.	Walker	13.37
19.	Ball	14.12

University of North Carolina Women's Soccer
2001 Fall Fit Test Revised

Vert Jump

Rank	Player	(in)
1.	Tomecka	27.0
2.	DePlatchett	25.0
3.	Morrell	23.5
4.	Gaston	22.0
5.	Borgman	21.5
5.	Reddick	21.5
5.	Remy	21.5
5.	Smith	21.5
9.	Bush	21.0
10.	Kluegel	20.5
11.	Costa	20.0
12.	Branam	19.5
12.	McDowell	19.5
12.	Randolph	19.5
12.	Walker	19.5
12.	Whittier	19.5
17.	Felts	19.0
18.	EB	18.5
18.	Simmons	18.5
20.	Gervais	18.0
21.	Blomgren	17.0
22.	Ball	15.5
23.	Winslow	15.5
24.	Winget	14.0
	Ramsey	
	Watley	

Agility

Rank	Player	(seconds)
1.	Bush	15.24
2.	Randolph	15.37
3.	Borgman	15.55
4.	Tomecka	15.99
5.	Branam	16.09
6.	Remy	16.14
7.	Kluegel	16.17
7.	Smith	16.17
9.	Reddick	16.19
10.	Winslow	16.20
11.	Whittier	16.22
12.	Gaston	16.23
13.	Morrell	16.24
14.	Gervais	16.25
15.	McDowell	16.28
16.	DePlatchett	16.32
17.	Blomgren	16.35
18.	Felts	16.40
19.	EB	16.41
20.	Walker	16.84
21.	Costa	16.90
22.	Ball	17.26
23.	Simmons	18.44
24.	Winget	19.16
	Ramsey	
	Watley	

Acceleration

Rank	Player	(m/s)
1.	Blomgren	5.760
2.	Gaston	5.540
3.	Bush	5.537
4.	Smith	5.473
5.	Randolph	5.464
6.	Branam	5.456
7.	Remy	5.447
8.	EB	5.441
9.	DePlatchett	5.405
10.	Whittier	5.388
11.	Costa	5.368
12.	Borgman	5.365
13.	Gervais	5.353
14.	Tomecka	5.336
15.	McDowell	5.294
16.	Kluegel	5.184
17.	Felts	5.168
18.	Reddick	5.160
19.	Winslow	5.157
20.	Ball	5.155
21.	Simmons	5.147
22.	Morrell	5.074
23.	Walker	4.985
24.	Winget	4.965
	Ramsey	
	Watley	

Fastest Speed

Rank	Player	(m/s)
1.	Borgman	6.80
2.	Gaston	6.61
3.	DePlatchett	6.59
3.	Kluegel	6.59
5.	Whittier	6.57
6.	Bush	6.55
7.	Randolph	6.53
8.	Remy	6.51
9.	Smith	6.49
10.	Blomgren	6.46
11.	Branam	6.44
12.	McDowell	6.40
13.	EB	6.38
13.	Winslow	6.38
15.	Tomecka	6.34
16.	Gervais	6.33
17.	Reddick	6.32
18.	Costa	6.31
19.	Morrell	6.18
20.	Felts	6.16
21.	Walker	6.05
22.	Simmons	5.92
22.	Winget	5.92
24.	Ball	5.75
	Ramsey	
	Watley	

Ave Speed

Rank	Player	(m/s)
1.	Bush	6.39
2.	Borgman	6.37
3.	Kluegel	6.36
4.	Gaston	6.28
4.	McDowell	6.28
6.	Randolph	6.27
7.	Remy	6.25
8.	DePlatchett	6.11
8.	Whittier	6.11
10.	Reddick	6.10
11.	Morrell	6.09
11.	Tomecka	6.09
13.	Costa	6.03
13.	Winslow	6.03
15.	Smith	5.97
16.	Felts	5.94
17.	Branam	5.93
18.	Walker	5.88
19.	Blomgren	5.82
20.	Gervais	5.76
21.	EB	5.73
22.	Ball	5.34
23.	Simmons	5.06
24.	Winget	4.59
	Ramsey	
	Watley	

Fatigue

Rank	Player	(%)
1.	Morrell	2.53
2.	McDowell	3.77
3.	Walker	4.07
4.	Reddick	4.61
5.	Kluegel	5.67
6.	Bush	5.94
7.	Tomecka	6.38
8.	Felts	6.81
9.	Remy	7.01
10.	Randolph	7.77
11.	Gaston	8.21
12.	Costa	9.57
13.	DePlatchett	11.02
14.	Smith	11.59
15.	Borgman	12.35
16.	Ball	12.97
17.	Branam	13.02
18.	Whittier	14.12
19.	Gervais	14.32
20.	Blomgren	15.37
21.	EB	17.02
22.	Winslow	21.43
23.	Simmons	28.61
24.	Winget	61.52
	Ramsey	
	Watley	

Beep

Rank	Player	(level)
1.	Kluegel	1920
2.	Borgman	1800
3.	McDowell	1700*
3.	Randolph	1700*
5.	Bush	1640
5.	Remy	1640
7.	Felts	1400*
7.	Gaston	1400
9.	Costa	1360
9.	Whittier	1360
11.	Smith	1280
12.	Reddick	1160
13.	Walker	1120
14.	DePlatchett	1080
15.	Morrell	960
16.	EB	880
17.	Blomgren	840
17.	Branam	840
17.	Tomecka	840
20.	Gervais	760
21.	Winslow	640
22.	Ball	600
23.	Simmons	360
24.	Winget	240
	Ramsey	
	Watley	

Ave Rank

Rank	Player	Ave Rank
1.	Bush	4.43
2.	Borgman	5.71
3.	Gaston	6.00
4.	Kluegel	6.43
4.	Randolph	6.43
6.	Remy	6.71
7.	McDowell	9.00
8.	DePlatchett	9.29
8.	Smith	9.29
10.	Tomecka	9.86
11.	Whittier	10.43
12.	Reddick	10.71
13.	Morrell	12.00
14.	Branam	12.14
15.	Costa	13.57
16.	Felts	14.71
17.	Blomgren	15.00
18.	Walker	15.71
19.	EB	16.57
20.	Winslow	17.14
21.	Gervais	17.43
22.	Ball	21.14
23.	Simmons	21.86
24.	Winget	23.71
	Ramsey	
	Watley	

* participants were stopped because of equipment failure and assigned ranks based on speculated finish

University of North Carolina Women's Soccer
Long Range Athletic Tracking

EB

	F 1998	W 1999	SP 1999	F 1999	W 2000	SP 2000	F 2000	W 2001	SP 2001	F 2001	
Weight (lb)					142	146					
Vert (in)				20.50	17.50	19.00	18.50	21.00	19.50	18.50	higher=better
Acceleration (m/s)				4.90	5.05	5.16	5.08	4.38	4.87	5.44	higher=better
Fastest Speed (m/s)				6.21	6.06	6.26	6.20	5.99	6.23	6.38	higher=better
Ave Speed (m/s)				5.39	5.58	5.70	5.68	5.47	5.80	5.73	higher=better
AA Fitness (fatigue) (%)				22.77	11.37	17.35	12.37	13.08	12.18	17.02	lower=better
Agility (s)				16.33	15.74	15.24	15.40	15.88	15.09	16.41	lower=better
Beep (m)				640	880	640	1080	1040	920	880	higher=better

Borgman

	F 1998	W 1999	SP 1999	F 1999	W 2000	SP 2000	F 2000	W 2001	SP 2001	F 2001	
Weight (lb)		149	154	149							
Vert (in)	22.00	21.50	20.50	20.50			22.00		21.50	21.50	higher=better
Acceleration (m/s)				5.43			5.42		5.39	5.36	higher=better
Fastest Speed (m/s)				6.58			6.69		6.81	6.80	higher=better
Ave Speed (m/s)		6.27	6.65	6.26			6.27		6.45	6.37	higher=better
AA Fitness (fatigue) (%)		9.59	8.42	7.89			8.54		9.20	12.35	lower=better
Agility (s)	16.90	16.10	16.20	15.03			15.30		14.78	15.55	lower=better
Beep (m)	1280	1420	1520	1400			1560		1680	1800	higher=better

Costa

	F 1998	W 1999	SP 1999	F 1999	W 2000	SP 2000	F 2000	W 2001	SP 2001	F 2001	
Weight (lb)		128	134		136	136					
Vert (in)	20.00	16.50	18.00	20.00	20.00	23.00	21.50	20.00	21.00	20.00	higher=better
Acceleration (m/s)				4.90	5.00	5.25	5.20	4.79	5.27	5.36	higher=better
Fastest Speed (m/s)				6.21	6.00	6.27	6.04	6.05	6.43	6.31	higher=better
Ave Speed (m/s)		5.83	6.14	5.93	5.88	6.16	5.95	5.78	6.21	6.03	higher=better
AA Fitness (fatigue) (%)		2.15	3.72	7.87	6.06	3.89	3.46	10.83	8.95	9.57	lower=better
Agility (s)	18.00	16.80	17.10	15.95	15.89	16.12	16.00	16.40	15.72	16.90	lower=better
Beep (m)	1000	1200	1280	880	1200	1200	1120	1440	1480	1360	higher=better

DePlatchett

	F 1998	W 1999	SP 1999	F 1999	W 2000	SP 2000	F 2000	W 2001	SP 2001	F 2001	
Weight (lb)		146	153		154	157					
Vert (in)	27.50	26.50	29.00		20.50	27.50	27.50	27.00	25.50	25.00	higher=better
Acceleration (m/s)					5.18	5.16	5.48	5.50	5.31	5.40	higher=better
Fastest Speed (m/s)					6.32	6.53	6.64	6.77	6.57	6.59	higher=better
Ave Speed (m/s)		6.02	6.34		5.70	5.96	6.32	6.25	6.29	6.11	higher=better
AA Fitness (fatigue) (%)		12.06	9.93		19.57	15.95	7.84	12.90	7.58	11.02	lower=better
Agility (s)	17.50	16.40	16.40		15.96	15.70	15.20	15.75	15.31	16.32	lower=better
Beep (m)	800	880	920		1040	1120	1320	1480	680	1080	higher=better

Florance

	F 1998	W 1999	SP 1999	F 1999	W 2000	SP 2000	F 2000	W 2001	SP 2001	F 2001	
Weight (lb)											
Vert (in)	20.50	18.50	20.50	20.00	17.50	21.50	18.50				higher=better
Acceleration (m/s)				5.02	5.18	5.31	5.33				higher=better
Fastest Speed (m/s)				6.40	6.18	6.58	6.52				higher=better
Ave Speed (m/s)		6.01	6.02	5.80	5.05	6.23	6.21				higher=better
AA Fitness (fatigue) (%)		13.90	9.05	16.84	11.76	9.35	8.67				lower=better
Agility (s)	17.50	16.90	16.70	15.99	15.88	15.13	15.30				lower=better
Beep (m)	760	1080	1080	1160	1280	1600	1680				higher=better

Kluegel

	F 1998	W 1999	SP 1999	F 1999	W 2000	SP 2000	F 2000	W 2001	SP 2001	F 2001	
Weight (lb)		127	127	124							
Vert (in)	25.00	22.50	22.50					22.50	21.50	20.50	higher=better
Acceleration (m/s)								5.15	5.33	5.18	higher=better
Fastest Speed (m/s)								6.58	6.77	6.59	higher=better
Ave Speed (m/s)		6.21	6.13					6.35	6.45	6.36	higher=better
AA Fitness (fatigue) (%)		10.61	9.15					5.96	8.48	5.67	lower=better
Agility (s)	17.30	16.80	16.50					15.78	16.35	16.17	lower=better
Beep (m)	1440	1760	1440					2080	1920	1920	higher=better

Remy

	F 1998	W 1999	SP 1999	F 1999	W 2000	SP 2000	F 2000	W 2001	SP 2001	F 2001	
Weight (lb)		127	127		118	119					
Vert (in)	21.50	21.50		22.50	21.50	24.00	21.50	22.00	22.00	21.50	higher=better
Acceleration (m/s)				5.29	5.05	5.44	5.03	4.80	5.26	5.44	higher=better
Fastest Speed (m/s)				6.40	6.11	6.56	6.18	6.01	6.50	6.51	higher=better
Ave Speed (m/s)		6.22		6.06	5.78	6.38	5.98	5.88	6.36	6.25	higher=better
AA Fitness (fatigue) (%)		14.13		11.37	12.97	4.78	5.93	4.59	4.29	7.01	lower=better
Agility (s)	17.60	17.00		16.09	15.92	15.60	15.70	16.25	15.66	16.14	lower=better
Beep (m)	1040	960		1280	1720	1560	1560	1640	1640	1640	higher=better

University of North Carolina Women's Soccer
Long Range Weight Room Tracking

EB

	SP 2001	F 2001	W 2002	SP 2002	F 2002	W 2003	SP 2003	F 2003	W 2004	SP 2004	
Bench Press (lb)		85.00	110.00								higher=better
Squat (lb)		115.00	215.00								higher=better
Broad Jump (in)	82.00	85.00	84.00								higher=better
Quick Feet (rep/min)		151.00	182.00								higher=better
Vertical Jump (in)											
Seated MB Throw (ft)		14.00									higher=better

Ball

	SP 2001	F 2001	W 2002	SP 2002	F 2002	W 2003	SP 2003	F 2003	W 2004	SP 2004	
Bench Press (lb)		60.00	70.00								higher=better
Squat (lb)		80.00	130.00								higher=better
Broad Jump (in)	70.00	76.50	70.00								higher=better
Quick Feet (rep/min)		132.00	162.00								higher=better
Vertical Jump (in)											
Seated MB Throw (ft)		11.60									higher=better

Blomgren

	SP 2001	F 2001	W 2002	SP 2002	F 2002	W 2003	SP 2003	F 2003	W 2004	SP 2004	
Bench Press (lb)		65.00	75.00								higher=better
Squat (lb)		75.00	180.00								higher=better
Broad Jump (in)		74.50	81.00								higher=better
Quick Feet (rep/min)		145.00	180.00								higher=better
Vertical Jump (in)											
Seated MB Throw (ft)		10.00									higher=better

Branam

	SP 2001	F 2001	W 2002	SP 2002	F 2002	W 2003	SP 2003	F 2003	W 2004	SP 2004	
Bench Press (lb)		105.00									higher=better
Squat (lb)		115.00									higher=better
Broad Jump (in)	81.00	81.50									higher=better
Quick Feet (rep/min)		152.00									higher=better
Vertical Jump (in)											
Seated MB Throw (ft)		17.00									higher=better

Bush

	SP 2001	F 2001	W 2002	SP 2002	F 2002	W 2003	SP 2003	F 2003	W 2004	SP 2004	
Bench Press (lb)		85.00									higher=better
Squat (lb)		90.00									higher=better
Broad Jump (in)	75.00	83.00									higher=better
Quick Feet (rep/min)		159.00									higher=better
Vertical Jump (in)											
Seated MB Throw (ft)		13.00									higher=better

University of North Carolina Women's Soccer
Long Range Technical Tracking

EB

	W2001	S2001	F2001	W2002	S2002	F2002	W2003	S2003	F2003	W2004	
Bogies offense (% scoring)			6.09								higher=better
Bogies defense (shutout %)			75.00								higher=better
Top Gun (% won)			55.60								higher=better
1v1 to Goal offense (% scoring)		54.40	64.70								higher=better
1v1 to Goal defense (shutout %)		52.30	64.30								higher=better
Shooting (% scoring)			15.00								higher=better
Triangle Passing (success pass/session)	2.20		2.90								higher=better
LS/LR 20 yds (succ serves/session)	8.80	9.50	8.60								higher=better
LS/LR 30 yds (succ serves/session)	7.60	5.50	6.60								higher=better
LS/LR 45 yds (succ serves/session)	2.00	1.50	3.10								higher=better
Long Service R (yards)	42.00	46.00	47.00								higher=better
Long Service L (yards)	33.00	35.00	40.00								higher=better
Power Heading (yards)	20.00	27.50	24.50								higher=better

Kluegel

	W2001	S2001	F2001	W2002	S2002	F2002	W2003	S2003	F2003	W2004	
Bogies offense (% scoring)			32.31								higher=better
Bogies defense (shutout %)			100.00								higher=better
Top Gun (% won)			66.70								higher=better
1v1 to Goal offense (% scoring)		44.20	46.70								higher=better
1v1 to Goal defense (shutout %)		52.80	71.20								higher=better
Shooting (% scoring)			6.30								higher=better
Triangle Passing (success pass/session)	1.70		2.80								higher=better
LS/LR 20 yds (succ serves/session)	10.00	8.50	8.00								higher=better
LS/LR 30 yds (succ serves/session)	6.40	4.00	6.10								higher=better
LS/LR 45 yds (succ serves/session)	1.60	1.50	1.90								higher=better
Long Service R (yards)	36.00	45.00	48.00								higher=better
Long Service L (yards)	23.00	38.00	38.00								higher=better
Power Heading (yards)	20.80	20.75	21.80								higher=better

Ramsey

	W2001	S2001	F2001	W2002	S2002	F2002	W2003	S2003	F2003	W2004	
Bogies offense (% scoring)			11.25								higher=better
Bogies defense (shutout %)			93.33								higher=better
Top Gun (% won)			76.70								higher=better
1v1 to Goal offense (% scoring)		66.10	57.70								higher=better
1v1 to Goal defense (shutout %)		71.90	78.60								higher=better
Shooting (% scoring)			30.00								higher=better
Triangle Passing (success pass/session)	2.20		2.80								higher=better
LS/LR 20 yds (succ serves/session)	10.80	7.50	11.40								higher=better
LS/LR 30 yds (succ serves/session)	6.40	4.00	7.80								higher=better
LS/LR 45 yds (succ serves/session)	1.20	0.50	4.30								higher=better
Long Service R (yards)	43.00	45.00	50.00								higher=better
Long Service L (yards)	32.00	36.00	34.00								higher=better
Power Heading (yards)	21.00	28.25	24.30								higher=better

Reddick

	W2001	S2001	F2001	W2002	S2002	F2002	W2003	S2003	F2003	W2004	
Bogies offense (% scoring)			21.60								higher=better
Bogies defense (shutout %)			87.62								higher=better
Top Gun (% won)			78.60								higher=better
1v1 to Goal offense (% scoring)		71.10	75.00								higher=better
1v1 to Goal defense (shutout %)		86.30	78.30								higher=better
Shooting (% scoring)			10.00								higher=better
Triangle Passing (success pass/session)	2.40		3.10								higher=better
LS/LR 20 yds (succ serves/session)	10.00	9.00	11.30								higher=better
LS/LR 30 yds (succ serves/session)	6.00	6.00	9.80								higher=better
LS/LR 45 yds (succ serves/session)	1.20	2.00	3.80								higher=better
Long Service R (yards)	48.00	50.00	53.00								higher=better
Long Service L (yards)	36.00	38.00	40.00								higher=better
Power Heading (yards)	22.40	27.25	26.70								higher=better

Remy

	W2001	S2001	F2001	W2002	S2002	F2002	W2003	S2003	F2003	W2004	
Bogies offense (% scoring)			28.85								higher=better
Bogies defense (shutout %)			93.33								higher=better
Top Gun (% won)			58.30								higher=better
1v1 to Goal offense (% scoring)		51.30	48.70								higher=better
1v1 to Goal defense (shutout %)		59.60	71.40								higher=better
Shooting (% scoring)			38.90								higher=better
Triangle Passing (success pass/session)	3.10		2.70								higher=better
LS/LR 20 yds (succ serves/session)	8.80	4.50	10.10								higher=better
LS/LR 30 yds (succ serves/session)	4.40	5.50	6.90								higher=better
LS/LR 45 yds (succ serves/session)	1.60	0.50	1.50								higher=better
Long Service R (yards)	35.00	40.00	38.00								higher=better
Long Service L (yards)	23.00	34.00	31.00								higher=better
Power Heading (yards)	24.60	23.75	21.60								higher=better

(2001) Summer Training Program
Start Now!

The summer preseason is broken down into 12 weeks. This would be the ideal training rhythm during the weeks you are not tapering into meaningful games. What would also be ideal is if you could organize your time to get the six fitness requirements done in the morning and in weeks 7, 8, and 9 get the weight training done following your "ball workouts" or games in the evening. This is different than last summer...weeks 1, 2, and 3 are easy but it will get you ready for the summer push; we don't want anyone to get hurt. Weeks 10, 11, and 12 are also a bit of a taper into the preseason so you can come in ready to rip heads off.

Weeks 1, 2, and 3, May 14–20, May 21–May 27, May 28–June 3:
  NCSCP (ball work 2 times per week, jumps 1 time per week)
  Lateral Speed and Agility* – 1st Block (1 time a week)
  Cones (1 time a week, 35 sec. work + 25 sec. rest x 6; 40 sec. work + 20
    sec. rest x 4; 2 extra rest – 15 seconds) OR 40-yard shuttles OR 20-
    minute fartlek (your choice, do a different one each week)
  Weight Training (2 times a week)

Weeks 4, 5, and 6, June 4–10, June 11–17, June 18–24:
  NCSCP (ball work 2 times per week, jumps 1 time per week)
  Speed Training (1 time a week, combine with (LSA)*...do it on the same
    day)
  Lateral Speed and Agility – 2nd Block (1 time a week)
  Cones (1 time a week, 35 sec. work + 25 sec. rest x 8; 40 sec. work + 20
    sec. rest x 2; 2 extra rest – 15 seconds) OR 50-yard cone drill (1 time
    a week) OR 40-yard shuttle (your choice, do a different one each
    week)
  Weight Training (2 times a week)

---

* Lateral Speed and Agility (see page 315).

Weeks 7, 8, and 9, June 25–July 1, July 2–8, July 9–15:
  NCSCP** (ball work 2 times per week, jumps 1 time per week)
  Speed training (1 time a week)
  Lateral Speed and Agility – 3rd Block (1 time a week)
  120s (1 time a week, 18 sec. work + 60 sec. rest x 10
                  jog back to starting line in 30 seconds)
  Super Set (1 time a week) (50-yard shuttle)
  Weight Training (2 times a week)**

Weeks 10, 11, and 12, July 16–22, July 23–29, July 30–August 5:
  NCSCP** (ball work 2 times per week, jumps 1 time per week)
  Speed Training (1 time a week, combine with LSA*...do it on the same
    day)
  Lateral Speed and Agility – 4th Block (1 time a week)
  120s (1 time a week, 18 sec. work + 60 sec. rest x 10; jog back to starting
    line in 30 seconds) OR Jingle Jangle*** (your choice, do a different
    one each week)
  Weight Training (2 times a week)

This will give you a seven-day taper into the preseason. By this time you should know what to do to keep yourself fit and strong for the last week as you get focused and rested for preseason.

If you are not training alone, what I have included is the original U.S. Women's National Team "Self Coach" philosophy for your personal development. Mix in the basic core from above with the things on the next page (Self Coach) to make your training more vibrant and enjoyable. Develop a "training mentality" to do something six days a week (take one full day off a week where you literally do nothing). And on days where you feel energetic, train twice (morning and evening) but never train for longer than one and one-half hours in a row—don't burn out!

---

* Lateral Speed and Agility (see page 315).
** North Carolina Summer Conditioning Program.
*** Jingle Jangle = out and back, 10y, x 10, within a given time (at UNC, it is 50–55 secs.). Do 5 sets.

The Self-Coach for the Field Player

There is only a certain amount of time in each day. Organize your time to achieve peak performance. Understand what is important, what is not; what to do first, what to do last; what to do every day; what to do once a week; what things you can do in the morning and then still be able to train with intensity in the evening with something else. Envision that you are a coach trying to get you, as a player, to be the best you can be. Also understand that if you train for longer than one and one-half hours you will eventually burn yourself out, and if you go twice a day, each session should be 1 hour 15 minutes or less. Understand that intensity in training enables you to be the margin of victory, so get after it when you train.

Priority Training—I have ranked in order of importance what will impact on your development the most to help you organize your day and week. Please understand THE BALL IS MOST IMPORTANT and even though we can't measure that development as easily, it is your skill that is going to get you on the field and be your measure as you climb in this game and make your mark.

	Maximum Ideal Repetitions Per Week
1. Competitive 11 v 11 match	2
2. Organized training session (1 1/2 hours)	5 or 6
3. Competitive pickup game (4 v 4 is ideal, with goalkeepers and regulation goals even better) where score is kept and you play with lines (30 minutes to 1 hour)	6
4. 1 v 1: keep score, play every day (3 minutes to 20 minutes)	6
5. North Carolina Summer Conditioning Program (NCSCP) (1 hour and at least twice per week)	2
6. Skill section of the NCSCP (30 minutes)	4
7. a. Coerver workout (15 minutes); this is a critical agility component, don't underestimate its value	6
b. User-friendly flighted balls with backspin (in pairs, as we did in the spring) (10 minutes)	6

c. Racquetball court or wall "shooting workout"   2
(20 minutes)
d. Heading (10 minutes)
8. a. Speed training 20s, 40s, 60s, 80s, 100s (30 minutes   2
to 1 hour 15 minutes)
b. Lateral Speed and Agility
c. 40-yard shuttles (45 seconds work, 45 seconds rest)   2
d. 50-yard cone drills (1 minute work, 1 minute rest)   1
e. Super Set (120s/40 yard shuttle...18 seconds work,   1
30 seconds jog back, 45 seconds work, 1:15 rest)
f. Jingle Jangle (50–55 seconds work, 1 minute rest)   1
g. Cones (five cones five yards apart...shuttle   1
runs, 40 seconds work, 20 seconds rest or 35
seconds work, 25 seconds rest. Total # of shuttles 10)
h. 120s (120 yd. sprint in 18 seconds, 30 seconds   1
jog back to starting line—30 seconds rest,
repeat 10 times)
i. 20–30 minute run (push yourself) and make it   when you
fartlek...sprint parts of it...vary speeds...then   can't do
it becomes more soccer-like.   anything else
9. Weight training (30 minutes to 1 hour)   2

Obviously in an organized training session, Nos. 3, 4, 5, 6, 7a & b, 8b or 8c might all be involved, so don't be confused by the "Maximum Ideal Repetitions Per Week." Don't do more than the maximum numbers in any area in any given week. You can do less if you select to bounce around in the different areas listed. For the 120s, cones and speed training you should try to give yourself two days in between, with other kinds of workouts to recover, because if you go after it in those areas it should take some time to regenerate.

We all look forward to the fall. Please call if you need help setting up your ideal environment. We would love to help you.

University of North Carolina Women's Soccer Summer Skill/Conditioning Program

Ball Control and Agility

1 minute – Jog while dribbling ball with quick touches, changing direction and speed. Do this in a confined space where many changes and touches are necessary.

1 minute – Head juggling.

1 minute – Throw ball up, jump and while you are in the air trap the ball with your head, settle the ball to your feet, and move off quickly—repeat.

1 minute – Thigh juggling.

1 minute – Throw ball up, jump, and while you are in the air trap the ball with your chest, settle the ball to your feet, and move off quickly—repeat.

1 minute – Foot juggling with no spin on the ball.

2 minutes –Starting in a sitting position, throw ball up, get up and stop the ball before it hits the ground, settle it to your feet, and move off quickly. Repeat using head, chest, each thigh, each foot—in that order—to trap the ball.

Technical Speed, Pure Speed, and Endurance

1. Dribble in a figure 8, use just the inside of your feet for 6 figure 8s, then use the outside of both feet for 6 more. The markers you dribble around should be 15 yards apart. As you dribble around one marker, accelerate to the other as if you were beating an opponent. As you round the marker, use quick touches to improve technical speed.
2. Rest by walking for 30 seconds.
3. Set a marker out about 25 yards from a starting point:
   a. Sprint dribble to marker
   b. Sprint backward to starting point
   c. Sprint to ball
   d. Collect ball and sprint dribble back to starting point
4. Rest by walking for 30 seconds.

5. Set ball on the ground to your left and set a marker out to your right about 10 yards. Move 10 times from side to side, using the slide method of moving, without crossing legs. Move as quickly as you can.
6. Rest by walking for 30 seconds.
7. To ten-yard marker and back: two leg explosive jumps. To marker and back: single leg explosive hopping. Left foot first, then right, out and back.
8. Rest by walking for 30 seconds.
9. Carioca (lateral running crisscrossing legs) to ten-yard marker and back. Move 10 times from side to side as quickly as possible.
10. Rest by walking for 30 seconds.
11. From the starting point:
    a. Pass the ball to the 25-yard marker
    b. Sprint to the ball
    c. Collect ball and accelerate to starting line
    d. Make 3 passes

Strength and Flexibility

60 jumps – Two-foot jumping forward and backward over the ball.
15 figure 8s – Standing position with legs spread and knees straight, roll the ball with your hands in a figure 8 pattern around your legs.
60 jumps – Two-foot jumping side to side over the ball.
15 roll arounds – Sitting position with legs extended, roll the ball with your hands around the soles of your feet and then back around your back.
60 jumps – Throw the ball up in the air, jump, catch the ball, and throw it back up before you hit the ground. Remember to "hang" in the air.
30 sit-ups – Touch the ball on the ground over your head and back up and touch your toes.
60 touch and jumps – Start in a standing position with the ball in your hands. Touch ball on the ground by bending at the knees so thighs are parallel to the ground and then vigorously extend jumping high with ball over your head. Don't just bend over and touch the ground; get your rear end as low as possible.
30 push-ups

Shooting and Heading

For this section of the exercise, a soccer kick wall, the side of a gymnasium, a tennis wall, racquetball court, etc., will be necessary.

1. Technique work: Get 5 to 7 yards from the wall and shoot the ball first time at the wall, making sure the foot is pointed, knee is over the ball, center of your foot is striking the center of the ball, and that all the power is derived from a quick snapping motion of the lower leg. (2 minutes)

2. First time shooting with power: Back off 20 yards and shoot the ball first time at the wall. Strike the ball as hard as you can regardless of the bounce, height, speed, etc., so that the ball comes to you. Pick a spot on the wall to shoot at each time and keep the ball low. (6 minutes)

3. Trapping and shooting: again at 20 yards, strike the ball with power, and as it comes off the wall, trap in cleanly and *quickly.* Fire another shot at the wall. The point of the drill is to develop a sound, clean trap and quick, hard shot. (6 minutes)

4. From one to two yards away, first-time head juggling against the wall. (1 minute)

5. Back off between 5 and 7 yards, throw the ball up against the wall and as it comes off, head with power, getting your entire body into the heading motion. (2 minutes)

6. Get within 5 yards of the wall—toss the ball against the wall to force you to jump to head the ball back at the wall. Catch the ball after you have headed it each time. Make sure your toss forces you to the peak of your jump. Remember your technique and head with power. (3 minutes)

This entire fitness program should take 45 minutes to an hour. It is important that you go through the entire program without pause other than at planned rest intervals.

Ideally, a short 4-a-side game would be a fine way to finish your training. If you are alone, this will be impossible, and I would suggest working on a weak aspect of your game. Also, never underestimate playing 1 v 1. There is nothing better, and even a short series of 1 v 1 contests against anyone you are with will be very helpful. Three 4-minute 1 v 1 games with rest in between would be excellent. If your opponent is superior (an excellent male soccer player) make your goal small (a cone) and his large (a regulation goal). If you are superior, do the same in reverse, or play 1 v 2. Playing males is why most women on the U.S. Olympic Team are as good as they are 1 v 1. Playing 1 v 2 is why George Best, in his day, was the best male dribbler in the world. He claimed 1 v 1 was too easy for him.

GOOD LUCK, YOU HARDWORKING TAR HEELS!

University of North Carolina
Summer Speed Program

This is for your *anaerobic fitness base* and also for your *speed development* (to be able to sprint for 90 minutes and still have your legs for a game the next day). This does not help your wind (aerobic base), but it is just as critical for the way we play our game (at a sprint). If done properly and consistently (explosively and as fast as you can go) this will also improve your speed through the summer. Remember, this is just part of what you have to do. You must continue training with the ball and playing shortsided games. This speed training does not help change of direction (strength in cutting, etc.). In fact, without anything else your speed training will hurt your agility.

SPRINT ALL-OUT ON EVERY SPRINT! — Do not pace yourself.

TAKE FULL REST PERIOD! (not less)

CONCENTRATE ON EXPLOSIVE STARTS! (driving knees, leaning forward, pumping arms). Keep stride smooth and powerful throughout sprint.

Week 4	**Week 5**	**Week 6**
May 15–May 28	May 29–June 4	June 6–June 11
8 x 20 yds	10 x 20 yds	12 x 20 yds
6 x 40 yds	8 x 40 yds	10 x 40 yds
4 x 60 yds	6 x 60 yds	6 x 60 yds
2 x 80 yds	4 x 80 yds	4 x 80 yds
1 x 100 yds	2 x 100 yds	3 x 100 yds
1 time per week	1 time per week	1 time per week

Week 7	**Week 8 & 12**	**Week 9 & 11**
June 12–June 25	July 2–July 9	July 10–July 23
14 x 20 yds	16 x 20 yds	18 x 20 yds
10 x 40 yds	10 x 40 yds	10 x 40 yds
8 x 60 yds	8 x 60 yds	8 x 60 yds
6 x 80 yds	6 x 80 yds	6 x 80 yds
4 x 100 yds	4 x 100 yds	4 x 100 yds
1 time per week	1 time per week	1 time per week

Week 10
July 24–August 6
20 x 20 yds
10 x 40 yds
8 x 60 yds
6 x 80 yds
4 x 100 yds
1 time per week

Rest Period Weeks 4–7
30 seconds for 20s
45 seconds for 40s
60 seconds for 60s
75 seconds for 80s
90 seconds for 100s

Rest Period Weeks 8–12
20 seconds for 20s
30 seconds for 40s
45 seconds for 60s
60 seconds for 80s
75 seconds for 100s

University of North Carolina
Women's Soccer
Lateral Speed and Agility (LSA) Development
Summer Program

General Information

1. This should be a major portion of your program for the summer, as the game is played in multidirections. Your ability to decelerate, stop momentarily, and reaccelerate, will be critical to your success on the field.
2. At each block interval you need to be a self-evaluator of your progress by timing yourself on the drills. Adjust your training if necessary.
3. There shouldn't be more than a 10% drop in your performance from your last test evaluation (agility cone test).
4. Perform the warm-up prescribed before each LSA session (this includes the functional stretches listed).

LSA—Dynamic Warm-Up
(20–30 yard distance on field/track)

(5–10 minutes) Functional stretches (see attached)
(10 minutes) Active Warm-up:

a. "S" run (forward/backward)—Work arms in overhead, cross body, or alternation swinging fashion as you move.
b. Carioca
c. Skip (forward/backward)
d. Alternation Step & Touch (forward lunge and touch foot with opposite hand each step)
e. Diagonal plant and cut
f. 360 run (turn while you run)
g. Sprint to Backpedal
h. Backpedal to Sprint
i. Lateral shuffle (10 yards) to sprint
j. Carioca (10 yards) to sprint

(5 minutes)   Footwork Drills
                (Speed ladder/line on the ground)
                Do single/double foot movements
                4–5 drills repeat each twice

LSA 1st Block

Active Warm-up: (20 yards)

1. Jog and Twist (forward/backward)
2. Skip (forward/backward)
3. Backward run
4. Carioca
5. Power skip (for height)

Starts: (10-yard distance working fast hands and feet)
    Repeat each start twice

1. Soccer start (athletic position)
2. Staggered stance
3. Balanced start (off one leg)
4. Lateral start (lead foot stepping first)
5. Crossover start (back foot crossing over front foot)
6. Back step (drop right/left foot back, turn, and accelerate)

LSA 2nd Block

Functional stretch and warm-up

Drills

Wheel Drill (courtesy of Vern Gambetta)

1. Start in the middle of the wheel with an
   athletic stance.
2. Work around the wheel in a clockwise
   fashion for the right foot (counterclockwise for the left).
3. Begin drill by stepping with right leg at
   spoke #1. Take one step and hold for 3
   seconds.

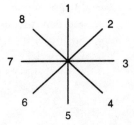

4. Check for good posture and balance during stepping motion.
5. Return to center after each step.
6. Repeat using left leg at spokes 1,8,7,6, and 5.
7. At spokes 3 & 7 use both lateral open step and crossover step.
8. As you increase control of your movement, use 3 steps at each spoke, then 5 steps. Increase the speed of your movements as you improve.

Repeat each drill twice on each leg.

Plant & Cut

6 cones set at various distances apart

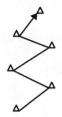

1. Run at each cone (plant) and hold for 3 seconds x 4.
2. Run and cut at cones with no stopping x 4 (control base of support at each cut).
3. Change cone distances x 3.

4-Cone Drill

(Sprint-shuffle, backpedal-carioca) x 4 change starting point.

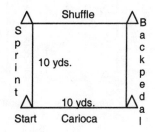

Test and evaluate each drill weekly by timing the drills.

LSA 3rd Block

Drill:

5-10-15 drill

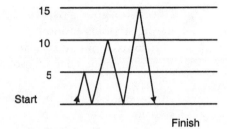

Variations:

1. Sprint-turn – sprint back
2. Sprint out – backpedal back
3. Backpedal out – sprint back
4. Shuffle out – carioca back

- Each run is performed in a shuttle fashion (down and back).
- Time each run weekly for an evaluation of progress.

12 Cone Shuffle/Weave/Slalom Drill

Do each drill x 2

1 Shuffle

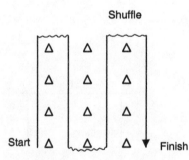

Sprint-shuffle-backpedal
(reverse on 2nd run)

2 Weave

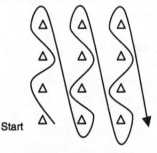

(change sides on 2nd run)

3 Slalom

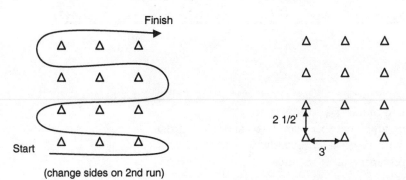

Start

(change sides on 2nd run)

2 1/2'

3'

LSA 4th Block

Drill:

Mirror Drill (with partner)

1. Move same direction as partner 3 x 15 seconds.
2. Move opposite direction of partner 3 x 15 seconds.
3. Incorporate the ball while moving 3 x 15 seconds.

• Keepers involve reacting off a shot on goal at this point.

50-yard "Ajax" shuttle

Perform (5) repeats (shuttle fashion) for time.
Do this drill twice per session.

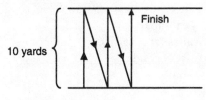

10 yards

Finish

Start

University of North Carolina
Summer Anaerobic/Aerobic Fitness Shuttles

40-Yard Shuttles
 – two markers 40 yards apart
 – up and back three times (total of 240 yards)
 – work interval 45 seconds
 – rest interval 45 seconds
 – start at 6 sets, work up to 10
 – extra rest every three (15 seconds extra rest), so after 3, 6, and 9

50-Yard Cone Drill
 – six markers at ten-yard intervals
 – 10 and back, 20 and back, 30 and back, 40 and back, 50 and back (total of 300 yards)
 – work interval - 1 minute
 – rest interval - 1 minute
 – start at 6 sets, work up to 8
 – extra rest every three (15 seconds extra rest), so after 3 and 6

Super Set
 – 120 yards sprint in 18 seconds
 – 120 yards back in 30 seconds
 – rest interval on the line 25 seconds
 – 40-yard shuttle (45 seconds to 47 seconds work)
 – rest interval 1:15
 – five complete sets

Jingle Jangle
 – two markers 10 yards apart
 – up and back 10 times (200 yards)
 – work interval 50–55 seconds
 – rest interval – 1 minute
 – start at 8 sets, work up to 10
 – extra rest every three (15 seconds extra rest), so after 3, 6, and 9

University of North Carolina Women's Soccer Summer Strength Program

The road to victory begins today!

Training Tips:

1. Follow training protocol listed.
2. Train with high intensity! You're a champion—train like one!
3. Increase the load as the weight becomes easier to move (set to set if possible).
4. Your peak strength and power should be during the last block of training.
5. Be aware of your technique. Don't sacrifice it for heavier weight!

Greg Gatz, c.s.c.s
Director of Strength and Conditioning for Olympic Sports

Weeks 1, 2, 3, and 4

PURPOSE: General Conditioning and Build Work Capacity

Core Training/Circuit Training

Day 1

Wtd.* Twists (standing) 2 x 30
Reverse Hypers 2 x 15
Push-ups 2 x 15-20

Quick foot drills x 6 drills
(12 seconds each)

Day 2

Back extension 2 x 15-20
Walking med ball lunge with
twist 2 x 8 each leg

Speed ladder x 6 drills 2 reps each
(1 foot; 2 feet; lateral 2 foot;
diagonal forward; carioca;
in, in, out, out forward)

---

* Wtd. = weighted (medicine ball, barbell, or other resistance).

Leg Circuit:

A
Bodyweight Squat x 20
Alt. Lunge x 20
Alt. Step-up x 20
Straight leg jumps x 10

B
Wide stance side squat x 20
Alt. Side lunge x 20
Alt. Side box hops x 20
Ice skaters x 20

C
Turn 180 and squat (rt/lft) x 20
Turn 180 and lunge (rt/lft) x 20
Alt. 45 box hops x 20
Alt. 270 jumps x 10

Total Body Circuit:
1. Med ball squat + overhead press
2. Push-ups
3. Body-weight Squat (wide stance)
4. DB** bent over row
5. Ice skaters***
6. DB curl and press
7. Squat thrust and jump
8. Alt. Power step-up
9. Pull-ups
10. DB front lunge w/reach, curl and press

30 seconds work/15 seconds rest, repeat 2–3 times (work down the list 1–10 = 1 time)

Week 1 = A-B-C 1 x 45 seconds rest between
Week 2 = A-B-C 2 x 30 seconds rest between
Week 3 = A-B-C 3 x 30 seconds rest between
Week 4 = A-B-C 3 x 15 seconds rest between

Weeks 5, 6, 7, and 8

PURPOSE: Hypertrophy/Increase Strength

Day 1

Warm-up:
Combo Lift
DB power pull
DB hang clean

Day 2

Warm-up:
Combo Lift
DB upright row
DB side lunge and press

** DB = dumbbell
*** Ice skaters = Lateral jumps alternating from one leg to the other, landing on one foot with the knee bent.

DB squat and press
3 x 6-6-6 (40% of body weight)
Do all 3 exercises for 1 set

DB push press
3 x 6-6-6 (40% of body weight)
(increase weight 5% every
    other week)

Strength   Bench press
               DB lunge and
                  overhead press

Strength   Squat (DB or BB)*
               Incline Press
               Pull-up (Incline)

Power   DB Snatch

Power   DB Push Jerk

Aux**   Push-ups x 30 reps

   Wtd. Crunches*** x
      50 reps
   Strength = 3 x 6
   Power = 4 x 3
   Aux = as listed

Aux   Incline push-ups x
             30 reps
          Back extension x
             30 reps
          Strength = 3 x 6
          Power = 4 x 3
          Aux = as listed

Weeks 9, 10, 11, and 12

PURPOSE: Convert strength to explosive power

Day 1

Day 2

Warm-up: Quick foot drills x
   6 (10 sec)

Warm-up: same as Day 1

Bench press and power push-up
DB pullover and medicine ball
   soccer throw
BB Frt. Lunge/alt. Split jumps
Medicine ball twists (standing)/
   180 jumps

DB squat/squat jump (bodyweight)
DB side lunge/ice skater
DB incline/medicine ball chest pass
DB snatch/squat thrust and jump

Combine each lift with an explosive movement.
Each exercise should be done with quick tempo.
Reps/sets = 3 sets 5 reps weights/30 jumps or throws

---

* BB = barbell.
** Aux = Auxiliary, or secondary exercise.
*** Weighted crunches (med. ball, barbell, or other resistance).

Functional Stretches (*courtesy of Gary Gray, PT*)

A. Calf Group (gastroc/soleus)
   1. Stand in front of a wall or area where you can use the hands to balance.
   2. Extend arms overhead against wall while the legs are in a traditional calf stretch position.
   3. Back heel should be against the ground.
   4. Opposite knee held high.
   5. Move raised leg in a side-to-side swinging motion, while stretching back calf/ankle.
   6. Do one set with heel flat and one with heel raised.

B. IT Band
   1. Bend stretching leg knee 15–20°.
   2. Evert (push outward) the heel of the front foot.
   3. Step back a short step with opposite leg.
   4. Lead slightly forward and across to the stretching leg with opposite arm.

C. Illioposas
   1. Stand with one leg on chair or bench as shown.
   2. Bring arms overhead and behind.

D. Adductors
   1. Stride with stretching leg forward and foot turned in.
   2. Swing arms side-to-side.

University of North Carolina
Women's Soccer
Self/Peer Evaluation

Creating Community Character

Instructions

- Appraise each team member's ATTITUDE, PERFORMANCE, CHARACTER, and DISCIPLINE.
- Rate yourself.

Descriptions

A. Excellent Performance.
B. Good Performance, but could use a little improvement.
C. Fair Performance, but definitely needs improvement.
D. Poor Performance, with serious problem areas.

Attitude

1. TEAMMATES—Being friendly/helpful/responsive and caring to teammates.
2. COACHES—Respecting and supporting coaching decisions and directions.
3. PROFESSORS—Respecting and cooperating with.
4. PROGRAM—Contributing to the reputation and growth of the soccer program by being a positive life force.
5. SELF-DEVELOPMENT—Having the desire to take specific steps to improve as a player.

Performance

6. ACADEMICS—100% effort/attending classes/using available resources (library, etc.)
7. PRACTICE—Tough practice player/hustling 100%.

8. TRAINING—Following a rigorous weight program to protect yourself from injury and improve your general athleticism, always pushing yourself and others.
9. COMMUNITY—Being a responsible role model at all times, giving back to the communities that helped build you.
10. CONFIDENCE—Having faith in your abilities without being conceited/arrogant.

Character

11. MENTAL TOUGHNESS—Staying focused/not getting down on yourself, teammates, coaches, etc., ...taking responsibility rather than distributing blame when the going gets tough.
12. RELIABILITY—Making curfews/coming to practices, meetings, games on time/returning equipment.
13. LOYALTY—Saying positive things about teammates, staff, and program "behind their backs," to maintain a close family atmosphere of support.
14. CONDUCT—Displaying behavior consistent with program philosophy/moral principles.
15. STRENGTH—Being a positive force instead of a selfish clod of ailments and grievances, complaining that the world will not devote itself to making you happy.

Discipline

16. FITNESS BASING—Having the capacity to stay fit year-round—consistently training aerobically, anaerobically and in the weight room, and doing this on a regular basis, working hard to be the best you can be.
17. HARD-BODY/HEALTH—Having the discipline to eat the best foods in the correct amounts to stay and live at an optimum body weight to feel good, look good, and perform at optimum levels, not just here, but for life.
18. SELF-DEVELOPMENT—Having the ambition to become the best soccer player you can be; working on and correcting technical weaknesses as well as improving all fitness bases and playing the game on a regular basis wherever you are, even in soccer deserts where you have to create your own training environments (finding kick walls to shoot on your own, etc.).

19. THE WILL TO PREPARE TO WIN—Having the understanding that everybody wants to win, but what distinguishes the champions from everyone else is that the champions have daily, weekly, monthly, and yearly plans on what they are going to do to become the best, and then they carry out these plans. Discipline yourself to be a champion. It is not easy, but it will always distinguish you from everyone else.

"What is it that binds us to this place as to no other? It is not the well or the bell or the stone walls or the crisp October nights or the memory of dogwoods blooming here on the crest of New Hope Chapel Hill...our love for this place is based on the fact that it is as it was meant to be...the university of the people."

CHARLES KURALT
UNC 1959

Photo Credits

Page number	Credit
xxiv	Brett Whitesell
2	Sports Information Office at the University of North Carolina
5	Sports Information Office at the University of North Carolina
10	Brad Smith
39	Sports Information Office at the University of North Carolina
52	John Gardiner
57	Brett Whitesell
60	Bill Richards
70	David Minton
80	Brad Smith
81	Brett Whitesell
105	Jeff Camarati
109	David Minton
133	Sports Information Office at the University of North Carolina
135	Abbey Burns
160	Brett Whitesell
162	Jeff Camarati
173	Jeff Camarati
178	Brett Whitesell
192	Brett Whitesell
201	Brett Whitesell
212	Nell Rittenbury
219	Brett Whitesell
239	Brett Whitesell
244	Brett Whitesell
249	Scott Sharpe
255	Jeff Camarati
275	Brett Whitesell